# Uniform System of Accounts for the Lodging Industry

# Uniform System of Accounts for the Lodging Industry

## Eleventh Revised Edition

Hotel Association of New York City
New York, New York

Hospitality Financial and Technology Professionals
Austin, Texas

American Hotel & Lodging Educational Institute
Orlando, Florida

# Disclaimer

This publication is designed to provide accurate and authoritative information in regard to the subject matter covered. It is sold with the understanding that the publisher is not engaged in rendering legal, accounting, or other professional service. If legal advice or other expert assistance is required, the services of a competent professional person should be sought.

> —*From the Declaration of Principles jointly adopted by the American Bar Association and a Committee of Publishers and Associations.*

Nothing contained in this publication shall constitute an endorsement by the American Hotel & Lodging Educational Institute (the Institute), the American Hotel & Lodging Association (AH&LA), Hospitality Financial and Technology Professionals (HFTP) or the Hotel Association of New York City (HANYC) of any information, opinion, procedure, or product mentioned, and the Institute, AH&LA, HFTP, and HANYC disclaim any liability with respect to the use of such information, procedure, or product, or reliance thereon.

©2014
By the HOTEL ASSOCIATION of NEW YORK CITY, INC.
320 Park Avenue, 22nd Floor
New York, New York 10022

Published by the
AMERICAN HOTEL & LODGING EDUCATIONAL INSTITUTE
2113 N. High Street
Lansing, Michigan  48906

With support from
HOSPITALITY FINANCIAL and TECHNOLOGY PROFESSIONALS
11709 Boulder Lane, Suite110
Austin, Texas 78726

**Printed in the United States of America**
 2  3  4  5  6  7  8  9  10  11  12  13  22  21  20  19  18  17  16  15  14

ISBN:    978-0-86612-447-8 (hardcover)
         978-0-86612-448-5 (digital)

## A few words from the sponsor of this edition of the
### *Uniform System of Accounts for the Lodging Industry*

Hospitality Financial and Technology Professionals is the international society for financial and technology professionals in the hospitality industry. Serving the industry since 1953, HFTP provides outstanding educational programs, networking opportunities, and information resources to hospitality professionals around the world. HFTP also awards the Certified Hospitality Accountant Executive (CHAE) and Certified Hospitality Technology Professional (CHTP) designations. HFTP has more than 70 chapters representing 56 countries. By the end of 2014, HFTP will have offices in the United States, Europe, and Asia.

The goal of HFTP is to be recognized by the global business community as the authoritative information source on finance and technology for the hospitality industry. We are reaching that goal through the following.

### Invaluable Resources

- *www.hftp.org.* The HFTP website provides members with convenient access to industry checklists, forms, and tips; streaming video and audio educational sessions; CHAE and CHTP reviews; online meeting registration; publication archives; Job Mart; membership directory and ability for members to update their profiles; and resources for chapter leaders.

- *The Bottomline.* Produced eight times a year, HFTP's professional journal provides members with industry news covering everything from taxes and technology to HR and accounting issues.

- *Infoline.* HFTP's bimonthly newsletter notifies members of association activities on both the local and international levels, providing well-deserved recognition to chapters and individual members for their contributions to the hospitality industry.

- *Industry Partnerships.* We pride ourselves on enhancing the image of financial and technology professionals through increased visibility, support, and networking in the hospitality industry. HFTP represents members at industry meetings and associations, and has collaborated with other organizations to conduct industry research in the areas of hospitality salaries, technology, capital, and e-business.

## Education and Technology

- *HITEC (Hospitality Industry Technology Exposition and Conference): www. hitec.org.* Internationally known, this conference offers industry professionals the largest, most comprehensive coverage of hospitality technology of its kind in the world. HITEC offers live demonstrations of the latest in hospitality technology, equipment, products and services, first-rate educational programs, and networking.

- *Annual Convention & Tradeshow.* Members attend the Annual Convention & Tradeshow each year to participate in information-sharing, educational sessions, and fun-filled entertainment.

- *Professional Development Seminars.* Each year, a series of specialized educational opportunities are offered to various segments of the hospitality industry, including the Club Controllers Conference, Hotel Controllers Conference, and Casino Controllers Conference.

- *Online Master's Program.* HFTP has collaborated with the University of Nevada, Las Vegas to provide an online master's degree in hospitality administration (finance or technology concentration). HFTP members are eligible for tuition discounts.

## Professional Opportunities

- *Certification.* The Certified Hospitality Accountant Executive (CHAE) designation is recognized worldwide as a symbol of achievement and competence. The Certified Hospitality Technology Professional (CHTP) designation—co-sponsored with the Educational Institute—symbolizes a high level of competency and professionalism in hospitality technology. Individuals who earn these designations are respected by employers and colleagues for their high level of commitment and dedication.

- *Networking.* The Colleague Advisory Network connects members who have expressed experience on particular subjects with members who have questions in that area. In addition, local chapters around the world provide members with leadership opportunities, discussion forums, and social activities.

*For more information, contact HFTP at 11709 Boulder Lane, Ste. 110, Austin, TX 78726, membership@hftp.org, 800-646-4387, fax: 512-249-1533, or visit www.hftp.org and www.hitec.org.*

# Contents

# Preface

The first edition of the *Uniform System of Accounts for Hotels* was published in 1926 by the Hotel Association of New York City. It represented the first successful organized effort to establish a uniform responsibility accounting system for the lodging industry and one of the first such efforts in any industry.

All members of the original committees, appointed by the Hotel Association of New York City to prepare a uniform system of accounts for hotels, deserve commendation for their untiring devotion to the completion of this task. The personnel of these committees were as follows:

## Proprietor's Committee

E. M. Statler, Chairman—Hotel Pennsylvania

| | |
|---|---|
| L. M. Boomer—The Waldorf-Astoria | Julius Manger—Hotel Times Square |
| I. Fluegelman—12 East 86th Street | Fred A. Muschenheim—Hotel Astor |
| David H. Knott—Hotel Albert | Charles G. Stamm—Hotel Willard |
| Arthur L. Lee—Hotel McAlpin | George W. Sweeney—Hotel Commodore |

## Accountants' Committee

William J. Forster, CPA, Chairman

| | |
|---|---|
| R. H. Browne | Hotel McAlpin |
| W. E. Dodd | Hotel San Remo |
| R. E. Frederickson | Hotel Astor |
| C. W. Kramer | Hotel Pennsylvania |
| E. E. Lightburne | The Waldorf-Astoria |
| H. M. Phelps | The Waldorf-Astoria |
| W. M. Ross, CPA | The Biltmore |
| Thomas E. Ross, CPA | The Biltmore |
| R. Schickler | The Plaza |
| F. W. Squires, CPA | Hotel Astor |
| C. B. Stoner | Hotels Statler Company Inc. |

## Accounting Societies

Chester P. Child, CPA, representing N.Y. State Society of CPAs
W. D. Cranstoun, CPA, representing American Institute of Accountants

One of the important results of the work of the Accountants' Committee was the organization of the Hotel Accountants Association of New York City. After the printing of the first edition of the manual, a Manual Committee of the Association was formed, which has been the medium through which the work of the original group has been continued. The Hotel Accountants Association of New York

City became the founding chapter of the organization now known as Hospitality Financial and Technology Professionals. The names of those who worked on previous revisions of the uniform systems can be found in each of those revisions.

In 1961, to meet the needs of its members, the American Hotel & Lodging Association appointed the National Association of Accountants to develop a uniform system of accounts for small hotels and motels. In 1979 and again in 1986, members of the Committee on Financial Management of the American Hotel & Lodging Association revised the original uniform system of accounts for small hotels to reflect the changes in terminology used in the lodging industry. The names of the committee members involved in these publications can be found in the respective editions.

In 1996, a decision was made to combine the two uniform system books into one publication, called the *Uniform System of Accounts for the Lodging Industry*. A subcommittee of the Committee on Financial Management of the American Hotel & Lodging Association, with representation from the Hotel Association of New York City and Hospitality Financial and Technology Professionals, worked to produce the new guide. The names of those involved in the publication can be found in that book.

The members of the Financial Management Committee of the American Hotel & Lodging Association responsible for the Eleventh Revised Edition are:

Michael K. Craft, CPA, CHAE, CHTP, Chair ....... Peabody Hotel Group
Ralph R. Miller, CPA, CA, CBV, CHA, CHAE, Vice-Chair
................................................Inntegrated Hospitality Management, Ltd.

Kapila K. Anand, CPA..............................................................KPMG, LLP
John Baldante, CPA..................................................PKF O'Connor Davies
Cindy Braak ......................................................Marriott International, Inc.
Jeffrey C. Carter............................CW Capital Asset Management, LLC
Chad Crandall ......................................Capital Hotel Management, LLC
Michael DeNicola..............................FelCor Lodging Trust Incorporated
Dennis DuBois.........................................Carlson Rezidor Hotel Group
Christopher Garland................................... Four Seasons Hotels Limited
Brad Garner..............................................................Smith Travel Research
Kim Gauthier, CHAM, CHA ..............................Thayer Lodging Group
Alessandro Grassivaro ......Starwood Hotels & Resorts Worldwide, Inc.
Howard Isaacson............................................................ RLJ Lodging Trust
Larry Kaminsky, CPA.......................................... LaSalle Hotel Properties
Robert Mandelbaum................................PKF Hospitality Research, LLC
Raymond D. Martz ...............................................Pebblebrook Hotel Trust
Craig Mason, CHAM, CHA, CCIM, CPM... Host Hotels & Resorts, Inc.
Timothy Morrey .........................................................................JHM Hotels
Terry Murray, CPA, CMA, MBA...........................FRHI Hotels & Resorts
Louis Petruzzelli................................................Mohonk Mountain House

Gordon Potter, CPA, Ph.D. ..........................................Cornell University
Victoria Richman................................................ HVS Hotel Management
Michelle Russo................................Hotel Asset Value Enhancement, Inc.
Raymond Schmidgall, Ph.D., CPA .................Michigan State University
Gina Tallarico.....................................................Hyatt Hotels Corporation
W. Peter Temling, CPA ...................................... The Temling Group, LLC
Melvyn M. Wilinsky, CPA (retired) .. Outrigger Enterprises Group, Inc.

This publication is the result of cooperation between the Hotel Association of New York City, which owns the copyright to the publication, the American Hotel & Lodging Educational Institute, which has agreed to publish and distribute the work, and the sponsorship of the Hospitality Financial and Technology Professionals.

# The Eleventh Revised Edition

## The Process

The Financial Management Committee (FMC) of the American Hotel & Lodging Association is charged with the responsibility of maintaining the *Uniform System of Accounts for the Lodging Industry* and revising the document as needed. The FMC comprises professionals involved in the lodging industry and includes representatives from hotel owners, asset managers, hospitality management companies, brand franchising organizations, independent properties, owner-operated hotels, consultants, benchmark reporting firms, academia, and certified public accountants. The FMC strives to maintain a balance of members from each of these industry segments in order to benefit from the variety of industry knowledge and expertise and to address the concerns of all parties. Industry trade associations from around the world also participated in the process.

## Purpose and Presentation

For the Eleventh Revised Edition, the FMC re-affirmed that the primary purpose of the *Uniform System* is to provide operating statements that are formatted to provide hotel owners, managers, and other interested parties with information and data that are pertinent to the unique operating environment of the lodging industry. The terminology and guidance of the *Uniform System* are intended to be consistent with accounting principles generally accepted in the United States of America (GAAP). Throughout the text of the *Uniform System,* any reference to GAAP refers to US GAAP. In an effort to make the *Uniform System* applicable to hotel operations throughout the world, certain language has been adjusted to be more global in nature.

Because the *Uniform System* is referenced in many industry contracts and documents, the format and terminology of the Eleventh Revised Edition must be followed in order for an operating statement to be presented "in conformity with the *Uniform System of Accounts for the Lodging Industry."* To reflect their unique operating conditions, lodging properties are encouraged to develop sub-accounts and sub-schedules that provide more detail related to a particular revenue or expense item. However, these sub-accounts and sub-schedules must then roll into the appropriate line item on either a departmental schedule or the Summary Operating Statement.

The effective date of this *Uniform System* is January 1, 2015. Note that during the initial year of implementation, comparisons to prior performance may be distorted if the historical data cannot be adjusted to conform to the Eleventh Revised Edition.

# Select Changes from the Tenth Revised Edition

The *Uniform System* is periodically revised to reflect changes in industry practice and to address issues that arise as the industry develops. Examples of contemporary industry issues and practices considered and addressed in this Eleventh Revised Edition include, but are not limited to, the following:

- Technology updates
- Sustainability
- Globalization
- New terminology
- Cluster services
- Distribution channels
- Enhanced ratio analysis

The following paragraphs and bullet statements highlight the *material* changes from the Tenth Revised Edition that are incorporated in the Eleventh Revised Edition. Be advised that additional changes are presented throughout the book.

## Summary Operating Statement

The following statements highlight the *material* changes made to the presentation of the Summary Operating Statement.

- "Rentals and Other Income" has been changed to "Miscellaneous Income."
- "Revenue" has been changed to "Operating Revenue" and "Total Revenue" has been changed to "Total Operating Revenue."
- "Information and Telecommunications Systems" has been added as a fifth Undistributed Operating Department (see *Part I, Schedule 6).*
- "Fixed Charges" has been changed to "Non-Operating Income and Expenses" (see *Part I, Schedule 11).*
- "Net Operating Income" has been changed to "Earnings Before Interest, Taxes, Depreciation and Amortization," commonly called EBITDA.
- Two Summary Operating Statement formats have been developed:
  - For operators, a Replacement Reserve is deducted from EBITDA, and the bottom line is "EBITDA less Replacement Reserve."
  - For owners, Interest, Depreciation, Amortization, and Income Taxes are deducted from EBITDA, and the bottom line is "Net Income."

# Operating Schedules

The following statements highlight the *material* changes contained in the operating schedules.

## Multiple Departments

- In all departments, readers are advised to refer to Part V of the book, which provides enhanced guidance on the reporting of revenues and expenses on a gross versus net basis.

- Additional guidance is provided in each revenue-producing department regarding the handling of surcharges, service charges, and gratuities.

- Categories have been added to each department schedule to provide additional information regarding Labor Costs and Related Expenses:

  - The aggregated salaries and wages of management and non-management personnel are presented on the department schedule.

  - Service Charge Distribution is presented as a distinct cost category within Salaries, Wages, Service Charges, Contracted Labor and Bonuses. It has been moved from Payroll-Related Expenses—Supplemental Pay.

  - Contracted, leased, and outsourced labor costs are presented independently.

- New expense categories have been added to account for cluster services and department-specific reservations expenses.

- Administrative telecommunications expenses are no longer recorded within each department. All administrative telecommunications expenses are now recorded in the new *Information and Telecommunications Systems—Schedule 6.*

## Rooms Department

- The segmentation that is used to record rooms revenue reflects efforts to provide greater detail and definitions and to align with industry practices.

- Resort fees are now recorded in *Miscellaneous Income—Schedule 4.* They are not included in the calculation of average daily rate.

- Enhanced guidance is provided regarding the handling of revenues and expenses associated with mixed-ownership lodging facilities.

- Enhanced guidance is provided regarding the allocation of package revenues and the handling of package breakage, which has moved to *Miscellaneous Income—Schedule 4.*

## Food and Beverage Department

- *Food and Beverage—Schedule 2* presents the revenues from both food and beverage venues. Separate food and beverage department schedules are not mandatory.

- Enhanced guidance is provided regarding the handling of gift certificate revenue.

- The term "cover" has been replaced with the term "customer" to reflect the number of people served.

## Other Operated Departments

- Telecommunications is no longer an Other Operated Department. Guest-room-generated revenues and cost of sales are now accounted for in Guest Communications on *Minor Operated Departments—Schedule 3-xx*. Function room-generated revenues and cost of sales are accounted for in Audiovisual on *Food and Beverage—Schedule 2*. All telecommunications-related labor expenses, administrative telecommunications costs, and the costs associated with complimentary phone and Internet services are recorded on the new *Information and Telecommunications Systems—Schedule 6*.

## Miscellaneous Income

- All resort fees and package breakage are recorded in *Miscellaneous Income—Schedule 4*.

- Additional guidance is provided regarding the handling of commissions, business interruption insurance, foreign currency exchange, unused or forfeited gift certificates, and interest income.

## Undistributed Departments

- The information and telecommunications systems department has been created to consolidate all system-related technology expenses.

- Additional guidance is provided regarding the handling of non-guest-related foreign currency exchange income and expenses.

- The segregation of sales and marketing expenses was eliminated.

- Revenue management and catering sales functions have been clarified as sales and marketing expenses.

- Utility Taxes was eliminated as a separate expense category on *Utilities—Schedule 9*.

- Contract Services was added as an expense category on *Utilities—Schedule 9* to incorporate the cost of energy audits.

## Non-Operating Income and Expenses

- The net revenue generated by ownership that is not managed or maintained by the hotel is recorded as Non-Operating Income.

- An Owner Expense category has been added to account for such items as asset management fees, receiver fees, and owner-directed market studies and audits.

- Additional guidance is provided regarding the handling of equipment rental, unique municipal charges, and various employee housing expenses.

## Financial Statements

The following statements highlight the *material* changes contained in the financial statements.

- Revenue and expense categories have been added to the Income Statement to reflect changes made to the Summary Operating Statement.

- A Statement of Comprehensive Income has been added to supplement the Income Statement. An illustrative statement is provided.

- A reference to International Financial Reporting Standards (IFRS) was added.

- Gift certificates and cards have been removed from Other Current Liabilities and made a separate line item.

- Additional guidance is provided regarding the handling of inventories, operating equipment, and pre-opening expenses.

## Financial Ratios and Operating Metrics

The following statements highlight the *material* changes contained in Part III.

- In recognition of the importance of operational and financial analysis, the name of this section has been changed from "Ratios and Statistics" to "Financial Ratios and Operating Metrics."

- Ratios are presented for both operating departments and undistributed departments.

- For each department, a recommended schedule of key ratios is provided.

- A recommended labor cost schedule is provided that presents detailed labor cost data for each department.

- Additional utility and waste consumption ratios are provided, as is a discussion regarding the growing trend to measure sustainability and environmental impact.

## Revenue and Expense Guide

The following statements highlight the *material* changes contained in the Revenue and Expense Guide.

- Guidance is provided regarding the proper recording of both revenues and expenses.

- The Revenue and Expense Guide is now available in an electronic format that is both sortable and searchable.

# Introduction

A uniform system of accounts establishes standardized formats and account classifications to guide individuals in the preparation and presentation of financial statements. The information set forth in this uniform system is based on a consensus of hotel owners, asset managers, hospitality management companies, brand franchising organizations, independent properties, owner-operated hotels, consultants, benchmark reporting firms, academia, and certified public accountants, and is intended to be consistent with accounting principles generally accepted in the United States of America (GAAP).

The resulting standardization established by the uniform system of accounts permits internal and external users of financial statements to compare the financial position and operational performance of a particular property with similar types of properties in the lodging industry.

*Uniform System of Accounts for the Lodging Industry,* Eleventh Revised Edition, is divided into five parts. Part I details the financial reports related to the operational activities of a lodging property, as shown in the Summary Operating Statements and its supporting schedules. It details the required format and explains the line items for departmental statements essential in the reporting and analyzing of operating results.

The Summary Operating Statements are not a GAAP financial statement, but rather a statement that displays operating results, including property taxes, insurance costs, and replacement reserves. Terms such as Gross Operating Profit, Income Before Non-Operating Income and Expenses, and EBITDA Less Replacement Reserve, which are used in the Summary Operating Statement, are not GAAP terms, but are used within the hospitality industry.

The statements provided were developed with full-service lodging properties operating food and beverage venues in mind, but can be easily adapted to other types of properties. For example, limited-service properties would delete those schedules that do not apply to their business, such as the food and beverage schedule.

Likewise, individual properties may delete irrelevant line items, but the *Uniform System* does not provide for the addition or substitution of other revenue and expense line items. Rather, if a property determines that more detailed information is required, sub-accounts/sub-schedules may be prepared. These sub-accounts/sub-schedules are then to be rolled into the appropriate line items detailed in the *Uniform System.*

Since the *Uniform System of Accounts for the Lodging Industry* is used by lending institutions and specifically cited in many management contracts, those preparing both the Summary Operating Statements and their supporting schedules, and financial statements, must adhere to the prescribed statement formats and the classification of revenue and expense items if the financial statements are to be "in conformity with the *Uniform System.*"

Part II presents the formats and explains the line items appearing on the basic Financial Statements produced for external users, such as lenders and stockholders. The statements include:

- Balance Sheet

- Statement of Income

- Statement of Comprehensive Income

- Statement of Owners' Equity

- Statement of Cash Flows

- Notes to the Financial Statements

The format and level of detail for these basic financial statements should be developed to meet an owner's Financial Statement needs, while remaining consistent with GAAP.

Part III deals with Financial Ratios and Operating Metrics and presents a series of ratios and other information useful in analyzing the financial and operating statements in both Part I and Part II.

Part IV contains the Revenue and Expense Guide.

Part V examines gross versus net reporting, as well as the treatment of surcharges, service charges, and gratuities.

## Format of Accounts Outside the United States

The examples and formats used throughout this book follow U.S. accounting standards for the presentation of Financial Statements. Users of the book outside the United States should be aware that the accounting requirements of their own jurisdictions will not necessarily follow those of the United States. The laws of other jurisdictions and the application of accounting standards may significantly affect the format and presentation of financial statements.

In an effort to make the *Uniform System* applicable to hotel operations throughout the world, certain language relative to the Operating Statements has been adjusted to be more global in nature.

# Part I
# Operating Statements

There are two versions of the Summary Operating Statement, one for operators and one for owners. Both statements are designed to:

- Provide management with information regarding the results of operations, and

- Facilitate the comparison of such results among different lodging properties.

The two Summary Operating Statements are identical through Earnings before Interest, Taxes, Depreciation, and Amortization. Thereafter, the presentations differ:

- The Operator's Statement deducts a replacement reserve from EBITDA to reflect what is understood in the industry as "the operating income" of the property.

- The Owner's Statement deducts all remaining expenses (interest, depreciation, amortization, and income taxes) from EBITDA to reflect the net income of the entity.

The proper formats for the two versions of the Summary Operating Statement are shown on the following pages. While properties may choose to delete some of the columns or to show them in a different order, the revenue and expenses lines, unless they are irrelevant, are to be included exactly as presented if the Summary Operating Statement is to be "in conformity with the *Uniform System.*"

# Summary Operating Statement [For Operators][1]

| | Period Of | | | | | |
|---|---|---|---|---|---|---|
| | Current Period | | | Year-To-Date | | |
| | Actual | Forecast/ Budget | Prior Year | Actual | Forecast/ Budget | Prior Year |
| Rooms Available: | | | | | | |
| Rooms Sold: | | | | | | |
| Occupancy: | | | | | | |
| ADR: | | | | | | |
| Rooms RevPAR: | | | | | | |
| Total RevPAR: | | | | | | |

| | Period Of | | | | | | | | | | | |
|---|---|---|---|---|---|---|---|---|---|---|---|---|
| | Current Period | | | | | | Year-To-Date | | | | | |
| | Actual | | Forecast/ Budget | | Prior Year | | Actual | | Forecast/ Budget | | Prior Year | |
| | $ | %[2] | $ | %[2] | $ | %[2] | $ | %[2] | $ | %[2] | $ | %[2] |
| Operating Revenue | | | | | | | | | | | | |
|   Rooms | | | | | | | | | | | | |
|   Food and Beverage | | | | | | | | | | | | |
|   Other Operated Departments | | | | | | | | | | | | |
|   Miscellaneous Income | | | | | | | | | | | | |
| Total Operating Revenue | | | | | | | | | | | | |
| Departmental Expenses | | | | | | | | | | | | |
|   Rooms | | | | | | | | | | | | |
|   Food and Beverage | | | | | | | | | | | | |
|   Other Operated Departments | | | | | | | | | | | | |
| Total Departmental Expenses | | | | | | | | | | | | |
| Total Departmental Profit | | | | | | | | | | | | |
| Undistributed Operating Expenses | | | | | | | | | | | | |
|   Administrative and General | | | | | | | | | | | | |
|   Information and Telecommunications Systems | | | | | | | | | | | | |
|   Sales and Marketing | | | | | | | | | | | | |
|   Property Operation and Maintenance | | | | | | | | | | | | |
|   Utilities | | | | | | | | | | | | |
| Total Undistributed Expenses | | | | | | | | | | | | |
| Gross Operating Profit | | | | | | | | | | | | |
| Management Fees | | | | | | | | | | | | |
| Income Before Non-Operating Income and Expenses | | | | | | | | | | | | |
| Non-Operating Income and Expenses | | | | | | | | | | | | |
|   Income | | | | | | | | | | | | |
|   Rent | | | | | | | | | | | | |
|   Property and Other Taxes | | | | | | | | | | | | |
|   Insurance | | | | | | | | | | | | |
|   Other | | | | | | | | | | | | |
| Total Non-Operating Income and Expenses | | | | | | | | | | | | |
| Earnings Before Interest, Taxes, Depreciation, and Amortization | | | | | | | | | | | | |
| Replacement Reserve | | | | | | | | | | | | |
| EBITDA Less Replacement Reserve | | | | | | | | | | | | |

[1] For a complete Statement of Income, refer to Part II.
[2] All revenues and expenses should be shown as a percentage of total operating revenue, except departmental expenses, which should be shown as a percentage of their respective departmental revenue.

# Summary Operating Statement [For Owners][1]

| | PERIOD OF | | | | | |
| --- | --- | --- | --- | --- | --- | --- |
| | CURRENT PERIOD | | | YEAR-TO-DATE | | |
| | ACTUAL | FORECAST/ BUDGET | PRIOR YEAR | ACTUAL | FORECAST/ BUDGET | PRIOR YEAR |
| ROOMS AVAILABLE: | | | | | | |
| ROOMS SOLD: | | | | | | |
| OCCUPANCY: | | | | | | |
| ADR: | | | | | | |
| ROOMS RevPAR: | | | | | | |
| TOTAL RevPAR: | | | | | | |

| | PERIOD OF | | | | | | | | | | | |
| --- | --- | --- | --- | --- | --- | --- | --- | --- | --- | --- | --- | --- |
| | CURRENT PERIOD | | | | | | YEAR-TO-DATE | | | | | |
| | ACTUAL | | FORECAST/ BUDGET | | PRIOR YEAR | | ACTUAL | | FORECAST/ BUDGET | | PRIOR YEAR | |
| | $ | %[2] | $ | %[2] | $ | %[2] | $ | %[2] | $ | %[2] | $ | %[2] |
| OPERATING REVENUE | | | | | | | | | | | | |
| Rooms | | | | | | | | | | | | |
| Food and Beverage | | | | | | | | | | | | |
| Other Operated Departments | | | | | | | | | | | | |
| Miscellaneous Income | | | | | | | | | | | | |
| TOTAL OPERATING REVENUE | | | | | | | | | | | | |
| DEPARTMENTAL EXPENSES | | | | | | | | | | | | |
| Rooms | | | | | | | | | | | | |
| Food and Beverage | | | | | | | | | | | | |
| Other Operated Departments | | | | | | | | | | | | |
| TOTAL DEPARTMENTAL EXPENSES | | | | | | | | | | | | |
| TOTAL DEPARTMENTAL PROFIT | | | | | | | | | | | | |
| UNDISTRIBUTED OPERATING EXPENSES | | | | | | | | | | | | |
| Administrative and General | | | | | | | | | | | | |
| Information and Telecommunications Systems | | | | | | | | | | | | |
| Sales and Marketing | | | | | | | | | | | | |
| Property Operation and Maintenance | | | | | | | | | | | | |
| Utilities | | | | | | | | | | | | |
| TOTAL UNDISTRIBUTED EXPENSES | | | | | | | | | | | | |
| GROSS OPERATING PROFIT | | | | | | | | | | | | |
| MANAGEMENT FEES | | | | | | | | | | | | |
| INCOME BEFORE NON-OPERATING INCOME AND EXPENSES | | | | | | | | | | | | |
| NON-OPERATING INCOME AND EXPENSES | | | | | | | | | | | | |
| Income | | | | | | | | | | | | |
| Rent | | | | | | | | | | | | |
| Property and Other Taxes | | | | | | | | | | | | |
| Insurance | | | | | | | | | | | | |
| Other | | | | | | | | | | | | |
| TOTAL NON-OPERATING INCOME AND EXPENSES | | | | | | | | | | | | |
| EARNINGS BEFORE INTEREST, TAXES, DEPRECIATION, AND AMORTIZATION | | | | | | | | | | | | |
| INTEREST, DEPRECIATION, AND AMORTIZATION | | | | | | | | | | | | |
| Interest | | | | | | | | | | | | |
| Depreciation | | | | | | | | | | | | |
| Amortization | | | | | | | | | | | | |
| TOTAL INTEREST, DEPRECIATION, AND AMORTIZATION | | | | | | | | | | | | |
| INCOME BEFORE INCOME TAXES | | | | | | | | | | | | |
| Income Taxes | | | | | | | | | | | | |
| NET INCOME | | | | | | | | | | | | |

[1] For a complete Statement of Income, refer to Part II.
[2] All revenues and expenses should be shown as a percentage of total operating revenue, expcept departmental expenses, which should be shown as a percentage of their respective departmental revenue.

The Summary Operating Statements are divided into sections: Operating Revenue, Departmental Expenses, Undistributed Operating Expenses, Management Fees, Non-Operating Income and Expenses, and either Replacement Reserve or Interest, Depreciation, and Amortization and Income Taxes. The following paragraphs describe the content of each of these sections.

## Operating Revenue

The *Uniform System* includes only four revenue categories. The first two categories, Rooms and Food and Beverage, report the results of those departments. Operating revenue from any other department included in property operations—for example, a golf course, spa, or parking—is included in Other Operated Departments. The fourth revenue category is Miscellaneous Income, which includes such items as space rental, commissions, and interest income.

Total Operating Revenue is the sum of the amounts for all four categories of revenue. The Total Operating Revenue line is considered to be 100 percent, and the percentage for each revenue category is determined by dividing the dollar amount for that revenue category by Total Operating Revenue.

## Departmental Expenses

There are three categories of departmental expenses, each of which relates to an operated department revenue category. In the schedules that accompany the Summary Operating Statements, departmental expenses are separated into as many as four groups: Cost of Sales, Cost of Other Revenue, Labor Costs and Related Expenses, and Other Expenses. The total of these groups of expenses for each category of revenue is the amount reported on the respective line of the Summary Operating Statements.

The percentage for each departmental expense is calculated by dividing the dollar amount of the expense by the corresponding revenue dollar amount.

Total Departmental Expenses is the sum of the amounts for all categories of departmental expenses. The percentage for Total Departmental Expenses is calculated by dividing Total Departmental Expenses by Total Operating Revenue.

## Total Departmental Profit

Total Departmental Profit is calculated by subtracting Total Departmental Expenses from Total Operating Revenue. The Total Departmental Profit percentage is calculated by dividing the dollar amount of Total Departmental Profit by Total Operating Revenue.

## Undistributed Operating Expenses

The Undistributed Operating Expenses section reports expenses that are considered applicable to the entire property. In order to achieve uniformity, it is not appropriate to allocate these types of expenses to specific departments. The Undistributed Operating Expenses are separated into five categories: Administrative and General, Information and Telecommunications Systems, Sales and Marketing, Property Operation and Maintenance, and Utilities.

The percentage for each Undistributed Operating Expense is calculated by dividing the dollar amount of the expense by Total Operating Revenue.

Total Undistributed Expenses is the sum of the amounts for all five categories of Undistributed Operating Expenses. The percentage for Total Undistributed Expenses is calculated by dividing Total Undistributed Expenses by Total Operating Revenue.

## Gross Operating Profit

Gross Operating Profit is calculated by subtracting Total Undistributed Expenses from Total Departmental Profit. The Gross Operating Profit percentage is calculated by dividing the dollar amount of Gross Operating Profit by Total Operating Revenue.

## Management Fees

Management Fees represents the cost for management services performed by a management company to operate the property as a whole. If a management fee is paid to another entity for the oversight of a department other than Rooms within the property, such as Food and Beverage, that fee is charged to the specific department for which the fee is incurred. The percentage for Management Fees is determined by dividing the dollar amount of Management Fees by Total Operating Revenue.

## Income Before Non-Operating Income and Expenses

Income Before Non-Operating Income and Expenses is calculated by subtracting Management Fees from Gross Operating Profit. The percentage for Income Before Non-Operating Income and Expenses is calculated by dividing the dollar amount of Income Before Non-Operating Income and Expenses by Total Operating Revenue.

## Non-Operating Income and Expenses

The items included under Non-Operating Income and Expenses include nonoperating Income, Rent, Property and Other Taxes, Insurance, and Other nonoperating expenses. The percentage for each of these expenses is calculated by dividing the dollar amount of the expense by Total Operating Revenue.

Total Non-Operating Income and Expenses is the sum of the amounts shown for Rent, Property and Other Taxes, Insurance, and Other non-operating expenses offset by the non-operating Income amount. The Total Non-Operating Income and Expenses percentage is calculated by dividing the dollar amount for Total Non-Operating Income and Expenses by Total Operating Revenue.

## Earnings Before Interest, Taxes, Depreciation, and Amortization

Earnings Before Interest, Taxes, Depreciation, and Amortization (EBITDA) is determined by subtracting the Total Non-Operating Income and Expenses from Income Before Non-Operating Income and Expenses. The EBITDA percentage is calculated by dividing the dollar amount for EBITDA by Total Operating Revenue.

## *For Operators*
## Replacement Reserve

Many management contracts, loan agreements, and owners/operators specify the establishment of a reserve to accumulate the funds required for future replacements of furniture, fixtures, and equipment. These funds may also provide for certain capital improvements and the replacement of existing assets such as the major building systems. Replacement Reserve indicates the amount set aside for the period covered by the Summary Operating Statement, whether or not the reserve is actually funded. The percentage for Replacement Reserve is calculated by dividing the dollar amount of the reserve by Total Operating Revenue.

## EBITDA Less Replacement Reserve

EBITDA Less Replacement Reserve is determined by subtracting Replacement Reserve from EBITDA. The EBITDA Less Replacement Reserve percentage is calculated by dividing the dollar amount for EBITDA Less Replacement Reserve by Total Operating Revenue.

## *For Owners*
## Net Income

To reconcile the Net Income presented on the Summary Operating Statement to the Net Income presented on the Statement of Income (see Part II), expenses typically paid by the owner are deducted from EBITDA. These expenses include Interest, Depreciation, Amortization, and Income Taxes. Total Interest, Depreciation and Amortization is deducted from EBITDA to calculate Income Before Income Taxes. Income Taxes are then deducted from Income Before Income Taxes to calculate Net Income. The Net Income percentage is calculated by dividing the dollar amount for Net Income by Total Operating Revenue.

# ROOMS—SCHEDULE 1

| | PERIOD OF | | | | | | | | | | | |
| --- | --- | --- | --- | --- | --- | --- | --- | --- | --- | --- | --- | --- |
| | CURRENT PERIOD | | | | | | YEAR-TO-DATE | | | | | |
| | ACTUAL | | FORECAST/ BUDGET | | PRIOR YEAR | | ACTUAL | | FORECAST/ BUDGET | | PRIOR YEAR | |
| | $ | % | $ | % | $ | % | $ | % | $ | % | $ | % |
| REVENUE | | | | | | | | | | | | |
| Transient Rooms Revenue | | | | | | | | | | | | |
| Retail | | | | | | | | | | | | |
| Discount | | | | | | | | | | | | |
| Negotiated | | | | | | | | | | | | |
| Qualified | | | | | | | | | | | | |
| Wholesale | | | | | | | | | | | | |
| Total Transient Rooms Revenue | | | | | | | | | | | | |
| Group Rooms Revenue | | | | | | | | | | | | |
| Corporate | | | | | | | | | | | | |
| Association/Convention | | | | | | | | | | | | |
| Government | | | | | | | | | | | | |
| Tour/Wholesalers | | | | | | | | | | | | |
| SMERF | | | | | | | | | | | | |
| Total Group Rooms Revenue | | | | | | | | | | | | |
| Contract Rooms Revenue | | | | | | | | | | | | |
| Other Rooms Revenue | | | | | | | | | | | | |
| Less: Allowances | | | | | | | | | | | | |
| TOTAL ROOMS REVENUE | | | | | | | | | | | | |
| EXPENSES | | | | | | | | | | | | |
| Labor Costs and Related Expenses | | | | | | | | | | | | |
| Salaries, Wages, Service Charges, Contracted Labor and Bonuses | | | | | | | | | | | | |
| Salaries and Wages | | | | | | | | | | | | |
| Management | | | | | | | | | | | | |
| Non-Management | | | | | | | | | | | | |
| Complimentary F&B | | | | | | | | | | | | |
| Front Office | | | | | | | | | | | | |
| Guest Services | | | | | | | | | | | | |
| Housekeeping | | | | | | | | | | | | |
| Laundry | | | | | | | | | | | | |
| Reservations | | | | | | | | | | | | |
| Transportation | | | | | | | | | | | | |
| Sub-Total: Salaries and Wages | | | | | | | | | | | | |
| Service Charge Distribution | | | | | | | | | | | | |
| Contracted, Leased and Outsourced Labor | | | | | | | | | | | | |
| Bonuses and Incentives | | | | | | | | | | | | |
| Total Salaries, Wages, Service Charges, Contracted Labor and Bonuses | | | | | | | | | | | | |
| Payroll-Related Expenses | | | | | | | | | | | | |
| Payroll Taxes | | | | | | | | | | | | |
| Supplemental Pay | | | | | | | | | | | | |
| Employee Benefits | | | | | | | | | | | | |
| Total Payroll-Related Expenses | | | | | | | | | | | | |
| Total Labor Costs and Related Expenses | | | | | | | | | | | | |
| Other Expenses | | | | | | | | | | | | |
| Cleaning Supplies | | | | | | | | | | | | |
| Cluster Services | | | | | | | | | | | | |

*(continued)*

## ROOMS—SCHEDULE 1 *(continued)*

| | PERIOD OF | | | | | |
|---|---|---|---|---|---|---|
| | CURRENT PERIOD | | | YEAR-TO-DATE | | |
| | ACTUAL | FORECAST/ BUDGET | PRIOR YEAR | ACTUAL | FORECAST/ BUDGET | PRIOR YEAR |
| | $    % | $    % | $    % | $    % | $    % | $    % |
| Commissions | | | | | | |
| Commissions and Fees—Group | | | | | | |
| Complimentary Food and Beverage | | | | | | |
| Complimentary In-Room/Media Entertainment | | | | | | |
| Complimentary Services and Gifts | | | | | | |
| Contract Services | | | | | | |
| Corporate Office Reimbursables | | | | | | |
| Decorations | | | | | | |
| Dues and Subscriptions | | | | | | |
| Entertainment—In-House | | | | | | |
| Equipment Rental | | | | | | |
| Guest Relocation | | | | | | |
| Guest Supplies | | | | | | |
| Guest Transportation | | | | | | |
| Laundry and Dry Cleaning | | | | | | |
| Licenses and Permits | | | | | | |
| Linen | | | | | | |
| Miscellaneous | | | | | | |
| Operating Supplies | | | | | | |
| Postage and Overnight Delivery Charges | | | | | | |
| Printing and Stationery | | | | | | |
| Reservations | | | | | | |
| Royalty Fees | | | | | | |
| Training | | | | | | |
| Travel—Meals and Entertainment | | | | | | |
| Travel—Other | | | | | | |
| Uniform Costs | | | | | | |
| Uniform Laundry | | | | | | |
| Total Other Expenses | | | | | | |
| TOTAL EXPENSES | | | | | | |
| DEPARTMENTAL PROFIT | | | | | | |

*Rooms—Schedule 1* reflects the proper format for a Rooms department and designates the revenue and expense accounts that are approved as line items in the *Uniform System.* Individual properties may delete irrelevant line items, but the *Uniform System* does not provide for the addition or substitution of other revenue or expense line items. Rather, properties may choose to develop a sub-account/sub-schedule to provide more detail related to a particular revenue or expense item. This sub-account/sub-schedule is then to be rolled into the appropriate line item. Additionally, properties may choose to delete some of the columns or to show them in a different order and remain "in conformity with the *Uniform System.*"

    *Rooms—Schedule 1* is designed to reflect a minimum standard of reporting. Properties may develop additional support schedules to provide additional information necessary to properly evaluate and benchmark operations within the Rooms department.

Refer to Part III for recommended operating metrics that are pertinent to the Rooms department.

The line items for *Rooms—Schedule 1* are defined in the following pages.

# Revenue

The primary source of revenue for a lodging property generally arises from the rental of rooms and suites to guests. Rooms Revenue is divided into four parts: Transient Rooms Revenue, Group Rooms Revenue, Contract Rooms Revenue, and Other Rooms Revenue.

## Transient Rooms Revenue

Transient Rooms Revenue commonly includes revenue derived from rental of rooms and suites by individuals or groups occupying fewer than 10 rooms per night. It also includes rooms leased to guests who have established permanent residence, with or without a contract. Transient stays typically include the following categories:

- *Retail*: A market positioned, seasonally priced room rate for transient business. It is a non-discounted, non-qualified rate that is always available when the hotel has rooms to sell.

- *Discount*: A rate open to the general public (non-qualified) under which the guest pays less than the Retail rate. Examples include advance purchase, loyalty redemptions or offers, packages, promotions, and online travel agency (OTA) opaque.

- *Negotiated*: A rate negotiated with special (typically corporate) accounts. Identification with a particular company or organization is required to obtain this rate.

- *Qualified*: A rate that requires the customer to be associated with a particular organization or to have a specific affiliation in order to book. Identification is required upon check-in. Examples include senior citizen, AAA, government, and employee rate.

- *Wholesale*: A discounted room rate packaged with outside travel and/or car rental prior to being sold to the guest. The rate is not visible to the guest.

## Group Rooms Revenue

Group Rooms Revenue includes revenue derived from renting blocks of rooms or suites to a group. A group is typically defined as 10 or more rooms per night sold pursuant to a contract. Group Rooms Revenue is recorded net of discounts to wholesalers for selling large blocks of rooms. Rebates or subsidies granted directly to a group should be recorded as contra revenue. To facilitate effective sales and marketing efforts, Group Rooms Revenue is generally segregated by market segment. Market segments typically include the following categories:

- *Corporate*: A negotiated rate for a block of rooms associated with a company related to industries such as, but not limited to, manufacturing, retail, healthcare, insurance, financial, law firms, professional sports organizations, entertainment companies, and transportation corporations.

- *Association/Convention*: A negotiated rate for a block of rooms associated with a trade, professional, or philanthropic association.

- *Government*: A negotiated rate for a block of rooms associated with qualifying government agencies including, but not limited to, active military, national security, and health and human services.

- *Tour/Wholesalers*: A negotiated rate for a block of rooms associated with tour operators/wholesalers who package together travel components and sell them as escorted tour group, escorted tour series, or inbound ad hoc group.

- *SMERF (Social, Military, Educational, Religious, Fraternal)*: A negotiated rate for a block of rooms associated with organizations that fall into the categories of social (a celebratory or personal event), military (veterans, support, and social groups), education (private or public organizations founded and united for the specific purpose to educate), religious (faith-specific organizations), and fraternal (honor societies, fraternities, sororities, unions, and unique forms of organizations that limit membership to specific fields of study, expertise, or employment).

## Contract Rooms Revenue

Contract Rooms Revenue includes revenue derived from a contract with another entity for a consistent block of rooms for an extended period over 30 days. Contract Rooms Revenue is recorded net of discounts. Examples include domiciled airline crews, ongoing corporate training seminars, and incentive-based benefit programs.

## Other Rooms Revenue

Other Rooms Revenue is miscellaneous revenue associated with guestrooms. This revenue is included in determining Total Rooms Revenue and is used in the calculation of average daily rate (ADR). Items associated with Other Rooms Revenue include:

- *No-shows.* This is revenue derived from a transient or group guest who has individually guaranteed payment to reserve a room, but has failed to occupy the room. No room nights are to be recorded for a no-show. Group attrition and cancellation and transient guest cancellation after the cutoff date are included in Attrition Fees and Cancellation Fees on *Miscellaneous Income — Schedule 4*, not Other Rooms Revenue.

- *Day use.* This is revenue derived from sources such as rooms used for hospitality suites, dressing rooms, employment interviews, movie auditions, and wholesale distributors (for example, clothing, toys, other merchandise). No Food and Beverage services should be included.

- *Early departure fees.*

- *Late check-out fees.*

- *Rental of rollaway beds and cribs.*

- *Surcharges and service charges.* These charges generally include any mandatory, non-discretionary, or other charge automatically added to a customer account in respect of the service or use of an amenity. Service charges in the Rooms department are common in certain geographic areas. Resort fees are not part of Rooms service charges and should be included in *Miscellaneous Income—Schedule 4*. The key determining factors for the recording of surcharges and service charges (versus gratuities) are set out in Part V.

Items placed in the guestroom for sale to guests are not included in the calculation of Other Rooms Revenue. For example, bottled water or packaged food items that are charged to guests if consumed are considered Mini Bar Food Revenue on *Food and Beverage—Schedule 2*. Non–food and beverage items sold in the room are credited to Miscellaneous Other Revenue on *Food and Beverage—Schedule 2*. Properties without food and beverage operations would show commission income on *Miscellaneous Income—Schedule 4*. However, if the property earns revenue and incurs expenses, the gross amounts should be reported in Other Operated Departments.

## Other Rooms Department Considerations

This section discusses other issues affecting the Rooms department. These include package revenues, barter transactions, sales and excise taxes and transient occupancy taxes, loyalty programs, wholesaler revenues, and e-channel revenues.

*Package Revenues.* Package revenues are lodging accommodations sold in conjunction with other services provided by either the property or third parties as part of a single transaction with the customer. For example, a guest could obtain accommodations, meals, golf, spa treatment, and a rental vehicle for a single price. Care needs to be taken to ensure that revenues are appropriately allocated among departments.

Where properties provide incidental (gratis) food and/or beverages to a guest, or where the guest cannot opt out of the food program, or where meals are provided as part of a franchise company brand standard, the cost of the food and/or beverage item is charged to the Rooms department, and no allocation of revenues should be made to the Food and Beverage department. In all other situations, such as resorts that market their room product on a Modified American Plan basis, it is appropriate to allocate the food and/or beverage revenue to the Food and Beverage department.

In the case where interdepartmental allocations are necessary (for example, where revenues have to be allocated between Rooms and Food and Beverage or other departments), the allocation is made proportionately based on the theoretical "market" values for the separate services if marketed on a standalone basis. The "market" values represent average realized amounts achieved by the property for similar services. The packaged revenue is then allocated based on the ratio among these market values. Ratios should be analyzed at least annually and modified more frequently if there are material changes to the market values (e.g., for highly seasonal hotels like resorts).

Market values should be driven by the revenue component of the item, not by the profit margin or cost of the item. The intent is to not inflate Rooms revenue by leaving revenue belonging to other departments in Rooms.

As an example, consider the following spa package consisting of a guestroom for one night, four meals, and the use of the property's spa facilities at an inclusive price of $240, not including taxes, gratuities, or service charges. Despite the fact that the fair market value of the package is $320, only the $240 total amount will show on the guest account plus sales, excise, and transient taxes as applicable to each category of revenue. Special attention must be taken to ensure that the taxes charged meet the requirements of the taxing authorities. The property computes the departmental allocations of the $240 sales price as follows:

| Department | Market Value | Ratio | Package Allocations |
|------------|--------------|-------|---------------------|
| Rooms | $160 | 50% | $120 |
| Food | $112 | 35% | 84 |
| Spa | 48 | 15% | 36 |
| Total | $320 | 100% | $240 |

In the case of packages that include a third-party vendor, the rate for the provision of the third-party service will likely be established by contractual arrangement. The third-party portion of a package should be recognized as revenue in the appropriate department and the remaining price of the package should be allocated to the respective departments based on their relative market value.

In some circumstances, the guests will either not consume all of the components that are included in the package or will spend more than the market value allocated to the non-rooms component of the package. If the hotel elects not to charge or refund the guest, the residual value that remains is commonly referred to as package breakage. Package breakage should be recorded to *Miscellaneous Income—Schedule 4*, regardless of whether it is a surplus or deficit. In cases where breakage is either significant or consistently negative, the package structure and pricing should be reviewed and adjusted accordingly.

***Barter Transactions.*** Lodging properties often enter into barter transactions. Typically, these arrangements require the property to provide accommodations and possibly food, beverages, golf packages, and other services in exchange for other services, such as advertising. These are non-monetary transactions that are settled through the provision of goods and services. While the form and details of barter transactions vary, they typically occur during periods of low occupancy.

Generally accepted accounting principles require that revenue and expenses associated with barter transactions be recognized. Typically, this means that Prepaid Expenses will be charged with the value of the services to be received by the property and Other Liabilities will be credited with the value of the services to be provided by the property. As the property receives the services agreed to in the barter transaction, it expenses the value of those services, leaving in Prepaid Expenses only the unused value of the barter transaction. Similarly, as the property provides the services agreed to in the barter transaction, it recognizes the revenue by writing down the liability, leaving only the unredeemed value of the services in Other Liabilities. The value assigned within the barter agreement to the services received should, accordingly, be a conservative average of the market rate for similar accommodations or services at the property. When rooms are part of a barter transaction, they are counted as occupied rooms and the corresponding statistics included.

*Sales and Excise Taxes and Transient Occupancy Taxes.* Most jurisdictions levy sales or excise taxes on revenues. In addition, many jurisdictions assess a transient occupancy, value added, accommodations, or resort tax on certain lodging revenues. In these cases, the property merely acts as a conduit in the collection of taxes for the taxing authority. The property is required to pay the taxes to the taxing authority regardless of whether the tax is charged to the guest. No revenue is recognized. Special attention must be taken with regard to the treatment of complimentary rooms by the taxing authorities.

*Loyalty Programs.* In an attempt to build customer loyalty and repeat business, some properties and chains have implemented loyalty programs where low-priced or free accommodations or services are provided to frequent guests based on points earned at various levels of patronage. The value of the loyalty program points is charged as a marketing expense when the points are issued with a corresponding credit to a liability account. When a guest redeems the points, the value of the points is credited to Rooms Revenue and debited to the liability account if the loyalty program is solely at the property level, or to a receivable account if the program is operated at a chain level. In the latter case, the cost is passed on to the chain to reimburse the property. Special attention must be paid so that the value assigned to points issued covers the liability associated with the estimated redemption of points. When rooms are part of a loyalty program, they are counted as occupied rooms and included in the corresponding statistics.

*Wholesaler and OTA Revenues.* Many lodging properties use the services of a wholesaler in connection with the sale and distribution of guestrooms. In turn, wholesalers generally market the rooms on behalf of the properties to retail travel agents. To entice wholesalers to perform the marketing function, they are offered a block or a set number of rooms at a discounted price. The rate offered to the wholesaler is typically a discount off of the rack or posted room rate for the rooms in the block. The block is typically non-binding, which means that the wholesaler is not obligated to purchase any of the allotted rooms in the block. The marketing and packaging efforts carried out by wholesalers are at no direct cost to the property. From the property's perspective, the marketing efficiency that a wholesaler represents justifies the lower rate charged to the wholesaler. The property does not exercise control over the pricing a wholesaler charges its customer.

Internet wholesalers focus not on travel agents, but rather on the end consumer whom they reach by marketing over the Internet. However, OTA wholesalers are no different from traditional wholesalers, and therefore the accounting for an OTA wholesaler is the same as that afforded to traditional wholesalers.

The fact that a wholesaler or an OTA wholesaler resells a room product either in combination with other travel services or alone is irrelevant to the way a property records the revenue received from a wholesaler. Guestroom sales to wholesalers and other similar entities are recorded at the net rate received by the property for the room, exclusive of any taxes or other charges, such as porterage, which may be added to the sale. It is not appropriate for a property to record a sale to a wholesaler at rack rates, which would have the effect of overstating revenues, average daily rate, RevPAR, and expenses, by virtue of recording an artificial expense, or commission, which would be implicit if the sale were grossed up. From a property's perspective, the sale occurs not to the end user, the consumer, but to the wholesaler. It is at this point in the revenue cycle that the sale occurs, and it is with the wholesaler that the property bears the risk of collection. Hence, it is at this time that the sale is recorded on the books of the property and at the contracted price with the wholesaler. What happens beyond that initial sale is not part of the revenue cycle for the property and is therefore not reflected on the books of the property.

Commissions paid to travel agents and meeting planners are not synonymous with the marketing services performed by a wholesaler. Travel agents are not afforded special rates for individual bookings, as there is no marketing efficiency brought to the hotel by a travel agent, unlike a wholesaler. Accordingly, commissions are not treated as reductions in room rates, but are charged to the appropriate commissions expense account in the Rooms department.

***Mixed-Ownership Lodging Facilities.*** Properties of all types and sizes are building or converting rooms into residential units creating "mixed-ownership" entities. These facilities may be timeshares, strata, fractional use, or whole ownership. Merely operating these mixed-ownership projects as a lodging operation does not in and of itself qualify the revenue stream to be recorded in the Rooms department. Consideration must be given to the individual facts and circumstances of each project.

The first step in identifying the revenue treatment of the mixed ownership or residential rental component is to determine if the reporting should be gross or net (see Part V). When working through the criteria for gross versus net, weight should be given to which party incurs the predominant economic loss if the renter fails to pay.

Once the revenue treatment is determined, there are three scenarios for inclusion in the Statement of Income.

*Scenario 1: Property assumes the predominant economic risk long term:* The property enters into an agreement with the third-party unit owner that extends one year or beyond and the units are included in the hotel room inventory for the full year. Under the terms of the agreement, the property assumes the economic risk associated with operating the third-party-owned units pursuant to the contractual relationship. The associated revenue stream is recorded in the Rooms department within the Transient, Group, Contract, and Other revenue categories as described previously in this section and the units are considered available rooms in the property room inventory. Alternately, a property could create a sub-schedule for "mixed ownership" revenue and roll up the individual revenues and expenses into the appropriate revenue and expense categories in the Rooms department. Where the contract permits the unit owner a limited number of nights in the unit, the unit owner would remain in the available room and would be recorded as a complimentary room. Rental payments (or a proportionate share thereof) to third-party owners due under the contractual agreement would be a Rent expense on *Non-Operating Income and Expenses — Schedule 11.*

*Scenario 2: Property assumes the predominant economic risk short term:* The property enters into an agreement with the third-party unit owner, whereby the unit owner places the unit into a rental program during part, but not all, of the year. Under the terms of the agreement, the property assumes the predominant economic risk associated with operating the third-party-owned units pursuant to the contractual relationship. For example, the property is responsible to reimburse or pay a rental/use fee to the third-party unit owner each time the unit is rented, even if the revenue is not collected by the property. The associated revenue stream is recorded in the Other Operated Departments section of the Summary Operating Statement. The property may choose to track the revenue and statistics as Transient, Group, Contract, and Other revenue within the Other Operated Department. However, due to the temporary nature of the room availability, such rooms are not considered property room inventory and are not included in room occupancy, ADR, and RevPAR statistics. Rental payments, either fixed or a percentage of net revenue, to third-party owners due under the contractual agreement would be a Rent expense on *Non-Operating Income and Expenses — Schedule 11.*

Labor costs and related expenses and operating expenses incurred by the property to rent and service the units would be recorded in the expenses of the Other Operated Department.

*Scenario 3: Third-party unit owner assumes the predominant economic risk:* The third-party owner assumes the predominant economic risk for renting the unit and reimburses the property for all expenses incurred by the property. The net revenue received by the property as an agent is the commission revenue on the rental. The recovery of any operating expenses or common area maintenance ("CAM") reimbursements is considered revenue received by the property and is recorded in *Minor Operated Departments — Schedule 3-xx* if the property earns a profit for providing the services, or *Non-Operating Income and Expenses — Schedule 11* if the property recovers the expenses without a profit. Examples of reimbursements would be maintenance/cleaning fees for the room rental, reservations charges, and administrative fees associated with the rental of the unit.

Labor costs and related expenses and operating expenses incurred by the property to rent and service the units would be recorded in the expenses of the Minor Operated Department or on *Non-Operating Income and Expenses — Schedule 11*, depending upon where the revenue is recorded as noted above.

Average rate and occupancy statistics are affected depending upon the facts and circumstances. If the relationship between property and owner qualifies for inclusion in the Rooms department (Scenario 1 above), then it is appropriate to record the available and occupied third-party-owned units in the total rooms available and total occupied rooms statistics of the property. Failing to meet the criteria set forth with respect to inclusion of such rental revenue in the Rooms department warrants the exclusion of the third-party-owned units from the Rooms department operating statistics. Instead, such statistics are recorded on a supplemental basis as discussed in Part III.

As indicated in the three scenarios above, under certain circumstances, mixed ownership revenue in its entirety may be reported on a net basis within *Miscellaneous Income—Schedule 4* and in other circumstances may be reported on a gross basis in the Rooms department or Other Operated Departments. For additional information, see Part V.

## Allowances

Allowances refers to a reduction in revenue due to a service problem, not an error in posting. Errors in posting, such as posting an incorrect rate, are treated as adjustments to revenue, regardless of the accounting period in which the error occurred.

## Total Rooms Revenue

Total Rooms Revenue is calculated by summing Transient Rooms Revenue, Group Rooms Revenue, Contract Rooms Revenue, and Other Rooms Revenue and subtracting Allowances. Total Rooms Revenue is the amount that appears on the Summary Operating Statement under Operating Revenue—Rooms.

In completing the revenue section of Schedule 1, consider the Total Rooms Revenue line to be 100 percent. The percentage for each source of revenue is determined by dividing the dollar amount for that revenue source by Total Rooms Revenue.

# Expenses

Rooms department expenses are separated into two major categories: Labor Costs and Related Expenses and Other Expenses.

## Labor Costs and Related Expenses

Labor Costs and Related Expenses includes all of the payroll expenses associated with Salaries, Wages, Service Charges, Contracted Labor, Bonuses, and Payroll-Related Expenses for employees and contractors. A list of the positions typically included in the Rooms department is provided in the Department Payroll Titles section at the end of Part I.

*Salaries and Wages.* Includes the earnings paid to employees for duties that relate to the operation of the property, such as regular pay, overtime pay, and shift differential pay. If an employee works in a department other than his or her regular home department, his or her earnings must be charged as Salaries and Wages in that other department, regardless of the duties being performed. For example, if a Rooms department employee works as a server at a Food and Beverage function, his or her earnings for the function are charged to Salaries and Wages in the Food and Beverage department, not to his or her home department.

Salaries and Wages should be delineated by significant management and non-management payroll titles within the department. If necessary, payroll titles should be aggregated to preserve the confidentiality of a specific employee's payroll.

Salaries and Wages includes the earnings associated with temporary employees when such expenses are processed through the property's payroll system.

***Service Charge Distribution.*** Includes the cost of service charges paid through the payroll system for hotel employees.

***Contracted, Leased and Outsourced Labor.*** Includes the gross cost of contracted, leased, and outsourced labor incurred when a property enters into an agreement with a third-party contractor to provide employees to fill positions that would normally be held by individuals paid on the regular payroll. In these situations, the property records or tracks the hours worked and pays the third-party contractor on an hourly or other agreed basis. A typical example is the use of individuals brought into the property to fill in for a shortage of Rooms department staff.

Contracted, Leased and Outsourced Labor includes the gross cost associated with shared staffing arrangements when such arrangements are supported by formal agreements.

***Bonuses and Incentives.*** Includes bonuses (contractual and discretionary), incentive pay, and other types of performance pay designed to drive revenue through sales, profit, or guest satisfaction.

***Total Salaries, Wages, Service Charges, Contracted Labor and Bonuses.*** Calculated by summing Salaries and Wages, Service Charge Distribution, Contracted, Leased and Outsourced Labor, and Bonuses and Incentives.

***Payroll-Related Expenses.*** Includes amounts paid for an employee for duties that relate to the operation of the property and amounts paid for an employee who works in a department other than his or her regular home department regardless of the duties being performed. Payroll-Related Expenses includes the following items:

- *Payroll Taxes.* Includes the employer share of contributions to national and state retirement, unemployment, disability and medical insurance programs, and other mandated payroll-related taxes or social insurance items. (See *Payroll-Related Expenses — Schedule 14.*)

- *Supplemental Pay.* Includes personal days, vacation pay, sick pay, holiday pay, jury duty pay, relocation pay, paid time off, and severance pay. (See *Payroll-Related Expenses — Schedule 14.*)

- *Employee Benefits.* Includes all other payroll-related expenses, such as employer-paid health insurance expenses, pension contributions, and union dues and fees. (See *Payroll-Related Expenses — Schedule 14.*) The distribution of employee meal costs from *Staff Dining — Schedule 13* is charged to this line.

***Total Payroll-Related Expenses.*** Calculated by summing Payroll Taxes, Supplemental Pay, and Employee Benefits.

*Note regarding shared staffing arrangements and cluster services:* Where reasonable and easily identifiable, labor costs related to shared staffing arrangements and cluster services should be charged to salaries and wages or payroll-related expenses.

## Total Labor Costs and Related Expenses

Total Labor Costs and Related Expenses is calculated by summing Total Salaries, Wages, Service Charges, Contracted Labor and Bonuses and Total Payroll-Related Expenses. The percentage for each labor cost component as well as Total Labor Costs and Related Expenses is calculated by dividing the line item amount by Total Rooms Revenue. Refer to Part III for recommended operating metrics that are pertinent to Labor Costs and Related Expenses.

## Other Expenses

This expense grouping includes the significant Rooms department expenses approved as Other Expenses in the *Uniform System.* Individual properties may delete irrelevant line items, but the *Uniform System* does not provide for the addition or substitution of other expense line items. Rather, properties may choose to develop a sub-account/sub-schedule to provide more detail related to a particular expense item. This sub-account/sub-schedule is then to be rolled into the appropriate line item listed below.

*Cleaning Supplies.* Includes the cost of products used in cleansing, sweeping, polishing, waxing, and disinfecting areas associated with the Rooms department.

*Cluster Services.* Includes allocation for costs shared between hotels in a limited geographic area (as opposed to nationally consolidated services such as those chargeable to Corporate Office Reimbursables). Where reasonable and easily identifiable, labor costs and related expenses should be charged to their respective line item and only other expenses are charged to Cluster Services. Where not practical, the fair allocation of the total cluster service expenses should be recognized here.

*Commissions.* Includes the remuneration paid to authorized agents for securing rooms business for the property, such as travel agent commissions. Travel agent commissions are generally reflected as an expense of the Rooms department regardless of whether the commission relates to accommodations only or to other services as well. This practice is generally followed because allocations of these commissions to other departments would not be cost-effective.

In some properties, blocks of rooms are provided to travel agents, wholesalers, and consolidators at a negotiated rate. These rooms are subsequently remarketed to the eventual guest. Revenue from these transactions is to be recorded at the negotiated rate and no attempt made to record additional revenue based on a rack or normal rate with an offset to commission expense.

Commissions also includes remuneration paid to rental agents for permanent rooms business that may involve leases. In the case of leases, the remuneration is prorated over the term of the lease.

*Commissions and Fees—Group.* Includes payments made to third-party meeting planners who act as a liaison between a hotel and a group in finding suitable meeting and accommodation space for the group, as well as fees paid to third-party housing companies. Rebates or subsidies granted directly to a group should be recorded as contra revenue.

*Complimentary Food and Beverage.* Includes the cost of food and beverage items and related supplies provided on a gratis basis, such as a breakfast or an evening reception, often provided in a club/concierge/executive lounge, as long as these are not part of a package (e.g., weekend getaway). This also includes complimentary coffee, often offered in the hotel lobby. Where labor is provided by employees outside the Rooms department, refer to Labor Costs and Related Expenses for guidance on allocating/transferring labor costs.

*Complimentary In-Room/Media Entertainment.* Includes the cost of providing media services (e.g., cable, music, games, satellite video) to guestrooms. It does not include the cost associated with pay-for-a-fee media, which is charged to Other Operated Departments or netted against revenue in Miscellaneous Income, whichever is appropriate. When brand and/or hotel standards dictate complimentary Internet to all guests, the access expense should be recorded on *Information and Telecommunications Systems—Schedule 6.*

*Complimentary Services and Gifts.* Includes the cost of providing gift items used in gratis presentations for promotional purposes to guests and vendors of the Rooms department, such as the cost of newspapers provided to guests on a complimentary basis, VIP gifts, guestroom flowers, or a complimentary fruit basket sent to the room of a frequent guest.

*Contract Services.* Includes expenses for activities performed for the Rooms department by outside contractors and professional service providers rather than by hotel employees, unless identified in this department with a specific line item. Department-specific consulting services and the costs of contracting outside companies to clean carpets and rugs, to perform night cleaning of the hotel lobby, or to disinfect areas associated with the Rooms department are typical examples. If supplies are purchased for contract companies to use, the supplies are charged to the appropriate supply account. The cost of contracts for Rooms department laundry and dry cleaning is charged to Laundry and Dry Cleaning.

*Corporate Office Reimbursables.* Includes the allocations of salaries and expenses of corporate or management company Rooms department personnel billed to the property by the regional or corporate office or by the management company, consistent with any contractual arrangements. Travel expenses of corporate or management company Rooms department personnel that are incurred while visiting the property, including the costs of meals and other applicable services or amenities provided to corporate or management company staff while on business in the property for the benefit of the property, are also charged to this account.

*Decorations.* Includes the cost of decorative items used in Rooms department areas for holidays and special events. Decorations also includes the cost of fresh floral arrangements used in the public areas. Guestroom flowers should be included in Complimentary Services and Gifts.

*Dues and Subscriptions.* Includes the cost of representation of the Rooms department, or of members of the staff when authorized to represent the Rooms department, in business or professional organizations. Dues and Subscriptions is also charged with the cost of subscriptions to newspapers, magazines, and books for use by the staff of the Rooms department.

*Entertainment—In-House.* Includes the food and beverage at cost, gratuities, service charges, and sales taxes (if applicable) consumed in the entertainment of guests, vendors, and business clients in the property's food and beverage facilities.

*Equipment Rental.* Includes the costs of renting any type of equipment that may be used either sporadically in the Rooms department or as a replacement for equipment out of service on a temporary basis. Equipment lease payments made under a qualified operating lease are charged to Other Property and Equipment under the Rent section of *Non-Operating Income and Expenses—Schedule 11*.

*Guest Relocation.* Includes the cost of renting accommodations in other properties when a decision is made to move a guest (usually on arrival) to another property because of a lack of available rooms. This item also includes any incidental costs, gratuities, or compensation paid in connection with these circumstances.

*Guest Supplies.* Includes the cost of consumable supplies and amenities provided for guests in the guestroom, such as soaps, shampoos, lotions, toilet tissue, shoeshine mitts, shower caps, and writing materials. The costs of any complimentary or hotel/brand-required offering provided at no charge to all guests, such as bottled water and coffee provided in the guestroom, are also included in Guest Supplies.

*Guest Transportation.* Includes all costs associated with transporting guests to and from the property, such as fuel costs, costs of washing and cleaning vehicles, the occasional rental of vehicles for transporting large groups, and the costs of contracting guest transportation services. The costs of mechanical maintenance of vehicles used to transport guests are charged to *Property Operation and Maintenance—Schedule 8*. If a vehicle used to transport guests is leased, the cost of the lease is charged to Rent on *Non-Operating Income and Expenses—Schedule 11*.

*Laundry and Dry Cleaning.* Includes the cost of laundry and dry cleaning services applicable to the Rooms department, whether the services are performed by an in-house facility or are contracted to an outside company. If the services are performed by an in-house laundry, an allocation from *House Laundry—Schedule 12* is charged to Laundry and Dry Cleaning. This allocation is distributed to departments on an equitable basis reflecting usage, such as cost-per-pound, number of pieces cleaned, number of orders processed, etc. If the services are performed by an outside company, the amount charged to Laundry and Dry Cleaning should be based on invoices sent by the outside laundry. The cost of cleaning employee uniforms is charged to Uniform Laundry.

*Licenses and Permits.* Includes the cost of national and local jurisdiction licenses, including costs of inspections needed for licensing, for all activities of the Rooms department.

*Linen.* Includes the cost, whether purchased or rented, of towels, face cloths, bath mats, blankets, guest robes, pillowcases, sheets, comforters, duvets, and bedspreads used by the Rooms department. Also includes the cost of hand towels used in public restrooms.

*Miscellaneous.* Includes any expenses of the Rooms department that do not apply to the other line items discussed in this section.

*Operating Supplies.* Includes the cost of items needed to operate the Rooms department that are not included in the descriptions of specific supply accounts such as Guest Supplies, Cleaning Supplies, and Printing and Stationery. Examples are alarm clocks, irons, keycards, "Do-Not-Disturb" signs, ice buckets, drinking glasses, and all general office supplies. The cost of consumable supplies and amenities provided in guestrooms for guest use is charged to Guest Supplies.

*Postage and Overnight Delivery Charges.* Includes the cost of stamps and express mail charges specifically related to the Rooms department.

*Printing and Stationery.* Includes the cost of printed forms used in the Rooms department, whether they are purchased from an outside source or produced internally. The costs associated with providing a guestroom or service directory, including the binder and the contents pages, are included here. The cost of writing materials provided in guestrooms is charged to Guest Supplies.

*Reservations.* Includes the costs associated with participating in an internal or external central reservation system, such as any fees paid for chain reservation services. Reservations also includes the cost of any communication lines, including Internet site communications costs, that are dedicated to generating reservations. System costs (non-transactional) related to a reservation system are charged to *Information and Telecommunications Systems — Schedule 6.*

When the hotel operator or franchisor combines its reservation and marketing assessments, management should seek guidance from the hotel operator or franchisor regarding the percentage of the assessment attributable to reservations versus marketing activities. The assessment should then be allocated accordingly between the Rooms and Sales and Marketing departments. If management is unable to attain guidance from the hotel operator or franchisor, then the total assessment should be recorded as a Franchise and Affiliation Marketing expense on *Sales and Marketing — Schedule 7.*

*Royalty Fees.* Includes all costs associated with the right to use a brand name in connection with a Rooms department activity. An example would be the fees paid to a sports league for specialty themed guestrooms. The fees paid for the use of a hotel brand name are charged to Franchise and Affiliation Fees — Royalties on *Sales and Marketing — Schedule 7.*

*Training.* Includes the costs, other than payroll costs, that can be directly attributed to the training of employees in the Rooms department. Examples include the costs of training materials, supplies, certification programs, and instructor fees. The cost of employee wages incurred during training is charged to Salaries and Wages.

*Travel—Meals and Entertainment.* Includes the reimbursable cost of food, beverage, and entertainment expenses incurred by employees of the Rooms department traveling on property business.

*Travel—Other.* Includes the cost of travel and reimbursable expenditures (e.g., airfare, car rental, hotel room and tax, guestroom Internet, conference registration fees), other than food, beverage, and entertainment, by employees of the Rooms department traveling on property business

*Uniform Costs.* Includes the cost of employee uniforms used in the Rooms department, whether purchased or rented. Repair costs are also included in this line item. The cost of cleaning uniforms is charged to Uniform Laundry.

*Uniform Laundry.* Includes the cost of cleaning uniforms for employees of the Rooms department, whether performed by an in-hotel facility or contracted to an outside company.

### Total Other Expenses

Total Other Expenses is calculated by summing all items listed under Other Expenses. The percentage for each line item expense as well as Total Other Expenses is calculated by dividing the line item amount by Total Rooms Revenue.

## Total Expenses

Total Expenses is calculated by adding Total Labor Costs and Related Expenses to Total Other Expenses. The percentage for Total Expenses is calculated by dividing the dollar amount of Total Expenses by Total Rooms Revenue.

Total Expenses is the amount that appears on the Summary Operating Statement under Departmental Expenses—Rooms.

## Departmental Profit

Departmental Profit is calculated by subtracting Total Expenses from Total Rooms Revenue. The percentage for Departmental Profit is calculated by dividing Departmental Profit by Total Rooms Revenue.

# FOOD AND BEVERAGE—SCHEDULE 2

| | PERIOD OF | | | | | |
|---|---|---|---|---|---|---|
| | CURRENT PERIOD | | | YEAR-TO-DATE | | |
| | ACTUAL | FORECAST/ BUDGET | PRIOR YEAR | ACTUAL | FORECAST/ BUDGET | PRIOR YEAR |
| | $  % | $  % | $  % | $  % | $  % | $  % |
| **REVENUE** | | | | | | |
| Food Revenue | | | | | | |
| Venue Food Revenue | | | | | | |
| In-Room Dining Food Revenue | | | | | | |
| Banquet/Conference/Catering Food Revenue | | | | | | |
| Mini Bar Food Revenue | | | | | | |
| Other Food Revenue | | | | | | |
| Total Food Revenue | | | | | | |
| Beverage Revenue | | | | | | |
| Venue Beverage Revenue | | | | | | |
| In-Room Dining Beverage Revenue | | | | | | |
| Banquet/Conference/Catering Beverage Revenue | | | | | | |
| Mini Bar Beverage Revenue | | | | | | |
| Other Beverage Revenue | | | | | | |
| Total Beverage Revenue | | | | | | |
| Less: Allowances | | | | | | |
| Total Food and Beverage Revenue | | | | | | |
| Other Revenue | | | | | | |
| Audiovisual | | | | | | |
| Function Room Rental and Setup Charges | | | | | | |
| Cover Charges | | | | | | |
| Surcharges and Service Charges | | | | | | |
| Miscellaneous Other Revenue | | | | | | |
| Less: Allowances | | | | | | |
| Total Other Revenue | | | | | | |
| **TOTAL REVENUE** | | | | | | |
| **COST OF SALES AND OTHER REVENUE** | | | | | | |
| Cost of Food and Beverage Sales | | | | | | |
| Cost of Food Sales | | | | | | |
| Cost of Beverage Sales | | | | | | |
| Total Cost of Food and Beverage Sales | | | | | | |
| Cost of Other Revenue | | | | | | |
| Audiovisual Cost | | | | | | |
| Miscellaneous Cost | | | | | | |
| Total Cost of Other Revenue | | | | | | |
| **TOTAL COST OF SALES AND OTHER REVENUE** | | | | | | |
| **GROSS PROFIT** | | | | | | |
| **EXPENSES** | | | | | | |
| Labor Costs and Related Expenses | | | | | | |
| Salaries, Wages, Service Charges, Contracted Labor and Bonuses | | | | | | |
| Salaries and Wages | | | | | | |
| Management | | | | | | |
| Service | | | | | | |
| Kitchen | | | | | | |
| Non-Management | | | | | | |
| Banquet/Conference/Catering Service | | | | | | |
| Kitchen | | | | | | |
| Venues | | | | | | |
| Sub-Total: Salaries and Wages | | | | | | |
| Service Charge Distribution | | | | | | |

## FOOD AND BEVERAGE—SCHEDULE 2 *(continued)*

| | CURRENT PERIOD | | | | | | YEAR-TO-DATE | | | | | |
|---|---|---|---|---|---|---|---|---|---|---|---|---|
| | ACTUAL | | FORECAST/ BUDGET | | PRIOR YEAR | | ACTUAL | | FORECAST/ BUDGET | | PRIOR YEAR | |
| | $ | % | $ | % | $ | % | $ | % | $ | % | $ | % |
| Contracted, Leased and Outsourced Labor | | | | | | | | | | | | |
| Bonuses and Incentives | | | | | | | | | | | | |
| Total Salaries, Wages, Service Charges, Contracted Labor and Bonuses | | | | | | | | | | | | |
| Payroll-Related Expenses | | | | | | | | | | | | |
| Payroll Taxes | | | | | | | | | | | | |
| Supplemental Pay | | | | | | | | | | | | |
| Employee Benefits | | | | | | | | | | | | |
| Total Payroll Related Expenses | | | | | | | | | | | | |
| Total Labor Costs and Related Expenses | | | | | | | | | | | | |
| Other Expenses | | | | | | | | | | | | |
| Banquet Expenses | | | | | | | | | | | | |
| China | | | | | | | | | | | | |
| Cleaning Supplies | | | | | | | | | | | | |
| Cluster Services | | | | | | | | | | | | |
| Commissions | | | | | | | | | | | | |
| Complimentary Services and Gifts | | | | | | | | | | | | |
| Contract Services | | | | | | | | | | | | |
| Corporate Office Reimbursables | | | | | | | | | | | | |
| Decorations | | | | | | | | | | | | |
| Dishwashing Supplies | | | | | | | | | | | | |
| Dues and Subscriptions | | | | | | | | | | | | |
| Entertainment—In-House | | | | | | | | | | | | |
| Equipment Rental | | | | | | | | | | | | |
| Flatware | | | | | | | | | | | | |
| Glassware | | | | | | | | | | | | |
| Ice | | | | | | | | | | | | |
| Kitchen Fuel | | | | | | | | | | | | |
| Kitchen Smallwares | | | | | | | | | | | | |
| Laundry and Dry Cleaning | | | | | | | | | | | | |
| Licenses and Permits | | | | | | | | | | | | |
| Linen | | | | | | | | | | | | |
| Management Fees | | | | | | | | | | | | |
| Menus and Beverage Lists | | | | | | | | | | | | |
| Miscellaneous | | | | | | | | | | | | |
| Music and Entertainment | | | | | | | | | | | | |
| Operating Supplies | | | | | | | | | | | | |
| Paper and Plastics | | | | | | | | | | | | |
| Postage and Overnight Delivery Charges | | | | | | | | | | | | |
| Printing and Stationery | | | | | | | | | | | | |
| Reservations | | | | | | | | | | | | |
| Royalty Fees | | | | | | | | | | | | |
| Training | | | | | | | | | | | | |
| Travel—Meals and Entertainment | | | | | | | | | | | | |
| Travel—Other | | | | | | | | | | | | |
| Uniform Costs | | | | | | | | | | | | |
| Uniform Laundry | | | | | | | | | | | | |
| Utensils | | | | | | | | | | | | |
| Total Other Expenses | | | | | | | | | | | | |
| TOTAL EXPENSES | | | | | | | | | | | | |
| DEPARTMENTAL PROFIT | | | | | | | | | | | | |

*Food and Beverage—Schedule 2* reflects the proper format for a Food and Beverage department and designates the revenue and expense accounts that are approved as line items in the *Uniform System*. Individual properties may delete irrelevant line items, but the *Uniform System* does not provide for the addition or substitution of other revenue or expense line items. Rather, properties may choose to develop a sub-account/sub-schedule to provide more detail related to a particular revenue or expense item. This sub-account/sub-schedule is then to be rolled into the appropriate line item. Additionally, properties may choose to delete some of the columns or to show them in a different order and remain "in conformity with the *Uniform System*."

Food and Beverage—Schedule 2 is designed to reflect a minimum standard of reporting. Properties may develop additional support schedules, including but not restricted to individual venue or kitchen schedules, to provide additional information necessary to properly evaluate and benchmark individual venue operations within the Food and Beverage department. Where individual venue schedules are provided, they should be presented in the same format as *Food and Beverage—Schedule 2*.

Refer to Part III for recommended operating metrics that are pertinent to the Food and Beverage department.

The line items for *Food and Beverage—Schedule 2* are defined in the following pages.

# Revenue

Revenue includes all sales of food and beverages for consumption by guests as well as certain services, charges, and non-consumable goods sold or applied in the Food and Beverage department as Other Revenue.

Food Revenue and Beverage Revenue may include allocated portions of package revenues. As discussed under *Rooms—Schedule 1*, package revenues are lodging accommodations sold in conjunction with other services provided by either the property or third parties as part of a single transaction with the guest. Package revenues are allocated to other departments based on the relative market values of the items supplied by those departments.

For hotels that offer minor levels of food and beverage sales on an occasional basis, the revenue and associated expenses may be reported as a Minor Operated Department or the revenues may be reported on a net basis on *Miscellaneous Income—Schedule 4*. Further, some revenue items within the Food and Beverage department may be reported on a net basis within the department. For additional information, see Part V.

## Food Revenue

*Venue Food Revenue.* Includes sales of food and non-alcoholic beverages in and from specific dining areas in the property. Examples of venues are restaurants, lounges, delicatessens, bakeries, snack shops, pool areas, spas, fitness facilities, and golf courses. Take-out revenue associated with a particular service venue should be recorded as part of the business activities of the venue. Banquet rooms, guestrooms, and group functions outside the property are not considered venues.

*In-Room Dining Food Revenue.* Includes sales of food and non-alcoholic beverages that require delivery to guests in their guestrooms. In-Room Dining Food Revenue can also include sales that require delivery to other areas inside the hotel or outside as in the example of condominiums that may be located near a hotel. Group sales of food ordered from and serviced by the Banquet/Conference/Catering department and delivered to guestrooms/suites or outside locations are recorded as Banquet/Conference/Catering Food Revenue.

*Banquet/Conference/Catering Food Revenue.* Includes sales of food and non-alcoholic beverages in a property's banquet rooms and for group functions outside the property. The banquet designation is used for sales related to groups of guests occupying guestrooms, while catering sales are related to groups of guests who are not occupying guestrooms. Banquet/Conference/Catering Food Revenue also includes sales from food service performed by the Banquet/Conference/Catering department in a guestroom/suite.

*Mini Bar Food Revenue.* Includes sales of packaged food and non-alcoholic beverages—for example, candy, snacks, bottled water, and soft drinks—placed in a guestroom.

*Other Food Revenue.* Includes sales of consumable food and non-alcoholic beverage items not designated as Venue, In-Room Dining, Banquet/Conference/Catering, or Mini Bar revenues.

## Total Food Revenue

Total Food Revenue is calculated by summing Venue Food, In-Room Dining Food, Banquet/Conference/Catering Food, Mini Bar Food, and Other Food Revenue.

## Beverage Revenue

Beverage Revenue includes all sales of alcoholic beverages for consumption by guests.

*Venue Beverage Revenue.* Includes beverage sales in and from specific dining areas in the property. Examples of venues are restaurants, lounges, bars, pool areas, and golf courses. Take-out revenue associated with a particular service venue should be recorded as part of the business activities of the venue. Banquet rooms, guestrooms, and group functions outside the property are not considered venues.

*In-Room Dining Beverage Revenue.* Includes beverage sales that require delivery to guests in their guestrooms. In-Room Dining Beverage Revenue can also include sales that require delivery to other areas inside the hotel or outside as in the example of condominiums that may be located near a property. Group beverage sales ordered from and serviced by the Banquet/Conference/Catering department and delivered to outside locations are recorded as Banquet/Conference/Catering Beverage Revenue.

*Banquet/Conference/Catering Beverage Revenue.* Includes beverage sales in the property's banquet rooms and for group functions outside the hotel. The banquet designation is used for sales related to groups of guests occupying guestrooms, while catering sales are related to groups of guests who are not occupying guestrooms. Banquet/Conference/Catering Beverage Revenues also include sales from beverage service performed by the Banquet/Conference/Catering department in a guestroom/suite.

*Mini Bar Beverage Revenue.* Includes sales of packaged beverages (bottles and cans) placed in a guestroom.

*Other Beverage Revenue.* Includes sales of consumable beverage items not designated as Venue, In-Room Dining, Banquet/Conference/Catering, or Mini Bar revenues.

## Total Beverage Revenue

Total Beverage Revenue is calculated by summing Venue Beverage Revenue, In-Room Dining Beverage Revenue, Banquet/Conference/Catering Beverage Revenue, Mini Bar Beverage Revenue, and Other Beverage Revenue.

## Allowances

Allowances refers to a reduction in revenue due to a service problem, not an error in posting. Errors in posting, such as charging an incorrect amount on a guest check, are treated as adjustments to revenue, regardless of the accounting period in which the error occurred.

## Total Food and Beverage Revenue

Total Food and Beverage Revenue is calculated by summing Total Food Revenue and Total Beverage Revenue and subtracting Allowances.

## Other Revenue

Other Revenue includes sales of services and all products that are not consumable food and beverage items.

*Audiovisual.* Generally includes the revenues derived from supplying audiovisual equipment and services and Internet access revenue from banquet/conference/catering function guests, whether the equipment is owned by the property or rented from a third party. If the services and equipment are obtained from a third party, the costs incurred are charged to Audiovisual Cost.

In situations where the provision of audiovisual or Internet service is outsourced to a third-party contractor who pays the property a fee or commission, and the contractual arrangements are made directly between the guest and the contractor, and the credit risk and risk of loss reside with the contractor, only the net fee or commission would be reported as revenue in Audiovisual.

For properties that do not operate a Food and Beverage department, the net fee or commission from a third-party audiovisual contractor would be reported as Commissions on *Miscellaneous Income—Schedule 4.* For properties that do not operate a Food and Beverage department but do provide their own audiovisual services, revenues and expenses would be reported on a gross basis as a Minor

Operated Department on *Other Operated Departments—Schedule 3*. For additional information, see Part V.

*Function Room Rentals and Setup Charges.* Includes revenue derived from the rental of function rooms to guests. If a guestroom/suite is used as a function room and Banquet/Conference/Catering Food and Beverage Revenue occurs, the room rental revenue is recorded here. If Banquet/Conference/Catering Food and Beverage Revenue do not occur in the guestroom/suite, the room rental revenue is recorded as Other Rooms Revenue in the Rooms department.

Function room setup charges are charged to guests in addition to, or instead of, function room rentals and relate to the activities for the preparation of function rooms for the use intended by the guests. Such charges should be reported as Function Room Rentals and Setup Charges.

*Cover Charges.* Includes charges to guests for entrance to events where food and/or beverage is sold. Such events would typically provide some form of entertainment or show.

*Surcharges and Service Charges.* Generally includes any mandatory, non-discretionary, or other charge automatically added to a customer account in respect of a service or the use of an amenity. The key determining factors for the recording of surcharges and service charges are set out in Part V.

*Miscellaneous Other Revenue.* Includes all non–food and beverage and non-consumable items or services sold to guests (such as memorabilia, apparel, and logo merchandise) in the Food and Beverage department that are not included in Audiovisual, Function Room Rentals and Setup Charges, Cover Charges, or Surcharges and Service Charges. Miscellaneous Other Revenue also includes any other revenue generated by the sale of non–food and beverage items in the guestroom. Costs associated with providing these items and services are charged to Miscellaneous Cost.

*Allowances.* Refers to a reduction in revenue due to a service problem, not an error in posting. Errors in posting, such as charging an incorrect price, are treated as adjustments to revenue, regardless of the accounting period in which the error occurred.

## Total Other Revenue

Total Other Revenue is calculated by summing Audiovisual, Function Room Rentals and Setup Charges, Cover Charges, Surcharges and Service Charges, and Miscellaneous Other Revenue and subtracting Allowances.

# Total Revenue

Total Revenue is the sum of Total Food and Beverage Revenue and Total Other Revenue. Total Revenue is the amount that appears on the Summary Operating Statement under Operating Revenue—Food and Beverage.

In completing the revenue section of Schedule 2 or venue sub-schedules, the Total Revenue line is considered to be 100 percent, and the percentage for each source of revenue is determined by dividing the dollar amount for that revenue source by Total Revenue.

# Cost of Sales and Other Revenue

## Cost of Food and Beverage Sales

*Cost of Food Sales.* Includes the cost of food served to guests in all segments of food revenues. Cost of Food Sales also includes the cost of beverage items transferred from the beverage department and used in food preparation and service. Spoilage, waste, and spillage are included in Cost of Food Sales. Food cost includes the cost of coffee, tea, milk, juice, sodas, and other non-alcoholic beverages.

Cost of Food Sales does not include costs of food items that have been transferred to other departments to be used in preparation or decoration in those departments. Such transfers are charged directly to the appropriate cost accounts in the departments receiving the items. If food items are sold at cost and revenue is not recorded (commissary and steward's sales), the sale is credited to the Cost of Food Sales.

Cost of Food Sales does not include the cost of food used in the preparation of meals provided for employees during the workday, even if employees are charged for food consumed. The cost of employee meals and revenues collected from employees are both charged to the *Staff Dining—Schedule 13* for allocation to each department having employees. Cost of Food Sales does not include the cost associated with food inventory items used for gratis presentation to guests, vendors, employees, and third parties. The cost of this complimentary food is charged as an expense to Complimentary Services and Gifts, Staff Dining, or Entertainment—In-House, depending on who is entertained, in the department that makes the gratis presentation. Finally, if a vendor provides a rebate on food purchased, it is credited to the Cost of Food Sales.

The percentage for Cost of Food Sales is calculated by dividing Cost of Food Sales by Total Food Revenue.

*Cost of Beverage Sales.* Includes the cost of alcoholic beverages served to guests in all segments of beverage revenues. Cost of Beverage Sales also includes the cost of food items (including non-alcoholic beverages) transferred from the food department and used in alcoholic beverage preparation and service. Spoilage, waste, and spillage are included in Cost of Beverage Sales.

Cost of Beverage Sales does not include costs of beverage items that have been transferred to other departments to be used in preparation or decoration in those departments. Such transfers are charged directly to the appropriate cost accounts in the departments receiving the items. If beverage items are sold at cost and revenue is not recorded (commissary or steward's sales), the sale is credited to the Cost of Beverage Sales. Cost of Beverage Sales does not include the cost associated with beverage inventory items being used for gratis presentation to guests, vendors, employees, and third parties. The cost of this complimentary beverage is charged as an expense to Complimentary Services and Gifts, Staff Dining, or Entertainment—In-House, depending on who is entertained, in the department that makes the gratis presentation. Finally, if beverage vendor rebates are legal within a jurisdiction and a vendor provides a rebate on beverage purchased, it is credited to the Cost of Beverage Sales.

The percentage for Cost of Beverage Sales is calculated by dividing Cost of Beverage Sales by Total Beverage Revenue.

## Total Cost of Food and Beverage Sales

Total Cost of Food and Beverage Sales is calculated by summing Cost of Food Sales and Cost of Beverage Sales. The percentage for Total Cost of Food and Beverage Sales is calculated by dividing Total Cost of Food and Beverage Sales by Total Food and Beverage Revenue.

## Cost of Other Revenue

Cost of Other Revenue includes the costs associated with the sales of services and all products that are not consumable food and beverage items, such as memorabilia, apparel, and logo merchandise. The percentage for each item under Cost of Other Revenue is calculated by dividing the dollar cost by its corresponding revenue amount.

*Audiovisual Cost.* Includes the cost associated with providing audiovisual equipment and services to guests in the Food and Beverage department. The income received from charging guests for these services is recorded as Audiovisual under Other Revenue.

*Miscellaneous Cost.* Includes the cost associated with providing non–food and beverage items such as memorabilia, apparel, and logo merchandise and services other than audiovisual services to guests in the Food and Beverage department. The income received from charging guests for these items and services is recorded as Miscellaneous Other Revenue.

## Total Cost of Other Revenue

Total Cost of Other Revenue is calculated by summing Audiovisual Cost and Miscellaneous Cost. The percentage for Total Cost of Other Revenue is calculated by dividing Total Cost of Other Revenue by Total Other Revenue.

## Total Cost of Sales and Other Revenue

Total Cost of Sales and Other Revenue is the sum of Total Cost of Food and Beverage Sales and Total Cost of Other Revenue. The percentage for Total Cost of Sales and Other Revenue is calculated by dividing the dollar amount of Total Cost of Sales and Other Revenue by Total Revenue for the Food and Beverage department.

# Gross Profit

Gross Profit is calculated by subtracting Total Cost of Sales and Other Revenue from Total Revenue for the Food and Beverage department. The percentage for Gross Profit is calculated by dividing the dollar amount of Gross Profit by Total Revenue for the Food and Beverage department.

# Expenses

Food and Beverage department expenses are separated into two major categories: Labor Costs and Related Expenses and Other Expenses.

## Labor Costs and Related Expenses

Labor Costs and Related Expenses includes all of the payroll expenses associated with Salaries, Wages, Service Charges, Contracted Labor, Bonuses, and Payroll-Related Expenses for employees and contractors. A list of the positions typically included in the Food and Beverage department is provided in the Department Payroll Titles section at the end of Part I.

*Salaries and Wages.* Includes the earnings paid to employees for duties that relate to the operation of the property, such as regular pay, overtime pay, and shift differential pay. If an employee works in a department other than his or her regular home department, his or her earnings must be charged as Salaries and Wages in that other department, regardless of the duties being performed. For example, if a Food and Beverage department employee regularly works as a server in a venue and temporarily works for the Golf Course and Pro Shop department on a function, his or her earnings for the function are charged to Salaries and Wages of the Golf Course and Pro Shop, not to his or her home department.

Salaries and Wages should be delineated by significant management and non-management payroll titles within the department. If necessary, payroll titles should be aggregated to preserve the confidentiality of a specific employee's payroll.

Salaries and Wages includes the earning associated with temporary employees when such expenses are processed through the property's payroll system.

*Service Charge Distribution.* Includes the cost of service charges paid through the payroll system for hotel employees.

*Contracted, Leased and Outsourced Labor.* Includes the gross cost of contracted, leased, and outsourced labor incurred when a property enters into an agreement with a third-party contractor to provide employees to fill positions that would normally be held by individuals paid on the regular payroll. In these situations, the property records or tracks the hours worked and pays the third-party contractor on an hourly or other agreed basis. A typical example is the use of individuals brought into the property to fill in for a shortage of Food and Beverage department staff.

Contracted, Leased and Outsourced Labor includes the gross cost associated with shared staffing arrangements when such arrangements are supported by formal agreements.

*Bonuses and Incentives.* Includes bonuses (contractual and discretionary), incentive pay, and other types of performance pay designed to drive revenue through sales, profit, or guest satisfaction.

*Total Salaries, Wages, Service Charges, Contracted Labor and Bonuses.* Calculated by summing Salaries and Wages, Service Charge Distribution, Contracted, Leased and Outsourced Labor, and Bonuses and Incentives.

*Payroll-Related Expenses.* Includes amounts paid for an employee for duties that relate to the operation of the property and amounts paid for an employee who works in a department other than his or her regular home department regardless of the duties being performed. Payroll-Related Expenses includes the following items:

- *Payroll Taxes.* Includes the employer share of contributions to national and state retirement, unemployment, disability and medical insurance programs, and other mandated payroll-related taxes or social insurance items. (See *Payroll-Related Expenses—Schedule 14.*)

- *Supplemental Pay.* Includes personal days, vacation pay, sick pay, holiday pay, jury duty pay, relocation pay, paid time off, and severance pay. (See *Payroll-Related Expenses—Schedule 14.*)

- *Employee Benefits.* Includes all other payroll-related expenses, such as employer-paid health insurance expenses, cost of meals furnished to employees, pension contributions, and union dues and fees. (See *Payroll-Related Expenses—Schedule 14.*) The distribution of employee meal costs from *Staff Dining—Schedule 13* is charged to this line.

*Total Payroll-Related Expenses.* Calculated by summing Payroll Taxes, Supplemental Pay, and Employee Benefits.

*Note regarding shared staffing arrangements and cluster services:* Where reasonable and easily identifiable, labor costs related to shared staffing arrangements and cluster services should be charged to salaries and wages or payroll-related expenses.

## Total Labor Costs and Related Expenses

Total Labor Costs and Related Expenses is calculated by summing Total Salaries, Wages, Service Charges, Contracted Labor and Bonuses and Total Payroll-Related Expenses. The percentage for each labor cost component as well as Total Labor Costs and Related Expenses is calculated by dividing the line item amount by Total Revenue for the Food and Beverage department. Refer to Part III for recommended operating metrics that are pertinent to Labor Costs and Related Expenses.

## Other Expenses

This expense grouping includes the significant Food and Beverage department expenses approved as Other Expenses in the *Uniform System*. Individual properties may delete irrelevant line items, but the *Uniform System* does not provide for the addition or substitution of other expense line items. Rather, properties may choose to develop a sub-account/sub-schedule to provide more detail related to a particular expense item. This sub-account/sub-schedule is then to be rolled into the appropriate line item listed below.

*Banquet Expense.* Includes the cost of items used in providing banquet service for which matching Other Revenue and Cost of Other Revenue accounts cannot be identified. If expenses can be matched to specific Other Revenue accounts (Audiovisual or Miscellaneous), they are recorded as Cost of Other Revenue.

*China.* Includes the cost of purchased or rented table and service ware, plates, bowls, serving platters, etc., constructed from any material (ceramic, glass, metal, non-disposable plastic, etc.) and used in providing food service.

*Cleaning Supplies.* Includes the cost of products used in cleansing, sweeping, polishing, waxing, and disinfecting areas associated with the Food and Beverage department. The cost of cleaning supplies used in dishwashing is charged to Dishwashing Supplies.

*Cluster Services.* Includes allocation for costs shared between hotels in a limited geographic area (as opposed to nationally consolidated services such as Corporate Office Reimbursables). Where reasonable and easily identifiable, labor costs and related expenses should be charged to their respective line item and only other expenses are charged to Cluster Services. Where not practical, the fair allocation of the total cluster service expenses should be recognized here.

*Commissions.* Includes the remuneration paid to authorized agents for securing business strictly for the benefit of the Food and Beverage department. If an agent secures business that includes revenue for both the Rooms and Food and Beverage departments, then the entirety of the commission paid to that agent is recorded in the Rooms department.

*Complimentary Services and Gifts.* Includes the cost of providing gift items used in gratis presentations for promotional purposes to guests and vendors of the Food and Beverage department, such as the cost of food provided to guests on a complimentary basis during "Happy Hour" and VIP gifts.

*Contract Services.* Includes expenses for activities performed for the Food and Beverage department by outside contractors and professional service providers rather than by hotel employees. Engaging a third party to provide silent shopper services, department-specific consulting services, cleaning of function rooms and kitchens, and cleaning of the ducts and other components of the kitchen ventilation system are all examples of contract services. If supplies are purchased for contract companies to use, the supplies are charged to the appropriate supply account. The cost of contracts for Food and Beverage department laundry and dry cleaning is charged to Laundry and Dry Cleaning.

*Corporate Office Reimbursables.* Includes the allocations of salaries and expenses of corporate or management company Food and Beverage department personnel billed to the property by the regional or corporate office or by the management company, consistent with any contractual arrangements. Travel expenses of corporate or management company food and beverage personnel that are incurred while visiting the property, including the costs of meals and other applicable services or amenities provided to corporate or management company staff while on business in the property for the benefit of the property, are also charged to this account.

*Decorations.* Includes the cost of decorative items used in Food and Beverage department areas for holidays and special events that are not charged directly to banquet guests. (The cost of decorations charged to banquet guests is recorded as

Cost of Other Revenue.) Decorations also includes the costs of ice blocks used in decorative carvings.

***Dishwashing Supplies.*** Includes the cost of cleaning, rinsing, and soaking agents used specifically in washing china, glassware, flatware, and utensils in the Food and Beverage department.

***Dues and Subscriptions.*** Includes the cost of representation for the Food and Beverage department, or of members of the staff when authorized to represent the Food and Beverage department, in business or professional organizations. Dues and Subscriptions is also charged with the cost of subscriptions to newspapers, magazines, and books for use by the staff of the Food and Beverage department.

***Entertainment—In-House.*** Includes the food and beverage at cost, gratuities, service charges, and sales taxes (if applicable) consumed in the entertainment of guests, vendors, and business clients in the property's food and beverage facilities.

***Equipment Rental.*** Includes the costs of renting any type of equipment that may be used either sporadically in the Food and Beverage department or as a replacement for equipment out of service on a temporary basis. Equipment lease payments made under a qualified operating lease are charged to Other Property and Equipment under the Rent section of *Non-Operating Income and Expenses— Schedule 11.* The costs of equipment rental charged to banquet guests are recorded as Cost of Other Revenue.

***Flatware.*** Includes the cost of all flatware, silverware, and serving pieces (serving spoons, cake knives, ladles, etc.), either purchased or rented, used in providing food and beverage service.

***Glassware.*** Includes the cost of purchased or rented containers constructed from any material (glass, ceramic, metal, non-disposable plastic, etc.) used in the consumption of beverages. Service items such as pitchers and tea sets are charged to China, along with the costs of cups and mugs used for coffee service.

***Ice.*** Includes the cost of ice used in food and beverage service, storage, or preparation. The cost of ice blocks used in decorative carvings and not charged to banquet guests is recorded as Decorations.

***Kitchen Fuel.*** Includes the cost of such fuels as Sterno, propane, and charcoal used in the warming, or sometimes specialized cooking, of food.

***Kitchen Smallwares.*** Includes the cost of all kitchen smallwares (pots, pans, and other small cooking apparatuses not included in Utensils), either purchased or rented, used in the preparation of food products.

***Laundry and Dry Cleaning.*** Includes the cost of laundry and dry cleaning services applicable to the Food and Beverage department, whether the services are performed by an in-house facility or are contracted to an outside company. If the services are performed by an in-house laundry, an allocation from *House Laundry—Schedule 12* is charged to Laundry and Dry Cleaning. This allocation is distributed to departments on an equitable basis reflecting usage, such as cost-per-pound, number of pieces cleaned, number of orders processed, etc. If the services are performed by an outside company, the amount charged to Laundry and Dry

Cleaning should be based on invoices sent by the outside laundry. The cost of cleaning employee uniforms is charged to Uniform Laundry.

*Licenses and Permits.* Includes the cost of national and local jurisdiction licenses, including costs of inspections needed for licensing, for all activities of the Food and Beverage department.

*Linen.* Includes the cost, whether purchased or rented, of table cloths, napkins, table runners, table skirt clips, and skirting used by the Food and Beverage department.

*Management Fees.* Includes any amounts paid to a third-party individual or company to operate or manage a food and beverage venue within the property, whether the fees are computed as a fixed amount or a percentage of revenues or profit.

*Menus and Beverage Lists.* Includes all costs of designing and printing menus for the Food and Beverage department. The costs of decorative and protective covers are also charged to this line item.

*Miscellaneous.* Includes any expenses of the Food and Beverage department that do not apply to the other line items discussed in this section.

*Music and Entertainment.* Includes all costs of providing live or recorded entertainment, including BMI, ASCAP, and similar artist royalties within the Food and Beverage department. Entertainment costs charged to banquet guests are recorded as Cost of Other Revenue.

*Operating Supplies.* Includes the cost of items needed to operate the Food and Beverage department that are not included in the descriptions of specific supply accounts such as Cleaning Supplies, Menus and Beverage Lists, Paper and Plastics, and Printing and Stationery. An example would be general office supplies.

*Paper and Plastics.* Includes the cost of all general supplies for the Food and Beverage department made from paper, plastic, and Styrofoam that are not specifically assigned by definition to other line items. Items charged to this line include chef hats, paper bags, aluminum foil, cellophane wrap, can liners, disposable plastic utensils, disposable paper plates, stir sticks, paper napkins, and cocktail picks.

*Postage and Overnight Delivery Charges.* Includes the cost of stamps and express mail charges specifically related to the Food and Beverage department.

*Printing and Stationery.* Includes the cost of printed forms used in the Food and Beverage department, whether they are purchased from an outside source or produced internally. The cost of producing menus is charged to Menus and Beverage Lists.

*Reservations.* Includes the costs associated with venue-specific participation with third-party reservation or booking systems (e.g., OpenTable.com). The third-party systems may be electronic or personal. The fees may include transaction costs or commissions in addition to the cost of communication channels, mobile applications, or websites dedicated to the specific venue. System costs (non-transactional) related to a reservation system are to be charged to *Information and Telecommunications Systems—Schedule 6.*

*Royalty Fees.* Includes all costs associated with the right to use a brand name in connection with a Food and Beverage department activity. An example would be the fees paid for a freestanding restaurant brand to identify a property food and beverage venue. The fees paid for the use of a hotel brand name are charged to Franchise and Affiliation Fees—Royalties on *Sales and Marketing—Schedule 7.*

*Training.* Includes the costs, other than payroll cost, that can be directly attributed to the training of employees in the Food and Beverage department. Examples include the costs of training materials, supplies, and instructor fees. The cost of employee wages incurred during training is charged to Salaries and Wages.

*Travel—Meals and Entertainment.* Includes the reimbursable cost of food and beverage and entertainment expenses incurred by employees of the Food and Beverage department traveling on property business.

*Travel—Other.* Includes the cost of travel and reimbursable expenses (e.g., airfare, car rental, hotel room and tax, guestroom Internet, conference registration fees), other than food, beverage, and entertainment, by employees of the Food and Beverage department traveling on property business.

*Uniform Costs.* Includes the cost of employee uniforms used in the Food and Beverage department, whether purchased or rented. Repair costs are also included in this line item. The cost of cleaning uniforms is charged to Uniform Laundry.

*Uniform Laundry.* Includes the cost of cleaning uniforms for employees of the Food and Beverage department, whether performed by an in-hotel facility or contracted to an outside company.

*Utensils.* Includes the cost of kitchen utensils (strainers, wine openers, cutting boards/knives) used in food preparation, whether purchased or rented.

## Total Other Expenses

Total Other Expenses is calculated by summing all items listed under Other Expenses. The percentage for each line item expense as well as Total Other Expenses is calculated by dividing the line item amount by Total Revenue for the Food and Beverage department.

# Total Expenses

Total Expenses is calculated by adding Total Labor Costs and Related Expenses to Total Other Expenses. The percentage for Total Expenses is calculated by dividing Total Expenses by Total Revenue for the Food and Beverage department.

The sum of Total Cost of Sales and Other Revenue and Total Expenses is the amount that appears on the Summary Operating Statement under Departmental Expenses—Food and Beverage.

# Departmental Profit

Departmental Profit is calculated by subtracting Total Expenses from Gross Profit. The percentage for Departmental Profit is calculated by dividing Departmental Profit by Total Revenue for the Food and Beverage department.

## OTHER OPERATED DEPARTMENTS—SCHEDULE 3

| | PERIOD OF | | | | | |
| --- | --- | --- | --- | --- | --- | --- |
| | CURRENT PERIOD | | | YEAR-TO-DATE | | |
| | ACTUAL | FORECAST/ BUDGET | PRIOR YEAR | ACTUAL | FORECAST/ BUDGET | PRIOR YEAR |
| | $ \| % | $ \| % | $ \| % | $ \| % | $ \| % | $ \| % |
| **DEPARTMENTAL REVENUE** | | | | | | |
| Other Operated Department 1 | | | | | | |
| Other Operated Department 2 | | | | | | |
| - - - | | | | | | |
| Other Operated Department x | | | | | | |
| Minor Operated Departments | | | | | | |
| **TOTAL DEPARTMENTAL REVENUE** | | | | | | |
| **DEPARTMENTAL EXPENSES**[1] | | | | | | |
| Other Operated Department 1 | | | | | | |
| Other Operated Department 2 | | | | | | |
| - - - | | | | | | |
| Other Operated Department x | | | | | | |
| Minor Operated Departments | | | | | | |
| **TOTAL DEPARTMENTAL EXPENSES** | | | | | | |
| **DEPARTMENTAL PROFIT** | | | | | | |
| Other Operated Department 1 | | | | | | |
| Other Operated Department 2 | | | | | | |
| - - - | | | | | | |
| Other Operated Department x | | | | | | |
| Minor Operated Departments | | | | | | |
| **TOTAL OTHER OPERATED DEPARTMENT PROFIT** | | | | | | |

[1] Departmental Expenses is the sum of Cost of Sales (when applicable) and Total Expenses.

*Other Operated Departments—Schedule 3* illustrates the proper format for reporting the summary of the revenue and expense amounts for the Other Operated and Minor Operated Departments. Only the revenues and expenses from the Other Operated and Minor Operated Departments that exist at an individual property are included on Schedule 3. To provide more detail, properties must prepare a sub-schedule for each major Other Operated Department, as well as a summary sub-schedule inclusive of all Minor Operated Departments. The totals from these sub-schedules are then to be incorporated into the appropriate line items on Schedule 3. The names of the line items under Departmental Revenue and Departmental Expenses should be changed to the names of the actual other operated department (e.g., Parking). Properties may choose to delete some of the columns or to show them in a different order and remain "in conformity with the *Uniform System.*"

Total Departmental Revenue is the amount that appears on the Summary Operating Statement under Operating Revenue—Other Operated Departments. Total Departmental Expenses is the amount that appears on the Summary Operating Statement under Departmental Expenses—Other Operated Departments. All operated departments other than the Rooms and Food and Beverage departments are classified on the Summary Operating Statement as Other Operated Departments. The following guidelines define an Other Operated Department:

- The department should generate revenue, have direct operating expenses, and be operated with a motivation to make a profit or limit the loss.

- Revenues are reported on a gross basis without the deduction of operating expenses, commissions, or fees. (For guidance, see Part V.)

- A department that has no revenue and is operated solely to provide a complimentary guest service is not classified as an Other Operated Department. The net expense of such a department is allocated to the department(s) that benefits most from the service. For example, if a property provides complimentary guest parking but does not operate a for-pay parking operation, all expenses for the complimentary parking operation would be charged to the Rooms and/or Food and Beverage departments.

- The exceptions are the costs associated with offering complimentary guest calls and Internet connectivity. These costs should be recorded on *Information and Telecommunications Systems—Schedule 6.*

- If the majority of income to the property is "net revenue" (percent of income, percent of profit, commission revenue, etc.), then the net revenues received by the property are classified under *Miscellaneous Income—Schedule 4.* (For guidance, see Part V.)

- All of the expenses cannot be paid by third-party operators. If all of the expenses result from a third party performing the services, the activity cannot be classified as an Other Operated Department. (For guidance, see Part V.)

- If the vast majority of financial risk and liability for an operating department are assumed by a third-party management company (even though the department and equipment are owned by the hotel's owner), then the "net income" of that department is classified as *Miscellaneous Income—Schedule 4.* (For guidance, see Part V.)

## Other Operated Department Schedule Formats

A property must include a sub-schedule for each of the Other Operated Departments that it runs or manages and a consolidated schedule for all Minor Operated Departments. The total revenue and expenses for each Other Operated Department are added to the total revenues and expenses from all Minor Operated Departments on Schedule 3. The combined revenues and expenses for all Other Operated Departments as shown on Schedule 3 are then listed on the Summary Operating Statement.

The format for an Other Operated Department sub-schedule follows the same base outline as the departmental schedules for the Rooms and Food and Beverage departments. The following pages contain sample sub-schedules for Golf Course and Pro Shop, Health Club/Spa, and Parking. In addition, a generic sub-schedule is presented to provide guidance on the format of a sub-schedule for potential Other Operated Departments (e.g., Marina, Guest Laundry, Business Center,

Retail Store). Finally, a sub-schedule is provided that summarizes and aggregates all revenues and expenses for Minor Operated Departments.

# GOLF COURSE AND PRO SHOP—SUB-SCHEDULE 3-1

| | PERIOD OF | | | | | | | | | | | |
|---|---|---|---|---|---|---|---|---|---|---|---|---|
| | CURRENT PERIOD | | | | | | YEAR-TO-DATE | | | | | |
| | ACTUAL | | FORECAST/ BUDGET | | PRIOR YEAR | | ACTUAL | | FORECAST/ BUDGET | | PRIOR YEAR | |
| | $ | % | $ | % | $ | % | $ | % | $ | % | $ | % |
| **REVENUE** | | | | | | | | | | | | |
| Greens Fee Revenue | | | | | | | | | | | | |
| Tournament Fee Revenue | | | | | | | | | | | | |
| Golf Cart Rental Revenue | | | | | | | | | | | | |
| Golf Equipment Rental Revenue | | | | | | | | | | | | |
| Practice Range Fee Revenue | | | | | | | | | | | | |
| Lesson Fee Revenue | | | | | | | | | | | | |
| Golf Club Maintenance Revenue | | | | | | | | | | | | |
| Storage Fee Revenue | | | | | | | | | | | | |
| Membership Fee Revenue | | | | | | | | | | | | |
| Merchandise Revenue | | | | | | | | | | | | |
| Clothing Revenue | | | | | | | | | | | | |
| Other Revenue | | | | | | | | | | | | |
| Less: Allowances | | | | | | | | | | | | |
| **TOTAL GOLF COURSE AND PRO SHOP REVENUE** | | | | | | | | | | | | |
| **COST OF SALES** | | | | | | | | | | | | |
| Cost of Merchandise Sales | | | | | | | | | | | | |
| Cost of Clothing Sales | | | | | | | | | | | | |
| **TOTAL COST OF SALES** | | | | | | | | | | | | |
| **GROSS PROFIT** | | | | | | | | | | | | |
| **EXPENSES** | | | | | | | | | | | | |
| Labor Costs and Related Expenses | | | | | | | | | | | | |
| Salaries, Wages, Service Charges, Contracted Labor and Bonuses | | | | | | | | | | | | |
| Salaries and Wages | | | | | | | | | | | | |
| Management | | | | | | | | | | | | |
| Non-Management | | | | | | | | | | | | |
| Golf Pros/Operations | | | | | | | | | | | | |
| Greens/Maintenance | | | | | | | | | | | | |
| Pro Shop | | | | | | | | | | | | |
| Sub-Total: Salaries and Wages | | | | | | | | | | | | |
| Service Charge Distribution | | | | | | | | | | | | |
| Contracted, Leased and Outsourced Labor | | | | | | | | | | | | |
| Bonuses and Incentives | | | | | | | | | | | | |
| Total Salaries, Wages, Service Charges, Contracted Labor and Bonuses | | | | | | | | | | | | |
| Payroll-Related Expenses | | | | | | | | | | | | |
| Payroll Taxes | | | | | | | | | | | | |
| Supplemental Pay | | | | | | | | | | | | |
| Employee Benefits | | | | | | | | | | | | |
| Total Payroll Related Expenses | | | | | | | | | | | | |
| Total Labor Costs and Related Expenses | | | | | | | | | | | | |
| Other Expenses | | | | | | | | | | | | |
| Cleaning Supplies | | | | | | | | | | | | |
| Cluster Services | | | | | | | | | | | | |

*(continued)*

## GOLF COURSE AND PRO SHOP—SUB-SCHEDULE 3-1 *(continued)*

| | PERIOD OF | | | | | |
| --- | --- | --- | --- | --- | --- | --- |
| | CURRENT PERIOD | | | YEAR-TO-DATE | | |
| | ACTUAL | FORECAST/ BUDGET | PRIOR YEAR | ACTUAL | FORECAST/ BUDGET | PRIOR YEAR |
| | $   % | $   % | $   % | $   % | $   % | $   % |
| Complimentary Services and Gifts | | | | | | |
| Contract Services | | | | | | |
| Corporate Office Reimbursables | | | | | | |
| Decorations | | | | | | |
| Dues and Subscriptions | | | | | | |
| Entertainment—In-House | | | | | | |
| Equipment Rental | | | | | | |
| Gasoline and Lubricants | | | | | | |
| Grounds Maintenance and Landscaping | | | | | | |
| Irrigation | | | | | | |
| Laundry and Dry Cleaning | | | | | | |
| Licenses and Permits | | | | | | |
| Linen | | | | | | |
| Management Fees | | | | | | |
| Miscellaneous | | | | | | |
| Operating Supplies | | | | | | |
| Printing and Stationery | | | | | | |
| Reservations | | | | | | |
| Royalty Fees | | | | | | |
| Tournament Expenses | | | | | | |
| Training | | | | | | |
| Transportation | | | | | | |
| Travel—Meals and Entertainment | | | | | | |
| Travel—Other | | | | | | |
| Uniform Costs | | | | | | |
| Uniform Laundry | | | | | | |
| Vehicle Repairs and Maintenance | | | | | | |
| Water | | | | | | |
| Total Other Expenses | | | | | | |
| TOTAL EXPENSES | | | | | | |
| DEPARTMENTAL PROFIT | | | | | | |

*Golf Course and Pro Shop—Sub-schedule 3-1* reflects the proper format for a Golf Course and Pro Shop department and designates the revenue and expense accounts that are approved as line items in the *Uniform System.* Individual properties may delete irrelevant line items, but the *Uniform System* does not provide for the addition or substitution of other revenue or expense line items. Rather, properties may choose to develop a sub-account/sub-schedule to provide more detail related to a particular revenue or expense item. This sub-account/sub-schedule is then to be rolled into the appropriate line item. Additionally, properties may choose to delete some of the columns or to show them in a different order and remain "in conformity with the *Uniform System.*"

Refer to Part III for operating ratios and statistics that are pertinent to the Golf Course and Pro Shop Department.

The Total Golf Course and Pro Shop Revenue, Total Expenses (including Total Cost of Sales), and Departmental Profit shown on Sub-schedule 3-1 are then reported on Schedule 3.

The line items for *Golf Course and Pro Shop—Sub-schedule 3-1* are defined in the following pages.

# Revenue

Revenue from the Golf Course and Pro Shop department is classified into many categories. These are defined below.

Golf Course and Pro Shop Revenue may include an allocated portion of package revenues. As discussed under *Rooms—Schedule 1*, package revenues are lodging accommodations sold in conjunction with other services provided by either the property or third parties as part of a single transaction with the guest. Package revenues are allocated to other departments based on the relative market values of the items supplied by those departments.

Under certain circumstances, golf course and pro shop revenue in its entirety may be reported on a net basis on *Miscellaneous Income—Schedule 4.* Further, some revenue items within the Golf Course and Pro Shop department may be reported on a net basis within the department. For additional information, see Part V.

## Greens Fee Revenue

Greens Fee Revenue includes revenue derived from charges to customers for playing golf on the golf course. Examples of greens fees charged to this account are those for hotel guests, club members, and general public. To the extent the golf operations has a variety of users, such as member guest, resort guest and outside/public guest, the revenues from greens fees can be recorded in a sub-schedule within Greens Fee Revenue to track these individual guests.

## Tournament Fee Revenue

Tournament Fee Revenue includes revenue derived from charges to customers for the playing of golf in organized tournaments.

## Golf Cart Rental Revenue

Golf Cart Rental Revenue includes revenue derived from the rental of electric or gasoline-powered golf carts to customers of the Golf department.

## Golf Equipment Rental Revenue

Golf Equipment Rental Revenue includes revenue derived from rental of all items used to play golf, such as clubs and pull carts.

## Practice Range Fee Revenue

Practice Range Fee Revenue includes revenue derived from the use of golf practice facilities of any kind (driving, putting, etc.) whether the facilities are located indoors or outdoors.

## Lesson Fee Revenue

Lesson Fee Revenue includes revenue derived from all golf lessons given to customers whether on the golf course or practice range.

## Golf Club Maintenance Revenue

Golf Club Maintenance Revenue includes revenue derived from the cleaning and repair of golf clubs for customers.

## Storage Fee Revenue

Storage Fee Revenue includes revenue derived from renting personal lockers or golf cart space to customers.

## Membership Fee Revenue

Membership Fee Revenue includes revenue derived from charging customers for a "membership" at the golf course, which normally allows the customer "member" to exercise privileges not given to the general public. Examples of privileges might be preferred tee times or discounts for golf or merchandise. To the extent the golf operations offers a tiered membership program, such as full member and social member, consider using a sub-schedule within Membership Fee Revenue to track these revenues.

## Merchandise Revenue

Merchandise Revenue includes revenue derived from all sales of non-clothing items in the golf shop or anywhere on the golf course. Examples of merchandise would be clubs, bags, and balls.

## Clothing Revenue

Clothing Revenue includes revenues derived from all sales of clothing items in the golf shop or anywhere on the golf course.

## Other Revenue

Other Revenue includes revenue from any services or charges not previously specified, such as surcharges and service charges. Surcharges and service charges generally include any mandatory, non-discretionary, or other charge automatically added to a customer account in respect of the service or use of an amenity. The key determining factors for the recording of surcharges and service charges (versus gratuities) are set out in Part V.

Revenue from food and beverage items sold on the golf course (e.g., from golf carts on the golf course) is reported on *Food and Beverage—Schedule 2.*

## Allowances

Allowances refers to a reduction in revenue due to a service problem, not an error in posting. Errors in posting, such as charging an incorrect amount, are treated as adjustments to revenue, regardless of the accounting period in which the error occurred.

## Total Golf Course and Pro Shop Revenue

Total Golf Course and Pro Shop Revenue is calculated by summing the revenue items listed above and subtracting Allowances. This amount is shown on Schedule 3 as Departmental Revenue—Golf Course and Pro Shop.

In completing the revenue section of Sub-schedule 3-1, the Total Golf Course and Pro Shop Revenue line is considered to be 100 percent, and the percentage for each source of revenue is determined by dividing the dollar amount for that revenue source by Total Golf Course and Pro Shop Revenue.

# Cost of Sales

Cost of Sales is divided into two categories: Cost of Merchandise Sales and Cost of Clothing Sales. The percentage for each of the costs of sales is calculated by dividing the dollar cost by its corresponding revenue amount.

## Cost of Merchandise Sales

Cost of Merchandise Sales includes the cost of non-clothing items sold to customers of the Golf Course and Pro Shop department. Inventory losses due to damaged or missing items are also charged to the Cost of Merchandise Sales. Cost of Merchandise Sales does not include the cost associated with non-clothing items used for gratis presentation to customers, vendors, and employees of any department in the property. The cost of any complimentary items is charged as an expense to Complimentary Services and Gifts for the department that makes the gratis presentation.

## Cost of Clothing Sales

Cost of Clothing Sales includes the cost of clothing items sold to customers of the Golf Course and Pro Shop department. Inventory losses due to damaged or missing items are also charged to the Cost of Clothing Sales. Cost of Clothing Sales does not include the cost associated with clothing items used for gratis presentation to customers, vendors, and employees of any department in the property. The cost of any complimentary clothing items is charged as an expense to Complimentary Services and Gifts expense for the department that makes the gratis presentation.

## Total Cost of Sales

Total Cost of Sales is the sum of Cost of Merchandise Sales and Cost of Clothing Sales. The percentage for Total Cost of Sales is calculated by dividing Total Cost of Sales by the sum of Merchandise Revenue and Clothing Revenue.

# Gross Profit

Gross Profit is calculated by subtracting Total Cost of Sales from Total Golf Course and Pro Shop Revenue. The percentage for Gross Profit is calculated by dividing Gross Profit by Total Golf Course and Pro Shop Revenue.

# Expenses

Golf Course and Pro Shop department expenses are separated into two major categories: Labor Costs and Related Expenses and Other Expenses.

## Labor Costs and Related Expenses

Labor Costs and Related Expenses includes all of the payroll expenses associated with Salaries, Wages, Service Charges, Contracted Labor, Bonuses, and Payroll-Related Expenses for employees and contractors. A list of the positions typically included in the Golf Course and Pro Shop department is provided in the Department Payroll Titles section at the end of Part I.

*Salaries and Wages.* Includes the earnings paid to employees for duties that relate to the operation of the property, such as regular pay, overtime pay, and shift differential pay. If an employee works in a department other than his or her regular home department, his or her earnings must be charged as Salaries and Wages in that other department, regardless of the duties being performed. For example, if a Golf Course and Pro Shop department employee regularly works as a caddie in the Golf Course and Pro Shop Department and temporarily works for the Food and Beverage department on a function, his or her earnings for the function are charged to Salaries and Wages in the Food and Beverage department, not to his or her home department.

Salaries and Wages should be delineated by significant management and non-management payroll titles within the department. If necessary, payroll titles should be aggregated to preserve the confidentiality of a specific employee's payroll.

Salaries and wages include the earnings associated with temporary employees when such expenses are processed through the property's payroll system.

*Service Charge Distribution.* Includes the cost of service charges paid through the payroll system for hotel employees.

*Contracted, Leased and Outsourced Labor.* Includes the gross cost of contracted, leased, and outsourced labor incurred when a property enters into an agreement with a third-party contractor to provide employees to fill positions that would normally be held by individuals paid on the regular payroll. In these situations, the property records or tracks the hours worked and pays the third-party contractor on an hourly or other agreed basis. A typical example is the use of individuals brought into the property to fill in for a shortage of tournament staff.

Contracted, Leased and Outsourced Labor includes the gross cost associated with shared staffing arrangements when such arrangements are supported by formal agreements.

**Bonuses and Incentives.** Includes bonuses (contractual and discretionary), incentive pay, and other types of performance pay designed to drive revenue through sales, profit, or guest satisfaction.

**Total Salaries, Wages, Service Charges, Contracted Labor and Bonuses.** Calculated by summing Salaries and Wages, Service Charge Distribution, Contracted, Leased and Outsourced Labor, and Bonuses and Incentives.

**Payroll-Related Expenses.** Includes amounts paid for an employee for duties that relate to the operation of the property and amounts paid for an employee who works in a department other than his or her regular home department regardless of the duties being performed. Payroll-Related Expenses includes the following items:

- *Payroll Taxes.* Includes the employer share of contributions to national and state retirement, unemployment, disability and medical insurance programs, and other mandated payroll-related taxes or social insurance items. (See *Payroll-Related Expenses—Schedule 14.*)

- *Supplemental Pay.* Includes personal days, vacation pay, sick pay, holiday pay, jury duty pay, relocation pay, paid time off, and severance pay. (See *Payroll-Related Expenses—Schedule 14.*)

- *Employee Benefits.* Includes all other payroll-related expenses, such as employer-paid health insurance expenses, cost of meals furnished to employees, pension contributions, and union dues and fees. (See *Payroll-Related Expenses—Schedule 14.*) The distribution of employee meal costs from *Staff Dining—Schedule 13* is charged to this line.

**Total Payroll-Related Expenses.** Calculated by summing Payroll Taxes, Supplemental Pay, and Employee Benefits.

*Note regarding shared staffing arrangements and cluster services:* Where reasonable and easily identifiable, labor costs related to shared staffing arrangements and cluster services should be charged to salaries and wages or payroll-related expenses.

## Total Labor Costs and Related Expenses

Total Labor Costs and Related Expenses is calculated by summing Total Salaries, Wages, Service Charges, Contracted Labor and Bonuses and Total Payroll-Related Expenses. The percentage for each labor cost component as well as Total Labor Costs and Related Expenses is calculated by dividing the line item amount by Total Golf Course and Pro Shop Revenue. Refer to Part III for recommended operating metrics that are pertinent to Labor Costs and Related Expenses.

## Other Expenses

This expense grouping includes the significant Golf Course and Pro Shop department expenses approved as Other Expenses in the *Uniform System*. Individual properties may delete irrelevant line items, but the *Uniform System* does not provide for the addition or substitution of other expense line items. Rather, properties may choose to develop a sub-account/sub-schedule to provide more detail related to a particular expense item. This sub-account/sub-schedule is then to be rolled into the appropriate line item listed below.

*Cleaning Supplies.* Includes the cost of products used in cleansing, sweeping, polishing, waxing, and disinfecting areas associated with the Golf Course and Pro Shop department.

*Cluster Services.* Includes allocation for costs shared between hotels in a limited geographic area (as opposed to nationally consolidated services such as Corporate Office Reimbursables). Where reasonable and easily identifiable, labor costs and related expenses should be charged to their respective line item and only other expenses are charged to Cluster Services. Where not practical, the fair allocation of the total cluster service expenses should be recognized here.

*Complimentary Services and Gifts.* Includes the cost of providing gift items used in gratis presentations for promotional purposes to guests and vendors of the Golf Course and Pro Shop department, such as VIP gifts, golf balls, and sun visors.

*Contract Services.* Includes expenses for activities performed for the Golf Course and Pro Shop department by outside contractors and professional service providers rather than by hotel employees, unless identified in this department with a specific line item. The cost of contracting outside companies to clean the carpets in the pro shop and department-specific consulting services are typical examples. If supplies are purchased for contract companies to use, the supplies are charged to the appropriate supply account. The cost of contracts for the golf course and pro shop laundry and dry cleaning is charged to Laundry and Dry Cleaning.

*Corporate Office Reimbursables.* Includes the allocations of salaries and expenses of corporate or management company Golf Course and Pro Shop department personnel billed to the property by the regional or corporate office or by the management company, consistent with any contractual arrangements. Travel expenses of such corporate or management company personnel that are incurred while visiting the property, including the costs of meals and other applicable services or amenities provided to corporate or management company staff while on business in the property for the benefit of the property, are also charged to this account.

*Decorations.* Includes the cost of decorative items used in Golf Course and Pro Shop areas for holidays and special events.

*Dues and Subscriptions.* Includes the cost of representation of the Golf Course and Pro Shop department, or of members of the staff when authorized to represent the Golf Course and Pro Shop department, in business or professional organizations. Dues and Subscriptions is also charged with the cost of subscriptions to newspapers, magazines, and books for use by the staff of the Golf Course and Pro Shop department.

*Entertainment—In-House.* Includes the food and beverage at cost, gratuities, service charges, and sales taxes (if applicable) consumed in the entertainment of guests, vendors, and business clients in the property's food and beverage facilities.

*Equipment Rental.* Includes the costs of renting any type of equipment that may be used either sporadically in the Golf Course and Pro Shop department or as a replacement for equipment out of service on a temporary basis. Equipment lease payments made under a qualified operating lease are charged to Other Property and Equipment under the Rent section of *Non-Operating Income and Expenses— Schedule 11.*

*Gasoline and Lubricants.* Includes the cost of gasoline and lubricants for gasoline-powered golf carts, mowers, tractors, and trucks used in operating the golf course.

*Grounds Maintenance and Landscaping.* Includes the cost of maintaining the golf course and related roads and paths. Examples include fertilizers, insecticides, other chemicals, sand, topsoil, seeds, flowers, and shrubs.

*Irrigation.* Includes the cost of repairing golf course water and drainage systems, sprinklers, water controllers, and computerized water systems, as well as the cost for water treatment. The cost of the water used for irrigation is charged to the Water line item below.

*Laundry and Dry Cleaning.* Includes the cost of laundry and dry cleaning services applicable to the Golf Course and Pro Shop department, whether the services are performed by an in-house facility or are contracted to an outside company. If the services are performed by an in-house laundry, an allocation from *House Laundry—Schedule 12* is charged to Laundry and Dry Cleaning. This allocation is distributed to departments on an equitable basis reflecting usage, such as cost-per-pound, number of pieces cleaned, number of orders processed, etc. If the services are performed by an outside company, the amount charged to Laundry and Dry Cleaning should be based on invoices sent by the outside laundry. The cost of cleaning employee uniforms is charged to Uniform Laundry.

*Licenses and Permits.* Includes the cost of national and local jurisdiction licenses, including costs of inspections needed for licensing, for all activities of the Golf Course and Pro Shop department.

*Linen.* Includes the cost, whether purchased or rented, of towels, face cloths, bath mats, and table cloths used by the Golf Course and Pro Shop department.

*Management Fees.* Includes the fees charged by an organization (other than the hotel's management company) to manage the Golf Course and Pro Shop department operations.

*Miscellaneous.* Includes any expenses of the Golf Course and Pro Shop department that do not apply to the other line items discussed in this section.

*Operating Supplies.* Includes the cost of operating and general office supplies needed to operate the Golf Course and Pro Shop department that are not included in the descriptions of specific supply accounts such as Cleaning Supplies, Decorations, Grounds Maintenance, Linen and Landscaping, or Printing and Stationery. Examples are practice range balls and containers, golf flag pins, ice chests, course signage, and paper cups.

*Printing and Stationery.* Includes the cost of printed forms used in the Golf Course and Pro Shop department, whether they are purchased from an outside source or produced internally. Examples include scoring cards and pencils.

*Reservations.* Includes the cost associated with participation with third-party reservation or booking systems (e.g., Golfnow.com). The third-party systems may be electronic or personal. The fees may include transaction costs or commissions in addition to the cost of communication channels, mobile applications, or websites dedicated to the specific venue. System costs (non-transactional) related to a reservation system are charged to *Information and Telecommunications Systems—Schedule 6*.

*Royalty Fees.* Includes all costs associated with the right to use a brand name in connection with a Golf Course and Pro Shop department activity. An example would be the fees paid for use of a brand name to identify a golf course, including franchise fees. The fees paid for the use of a hotel brand name are charged to Franchise and Affiliation Fees—Royalties in *Sales and Marketing—Schedule 7*.

*Tournament Expenses.* Includes all costs associated with administering a golf tournament.

*Training.* Includes the costs, other than payroll cost, that can be directly attributed to the training of employees in the Golf Course and Pro Shop department. Examples include the costs of training materials, supplies, certification programs, and instructor fees. The cost of employee wages incurred during training is charged to Salaries and Wages.

*Transportation.* Includes all costs associated with transporting guests to and from a remote golf course, such as fuel costs, costs of washing and cleaning vehicles, or the occasional rental of vehicles for transporting large groups, or the costs of contracting guest transportation services. The cost of mechanical maintenance of vehicles used to transport guests is charged to *Property Operation and Maintenance—Schedule 8*. If a vehicle used to transport guests is leased, the cost of the lease is charged to Rent under *Non-Operating Income and Expenses —Schedule 11*.

Not included in this account are the costs associated with the maintenance of golf carts owned by the hotel. These costs are charges to Vehicle Repairs and Maintenance.

*Travel—Meals and Entertainment.* Includes the reimbursable cost of food and beverage expenditures for travel and entertainment by employees of the Golf Course and Pro Shop department traveling on property business.

*Travel—Other.* Includes the cost of travel and reimbursable expenses (e.g., airfare car rental, hotel room and tax, guestroom Internet, conference registration fees), other than food, beverage, and entertainment, incurred by employees of the Golf Course and Pro Shop department traveling on property business.

*Uniform Costs.* Includes the cost of employee uniforms used in the Golf Course and Pro Shop department, whether purchased or rented. Repair costs are also included in this line item. The cost of cleaning uniforms is charged to Uniform Laundry.

*Uniform Laundry.* This includes the cost of cleaning uniforms for employees of the Golf Course and Pro Shop department, whether performed by an in-hotel facility or contracted to an outside company.

*Vehicle Repairs and Maintenance.* Includes the cost of repairing and maintaining golf carts (including the cost of batteries for the golf carts along with the costs associated with charging the batteries), mowers, tractors, and trucks used in operating the golf course. The cost of building repairs and maintenance should be charged to the Property Operation and Maintenance department.

*Water.* Includes the cost of water used for irrigation and water features/hazards on the golf course.

## Total Other Expenses

Total Other Expenses is calculated by summing all items listed under Other Expenses. The percentage for each line item expense as well as Total Other Expenses is calculated by dividing the line item amount by Total Golf Course and Pro Shop Revenue.

# Total Expenses

Total Expenses is calculated by adding Total Labor Costs and Related Expenses to Total Other Expenses. The percentage for Total Expenses is calculated by dividing Total Expenses by Total Golf Course and Pro Shop Revenue.

The sum of Total Cost of Sales and Total Expenses is shown on Schedule 3 as Departmental Expenses—Golf Course and Pro Shop.

# Departmental Profit

Departmental Profit is calculated by subtracting Total Expenses from Gross Profit. The percentage for Departmental Profit is calculated by dividing Departmental Profit by Total Golf Course and Pro Shop Revenue. Departmental Profit is then shown on Schedule 3 as Departmental Profit—Golf Course and Pro Shop.

# HEALTH CLUB/SPA—SUB-SCHEDULE 3-2

| | PERIOD OF | | | | | | | | | | | |
|---|---|---|---|---|---|---|---|---|---|---|---|---|
| | CURRENT PERIOD | | | | | | YEAR-TO-DATE | | | | | |
| | ACTUAL | | FORECAST/ BUDGET | | PRIOR YEAR | | ACTUAL | | FORECAST/ BUDGET | | PRIOR YEAR | |
| | $ | % | $ | % | $ | % | $ | % | $ | % | $ | % |
| **REVENUE** | | | | | | | | | | | | |
| Massage and Body Treatment Revenue | | | | | | | | | | | | |
| Skin Care Revenue | | | | | | | | | | | | |
| Hair Care Revenue | | | | | | | | | | | | |
| Nail Care Revenue | | | | | | | | | | | | |
| Fitness Revenue | | | | | | | | | | | | |
| Health and Wellness Revenue | | | | | | | | | | | | |
| Membership Fee Revenue | | | | | | | | | | | | |
| Retail Revenue | | | | | | | | | | | | |
| Other Revenue | | | | | | | | | | | | |
| Less: Allowances | | | | | | | | | | | | |
| **TOTAL HEALTH CLUB/SPA REVENUE** | | | | | | | | | | | | |
| **COST OF SALES** | | | | | | | | | | | | |
| **GROSS PROFIT** | | | | | | | | | | | | |
| **EXPENSES** | | | | | | | | | | | | |
| Labor Costs and Related Expenses | | | | | | | | | | | | |
| Salaries, Wages, Service Charges, Contracted Labor and Bonuses | | | | | | | | | | | | |
| Salaries and Wages | | | | | | | | | | | | |
| Management | | | | | | | | | | | | |
| Non-Management | | | | | | | | | | | | |
| Attendant/Housekeeping | | | | | | | | | | | | |
| Fitness | | | | | | | | | | | | |
| Reception/Retail | | | | | | | | | | | | |
| Therapists/Technicians | | | | | | | | | | | | |
| Sub-Total: Salaries and Wages | | | | | | | | | | | | |
| Service Charge Distribution | | | | | | | | | | | | |
| Contracted, Leased and Outsourced Labor | | | | | | | | | | | | |
| Bonuses and Incentives | | | | | | | | | | | | |
| Total Salaries, Wages, Service Charges, Contracted Labor and Bonuses | | | | | | | | | | | | |
| Payroll-Related Expenses | | | | | | | | | | | | |
| Payroll Taxes | | | | | | | | | | | | |
| Supplemental Pay | | | | | | | | | | | | |
| Employee Benefits | | | | | | | | | | | | |
| Total Payroll Related Expenses | | | | | | | | | | | | |
| Total Labor Costs and Related Expenses | | | | | | | | | | | | |
| Other Expenses | | | | | | | | | | | | |
| Ambience | | | | | | | | | | | | |
| Athletic Supplies | | | | | | | | | | | | |
| Cleaning Supplies | | | | | | | | | | | | |
| Cluster Services | | | | | | | | | | | | |
| Complimentary Services and Gifts | | | | | | | | | | | | |
| Contract Services | | | | | | | | | | | | |

**HEALTH CLUB/SPA—SUB-SCHEDULE 3-2** *(continued)*

| | Current Period | | | | | | Year-To-Date | | | | | |
|---|---|---|---|---|---|---|---|---|---|---|---|---|
| | Actual | | Forecast/ Budget | | Prior Year | | Actual | | Forecast/ Budget | | Prior Year | |
| | $ | % | $ | % | $ | % | $ | % | $ | % | $ | % |
| Corporate Office Reimbursables | | | | | | | | | | | | |
| Decorations | | | | | | | | | | | | |
| Dues and Subscriptions | | | | | | | | | | | | |
| Entertainment—In-House | | | | | | | | | | | | |
| Equipment Rental | | | | | | | | | | | | |
| Health and Beauty Products | | | | | | | | | | | | |
| Laundry and Dry Cleaning | | | | | | | | | | | | |
| Licenses and Permits | | | | | | | | | | | | |
| Linen | | | | | | | | | | | | |
| Management Fees | | | | | | | | | | | | |
| Miscellaneous | | | | | | | | | | | | |
| Operating Supplies | | | | | | | | | | | | |
| Printing and Stationery | | | | | | | | | | | | |
| Reservations | | | | | | | | | | | | |
| Royalty Fees | | | | | | | | | | | | |
| Swimming Pool | | | | | | | | | | | | |
| Training | | | | | | | | | | | | |
| Travel—Meals and Entertainment | | | | | | | | | | | | |
| Travel—Other | | | | | | | | | | | | |
| Uniform Costs | | | | | | | | | | | | |
| Uniform Laundry | | | | | | | | | | | | |
| Total Other Expenses | | | | | | | | | | | | |
| **Total Expenses** | | | | | | | | | | | | |
| **Departmental Profit** | | | | | | | | | | | | |

*Health Club/Spa—Sub-schedule 3-2* reflects the proper format for a Health Club/Spa department and designates the revenue and expense accounts that are approved as line items in the *Uniform System*. Individual properties may delete irrelevant line items, but the *Uniform System* does not provide for the addition or substitution of other revenue or expense line items. Rather, properties may choose to develop a sub-account/sub-schedule to provide more detail related to a particular revenue or expense item. This sub-account/sub-schedule is then to be rolled into the appropriate line item. Additionally, properties may choose to delete some of the columns or to show them in a different order and remain "in conformity with the *Uniform System*."

Refer to Part III for operating ratios and statistics that are pertinent to the Health Club/Spa department.

The Total Health Club/Spa Revenue, Total Expenses (including Total Cost of Sales), and Departmental Profit shown on Sub-schedule 3-2 are then reported on Schedule 3.

The line items for *Health Club/Spa—Sub-schedule 3-2* are defined in the following pages.

# Revenue

Revenue from the Health Club/Spa department is classified into many categories. These are defined below.

Health Club/Spa Revenue may include an allocated portion of package revenues. As discussed under *Rooms—Schedule 1*, package revenues are lodging accommodations sold in conjunction with other services provided by either the property or third parties as part of a single transaction with the guest. Package revenues are allocated to other departments based on the relative market values of the items supplied by those departments.

Under certain circumstances, health club/spa revenue in its entirety may be reported on a net basis on *Miscellaneous Income—Schedule 4*. Further, some revenue items within the Health Club/Spa department may be reported on a net basis within the department. For additional information, see Part V.

## Massage and Body Treatment Revenue

Massage and Body Treatment Revenue includes revenue derived from fees charged to customers for massage and body treatment services.

## Skin Care Revenue

Skin Care Revenue includes revenue derived from facial treatments and waxing services.

## Hair Care Revenue

Hair Care Revenue includes revenue derived from styling, coloring, and chemical treatments.

## Nail Care Revenue

Nail Care Revenue includes revenue derived from manicures and pedicures.

## Fitness Revenue

Fitness Revenue includes revenue derived from personal training, fitness evaluations, and exercise classes.

## Health and Wellness Revenue

Health and Wellness Revenue includes revenue derived from programs such as medically supervised services, nutrition classes, wellness consultations, and wellness programs.

## Membership Fee Revenue

Membership Fee Revenue includes revenue derived from daily facility fees, guest fees, initiation fees, and membership dues.

## Retail Revenue

Retail Revenue includes revenue derived from the sales of apparel, gifts, accessories, products, sundries, and other retail items.

## Other Revenue

Other Revenue includes revenue from any other services and charges not previously specified, such as surcharges and service charges. Surcharges and service charges generally include any mandatory, non-discretionary, or other charge automatically added to a customer account in respect of the service or use of an amenity. The key determining factors for the recording of surcharges and service charges (versus gratuities) are set out in Part V.

Revenue from food and beverage sales sold in the Health Club/Spa department is reported on *Food and Beverage—Schedule 2.*

## Allowances

Allowances refers to a reduction in revenue due to a service problem, not an error in posting. Errors in posting, such as charging an incorrect amount, are treated as adjustments to revenue, regardless of the accounting period in which the error occurred.

## Total Health Club/Spa Revenue

Total Health Club/Spa Revenue is calculated by summing the revenue items listed above and subtracting Allowances. This amount is shown on Schedule 3 as Departmental Revenue—Health Club/Spa.

In completing the revenue section of Sub-schedule 3-2, the Total Health Club/Spa Revenue line is considered to be 100 percent, and the percentage for each source of revenue is determined by dividing the dollar amount for that revenue source by Total Health Club/Spa Revenue.

# Cost of Sales

Cost of Sales includes the cost of apparel, gifts, accessories, products, sundries, and other retail items sold to customers of the Health Club/Spa department. Inventory losses due to damaged or missing items are also charged to the Cost of Sales. Cost of Sales does not include the cost associated with items used for gratis presentation to customers, vendors, and employees of any department in the property. The cost of any complimentary items is charged as an expense to Complimentary Services and Gifts expense for the department that makes the gratis presentation.

The percentage for Cost of Sales is calculated by dividing Cost of Sales by Retail Revenue.

# Gross Profit

Gross Profit is calculated by subtracting Cost of Sales from Total Health Club/Spa Revenue. The percentage for Gross Profit is calculated by dividing Gross Profit by Total Health Club/Spa Revenue.

# Expenses

Health Club/Spa department expenses are separated into two major categories: Labor Costs and Related Expenses and Other Expenses.

## Labor Costs and Related Expenses

Labor Costs and Related Expenses includes all of the payroll expenses associated with Salaries, Wages, Service Charges, Contracted Labor, Bonuses, and Payroll-Related Expenses for employees and contractors. A list of the positions typically included in the Health Club/Spa department is provided in the Department Payroll Titles section at the end of Part I.

*Salaries and Wages.* Salaries and Wages includes the earnings paid to employees for duties that relate to the operation of the property, such as regular pay, overtime pay, and shift differential pay. If an employee works in a department other than his or her regular home department, his or her earnings must be charged as Salaries and Wages in that other department, regardless of the duties being performed. For example, if a Health Club/Spa department employee regularly works as a spa technician in the Health Club/Spa Department and temporarily works for the Food and Beverage department on a function, his or her earnings for the function are charged to Salaries and Wages in the Food and Beverage department, not to his or her home department.

Salaries and Wages should be delineated by significant management and non-management payroll titles within the department. If necessary, payroll titles should be aggregated to preserve the confidentiality of a specific employee's payroll.

Salaries and wages include the earnings associated with temporary employees when such expenses are processed through the property's payroll system.

*Contracted, Leased and Outsourced Labor.* Includes the gross cost of contracted, leased, and outsourced labor incurred when a property enters into an agreement with a third-party contractor to provide employees to fill positions that would normally be held by individuals paid on the regular payroll. In these situations, the property records or tracks the hours worked and pays the third-party contractor on an hourly or other agreed basis. Spa therapists and technicians frequently work as individual contracted labor. Payments made to these contracted employees should be recorded in this cost category.

Contracted, Leased and Outsourced Labor includes the gross cost associated with shared staffing arrangements when such arrangements are supported by formal agreements.

*Service Charge Distribution.* Includes the cost of service charges paid through the payroll system for hotel employees.

*Bonuses and Incentives.* Includes bonuses (contractual and discretionary), incentive pay, and other types of performance pay designed to drive revenue through sales, profit, or guest satisfaction.

*Total Salaries, Wages, Service Charges, Contracted Labor and Bonuses.* Calculated by summing Salaries and Wages, Service Charge Distribution, Contracted, Leased and Outsourced Labor, and Bonuses and Incentives.

*Payroll-Related Expenses.* Includes amounts paid for an employee for duties that relate to the operation of the property and amounts paid for an employee who works in a department other than his or her regular home department regardless of the duties being performed. Payroll-Related Expenses includes the following items:

- *Payroll Taxes.* Includes the employer share of contributions to national and state retirement, unemployment, disability and medical insurance programs, and other mandated payroll-related taxes or social insurance items. (See *Payroll-Related Expenses—Schedule 14.*)

- *Supplemental Pay.* Includes personal days, vacation pay, sick pay, holiday pay, jury duty pay, relocation pay, paid time off, and severance pay. (See *Payroll-Related Expenses—Schedule 14.*)

- *Employee Benefits.* Includes all other payroll-related expenses, such as employer-paid health insurance expenses, cost of meals furnished to employees, pension contributions, and union dues and fees. (See *Payroll-Related Expenses—Schedule 14.*) The distribution of employee meal costs from *Staff Dining—Schedule 13* is charged to this line.

*Total Payroll-Related Expenses.* Calculated by summing Payroll Taxes, Supplemental Pay, and Employee Benefits.

*Note regarding shared staffing arrangements and cluster services:* Where reasonable and easily identifiable, labor costs related to shared staffing arrangements and cluster services should be charged to salaries and wages or payroll-related expenses.

## Total Labor Costs and Related Expenses

Total Labor Costs and Related Expenses is calculated by summing Total Salaries, Wages, Service Charges, Contracted Labor and Bonuses and Total Payroll-Related Expenses. The percentage for each labor cost component as well as Total Labor Costs and Related Expenses is calculated by dividing the line item amount by Total Health Club/Spa Revenue. Refer to Part III for recommended operating metrics that are pertinent to Labor Costs and Related Expenses.

## Other Expenses

This expense grouping includes the significant Health Club/Spa department expenses approved as Other Expenses in the *Uniform System.* Individual properties may delete irrelevant line items, but the *Uniform System* does not provide for the addition or substitution of other expense line items. Rather, properties may choose to develop a sub-account/sub-schedule to provide more detail related to a particular expense item. This sub-account/sub-schedule is then to be rolled into the appropriate line item listed below.

*Ambience.* Includes the cost to provide the sensory environment within the spa, including background music, candles, aromatherapy oils, and diffusers.

*Athletic Supplies.* Includes the cost of non-capitalized gym equipment, as well as supplies used during fitness classes.

*Cleaning Supplies.* Includes the cost of products used in cleansing, sweeping, polishing, waxing, and disinfecting areas associated with the Health Club/Spa department.

*Cluster Services.* Includes allocation for costs shared between hotels in a limited geographic area (as opposed to nationally consolidated services such as Corporate Office Reimbursables). Where reasonable and easily identifiable, labor costs and related expenses should be charged to their respective line item and only other expenses are charged to Cluster Services. Where not practical, the fair allocation of the total cluster service expenses should be recognized here.

*Complimentary Services and Gifts.* Includes the cost of providing gift items used in gratis presentations for promotional purposes to guests and vendors of the health club/spa department, such as VIP gifts, razors and shaving cream, shampoo, Q-tips and cotton balls, fruit juices, and herbal teas.

*Contract Services.* Includes expenses for activities performed for the Health Club/Spa department by outside contractors and professional service providers rather than by hotel employees, unless identified in this department with a specific line item. The cost of contracting outside companies to clean the spa or whirlpool and department-specific consulting services are typical examples. If supplies are purchased for contract companies to use, the supplies are charged to the appropriate supply account. The cost of contracts for the Health Club/Spa department laundry and dry cleaning is charged to Laundry and Dry Cleaning.

*Corporate Office Reimbursables.* Includes the allocations of salaries and expenses of corporate or management company Health Club/Spa department personnel billed to the property by the regional or corporate office or by the management company, consistent with any contractual arrangements. Travel expenses of such corporate or management company personnel that are incurred while visiting the property, including the costs of meals and other applicable services or amenities provided to corporate or management company staff while on business in the property for the benefit of the property, are also charged to this account.

*Decorations.* Includes the cost of decorative items used in the Health Club/Spa areas for holidays and special events.

*Dues and Subscriptions.* Includes the cost of representation of the Health Club/Spa department, or of members of the staff when authorized to represent the Health Club/Spa department, in business or professional organizations. Dues and Subscriptions is also charged with the cost of subscriptions to newspapers, magazines, and books for use by the staff of the Health Club/Spa department.

*Entertainment—In-House.* Includes the food and beverage at cost, gratuities, service charges, and sales taxes (if applicable) consumed in the entertainment of guests, vendors, and business clients in the property's food and beverage facilities.

*Equipment Rental.* Includes the costs of renting any type of equipment that may be used either sporadically in the Health Club/Spa department or as a replacement for equipment out of service on a temporary basis. Equipment lease payments made under a qualified operating lease are charged to Other Property and Equipment under the Rent section of *Non-Operating Income and Expenses—Schedule 11.*

*Health and Beauty Products.* Includes the cost of items used in producing Massage and Body Treatment Revenue, Skin Care Revenue, Hair Care Revenue, and Nail Care Revenue. Items charged to this line include nail polish, face cream, shampoo, and massage oils.

*Laundry and Dry Cleaning.* Includes the cost of laundry and dry cleaning services applicable to the Health Club/Spa department, whether the services are performed by an in-house facility or are contracted to an outside company. If the services are performed by an in-house laundry, an allocation from *House Laundry—Schedule 12* is charged to Laundry and Dry Cleaning. This allocation is distributed to departments on an equitable basis reflecting usage, such as cost-per-pound, number of pieces cleaned, number of orders processed, etc. If the services are performed by an outside company, the amount charged to Laundry and Dry Cleaning should be based on invoices sent by the outside laundry. The cost of cleaning employee uniforms is charged to Uniform Laundry.

*Licenses and Permits.* Includes the cost of national and local jurisdiction licenses, including costs of inspections needed for licensing, for all activities of the Health Club/Spa department.

*Linen.* Includes the cost, whether purchased or rented, of towels, face cloths, bath mats, and bathrobes used by the Health Club/Spa department.

*Management Fees.* Includes the fees charged by an organization (other than the hotel's management company) to manage the Health Club/Spa department operations.

*Miscellaneous.* Includes any expenses of the Health Club/Spa department that do not apply to the other line items discussed in this section.

*Operating Supplies.* Includes the cost of items needed to operate the Health Club/Spa department that are not included in the descriptions of specific supply accounts such as Athletic Supplies, Cleaning Supplies, or Printing and Stationery. Examples would be toilet paper, life preservers, clothing hangers, and a weight scale.

*Printing and Stationery.* Includes the cost of printed forms used in the Health Club/Spa department, whether they are purchased from an outside source or produced internally. Examples are the forms used to track exercise routines, guest treatment forms, equipment instructions, file folders, and pencils.

*Reservations.* Includes the cost associated with participation with third-party reservation or booking systems (e.g., SpaFinder). The third-party systems may be electronic or personal. The fees may include transaction costs or commissions in addition to the cost of communication channels, mobile applications, or websites dedicated to the specific venue. System costs (non-transactional) related to a reservation system are to be charged to *Information and Telecommunications Systems—Schedule 6.*

*Royalty Fees.* Includes all costs associated with the right to use a brand name in connection with a Health Club/Spa department activity. An example would include the fees paid for use of a brand name to identify the health club/spa. The fees paid for the use of a hotel brand name are charged to Franchise and Affiliation Fees—Royalties in *Sales and Marketing—Schedule 7.*

*Swimming Pool.* Includes the cost of materials, supplies, pool chemicals, and contracts relating to the maintenance and repair of swimming pools when the Health Club/Spa department is responsible for managing the pool. If the Health Club/Spa department is not responsible for managing the pool, then these costs are recorded on *Property Operation and Maintenance—Schedule 8.*

*Training.* Includes the costs, other than payroll cost, that can be directly attributed to the training of employees in the Health Club/Spa department. Examples include the costs of training materials, supplies, certification programs, and instructor fees. The cost of employee wages incurred during training is charged to Salaries and Wages.

*Travel—Meals and Entertainment.* Includes the reimbursable cost of food and beverage expenses for travel and entertainment by employees of the Health Club/Spa department traveling on property business.

*Travel—Other.* Includes the cost of travel and reimbursable expenses (e.g., airfare car rental, hotel room and tax, guestroom Internet, conference registration fees), other than food, beverage, and entertainment, incurred by employees of the Health Club/Spa department traveling on property business.

*Uniform Costs.* Includes the cost of employee uniforms used in the Health Club/Spa department, whether purchased or rented. Repair costs are also included in this line item. The cost of cleaning uniforms is charged to Uniform Laundry.

*Uniform Laundry.* Includes the cost of cleaning uniforms for employees of the Health Club/Spa department, whether performed by an in-hotel facility or contracted to an outside company.

### Total Other Expenses

Total Other Expenses is calculated by summing all items listed under Other Expenses. The percentage for each line item expense as well as Total Other Expenses is calculated by dividing the line item amount by Total Health Club/Spa Revenue.

## Total Expenses

Total Expenses is calculated by adding Total Labor Costs and Related Expenses to Total Other Expenses. The percentage for Total Expenses is calculated by dividing Total Expenses by Total Health Club/Spa Revenue.

The sum of Cost of Sales and Total Expenses is shown on Schedule 3 as Departmental Expenses—Health Club/Spa.

# Departmental Profit

Departmental Profit is calculated by subtracting Total Expenses from Gross Profit. The percentage for Departmental Profit is calculated by dividing Departmental Profit by Total Health Club/Spa Revenue. Departmental Profit is then shown on Schedule 3 as Departmental Profit—Health Club/Spa.

# PARKING—SUB-SCHEDULE 3-3

| | PERIOD OF | | | | | | | | | | | |
|---|---|---|---|---|---|---|---|---|---|---|---|---|
| | CURRENT PERIOD | | | | | | YEAR-TO-DATE | | | | | |
| | ACTUAL | | FORECAST/ BUDGET | | PRIOR YEAR | | ACTUAL | | FORECAST/ BUDGET | | PRIOR YEAR | |
| | $ | % | $ | % | $ | % | $ | % | $ | % | $ | % |
| **REVENUE** | | | | | | | | | | | | |
| Self-Parking Revenue | | | | | | | | | | | | |
| Valet Parking Revenue | | | | | | | | | | | | |
| Other Revenue | | | | | | | | | | | | |
| Less: Allowances | | | | | | | | | | | | |
| **TOTAL PARKING REVENUE** | | | | | | | | | | | | |
| **COST OF SALES** | | | | | | | | | | | | |
| **GROSS PROFIT** | | | | | | | | | | | | |
| **EXPENSES** | | | | | | | | | | | | |
| Labor Costs and Related Expenses | | | | | | | | | | | | |
| Salaries, Wages, Service Charges, Contracted Labor and Bonuses | | | | | | | | | | | | |
| Salaries and Wages | | | | | | | | | | | | |
| Management | | | | | | | | | | | | |
| Non-Management | | | | | | | | | | | | |
| Sub-Total: Salaries and Wages | | | | | | | | | | | | |
| Service Charge Distribution | | | | | | | | | | | | |
| Contracted, Leased and Outsourced Labor | | | | | | | | | | | | |
| Bonuses and Incentives | | | | | | | | | | | | |
| Total Salaries, Wages, Service Charges, Contracted Labor and Bonuses | | | | | | | | | | | | |
| Payroll-Related Expenses | | | | | | | | | | | | |
| Payroll Taxes | | | | | | | | | | | | |
| Supplemental Pay | | | | | | | | | | | | |
| Employee Benefits | | | | | | | | | | | | |
| Total Payroll Related Expenses | | | | | | | | | | | | |
| Total Labor Costs and Related Expenses | | | | | | | | | | | | |
| Other Expenses | | | | | | | | | | | | |
| Cleaning Supplies | | | | | | | | | | | | |
| Cluster Services | | | | | | | | | | | | |
| Complimentary Services and Gifts | | | | | | | | | | | | |
| Contract Services | | | | | | | | | | | | |
| Corporate Office Reimbursables | | | | | | | | | | | | |
| Decorations | | | | | | | | | | | | |
| Dues and Subscriptions | | | | | | | | | | | | |
| Entertainment—In-House | | | | | | | | | | | | |
| Equipment Rental | | | | | | | | | | | | |
| Laundry and Dry Cleaning | | | | | | | | | | | | |
| Licenses and Permits | | | | | | | | | | | | |
| Management Fees | | | | | | | | | | | | |
| Miscellaneous | | | | | | | | | | | | |
| Operating Supplies | | | | | | | | | | | | |
| Printing and Stationery | | | | | | | | | | | | |
| Rent | | | | | | | | | | | | |
| Royalty Fees | | | | | | | | | | | | |

**PARKING—SUB-SCHEDULE 3-3** *(continued)*

| | PERIOD OF | | | | | |
| --- | --- | --- | --- | --- | --- | --- |
| | CURRENT PERIOD | | | YEAR-TO-DATE | | |
| | ACTUAL | FORECAST/ BUDGET | PRIOR YEAR | ACTUAL | FORECAST/ BUDGET | PRIOR YEAR |
| | $ \| % | $ \| % | $ \| % | $ \| % | $ \| % | $ \| % |
| Training | | | | | | |
| Travel—Meals and Entertainment | | | | | | |
| Travel—Other | | | | | | |
| Uniform Costs | | | | | | |
| Uniform Laundry | | | | | | |
| Total Other Expenses | | | | | | |
| TOTAL EXPENSES | | | | | | |
| DEPARTMENTAL PROFIT | | | | | | |

*Parking—Sub-schedule 3-3* reflects the proper format for a Parking department and designates the revenue and expense accounts that are approved as line items in the *Uniform System*. Individual properties may delete irrelevant line items, but the *Uniform System* does not provide for the addition or substitution of other revenue or expense line items. Rather, properties may choose to develop a sub-account/sub-schedule to provide more detail related to a particular revenue or expense item. This sub-account/sub-schedule is then to be rolled into the appropriate line item. Additionally, properties may choose to delete some of the columns or to show them in a different order and remain "in conformity with the *Uniform System*."

Refer to Part III for operating ratios and statistics that are pertinent to the Parking department.

The Total Parking Revenue, Total Expenses (including Cost of Sales), and Departmental Profit shown on Sub-schedule 3-3 are then reported on Schedule 3.

The line items for *Parking—Sub-schedule 3-3* are defined in the following pages.

# Revenue

Parking revenue is classified into Self-Parking Revenue, Valet Parking Revenue, and Other Revenue.

Parking Revenue may include an allocated portion of package revenues. As discussed under *Rooms—Schedule 1*, package revenues are lodging accommodations sold in conjunction with other services provided by either the property or third parties as part of a single transaction with the guest. Package revenues are allocated to other departments based on the relative market values of the items supplied by those departments.

Under certain circumstances, parking revenue in its entirety may be reported on a net basis on *Miscellaneous Income—Schedule 4*. Further, some revenue items within the Parking department may be reported on a net basis within the department. For additional information, see Part V.

### Self-Parking Revenue

Self-Parking Revenue includes revenue derived from use of the parking facilities by customers without valet service.

### Valet Parking Revenue

Valet Parking Revenue includes revenue derived from use of the parking facility by customers with valet service.

### Other Revenue

Other Revenue includes revenue from any other services or charges not previously specified. Examples would include surcharges and service charges, automobile repair, car washes, or gasoline sales. Surcharges and service charges generally include any mandatory, non-discretionary, or other charge automatically added to a customer account in respect of the service or use of an amenity. The key determining factors for the recording of surcharges and service charges (versus gratuities) are set out in Part V.

### Allowances

Allowances refers to a reduction in revenue due to a service problem, not an error in posting. Errors in posting, such as charging an incorrect amount, are treated as adjustments to revenue, regardless of the accounting period in which the error occurred.

### Total Parking Revenue

Total Parking Revenue is calculated by summing the revenue items listed above and subtracting Allowances. This amount is shown on Schedule 3 as Departmental Revenue—Parking.

In completing the revenue section of Sub-schedule 3-3, the Total Parking Revenue line is considered to be 100 percent, and the percentage for each source of revenue is determined by dividing the dollar amount for that revenue source by Total Parking Revenue.

## Cost of Sales

Cost of Sales includes the cost for any items sold when the revenue is included in Other Revenue. The cost of gasoline sold would be an example of a Cost of Sales. The percentage for Cost of Sales is calculated by dividing Cost of Sales by Other Revenue.

## Gross Profit

Gross Profit is calculated by subtracting Cost of Sales from Total Parking Revenue. The percentage for Gross Profit is calculated by dividing Gross Profit by Total Parking Revenue.

# Expenses

Parking expenses are separated into two categories: Labor Costs and Related Expenses and Other Expenses.

## Labor Costs and Related Expenses

Labor Costs and Related Expenses includes all of the payroll expenses associated with Salaries, Wages, Service Charges, Contracted Labor, Bonuses, and Payroll-Related Expenses for employees and contractors. A list of the positions typically included in the Parking department is provided in the Department Payroll Titles section at the end of Part I.

*Salaries and Wages.* Includes the earnings paid to employees for duties that relate to the operation of the property, such as regular pay, overtime pay, and shift differential pay. If an employee works in a department other than his or her regular home department, his or her earnings must be charged as Salaries and Wages in that other department, regardless of the duties being performed. For example, if a Parking department employee regularly works as a valet parker in the Parking department and temporarily works for the Food and Beverage department on a function, his or her earnings for the function are charged to Salaries and Wages in the Food and Beverage department, not to his or her home department.

Salaries and Wages should be delineated by significant management and non-management payroll titles within the department. If necessary, payroll titles should be aggregated to preserve the confidentiality of a specific employee's payroll.

Salaries and Wages includes the earnings associated with temporary employees when such expenses are processed through the property's payroll system.

*Service Charge Distribution.* Includes the cost of service charges paid through the payroll system for hotel employees.

*Contracted, Leased and Outsourced Labor.* Includes the gross cost of contracted, leased, and outsourced labor incurred when a property enters into an agreement with a third-party contractor to provide employees to fill positions that would normally be held by individuals paid on the regular payroll. In these situations, the property records or tracks the hours worked and pays the third-party contractor on an hourly or other agreed basis. A typical example is the use of individuals brought into the property to fill in for a shortage of valet parking staff.

Contracted, Leased and Outsourced Labor includes the gross cost associated with shared staffing arrangements when such arrangements are supported by formal agreements.

*Bonuses and Incentives.* Includes bonuses (contractual and discretionary), incentive pay, and other types of performance pay designed to drive revenue through sales, profit, or guest satisfaction.

*Total Salaries, Wages, Service Charges, Contracted Labor and Bonuses.* Calculated by summing Salaries and Wages, Service Charge Distribution, Contracted, Leased and Outsourced Labor, and Bonuses and Incentives.

*Payroll-Related Expenses.* Includes amounts paid for an employee for duties that relate to the operation of the property and amounts paid for an employee who works in a department other than his or her regular home department regardless of the duties being performed. Payroll-Related Expenses includes the following items:

- *Payroll Taxes.* Includes the employer share of contributions to national and state retirement, unemployment, disability and medical insurance programs, and other mandated payroll-related taxes or social insurance items. (See *Payroll-Related Expenses — Schedule 14.*)

- *Supplemental Pay.* Includes personal days, vacation pay, sick pay, holiday pay, jury duty pay, relocation pay, paid time off, and severance pay. (See *Payroll-Related Expenses — Schedule 14.*)

- *Employee Benefits.* Includes all other payroll-related expenses, such as employer-paid health insurance expenses, cost of meals furnished to employees, pension contributions, and union dues and fees. (See *Payroll-Related Expenses — Schedule 14.*) The distribution of employee meal costs from *Staff Dining — Schedule 13* is charged to this line.

*Total Payroll-Related Expenses.* Calculated by summing Payroll Taxes, Supplemental Pay, and Employee Benefits.

*Note regarding shared staffing arrangements and cluster services:* Where reasonable and easily identifiable, labor costs related to shared staffing arrangements and cluster services should be charged to salaries and wages or payroll-related expenses.

## Total Labor Costs and Related Expenses

Total Labor Costs and Related Expenses is calculated by summing Total Salaries, Wages, Service Charges, Contracted Labor and Bonuses and Total Payroll-Related Expenses. The percentage for each labor cost component as well as Total Labor Costs and Related Expenses is calculated by dividing the line item amount by Total Parking Revenue. Refer to Part III for recommended operating metrics that are pertinent to Labor Costs and Related Expenses.

## Other Expenses

This expense grouping includes the significant Parking department expenses approved as Other Expenses in the *Uniform System.* Individual properties may delete irrelevant line items, but the *Uniform System* does not provide for the addition or substitution of other expense line items. Rather, properties may choose to develop a sub-account/sub-schedule to provide more detail related to a particular expense item. This sub-account/sub-schedule is then to be rolled into the appropriate line item listed below.

*Cleaning Supplies.* Includes the cost of products used in cleansing, sweeping, polishing, waxing, and disinfecting areas associated with the Parking department.

*Cluster Services.* Includes allocation for costs shared between hotels in a limited geographic area (as opposed to nationally consolidated services such as Corporate Office Reimbursables). Where reasonable and easily identifiable, labor costs and related expenses should be charged to their respective line item and only other expenses are charged to Cluster Services. Where not practical, the fair allocation of the total cluster service expenses should be recognized here.

*Complimentary Services and Gifts.* Includes the cost of providing gift items used in gratis presentations for promotional purposes to guests and vendors of the Parking department and VIP gifts.

*Contract Services.* Includes expenses for activities performed for the parking department by outside contractors and professional service providers rather than by hotel employees, unless identified in this department with a specific line item. The cost of contracting outside companies to paint lines on the parking surface and department-specific consulting services are typical examples. If supplies are purchased for contract companies to use, the supplies are charged to the appropriate supply account. The cost of contracts for the Parking laundry and dry cleaning is charged to Laundry and Dry Cleaning.

*Corporate Office Reimbursables.* Includes the allocations of salaries and expenses of corporate or management company Parking department personnel billed to the property by the regional or corporate office or by the management company, consistent with any contractual arrangements. Travel expenses of such corporate or management company personnel that are incurred while visiting the property, including the costs of meals and other applicable services or amenities provided to corporate or management company staff while on business in the property for the benefit of the property, are also charged to this account.

*Decorations.* Includes the cost of decorative items used in Parking department areas for holidays and special events.

*Dues and Subscriptions.* Includes the cost of representation of the Parking department, or of members of the staff when authorized to represent the Parking department, in business or professional organizations. Dues and Subscriptions is also charged with the cost of subscriptions to newspapers, magazines, and books for use by the staff of the Parking department.

*Entertainment—In-House.* Includes the food and beverage at cost, gratuities, service charges, and sales taxes (if applicable) consumed in the entertainment of guests, vendors, and business clients in the property's food and beverage facilities.

*Equipment Rental.* Includes the costs of renting any type of equipment that may be used either sporadically in the Parking department or as a replacement for equipment out of service on a temporary basis. Equipment lease payments made under a qualified operating lease are charged to Other Property and Equipment under the Rent section of *Non-Operating Income and Expenses—Schedule 11.*

*Laundry and Dry Cleaning.* Includes the cost of laundry and dry cleaning services applicable to the Parking department, whether the services are performed by an in-house facility or are contracted to an outside company. If the services are performed by an in-house laundry, an allocation from *House Laundry—Schedule 12* is charged to Laundry and Dry Cleaning. This allocation is distributed to departments on an equitable basis reflecting usage, such as cost-per-pound, number of pieces cleaned, number of orders processed, etc. If the services are performed by an outside company, the amount charged to Laundry and Dry Cleaning should be based on invoices sent by the outside laundry. The cost of cleaning employee uniforms is charged to Uniform Laundry.

*Licenses and Permits.* Includes the cost of national and local jurisdiction licenses, including costs of inspections needed for licensing, for all activities of the Parking department.

*Management Fees.* Includes the fees charged by an organization (other than the hotel's management company) to manage Parking department operations.

*Miscellaneous.* Includes any expenses of the Parking department that do not apply to the other line items discussed in this section.

*Operating Supplies.* Includes the cost of items needed to operate the parking department that are not included in the descriptions of specific supply accounts such as Cleaning Supplies, Laundry Supplies, or Printing and Stationery. An example would be car wash supplies.

*Printing and Stationery.* Includes the cost of printed forms used in the Parking department, whether they are purchased from an outside source or produced internally. An example would be gate tickets.

*Rent.* Includes the costs associated with the temporary rental of additional parking spaces or a parking lot, usually to accommodate extra guests during special events or busy periods. Not included are the rental payments made for a long-term lease of parking spaces in a lot or garage that would be recorded in the Rent section of *Non-Operating Income and Expenses—Schedule 11*

*Royalty Fees.* Includes all costs associated with the right to use a brand name in connection with a Parking department activity. An example would include the fees paid for use of a brand name to identify the parking facility. The fees paid for the use of a hotel brand name are charged to Franchise and Affiliation Fees—Royalties in *Sales and Marketing—Schedule 7*.

*Training.* Includes the costs, other than payroll cost, that can be directly attributed to the training of employees in the Parking department. Examples include the costs of training materials, supplies, certification programs, and instructor fees. The cost of employee wages incurred during training is charged to Salaries and Wages.

*Travel—Meals and Entertainment.* Includes the reimbursable cost of food, beverage, and entertainment expenses incurred by employees of the Parking department traveling on property business.

*Travel—Other.* Includes the cost of travel and reimbursable expenses (e.g., airfare car rental, hotel room and tax, guestroom Internet, conference registration fees), other than food, beverage, and entertainment, incurred by employees of the Parking department traveling on property business.

*Uniform Costs.* Includes the cost of employee uniforms used in the Parking department, whether purchased or rented. Repair costs are also included in this line item. The cost of cleaning uniforms is charged to Uniform Laundry.

*Uniform Laundry.* Includes the cost of cleaning uniforms for employees of the Parking department, whether performed by an in-hotel facility or contracted to an outside company.

## Total Other Expenses

Total Other Expenses is calculated by summing all items listed under Other Expenses. The percentage for each line item expense as well as Total Other Expenses is calculated by dividing the line item amount by Total Parking Revenue.

# Total Expenses

Total Expenses is calculated by adding Total Labor Costs and Related Expenses to Total Other Expenses. The percentage for Total Expenses is calculated by dividing Total Expenses by Total Parking Revenue.

The sum of Cost of Sales and Total Expenses is shown on Schedule 3 as Departmental Expenses—Parking.

# Departmental Profit

Departmental Profit is calculated by subtracting Total Expenses from Gross Profit. The percentage for Departmental Profit is calculated by dividing Departmental Profit by Total Parking Revenue. Departmental Profit is then shown on Schedule 3 as Departmental Profit—Parking.

# OTHER OPERATED DEPARTMENTS—SUB-SCHEDULE 3-X *(Generic)*

| | PERIOD OF | | | | | | | | | | | |
| --- | --- | --- | --- | --- | --- | --- | --- | --- | --- | --- | --- | --- |
| | CURRENT PERIOD | | | | | | YEAR-TO-DATE | | | | | |
| | ACTUAL | | FORECAST/ BUDGET | | PRIOR YEAR | | ACTUAL | | FORECAST/ BUDGET | | PRIOR YEAR | |
| | $ | % | $ | % | $ | % | $ | % | $ | % | $ | % |
| REVENUE | | | | | | | | | | | | |
| Revenue | | | | | | | | | | | | |
| Less: Allowances | | | | | | | | | | | | |
| TOTAL [SCHEDULE NAME] REVENUE | | | | | | | | | | | | |
| COST OF SALES | | | | | | | | | | | | |
| GROSS PROFIT | | | | | | | | | | | | |
| EXPENSES | | | | | | | | | | | | |
| Labor Costs and Related Expenses | | | | | | | | | | | | |
| Salaries, Wages, Service Charges, Contracted Labor and Bonuses | | | | | | | | | | | | |
| Salaries and Wages | | | | | | | | | | | | |
| Management | | | | | | | | | | | | |
| Non-Management | | | | | | | | | | | | |
| Sub-Categories as needed | | | | | | | | | | | | |
| Sub-Total: Salaries and Wages | | | | | | | | | | | | |
| Service Charge Distribution | | | | | | | | | | | | |
| Contracted, Leased and Outsourced Labor | | | | | | | | | | | | |
| Bonuses and Incentives | | | | | | | | | | | | |
| Total Salaries, Wages, Service Charges, Contracted Labor and Bonuses | | | | | | | | | | | | |
| Payroll-Related Expenses | | | | | | | | | | | | |
| Payroll Taxes | | | | | | | | | | | | |
| Supplemental Pay | | | | | | | | | | | | |
| Employee Benefits | | | | | | | | | | | | |
| Total Payroll Related Expenses | | | | | | | | | | | | |
| Total Labor Costs and Related Expenses | | | | | | | | | | | | |
| Other Expenses | | | | | | | | | | | | |
| Cleaning Supplies | | | | | | | | | | | | |
| Cluster Services | | | | | | | | | | | | |
| Complimentary Services and Gifts | | | | | | | | | | | | |
| Contract Services | | | | | | | | | | | | |
| Corporate Office Reimbursables | | | | | | | | | | | | |
| Decorations | | | | | | | | | | | | |
| Dues and Subscriptions | | | | | | | | | | | | |
| Entertainment—In-House | | | | | | | | | | | | |
| Equipment Rental | | | | | | | | | | | | |
| Laundry and Dry Cleaning | | | | | | | | | | | | |
| Licenses and Permits | | | | | | | | | | | | |
| Linen | | | | | | | | | | | | |
| Management Fees | | | | | | | | | | | | |
| Miscellaneous | | | | | | | | | | | | |
| Operating Supplies | | | | | | | | | | | | |
| [Other detailed expenses as warranted] | | | | | | | | | | | | |
| Printing and Stationery | | | | | | | | | | | | |

**OTHER OPERATED DEPARTMENTS—SUB-SCHEDULE 3-X** *(Generic) (continued)*

| | PERIOD OF | | | | | | | | | | | |
|---|---|---|---|---|---|---|---|---|---|---|---|---|
| | CURRENT PERIOD | | | | | | YEAR-TO-DATE | | | | | |
| | ACTUAL | | FORECAST/ BUDGET | | PRIOR YEAR | | ACTUAL | | FORECAST/ BUDGET | | PRIOR YEAR | |
| | $ | % | $ | % | $ | % | $ | % | $ | % | $ | % |
| Royalty Fees | | | | | | | | | | | | |
| Training | | | | | | | | | | | | |
| Travel—Meals and Entertainment | | | | | | | | | | | | |
| Travel—Other | | | | | | | | | | | | |
| Uniform Costs | | | | | | | | | | | | |
| Uniform Laundry | | | | | | | | | | | | |
| Total Other Expenses | | | | | | | | | | | | |
| TOTAL EXPENSES | | | | | | | | | | | | |
| DEPARTMENTAL PROFIT | | | | | | | | | | | | |

The generic *Other Operated Departments — Sub-schedule 3-x* reflects the proper format for an Other Operated Department and designates the revenue and expense accounts that are approved as line items in the *Uniform System*. *Sub-schedule 3-x* in intended to be used for other operated departments other than the three already detailed (Golf Course and Pro Shop, Health Club/Spa, and Parking)—for example, a retail store, a marina, a business center, or a tennis and pro shop. The hotel should define its additional departments.

When the need for an additional department sub-schedule exists, use the generic format set forth in Sub-schedule 3-x. Because each Other Operated Department may have significant costs that are unique to that department, hotels *are permitted* in this one area only to insert additional Other Expense line items in Sub-schedule 3-x. These unique expenses should be added under Other Expenses as appropriate. Examples of potential unique expenses are provided in the descriptive paragraph for the bracketed line item labeled [Other detailed expenses as warranted]. Properties may choose to develop further sub-accounts to provide even more detail related to a particular revenue or expense item. These additional sub-accounts/sub-schedules are then to be rolled into the appropriate line item on Sub-schedule 3-x. Additionally, properties may choose to delete some of the columns or to show them in a different order and remain "in conformity with the *Uniform System*."

Refer to Part III for operating ratios and statistics that are pertinent to the Other Operated Departments.

The Total Revenue, Total Expenses (including any applicable cost of sales), and Departmental Profit shown on Sub-schedule 3-x are then reported on Schedule 3.

The following presents a description of the base revenue and expense items that should be included in the sub-schedules for Other Operated Departments. In addition, examples of other revenue and expense items that are commonly found in Other Operated Departments are provided.

## Special Notice for Mixed Ownership/Condominium Hotels

The revenues and direct operating expenses associated with the management of condominium units are recorded as an Other Operated Department unless the property has assumed an economic risk pursuant to a contractual relationship that extends for the full reporting year. If the property has assumed economic risk for the full year, then the revenues, expenses, and rooms statistics are recorded in their appropriate categories as prescribed by the *Uniform System.*

Under certain circumstances, other operated department revenue in its entirety may be reported on a net basis on *Miscellaneous Income—Schedule 4.* Further, some revenue items within the Other Operated Department may be reported on a net basis within the department. For additional information, see Part V.

## Special Notice for Casino Hotels

The *Uniform System of Accounts for the Lodging Industry* is not recommended for use by casino hotels with significant gaming operations. It is recommended that casino hotels use accounting classification systems specific to the gaming industry.

For hotels that receive minor revenue from gaming, revenues and direct operating expenses are recorded as an Other Operated Department. Examples include hotels with card rooms or gaming machines within the lounge.

# Revenue

Revenue consists of the gross sales derived from the department. The following list describes the revenue typically found in select other operated departments. The list is not intended to be all-inclusive. Additional significant revenues should be segregated in sub-schedules as warranted.

Other Operated Departments may include an allocated portion of package revenues. As discussed under *Rooms—Schedule 1*, package revenues are lodging accommodations sold in conjunction with other services provided by either the property or third parties as part of a single transaction with the guest. Package revenues are allocated to other departments based on the relative market values of the items supplied by those departments

Under certain circumstances, other operated department revenue in its entirety may be reported on a net basis on *Miscellaneous Income—Schedule 4.* Further, some revenue items within the Other Operated Department may be reported on a net basis within the department. For additional information, see Part V.

| Operated Department | Revenue |
|---|---|
| Transportation: | Usage Revenue, Special Vehicle Rentals |
| Guest Laundry: | Guest Dry Cleaning/Laundry, Alterations and Repairs |
| Swimming Pool/Beach: | Usage Revenue, Membership Fees, Equipment Rental, Lessons |
| Tennis and Pro Shop: | Court Rental, Retail Revenue, Lessons, Merchandise, Equipment Rental |

| Other Recreation: | Skeet Shooting, Ropes Course, Skiing, Rock Climbing |
|---|---|
| Business Center: | Typing Services, Document Printing |
| Marina: | Slip Rental, Gas, Groceries, Fishing Equipment Rental |
| Retail Store: | Clothing, Merchandise, Candy, Newspapers |
| Children's Camp: | Registration Fees, Day Care, Babysitting |
| Barber/Beauty Shop: | Hair Cuts/Styling, Merchandise |
| Mixed Ownership: | Room Rental |
| Gaming: | Card Games, Slot Machines |

If needed, an Other Revenue line may be added to capture revenue from any other services or charges not covered by the revenue line items chosen for the Other Operated Department, such as surcharges and service charges. Surcharges and service charges generally include any mandatory, non-discretionary, or other charge automatically added to a customer account in respect of the service or use of an amenity. The key determining factors for the recording of surcharges and service charges (versus gratuities) are set out in Part V.

## Allowances

Allowances refers to a reduction in revenue due to a service problem, not an error in posting. Errors in posting, such as charging an incorrect amount, are treated as adjustments to revenue, regardless of the accounting period in which the error occurred.

## Total Revenue

Total Revenue is calculated by summing the revenue items for a respective Other Operated Department and subtracting Allowances. This amount appears on Schedule 3 as Departmental Revenue—[Schedule Name].

In completing the revenue section of Sub-schedule 3-x, the Total [Schedule Name] Revenue line is considered to be 100 percent, and the percentage for each source of revenue is determined by dividing the dollar amount for that revenue source by Total [Schedule Name] Revenue.

# Cost of Sales

Cost of Sales includes the cost for any items sold. If individual merchandise items or categories of similar items are listed separately under Revenue, these same items or categories of items should also be listed separately under Cost of Sales. The percentage for Cost of Sales is calculated by dividing the cost by its corresponding revenue amount. If there are separate entries under Cost of Sales, the percentage for Total Cost of Sales is calculated by dividing the cost by the sum of the corresponding revenue amounts.

If a Cost of Sales line item is necessary, a Gross Profit line item is necessary as well. If an Other Operated Department does not have a cost of sales, the sub-schedule will not use the Cost of Sales and Gross Profit line items.

# Gross Profit

Gross Profit is calculated by subtracting Cost of Sales from Total Revenue. The percentage for Gross Profit is calculated by dividing Gross Profit by Total [Schedule Name] Revenue.

# Expenses

Other Operated Department expenses are separated into two major categories: Labor Costs and Related Expenses and Other Expenses.

## Labor Costs and Related Expenses

Labor Costs and Related Expenses includes all of the payroll expenses associated with Salaries, Wages, Service Charges, Contracted Labor, Bonuses, and Payroll-Related Expenses for employees and contractors.

*Salaries and Wages.* Includes the earnings paid to employees for duties that relate to the operation of the property, such as regular pay, overtime pay, and shift differential pay. If an employee works in a department other than his or her regular home department, his or her earnings must be charged as Salaries and Wages in that other department, regardless of the duties being performed. For example, if a Gift Shop Department employee regularly works as a clerk in the Gift Shop department and temporarily works for the Food and Beverage department on a function, his or her earnings for the function are charged to Salaries and Wages in the Food and Beverage department, not to his or her home department.

Salaries and Wages should be delineated by significant management and non-management payroll titles within the department. If necessary, payroll titles should be aggregated to preserve the confidentiality of a specific employee's payroll.

Salaries and Wages includes the earnings associated with temporary employees when such expenses are processed through the property's payroll system.

*Service Charge Distribution.* Includes the cost of service charges paid through the payroll system for hotel employees.

*Contracted, Leased and Outsourced Labor.* Includes the gross cost of contracted, leased, and outsourced labor incurred when a property enters into an agreement with a third-party contractor to provide employees to fill positions that would normally be held by individuals paid on the regular payroll. In these situations, the property records or tracks the hours worked and pays the third-party contractor on an hourly or other agreed basis. A typical example is the use of individuals brought into the property to fill in for a shortage of Gift Shop department staff.

Contracted, Leased and Outsourced Labor includes the gross cost associated with shared staffing arrangements when such arrangements are supported by formal agreements.

*Bonuses and Incentives.* Includes bonuses (contractual and discretionary), incentive pay, and other types of performance pay designed to drive revenue through sales, profit, or guest satisfaction.

*Total Salaries, Wages, Service Charges, Contracted Labor and Bonuses.* Calculated by summing Salaries and Wages, Service Charge Distribution, Contracted, Leased and Outsourced Labor, and Bonuses and Incentives.

*Payroll-Related Expenses.* Includes amounts paid for an employee for duties that relate to the operation of the property and amounts paid for an employee who works in a department other than his or her regular home department regardless of the duties being performed. Payroll-Related Expenses includes the following items:

- *Payroll Taxes.* Includes the employer share of contributions to national and state retirement, unemployment, disability and medical insurance programs, and other mandated payroll-related taxes or social insurance items. (See *Payroll-Related Expenses—Schedule 14.*)

- *Supplemental Pay.* Includes personal days, vacation pay, sick pay, holiday pay, jury duty pay, relocation pay, paid time off, and severance pay. (See *Payroll-Related Expenses—Schedule 14.*)

- *Employee Benefits.* Includes all other payroll-related expenses, such as employer-paid health insurance expenses, cost of meals furnished to employees, pension contributions, and union dues and fees. (See *Payroll-Related Expenses—Schedule 14.*) The distribution of employee meal costs from *Staff Dining—Schedule 13* is charged to this line.

*Total Payroll-Related Expenses.* Calculated by summing Payroll Taxes, Supplemental Pay, and Employee Benefits.

*Note regarding shared staffing arrangements and cluster services:* Where reasonable and easily identifiable, labor costs related to shared staffing arrangements and cluster services should be charged to salaries and wages or payroll-related expenses.

## Total Labor Costs and Related Expenses

Total Labor Costs and Related Expenses is calculated by summing Total Salaries, Wages, Service Charges, Contracted Labor and Bonuses and Total Payroll-Related Expenses. The percentage for each labor cost component as well as Total Labor Costs and Related Expenses is calculated by dividing the line item amount by Total [Schedule Name] Revenue. Refer to Part III for recommended operating metrics that are pertinent to Labor Costs and Related Expenses.

## Other Expenses

This expense grouping includes the significant Other Operated Department expenses approved as Other Expenses in the *Uniform System.* As always, properties may delete irrelevant line items. For Sub-schedule 3-x only, properties *also may insert* additional Other Expenses that are substantial and unique to an Other

Operated Department. Properties also may choose to develop a sub-account/sub-schedule to provide more detail related to a particular expense item. This sub-account/sub-schedule is then to be rolled into the appropriate line item listed below.

*Cleaning Supplies.* Includes the cost of products used in cleansing, sweeping, polishing, waxing, and disinfecting areas associated with the Other Operated Department.

*Cluster Services.* Includes allocation for costs shared between hotels in a limited geographic area (as opposed to nationally consolidated services such as Corporate Office Reimbursables). Where reasonable and easily identifiable, labor costs and related expenses should be charged to their respective line item and only other expenses are charged to Cluster Services. Where not practical, the fair allocation of the total cluster service expenses should be recognized here.

*Complimentary Services and Gifts.* Includes the cost of providing gift items used in gratis presentations for promotional purposes to guests and vendors of the Other Operated Department and VIP gifts.

*Contract Services.* Includes expenses for activities performed for the Other Operated Department by outside contractors and professional service providers rather than by hotel employees, unless identified in this department with a specific line item. The cost of contracting outside companies to clean the carpets in the Other Operated Department and department-specific consulting services are typical examples. If supplies are purchased for contract companies to use, the supplies are charged to the appropriate supply account. The cost of contracts for Other Operated Department laundry and dry cleaning is charged to Laundry and Dry Cleaning.

*Corporate Office Reimbursables.* Includes the allocations of salaries and expenses of corporate or management company personnel associated with the Other Operated Department billed to the property by the regional or corporate office or by the management company, consistent with any contractual arrangements. Travel expenses of such corporate or management company personnel that are incurred while visiting the property, including the costs of meals and other applicable services or amenities provided to corporate or management company staff while on business in the property for the benefit of the property, are also charged to this account.

*Decorations.* Includes the cost of decorative items used in the Other Operated Department for holidays and special events.

*Dues and Subscriptions.* Includes the cost of representation of the Other Operated Department, or of members of the staff when authorized to represent the Other Operated Department, in business or professional organizations. Dues and Subscriptions is also charged with the cost of subscriptions to newspapers, magazines, and books for use by the Other Operated Department staff.

*Entertainment—In-House.* Includes the food and beverage at cost, gratuities, service charges, and sales taxes (if applicable) consumed in the entertainment of guests, vendors, and business clients in the property's food and beverage facilities.

*Equipment Rental.* Includes the costs of renting any type of equipment that may be used either sporadically in the Other Operated Department or as a replacement for equipment out of service on a temporary basis. Equipment lease payments made under a qualified operating lease are charged to Other Property and Equipment under the Rent section of *Non-Operating Income and Expenses—Schedule 11.*

*Laundry and Dry Cleaning.* Includes the cost of laundry and dry cleaning services applicable to the Other Operated Department, whether the services are performed by an in-house facility or are contracted to an outside company. If the services are performed by an in-house laundry, an allocation from *House Laundry—Schedule 12* is charged to Laundry and Dry Cleaning. This allocation is distributed to departments on an equitable basis reflecting usage, such as cost-per-pound, number of pieces cleaned, number of orders processed, etc. If the services are performed by an outside company, the amount charged to Laundry and Dry Cleaning should be based on invoices sent by the outside laundry. The cost of cleaning employee uniforms is charged to Uniform Laundry.

*Licenses and Permits.* Includes the cost of national and local jurisdiction licenses, including costs of inspections needed for licensing, for all activities of the Other Operated Department.

*Linen.* Includes the cost, whether purchased or rented, of table cloths, napkins, table runners, and skirting used by the Other Operated Department.

*Management Fees.* Includes the fees charged by an organization (other than the hotel's management company) to manage the operations of the Other Operated Department.

*Miscellaneous.* Includes any expenses of the Other Operated Department that do not apply to the other line items discussed in this section.

*Operating Supplies.* Includes the cost of items needed to operate the Other Operated Department that are not included in the descriptions of specific supply accounts such as Cleaning Supplies or Printing and Stationery.

*Other Detailed Expenses as Warranted.* Includes significant expenses commonly found in specific Other Operated Departments. The following expenses, if they exist, are presented as examples of separate expense line items typically found in the associated Other Operated Department. The list is not exhaustive. Additional significant expenses should be segregated as warranted.

| Operated Department | Expense |
| --- | --- |
| Transportation: | Gas, Parts |
| Guest Laundry: | Cleaning Supplies, Chemicals |
| Swimming Pool/Beach: | Chemicals |
| Tennis and Pro Shop: | Nets and Tapes, Maintenance |
| Other Recreation: | Skeet Rifles, Ropes Course Equipment, Snow Shoes, Rock Climbing Gear |

| | |
|---|---|
| Business Center: | Copier/Printer/Computer Parts & Supplies |
| Marina: | Maintenance |
| Retail Store: | Display Equipment |
| Children's Camp: | Arts and Crafts Equipment, Kids' Meals |
| Barber/Beauty Shop: | Beauty Products |
| Mixed Ownership: | Operating expenses similar to Rooms department |
| Gaming: | Cards, Chips |

*Printing and Stationery.* Includes the cost of printed forms used in the Other Operated Department, whether they are purchased from an outside source or produced internally.

*Royalty Fees.* Includes all costs associated with the right to use a brand name in connection with an Other Operated Department activity. The fees paid for the use of a hotel brand name are charged to Franchise and Affiliation Fees—Royalties in *Sales and Marketing—Schedule 7.*

*Training.* Includes the costs, other than payroll cost, that can be directly attributed to the training of employees in the Other Operated Department. Examples include the costs of training materials, supplies, certification programs, and instructor fees. The cost of employee wages incurred during training is charged to Salaries and Wages.

*Travel—Meals and Entertainment.* Includes the reimbursable cost of food, beverage, and entertainment expenses incurred by employees of the Other Operated Department traveling on property business.

*Travel—Other.* Includes the cost of travel and reimbursable expenses (e.g., airfare car rental, hotel room and tax, guestroom Internet, conference registration fees), other than food, beverage, and entertainment, incurred by employees of the Other Operated Department traveling on property business.

*Uniform Costs.* Includes the cost of employee uniforms used in the Other Operated Department, whether purchased or rented. Repair costs are also included in this line item. The cost of cleaning uniforms is charged to Uniform Laundry.

*Uniform Laundry.* Includes the cost of cleaning uniforms for employees of the Other Operated Department, whether performed by an in-hotel facility or contracted to an outside company.

## Total Other Expenses

Total Other Expenses is calculated by summing all items listed under Other Expenses. The percentage for each line item expense as well as Total Other Expenses is calculated by dividing the line item amount by Total [Schedule Name] Revenue.

## Total Expenses

Total Expenses is calculated by adding Total Labor Costs and Related Expenses to Total Other Expenses. The percentage for Total Expenses is calculated by dividing Total Expenses by Total [Schedule Name] Revenue.

The sum of Total Cost of Sales (if any) and Total Expenses is shown on Schedule 3 as Departmental Expenses—[Schedule Name].

## Departmental Profit

Departmental Profit is calculated by subtracting Total Expenses from Gross Profit. The percentage for Departmental Profit is calculated by dividing Departmental Profit by Total [Schedule Name] Revenue. Departmental Profit is then shown on Schedule 3 as Departmental Profit—[Schedule Name].

## MINOR OPERATED DEPARTMENTS—SUB-SCHEDULE 3-XX

| | PERIOD OF | | | | | |
|---|---|---|---|---|---|---|
| | CURRENT PERIOD | | | YEAR-TO-DATE | | |
| | ACTUAL | FORECAST/ BUDGET | PRIOR YEAR | ACTUAL | FORECAST/ BUDGET | PRIOR YEAR |
| | $ \| % | $ \| % | $ \| % | $ \| % | $ \| % | $ \| % |
| DEPARTMENTAL REVENUE | | | | | | |
| Minor Operated Department 1 | | | | | | |
| Minor Operated Department 2 | | | | | | |
| - - - | | | | | | |
| Minor Operated Department x | | | | | | |
| Less: Allowances | | | | | | |
| TOTAL DEPARTMENTAL REVENUE | | | | | | |
| DEPARTMENTAL EXPENSES[1] | | | | | | |
| Minor Operated Department 1 | | | | | | |
| Minor Operated Department 2 | | | | | | |
| - - - | | | | | | |
| Minor Operated Department x | | | | | | |
| TOTAL MINOR OPERATED DEPARTMENTAL EXPENSES | | | | | | |
| DEPARTMENTAL PROFIT | | | | | | |
| Minor Operated Department 1 | | | | | | |
| Minor Operated Department 2 | | | | | | |
| - - - | | | | | | |
| Minor Operated Department x | | | | | | |
| TOTAL MINOR OPERATED DEPARTMENT PROFIT | | | | | | |

[1] Departmental Expenses is the sum of Cost of Sales (when applicable) and Total Expenses.

*Minor Operated Departments—Sub-schedule 3-xx* reflects the proper format for minor operated departments. The revenue and expense items shown in Sub-schedule 3-xx are totally at the discretion of an individual hotel. However, each revenue item must have a matching expense item and vice versa. Properties may choose to delete some of the columns or to show them in a different order and remain "in conformity with the *Uniform System.*"

Minor Operated Departments are sources of income that meet the guidelines to present revenues and expenses on a gross basis, yet generate limited income and incur minor direct operating expenses. The minor levels of revenues and expenses do not warrant the presentation of a full operated department sub-schedule. Operated departments with Labor Costs and Related Expenses should not be included in Minor Operated Departments. For additional information, see Part V.

Refer to Part III for recommended operating metrics that are pertinent to the Minor Operated Departments.

The Total Minor Operated Departmental Revenue, Total Minor Operated Departmental Expenses, and Total Minor Operated Departmental Profit from Sub-schedule 3-xx are then shown on Schedule 3.

Examples of income sources and the associated direct expenses that are frequently (but not always) classified as Minor Operated Departments are:

- Vending machines owned and stocked by the hotel will have Vending Revenue and Vending Expenses.

- Retail kiosks operated by front desk personnel and stocked by hotel will have Retail Kiosk Revenue and Retail Kiosk Expenses. Typical sale items include newspapers, soft drinks, toiletries, and microwave foods.

- Video game machines owned and maintained by the hotel will have Video Game Revenue and Video Game Expenses.

- In-Room Movie Rental systems owned and operated by the hotel will have Movie Rental Revenue and Movie Rental Expenses.

- Guest Laundry and Dry Cleaning provided by an outside vendor, but partially serviced by the hotel, will have Guest Laundry and Dry Cleaning Revenue and Guest Laundry and Dry Cleaning Expenses.

- Guest Communications includes revenues received from guests' use of telephones, fax machines, and the Internet in the guestroom. The gross or net (commission) revenue generated from Internet service charges in function rooms should be recorded as Audiovisual revenue in the Food and Beverage department. Only the cost of sales associated with guestroom-generated communications revenue should be included in the Minor Operated Department Expenses. The costs associated with offering complimentary guest calls and Internet connectivity anywhere within the property should be recorded on *Information and Telecommunications Systems—Schedule 6*, as should all labor- and maintenance-related expenses. Guestroom Communications will have Guestroom Telephone Revenue, Guestroom Internet Revenue, Guest Fax Revenue, Guestroom Telephone Cost of Sales, Guestroom Internet Cost of Sales, and Guest Fax Cost of Sales.

- Services and CAM (common area maintenance) charges sold to third-party unit owners at a profit will have Services and CAM Revenue and Services and CAM Expenses.

- Occasional food and beverage service provided by hotels that do not routinely sell food and beverage will have Occasional Food Revenue, Occasional Beverage Revenue, Occasional Room Rental Revenue, Occasional Food Cost of Sales, Occasional Beverage Cost of Sales, and Other Occasional Food and Beverage Expenses.

Some income sources may meet the requirement to be reported on a net basis on *Miscellaneous Income—Schedule 4*. See Part V for more information.

# MISCELLANEOUS INCOME—SCHEDULE 4

| | PERIOD OF | | | | | |
| --- | --- | --- | --- | --- | --- | --- |
| | CURRENT PERIOD | | | YEAR-TO-DATE | | |
| | ACTUAL | FORECAST/ BUDGET | PRIOR YEAR | ACTUAL | FORECAST/ BUDGET | PRIOR YEAR |
| | $ \| % | $ \| % | $ \| % | $ \| % | $ \| % | $ \| % |
| Attrition Fees | | | | | | |
| Cancellation Fees | | | | | | |
| Cash Discounts Earned | | | | | | |
| Commissions | | | | | | |
| Guest-Related Foreign Currency Transaction Gains (Losses) | | | | | | |
| Guest Laundry and Dry Cleaning | | | | | | |
| Interest Income | | | | | | |
| Net Revenue from Renting Mixed-Ownership Units | | | | | | |
| Other Breakage | | | | | | |
| Package Breakage | | | | | | |
| Proceeds from Business Interruption Insurance | | | | | | |
| Resort Fees | | | | | | |
| Space Rental and Concessions | | | | | | |
| Other | | | | | | |
| **TOTAL MISCELLANEOUS INCOME** | | | | | | |

*Miscellaneous Income—Schedule 4* reflects the proper format for a schedule supporting the Miscellaneous Income amount reported on the Summary Operating Statement. Individual properties may delete irrelevant line items, but the *Uniform System* does not provide for the addition or substitution of other income line items. Rather, properties may choose to develop a sub-account/sub-schedule to provide more detail related to a particular income item. This sub-account/sub-schedule is then to be rolled into the appropriate line item. Additionally, properties may choose to delete some of the columns or to show them in a different order and remain "in conformity with the *Uniform System.*"

Revenue is classified as Miscellaneous Income if it meets the standards for reporting revenues on a net basis. (Audiovisual net revenue is a potential exception; it is reported as Audiovisual on *Food and Beverage—Schedule 2* for properties that have a Food and Beverage department.) For additional information, see Part V.

Refer to Part III for operating ratios and statistics that are pertinent to Miscellaneous Income.

The line items for *Miscellaneous Income—Schedule 4* are defined in the following pages.

## Attrition Fees

Fee income received from groups that do not fulfill their guaranteed number of reservations for guestrooms, food and beverage, and other services is included in this line item.

# Cancellation Fees

Fee income received from transient guests and groups that cancel their reservations for guestrooms, food and beverage, and other services after a contracted or cutoff date is included in this line item. "No-show" revenue from individual guests who do not show for a guaranteed reservation and "early departure fees" from the guests who check out earlier than the scheduled departure date are included in Other Revenue in the Rooms department.

# Cash Discounts Earned

Discounts earned by the payment of hotel creditors' accounts within the discount period are included in this line item. The revenue recognized should be the amount of the cash discount earned. Sales and occupancy tax discounts resulting from the hotel remitting payments within the taxing jurisdiction's discount period are also included in this category.

When the hotel earns a cash discount on a purchase it makes, the discount is recorded as a deduction from cost of sales or in an individual expense item. It is not included in this revenue category.

# Commissions

Commissions received from third parties for services, such as leased gaming and vending machines, taxicab stands, parking lots, automobile rentals, non-owned or non-operated audiovisual services (for properties without a Food and Beverage department), guestroom Internet connectivity, automated teller machines, photography, and use of a payment (credit/debit) card purchasing service are included in this line item. Separate sub-categories could be used to identify significant revenue items.

For properties that operate a Food and Beverage department, the fee or commission revenue from a third-party audiovisual contractor would be reported as Other Revenue—Audiovisual on *Food and Beverage—Schedule 2.*

# Guest-Related Foreign Currency Transaction Gains (Losses)

Foreign currency gains or losses resulting from exchanging foreign currency for hotel guests, groups, and banquets into the local currency of the country are included in this line item.

Foreign currency gains or losses resulting from non-guest transactions should be reported on *Administrative and General—Schedule 5* or *Non-Operating Income and Expenses—Schedule 11.*

# Guest Laundry and Dry Cleaning

The net income earned for cleaning guest laundry from third-party-operated concessions is included in this line item.

## Interest Income

Interest earned on cash investments, bank deposits, notes receivable, accounts receivable, and from other sources is included in this line item. Interest earned from capital reserve accounts and any restricted funds accounts should be reported on *Non-Operating Income and Expenses — Schedule 11*.

## Net Revenue from Renting Mixed-Ownership Units

When it is determined that the mixed ownership rentals should be reported on a net basis, the net revenue received by the property as an agent is the commission revenue on the rental.

## Other Breakage

Unused or forfeited gift cards or gift certificates and un-presented or expired prepaid coupons, where escheat laws do not require them to be turned over to a government authority, should be recorded as revenue. As it relates to prepaid coupons, only the discounted value should be recorded as revenue.

## Package Breakage

When guests do not consume all of the components that are included in a package, or spend more than the market value allocated for the package, the surplus or deficit is commonly referred to as breakage. If the hotel elects not to charge or refund the guest for the breakage, the residual value should be recorded to Miscellaneous Income, regardless of whether it is a surplus or deficit. In cases where breakage is either significant or consistently negative, the package structure and pricing should be reviewed and adjusted accordingly.

## Proceeds from Business Interruption Insurance

The gross amount of the agreed settlement with an insurance company for a business interruption claim is included in the line item, less the extra expenses included in the settlement that are credited to accounts receivable. Extra expenses are those expenses that are a direct result of the insurable loss and not part of normal property operations, such as relocation of guests or professional fees to prepare the claim. The gross settlement net of the extra expenses is recorded to this account and the deductible portion of the claim is recorded as an insurance expense on *Non-Operating Income and Expenses — Schedule 11*.

## Resort Fees

Resort fees are mandatory fees charged at either a flat amount or a percentage of the room rate. They are charged per room night rather than per person and allow the guest to use services such as fitness facilities, spa, pool, local phone calls, Internet access, airport transportation, golf driving range, and other recreational facilities.

Subject to the determination to report revenue on a net or gross basis as outlined in Part V, if the resort fee covers guest use of a service provided by a third party, the amount of gross or net revenue attributable to the third-party service will be included in Resort Fee revenue. The amount due to the third-party service will be treated either as a cost in the appropriate department (gross revenue reporting) or as a pass through in the balance sheet (net revenue reporting).

## Space Rental and Concessions

Many properties wish to offer their guests services and/or merchandise that are not provided by the operated departments previously discussed. In these cases, properties contract the operations of such activities through rental or concession agreements. Space Rental and Concessions includes the revenue generated from the rental of space within the property. Examples are gifts shops, coffee kiosks, and car rental agencies that lease space from the hotel. The amount paid by tenants entering into leases with the property is amortized over the term of the lease and reported in Miscellaneous Income.

Rental revenue earned from commercial leases not directly associated with the operation of hotel and not managed or maintained by hotel management should be reported on *Non-Operating Income and Expenses—Schedule 11.* Examples include owner-directed office leases, billboards, and cell towers.

Commissions to renting agents are amortized over the term of the lease and are charged against Administrative and General—Professional Fees.

## Other

This line item includes any income not classified under another caption. Examples include in-room safes, safety deposit boxes, and in-room refrigerator rental.

## Total Miscellaneous Income

Total Miscellaneous Income is calculated by summing all of the amounts listed above. This amount appears on the Summary Operating Statement under Operating Revenue—Miscellaneous Income.

In completing Schedule 4, Total Miscellaneous Income is considered to be 100 percent, and the percentage for each source of income is determined by dividing the dollar amount of that source by Total Miscellaneous Income.

## ADMINISTRATIVE AND GENERAL—SCHEDULE 5

| | PERIOD OF | | | | | | | | | | | |
|---|---|---|---|---|---|---|---|---|---|---|---|---|
| | CURRENT PERIOD | | | | | | YEAR-TO-DATE | | | | | |
| | ACTUAL | | FORECAST/ BUDGET | | PRIOR YEAR | | ACTUAL | | FORECAST/ BUDGET | | PRIOR YEAR | |
| | $ | % | $ | % | $ | % | $ | % | $ | % | $ | % |
| **EXPENSES** | | | | | | | | | | | | |
| Labor Costs and Related Expenses | | | | | | | | | | | | |
| Salaries, Wages, Service Charges, Contracted Labor and Bonuses | | | | | | | | | | | | |
| Salaries and Wages | | | | | | | | | | | | |
| Management | | | | | | | | | | | | |
| Non-Management | | | | | | | | | | | | |
| Accounting | | | | | | | | | | | | |
| General Support | | | | | | | | | | | | |
| Human Resources | | | | | | | | | | | | |
| Purchasing/Receiving | | | | | | | | | | | | |
| Security | | | | | | | | | | | | |
| Sub-Total: Salaries and Wages | | | | | | | | | | | | |
| Service Charge Distribution | | | | | | | | | | | | |
| Contracted, Leased and Outsourced Labor | | | | | | | | | | | | |
| Bonuses and Incentives | | | | | | | | | | | | |
| Total Salaries, Wages, Service Charges, Contracted Labor and Bonuses | | | | | | | | | | | | |
| Payroll-Related Expenses | | | | | | | | | | | | |
| Payroll Taxes | | | | | | | | | | | | |
| Supplemental Pay | | | | | | | | | | | | |
| Employee Benefits | | | | | | | | | | | | |
| Total Payroll Related Expenses | | | | | | | | | | | | |
| Total Labor Costs and Related Expenses | | | | | | | | | | | | |
| Other Expenses | | | | | | | | | | | | |
| Audit Charges | | | | | | | | | | | | |
| Bank Charges | | | | | | | | | | | | |
| Cash Overages and Shortages | | | | | | | | | | | | |
| Centralized Accounting Charges | | | | | | | | | | | | |
| Cluster Services | | | | | | | | | | | | |
| Complimentary Services and Gifts | | | | | | | | | | | | |
| Contract Services | | | | | | | | | | | | |
| Corporate Office Reimbursables | | | | | | | | | | | | |
| Credit and Collection | | | | | | | | | | | | |
| Credit Card Commissions | | | | | | | | | | | | |
| Decorations | | | | | | | | | | | | |
| Donations | | | | | | | | | | | | |
| Dues and Subscriptions | | | | | | | | | | | | |
| Entertainment—In-House | | | | | | | | | | | | |
| Equipment Rental | | | | | | | | | | | | |
| Human Resources | | | | | | | | | | | | |
| Legal Services | | | | | | | | | | | | |
| Licenses and Permits | | | | | | | | | | | | |
| Loss and Damage | | | | | | | | | | | | |
| Miscellaneous | | | | | | | | | | | | |

**ADMINISTRATIVE AND GENERAL—SCHEDULE 5** *(continued)*

| | PERIOD OF | | | | | |
| --- | --- | --- | --- | --- | --- | --- |
| | CURRENT PERIOD | | | YEAR-TO-DATE | | |
| | ACTUAL | FORECAST/ BUDGET | PRIOR YEAR | ACTUAL | FORECAST/ BUDGET | PRIOR YEAR |
| | $ \| % | $ \| % | $ \| % | $ \| % | $ \| % | $ \| % |
| Non-Guest-Related Foreign Currency Exchange Gains (Losses) | | | | | | |
| Operating Supplies | | | | | | |
| Payroll Processing | | | | | | |
| Postage and Overnight Delivery Charges | | | | | | |
| Professional Fees | | | | | | |
| Provision for Doubtful Accounts | | | | | | |
| Security | | | | | | |
| Settlement Costs | | | | | | |
| Staff Transportation | | | | | | |
| Training | | | | | | |
| Travel—Meals and Entertainment | | | | | | |
| Travel—Other | | | | | | |
| Uniform Costs | | | | | | |
| Uniform Laundry | | | | | | |
| Total Other Expenses | | | | | | |
| TOTAL EXPENSES | | | | | | |

*Administrative and General—Schedule 5* reflects the proper format for an Administrative and General department and designates the expense accounts that are approved as line items in the *Uniform System.* Individual properties may delete irrelevant line items, but the *Uniform System* does not provide for the addition or substitution of other revenue or expense line items. Rather, properties may choose to develop a sub-account/sub-schedule to provide more detail related to a particular expense item. This sub-account/sub-schedule is then to be rolled into the appropriate line item. Additionally, properties may choose to delete some of the columns or to show them in a different order and remain "in conformity with the *Uniform System.*"

Refer to Part III for operating ratios and statistics that are pertinent to the Administrative and General department.

The line items for *Administrative and General—Schedule 5* are defined in the following pages.

# Expenses

Administrative and General expenses are separated into two major categories: Labor Costs and Related Expenses and Other Expenses.

## Labor Costs and Related Expenses

Labor Costs and Related Expenses includes all of the payroll expenses associated with Salaries, Wages, Service Charges, Contracted Labor, Bonuses, and

Payroll-Related Expenses for employees and contractors. A list of the positions typically included in the Administrative and General department is provided in the Department Payroll Titles section at the end of Part I.

*Salaries and Wages.* Includes the earnings paid to employees for duties that relate to the operation of the property, such as regular pay, overtime pay, and shift differential pay. If an employee works in a department other than his or her regular home department, his or her earnings must be charged as Salaries and Wages in that other department, regardless of the duties being performed. For example, if an Administrative and General department employee regularly works as an accounting clerk in the Administrative and General department and temporarily works for the Food and Beverage department on a function, his or her earnings for the function are charged to Salaries and Wages in the Food and Beverage department, not to his or her home department.

Salaries and Wages should be delineated by significant management and non-management payroll titles within the department. If necessary, payroll titles should be aggregated to preserve the confidentiality of a specific employee's payroll.

Salaries and Wages includes the earnings associated with temporary employees when such expenses are processed through the property's payroll system.

*Service Charge Distribution.* Includes the cost of service charges paid through the payroll system for hotel employees.

*Contracted, Leased and Outsourced Labor.* Includes the gross cost of contracted, leased, and outsourced labor incurred when a property enters into an agreement with a third-party contractor to provide employees to fill positions that would normally be held by individuals paid on the regular payroll. In these situations, the property records or tracks the hours worked and pays the third-party contractor on an hourly or other agreed basis. A typical example is the use of individuals brought into the property to fill in for a shortage of security staff.

Contracted, Leased and Outsourced Labor includes the gross cost associated with shared staffing arrangements when such arrangements are supported by formal agreements.

*Bonuses and Incentives.* Includes bonuses (contractual and discretionary), incentive pay, and other types of performance pay designed to drive revenue through sales, profit, or guest satisfaction.

*Total Salaries, Wages, Service Charges, Contracted Labor and Bonuses.* Calculated by summing Salaries and Wages, Service Charge Distribution, Contracted, Leased and Outsourced Labor, and Bonuses and Incentives.

*Payroll-Related Expenses.* Includes amounts paid for an employee for duties that relate to the operation of the property and amounts paid for an employee who works in a department other than his or her regular home department regardless of the duties being performed. Payroll-Related Expenses includes the following items:

- *Payroll Taxes.* Includes the employer share of contributions to national and state retirement, unemployment, disability and medical insurance programs, and other mandated payroll-related taxes or social insurance items. (See *Payroll-Related Expenses—Schedule 14.*)

- *Supplemental Pay.* Includes personal days, vacation pay, sick pay, holiday pay, jury duty pay, relocation pay, paid time off, and severance pay. (See *Payroll-Related Expenses—Schedule 14.*)

- *Employee Benefits.* Includes all other payroll-related expenses, such as employer-paid health insurance expenses, cost of meals furnished to employees, pension contributions, and union dues and fees. (See *Payroll-Related Expenses—Schedule 14.*) The distribution of employee meal costs from *Staff Dining—Schedule 13* is charged to this line.

*Total Payroll-Related Expenses.* Calculated by summing Payroll Taxes, Supplemental Pay, and Employee Benefits.

*Note regarding shared staffing arrangements and cluster services:* Where reasonable and easily identifiable, labor costs related to shared staffing arrangements and cluster services should be charged to salaries and wages or payroll-related expenses.

## Total Labor Costs and Related Expenses

Total Labor Costs and Related Expenses is calculated by summing Total Salaries, Wages, Service Charges, Contracted Labor and Bonuses and Total Payroll-Related Expenses. The percentage for each labor cost component as well as Total Labor Costs and Related Expenses is calculated by dividing the line item amount by Total Operating Revenue for the entire property. Refer to Part III for recommended operating metrics that are pertinent to Labor Costs and Related Expenses.

## Other Expenses

This expense grouping includes the significant Administrative and General department expenses approved as Other Expenses in the *Uniform System.* Individual properties may delete irrelevant line items, but the *Uniform System* does not provide for the addition or substitution of other expense line items. Rather, properties may choose to develop a sub-account/sub-schedule to provide more detail related to a particular expense item. This sub-account/sub-schedule is then to be rolled into the appropriate line item listed below.

*Audit Charges.* Includes the cost of any accounting audits, whether internal or external, performed for the property. Audits performed specifically at the request of and for the benefit of ownership would be recorded in Owner Expenses on *Non-Operating Income and Expenses—Schedule 11.*

*Bank Charges.* Includes bank charges assessed for banking services and transactions such as overdrafts, monthly service charges, stop payments, check charges, wire and bank transfer charges, and other related items.

*Cash Overages and Shortages.* Includes cashiers' overages and shortages.

*Centralized Accounting Charges.* Includes the cost of centralized accounting charges (e.g., fees for accounts payable, statement of income preparation, and payroll processing) and sales/use/occupancy tax preparation assessed by the corporate office or management company.

*Cluster Services.* Includes allocation for costs shared between hotels in a limited geographic area (as opposed to nationally consolidated services such as Corporate Office Reimbursables). Where reasonable and easily identifiable, labor costs and related expenses should be charged to their respective line item and only other expenses are charged to Cluster Services. Where not practical, the fair allocation of the total cluster service expenses should be recognized here.

*Complimentary Services and Gifts.* Includes the cost of providing gift items used in gratis presentations to guests or vendors associated with the Administrative and General department and VIP gifts. Complimentary Services and Gifts for promotional purposes should be coded to *Sales and Marketing — Schedule 7.*

*Contract Services.* Includes expenses for activities performed for the Administrative and General department by outside contractors and professional service providers rather than hotel employees, unless identified in this department with a specific line item. The costs of contracting outside companies for document retention services is an example. If supplies are purchased for contract companies to use, the supplies are charged to the appropriate supply account.

*Corporate Office Reimbursables.* Includes the allocations of salaries and expenses of corporate or management company administrative personnel billed to the property by the regional or corporate office or the management company, consistent with any contractual arrangements. Costs should be assigned to the Administrative and General department only when these salaries and expenses cannot be billed to this account in any other department in the property. Travel expenses of such corporate or management company personnel that are incurred while visiting the property, including the costs of meals and other applicable services or amenities provided to corporate or management company staff while on business in the property for the benefit of the property, are also charged to this account.

*Credit and Collection.* Includes the cost of collecting guest accounts, such as attorney's fees and credit and check verification services.

*Credit Card Commissions.* Includes the cost of commissions paid to credit card organizations.

*Decorations.* Includes the cost of decorative items used in the Administrative and General areas for holidays and special events.

*Donations.* Includes the cost of any contributions made by the property. Examples include charitable, political, social, and community donations.

*Dues and Subscriptions.* Includes the cost of representation of the Administrative and General department, or of members of the staff when authorized to represent the Administrative and General department, in business or professional organizations. Dues and Subscriptions is also charged with the cost of subscriptions to newspapers, magazines, and books for use by the staff of the Administrative and General department.

*Entertainment—In-House.* Includes the food and beverage at cost, gratuities, service charges, and sales taxes (if applicable) consumed in the entertainment of guests, vendors, and business clients in the property's food and beverage facilities.

*Equipment Rental.* Includes the costs of renting any type of equipment that may be used either sporadically in the Administrative and General department or as a replacement for equipment out of service on a temporary basis. Equipment lease payments made under a qualified operating lease are charged to Other Property and Equipment under the Rent section of *Non-Operating Income and Expenses—Schedule 11.*

*Human Resources.* Includes all costs directly related to the human resources function, such as recruitment, relocation, background checks, non-legal cost of Visa for an ex-pat employee, employee temporary housing, physician fees and medical supplies, and all expenses associated with the cost of house media, social and sports activities, employee awards, and events and activities intended to improve employee relations and morale. If these expenses are significant, a property may develop a sub-schedule to provide more detail, but the sub-schedule total must roll up into this line item.

*Legal Services.* Includes court costs and the cost of attorney fees, attorney retainers, fees associated with acquiring visas for ex-pats, expert witnesses, related travel, and other reimbursable expenses other than those incurred in connection with an insurance claim. Legal fees incurred for insurance-related matters are charged to the appropriate insurance category on *Non-Operating Income and Expenses—Schedule 11.*

*Licenses and Permits.* Includes the cost of national and local jurisdiction licenses, including costs of inspections needed for licensing, for all activities of the Administrative and General department.

*Loss and Damage.* Includes the payments made for guest property lost or damaged in excess of the amounts recovered from insurance companies.

*Miscellaneous.* Includes any Administrative and General department expenses that do not apply to the other line items discussed in this section. Volume rebate payments received from credit card organizations would be credited to this account unless clearly and easily identifiable to a particular expense category.

*Non-Guest-Related Foreign Currency Exchange Gains (Losses).* Foreign exchange (FX) gains or losses relating to hotel accounts receivable and accounts payable should be recorded here, while all other FX gains or losses not related to guest transactions should be recorded on *Non-Operating Income and Expenses—Schedule 11.*

*Operating Supplies.* Includes the cost of items needed to operate the Administrative and General department that are not included in the descriptions of specific supply accounts. Examples are general office supplies, such as facsimile machines and calculators, and expendable office supplies, such as notepads, pens, pencils, and paper clips. This account also includes the cost of printed forms used in the

Administrative and General department, whether they are purchased from an outside source or produced internally.

*Payroll Processing.* Includes the cost incurred when a third-party service is used to process payroll.

*Postage and Overnight Delivery Charges.* Includes the cost of stamps and express mail charges specifically related to the Administrative and General department.

*Professional Fees.* Includes the cost of public accountants (other than audit fees) and other professional consultants, excluding attorneys. The amount recorded includes professional fees, travel, and other reimbursable expenses. For example, amortization of commissions paid to rental agents who have assisted in securing tenants for space rented in the property is charged to this account. Department-specific consulting fees are charged to the appropriate department. Consulting fees incurred for insurance-related matters are charged to the appropriate Insurance category on *Non-Operating Income and Expenses—Schedule 11.*

*Provision for Doubtful Accounts.* Includes any charge made to provide for the probable loss on accounts and notes receivable.

*Security.* Includes the cost of contract security for onetime events and other related expenses, such as armored car service and safety and lock boxes. Full-time third-party security in lieu of hotel staff should be charged to Salaries and Wages.

*Settlement Costs.* Includes the costs associated with settling uninsurable claims, including damage awards in connection with the settling of a lawsuit and contractual disputes. For example, the costs associated with employee or other discrimination claim settlements are charged to this line item.

*Staff Transportation.* Includes the cost of transportation other than that directly related to guests, such as the costs associated with transporting employees to the property. Subsidized public transit passes given to staff as a recruiting or retention benefit are expensed to Employee Benefits in each department.

*Training.* Includes the costs, other than payroll costs, that can be directly attributed to the training of employees in the Administrative and General department. Examples include the costs of training materials, supplies, certification programs and instructor fees. The cost of employee wages incurred during training is charged to Salaries and Wages.

*Travel—Meals and Entertainment.* Includes the reimbursable cost of food, beverage, and entertainment expenses incurred by employees of the Administrative and General department traveling on property business.

*Travel—Other.* Includes the cost of travel and reimbursable expenses (e.g., airfare car rental, hotel room and tax, guestroom Internet, conference registration fees), other than food, beverage, and entertainment, incurred by employees of the Administrative and General department traveling on property business.

*Uniform Costs.* Includes the cost of employee uniforms used in the Administrative and General department, whether purchased or rented. Repair costs are also included in this line item. The cost of cleaning uniforms is charged to Uniform Laundry.

*Uniform Laundry.* Includes the cost of cleaning uniforms for employees of the Administrative and General department, whether performed by an in-hotel facility or contracted to an outside company.

## Total Other Expenses

Total Other Expenses is calculated by summing all items listed under Other Expenses. The percentage for each line item expense as well as Total Other Expenses is calculated by dividing the line item amount by Total Operating Revenue for the entire property.

# Total Expenses

Total Expenses is calculated by adding Total Labor Costs and Related Expenses to Total Other Expenses. The percentage for Total Expenses is calculated by dividing Total Expenses by Total Operating Revenue for the entire property.

Total Expenses is the amount that appears on the Summary Operating Statement under Undistributed Operating Expenses—Administrative and General.

# INFORMATION AND TELECOMMUNICATIONS SYSTEMS—SCHEDULE 6

| | PERIOD OF | | | | | |
| --- | --- | --- | --- | --- | --- | --- |
| | CURRENT PERIOD | | | YEAR-TO-DATE | | |
| | ACTUAL | FORECAST/ BUDGET | PRIOR YEAR | ACTUAL | FORECAST/ BUDGET | PRIOR YEAR |
| | $ \| % | $ \| % | $ \| % | $ \| % | $ \| % | $ \| % |
| **EXPENSES** | | | | | | |
| Labor Costs and Related Expenses | | | | | | |
| Salaries, Wages, Service Charges, Contracted Labor and Bonuses | | | | | | |
| Salaries and Wages | | | | | | |
| Management | | | | | | |
| Non-Management | | | | | | |
| Information Technology | | | | | | |
| Telecommunications | | | | | | |
| Sub-Total: Salaries and Wages | | | | | | |
| Service Charge Distribution | | | | | | |
| Contracted, Leased and Outsourced Labor | | | | | | |
| Bonuses and Incentives | | | | | | |
| Total Salaries, Wages, Service Charges, Contracted Labor and Bonuses | | | | | | |
| Payroll-Related Expenses | | | | | | |
| Payroll Taxes | | | | | | |
| Supplemental Pay | | | | | | |
| Employee Benefits | | | | | | |
| Total Payroll Related Expenses | | | | | | |
| Total Labor Costs and Related Expenses | | | | | | |
| Cost of Services | | | | | | |
| Cost of Cell Phones | | | | | | |
| Cost of Internet Services | | | | | | |
| Cost of Local Calls | | | | | | |
| Cost of Long Distance Calls | | | | | | |
| Other Cost of Services | | | | | | |
| Total Cost of Services | | | | | | |
| System Expenses | | | | | | |
| Administrative and General | | | | | | |
| Centralized Information System Charges | | | | | | |
| Energy Management | | | | | | |
| Food and Beverage | | | | | | |
| Golf | | | | | | |
| Hardware | | | | | | |
| Health Club/Spa | | | | | | |
| Human Resources | | | | | | |
| Information Security | | | | | | |
| Information Systems | | | | | | |
| Other | | | | | | |
| Parking | | | | | | |
| Property Operation and Maintenance | | | | | | |
| Rooms | | | | | | |
| Sales and Marketing | | | | | | |
| Telecommunications | | | | | | |
| Total System Expenses | | | | | | |

**INFORMATION AND TELECOMMUNICATIONS SYSTEMS—SCHEDULE 6** *(continued)*

| | PERIOD OF | | | | | |
| | CURRENT PERIOD | | | YEAR-TO-DATE | | |
| | ACTUAL | FORECAST/ BUDGET | PRIOR YEAR | ACTUAL | FORECAST/ BUDGET | PRIOR YEAR |
| | $ \| % | $ \| % | $ \| % | $ \| % | $ \| % | $ \| % |
| Other Expenses | | | | | | |
| Cluster Services | | | | | | |
| Contract Services | | | | | | |
| Corporate Office Reimbursables | | | | | | |
| Dues and Subscriptions | | | | | | |
| Entertainment—In-House | | | | | | |
| Equipment Rental | | | | | | |
| Miscellaneous | | | | | | |
| Operating Supplies | | | | | | |
| Other Equipment | | | | | | |
| System Storage and Optimization | | | | | | |
| Training | | | | | | |
| Travel—Meals and Entertainment | | | | | | |
| Travel—Other | | | | | | |
| Uniform Costs | | | | | | |
| Uniform Laundry | | | | | | |
| Total Other Expenses | | | | | | |
| TOTAL EXPENSES | | | | | | |

*Information and Telecommunications Systems—Schedule 6* reflects the proper format for an Information and Telecommunications Systems department and designates the expense accounts that are approved as line items in the *Uniform System.* Individual properties may delete irrelevant line items, but the *Uniform System* does not provide for the addition or substitution of other revenue or expense line items. Rather, properties may choose to develop a sub-account/sub-schedule to provide more detail related to a particular expense item. This sub-account/sub-schedule is then to be rolled into the appropriate line item. Additionally, properties may choose to delete some of the columns or to show them in a different order and remain "in conformity with the *Uniform System."*

Refer to Part III for operating ratios and statistics that are pertinent to the Information and Telecommunications Systems department.

The line items for *Information and Telecommunications Systems—Schedule 6* are defined in the following pages.

## Expenses

Information and Telecommunications Systems expenses are separated into four major categories: Labor Costs and Related Expenses, Cost of Services, System Expenses, and Other Expenses.

## Labor Costs and Related Expenses

Labor Costs and Related Expenses includes all of the payroll expenses associated with Salaries, Wages, Service Charges, Contracted Labor, Bonuses, and Payroll-Related Expenses for employees and contractors. A list of the positions typically included in the Information and Telecommunications Systems department is provided in the Department Payroll Titles section at the end of Part I.

*Salaries and Wages.* Includes the earnings paid to employees for duties that relate to the operation of the property, such as regular pay, overtime pay, and shift differential pay. If an employee works in a department other than his or her regular home department, his or her earnings must be charged as Salaries and Wages in that other department, regardless of the duties being performed. For example, if an Information and Telecommunications Systems department employee regularly works as a computer operator in the Information and Telecommunications Systems department and temporarily works for the Food and Beverage department on a function, his or her earnings for the function are charged to Salaries and Wages in the Food and Beverage department, not to his or her home department.

Salaries and Wages should be delineated by significant management and non-management payroll titles within the department. If necessary, payroll titles should be aggregated to preserve the confidentiality of a specific employee's payroll.

Salaries and Wages includes the earnings associated with temporary employees when such expenses are processed through the property's payroll system.

*Service Charge Distribution.* Includes the cost of service charges paid through the payroll system for hotel employees.

*Contracted, Leased and Outsourced Labor.* Includes the gross cost of contracted, leased, and outsourced labor incurred when a property enters into an agreement with a third-party contractor to provide employees to fill positions that would normally be held by individuals paid on the regular payroll. In these situations, the property records or tracks the hours worked and pays the third-party contractor on an hourly or other agreed basis. A typical example is the use of individuals brought into the property to fill in for a shortage of PBX operators.

Contracted, Leased and Outsourced Labor includes the gross cost associated with shared staffing arrangements when such arrangements are supported by formal agreements.

*Bonuses and Incentives.* Includes bonuses (contractual and discretionary), incentive pay, and other types of performance pay designed to drive revenue through sales, profit, or guest satisfaction.

*Total Salaries, Wages, Service Charges, Contracted Labor and Bonuses.* Calculated by summing Salaries and Wages, Service Charge Distribution, Contracted, Leased and Outsourced Labor, and Bonuses and Incentives.

*Payroll-Related Expenses.* Includes amounts paid for an employee for duties that relate to the operation of the property and amounts paid for an employee who works in a department other than his or her regular home department regardless of the duties being performed. Payroll-Related Expenses includes the following items:

- *Payroll Taxes.* Includes the employer share of contributions to national and state retirement, unemployment, disability and medical insurance programs, and other mandated payroll-related taxes or social insurance items. (See *Payroll-Related Expenses—Schedule 14.*)

- *Supplemental Pay.* Includes personal days, vacation pay, sick pay, holiday pay, jury duty pay, relocation pay, paid time off, and severance pay. (See *Payroll-Related Expenses—Schedule 14.*)

- *Employee Benefits.* Includes all other payroll-related expenses, such as employer-paid health insurance expenses, cost of meals furnished to employees, pension contributions, and union dues and fees. (See *Payroll-Related Expenses—Schedule 14.*) The distribution of employee meal costs from *Staff Dining—Schedule 13* is charged to this line.

**Total Payroll-Related Expenses.** Calculated by summing Payroll Taxes, Supplemental Pay, and Employee Benefits.

*Note regarding shared staffing arrangements and cluster services:* Where reasonable and easily identifiable, labor costs related to shared staffing arrangements and cluster services should be charged to salaries and wages or payroll-related expenses.

## Total Labor Costs and Related Expenses

Total Labor Costs and Related Expenses is calculated by summing Total Salaries, Wages, Service Charges, Contracted Labor and Bonuses and Total Payroll-Related Expenses. The percentage for each labor cost component as well as Total Labor Costs and Related Expenses is calculated by dividing the line item amount by Total Operating Revenue for the entire property. Refer to Part III for recommended operating metrics that are pertinent to Labor Costs and Related Expenses.

## Note Regarding Cost of Services, System Expenses, and Other Expenses

These expense groupings include the significant Information and Telecommunications Systems department expenses approved in the *Uniform System*. Individual properties may delete irrelevant line items, but the *Uniform System* does not provide for the addition or substitution of other expense line items. Rather, properties may choose to develop a sub-account/sub-schedule to provide more detail related to a particular expense item. This sub-account/sub-schedule is then to be rolled into the appropriate line item listed below.

## Cost of Services

*Cost of Cell Phones.* Includes the cost of cell phone plans and equipment for hotel employees.

*Cost of Internet Services.* Includes the cost of providing administrative and complimentary guest Internet services, such as access charges, miscellaneous equipment not eligible for capitalization, and fees.

*Cost of Local Calls.* Includes the cost of administrative and complimentary guest calls designated as non-toll calls by the service provider, such as the associated costs for any trunk lines, access charges, usage fees, and utility taxes.

*Cost of Long Distance Calls.* Includes the cost of administrative calls designated as toll calls by the service provider, such as the associated costs for any trunk lines, access charges, usage fees, and utility taxes.

*Other Cost of Services.* Includes any expense associated with providing telecommunications services that does not apply to the other line items discussed in this section.

## Total Cost of Services

Total Cost of Services is calculated by summing all items listed under Cost of Services. The percentage for each line item expense as well as Total Cost of Services is calculated by dividing the line item amount by Total Operating Revenue for the entire property.

## System Expenses

System Expenses for each area includes systems not specified elsewhere in the Information and Telecommunications Systems department that are used by and primarily benefit the area noted. System Expenses includes items such as software licenses and maintenance, software as a service fees, hosting storage fees, and technical support fees.

*Administrative and General.* Includes any expenses of an accounting system and security system for the property.

*Centralized Information System Charges.* Includes expenses for corporate or brand systems that provide for centralized information technology solutions.

*Energy Management.* Includes any expenses of an energy management system for the property.

*Food and Beverage.* Includes any expenses of a point-of-sale system or reservation system for the Food and Beverage department except transaction costs or commissions related to a venue-specific third-party reservation or booking system.

*Golf.* Includes any expenses of a point-of-sale or reservation system for a Golf Course and Pro Shop department on the property except transaction costs or commissions related to a venue-specific third-party reservation or booking system.

*Hardware.* Includes any expenses for non-capitalized equipment (e.g., keyboards, computer mouse, etc.)

*Health Club/Spa.* Includes any expenses of a point-of-sale or reservation system for a Health Club/Spa department except transaction costs or commissions related to a venue-specific third-party reservation or booking system.

*Human Resources.* Includes any expenses of a human resources system (e.g., payroll, HRIS, time clocks) for the property.

*Information Security.* Includes any expenses of the Information and Telecommunications Systems department that are for the purpose to secure information data (e.g., PCI compliance software and affiliated costs).

*Information Systems.* Includes any expenses of a local (LAN) or wide area network (WAN) system and e-mail for the property (e.g., hardware).

*Other.* Includes any expenses of a point-of-sale or reservation system for other facilities on the property except transaction costs or commissions related to a venue-specific third-party reservation or booking system.

*Parking.* Includes any expenses of a parking lot or valet parking system for the property.

*Property Operation and Maintenance.* Includes any expenses of a property or preventive maintenance system for the property that is used to track work orders and preventive maintenance items.

*Rooms.* Includes any expenses of a property management system and key coding system for the property.

*Sales and Marketing.* Includes any expenses of a sales, catering, and marketing system for the property.

*Telecommunications.* Includes any expenses of a telecommunications system for the hotel (e.g., VoIP, T-1).

## Total System Expenses

Total System Expenses is calculated by summing all items listed under System Expenses. The percentage for each line item expense as well as Total System Expenses is calculated by dividing the line item amount by Total Operating Revenue for the entire property.

## Other Expenses

*Cluster Services.* Includes allocation for costs shared between hotels in a limited geographic area (as opposed to nationally consolidated services such as Corporate Office Reimbursables). Where reasonable and easily identifiable, labor costs and related expenses should be charged to their respective line item and only other expenses are charged to Cluster Services. Where not practical, the fair allocation of the total cluster service expenses should be recognized here.

*Contract Services.* Includes expenses for activities performed for the Information and Telecommunications Systems department by outside contractors and professional service providers rather than by hotel employees, unless identified in this department with a specific line item. The cost of contracting outside companies for data backup and department-specific consulting services are typical examples. If supplies are purchased for contract companies to use, the supplies are charged to the appropriate supply account.

*Corporate Office Reimbursables.* Includes the allocations of salaries and expenses of corporate or management company Information and Telecommunications Systems department personnel billed to the property by the regional or corporate office or by the management company, consistent with any contractual arrangements. Travel expenses of such corporate or management company personnel that are incurred while visiting the property, including the costs of meals and other applicable services or amenities provided to corporate or management company staff while on business in the property for the benefit of the property, are also charged to this account.

*Dues and Subscriptions.* Includes the cost of membership of the Information and Telecommunications Systems department, or of members of the staff when authorized to represent the Information and Telecommunications Systems department, in business or professional organizations. Dues and Subscriptions is also charged with the cost of subscriptions to newspapers, magazines, and books for use by the Information and Telecommunications Systems department staff.

*Entertainment—In-House.* Includes the food and beverage at cost, gratuities, service charges, and sales taxes (if applicable) consumed in the entertainment of guests, vendors, and business clients in the property's food and beverage facilities.

*Equipment Rental.* Includes the costs of renting any type of equipment that may be used either sporadically in the Information and Telecommunications System department or as a replacement for equipment out of service on a temporary basis. Equipment lease payments made under a qualified operating lease are charged to Other Property and Equipment under the Rent section of *Non-Operating Income and Expenses—Schedule 11.*

*Miscellaneous.* Includes any expenses of the Information and Telecommunications Systems department that do not apply to the other line items discussed in this section.

*Operating Supplies.* Includes the cost of items needed to operate the Information and Telecommunications Systems department that are not included in the descriptions of specific supply accounts. An example would be general office supplies.

*Other Equipment.* Includes any purchases of small value equipment that cannot be assigned to a particular system and would not be capitalized for the Information and Telecommunications Systems department.

*System Storage and Optimization.* Includes any expenses related to an offsite or onsite repository/storage of data for the hotel.

*Training.* Includes the costs, other than payroll cost, that can be directly attributed to the training of employees in the Information and Telecommunications Systems department. Examples include the costs of training materials, supplies, certification programs and instructor fees. The cost of employee wages incurred during training is charged to Salaries and Wages.

*Travel—Meals and Entertainment.* Includes the reimbursable cost of food, beverage, and entertainment expenses incurred by employees of the Information and Telecommunications Systems department traveling on property business.

*Travel—Other.* Includes the cost of travel and reimbursable expenses (e.g., airfare car rental, hotel room and tax, guestroom Internet, conference registration fees), other than food, beverage, and entertainment, incurred by employees of the Information and Telecommunications Systems department traveling on property business.

*Uniform Costs.* Includes the cost of employee uniforms used in the Information and Telecommunications Systems department, whether purchased or rented. Repair costs are also included in this line item. The cost of cleaning uniforms is charged to Uniform Laundry.

*Uniform Laundry.* Includes the cost of cleaning uniforms for employees of the Information and Telecommunications Systems department, whether performed by an in-hotel facility or contracted to an outside company.

## Total Other Expenses

Total Other Expenses is calculated by summing all items listed under Other Expenses. The percentage for each line item expense as well as Total Other Expenses is calculated by dividing the line item amount by Total Operating Revenue for the entire property.

# Total Expenses

Total Expenses is calculated by summing Total Labor Costs and Related Expenses, Total Cost of Services, Total System Expenses, and Total Other Expenses. The percentage for Total Expenses is calculated by dividing Total Expenses by Total Operating Revenue for the entire property.

Total Expenses is the amount that appears on the Summary Operating Statement under Undistributed Operating Expenses—Information and Telecommunications Systems.

# SALES AND MARKETING—SCHEDULE 7

| | PERIOD OF | | | | | | | | | | | |
|---|---|---|---|---|---|---|---|---|---|---|---|---|
| | CURRENT PERIOD | | | | | | YEAR-TO-DATE | | | | | |
| | ACTUAL | | FORECAST/ BUDGET | | PRIOR YEAR | | ACTUAL | | FORECAST/ BUDGET | | PRIOR YEAR | |
| | $ | % | $ | % | $ | % | $ | % | $ | % | $ | % |
| EXPENSES | | | | | | | | | | | | |
| Labor Costs and Related Expenses | | | | | | | | | | | | |
| Salaries, Wages, Service Charges, Contracted Labor and Bonuses | | | | | | | | | | | | |
| Salaries and Wages | | | | | | | | | | | | |
| Management | | | | | | | | | | | | |
| Non-Management | | | | | | | | | | | | |
| Sub-Total: Salaries and Wages | | | | | | | | | | | | |
| Service Charge Distribution | | | | | | | | | | | | |
| Contracted, Leased and Outsourced Labor | | | | | | | | | | | | |
| Bonuses and Incentives | | | | | | | | | | | | |
| Total Salaries, Wages, Service Charges, Contracted Labor and Bonuses | | | | | | | | | | | | |
| Payroll-Related Expenses | | | | | | | | | | | | |
| Payroll Taxes | | | | | | | | | | | | |
| Supplemental Pay | | | | | | | | | | | | |
| Employee Benefits | | | | | | | | | | | | |
| Total Payroll Related Expenses | | | | | | | | | | | | |
| Total Labor Costs and Related Expenses | | | | | | | | | | | | |
| Other Expenses | | | | | | | | | | | | |
| Agency Fees | | | | | | | | | | | | |
| Cluster Services | | | | | | | | | | | | |
| Collateral Material | | | | | | | | | | | | |
| Complimentary Services and Gifts | | | | | | | | | | | | |
| Contract Services | | | | | | | | | | | | |
| Corporate Office Reimbursables | | | | | | | | | | | | |
| Decorations | | | | | | | | | | | | |
| Direct Mail | | | | | | | | | | | | |
| Dues and Subscriptions | | | | | | | | | | | | |
| Entertainment—In-House | | | | | | | | | | | | |
| Equipment Rental | | | | | | | | | | | | |
| Familiarization Trips | | | | | | | | | | | | |
| Franchise and Affiliation Marketing | | | | | | | | | | | | |
| Franchise and Affiliation Fees—Royalties | | | | | | | | | | | | |
| In-House Graphics | | | | | | | | | | | | |
| Loyalty Programs | | | | | | | | | | | | |
| Media | | | | | | | | | | | | |
| Miscellaneous | | | | | | | | | | | | |
| Operating Supplies | | | | | | | | | | | | |
| Outside Sales Representation | | | | | | | | | | | | |
| Outside Services Market Research | | | | | | | | | | | | |
| Outside Signage | | | | | | | | | | | | |
| Photography | | | | | | | | | | | | |
| Postage and Overnight Delivery Charges | | | | | | | | | | | | |
| Promotion | | | | | | | | | | | | |

**SALES AND MARKETING—SCHEDULE 7** *(continued)*

| | PERIOD OF | | | | | |
| --- | --- | --- | --- | --- | --- | --- |
| | CURRENT PERIOD | | | YEAR-TO-DATE | | |
| | ACTUAL | FORECAST/ BUDGET | PRIOR YEAR | ACTUAL | FORECAST/ BUDGET | PRIOR YEAR |
| | $ \| % | $ \| % | $ \| % | $ \| % | $ \| % | $ \| % |
| Trade Shows | | | | | | |
| Training | | | | | | |
| Travel—Meals and Entertainment | | | | | | |
| Travel—Other | | | | | | |
| Uniform Laundry | | | | | | |
| Website | | | | | | |
| Total Other Expenses | | | | | | |
| TOTAL EXPENSES | | | | | | |

*Sales and Marketing—Schedule 7* reflects the proper format for a Sales and Marketing department and designates the expense accounts that are approved as line items in the *Uniform System.* Individual properties may delete irrelevant line items, but the *Uniform System* does not provide for the addition or substitution of other revenue or expense line items. Rather, properties may choose to develop a sub-account/sub-schedule to provide more detail related to a particular expense item. This sub-account/sub-schedule is then to be rolled into the appropriate line item. Additionally, properties may choose to delete some of the columns or to show them in a different order and remain "in conformity with the *Uniform System.*"

Refer to Part III for operating ratios and statistics that are pertinent to the Sales and Marketing department.

The line items for *Sales and Marketing—Schedule 7* are defined in the following pages.

# Expenses

Sales and Marketing expenses are separated into two major categories: Labor Costs and Related Expenses and Other Expenses.

## Labor Costs and Related Expenses

Labor Costs and Related Expenses includes all of the payroll expenses associated with Salaries, Wages, Service Charges, Contracted Labor, Bonuses, and Payroll-Related Expenses for employees and contractors. A list of the positions typically included in the Sales and Marketing department is provided in the Department Payroll Titles section at the end of Part I.

*Salaries and Wages.* Includes the earnings paid to employees for duties that relate to the operation of the property, such as regular pay, overtime pay, and shift differential pay. If an employee works in a department other than his or her regular home department, his or her earnings must be charged as Salaries and Wages in that other department, regardless of the duties being performed. For example, if a Sales and Marketing department employee regularly works as an administrative assistant in the Sales and Marketing department and temporarily works for the Food and Beverage department on a function, his or her earnings for the function are charged to Salaries and Wages in the Food and Beverage department, not to his or her home department.

Salaries and Wages should be delineated by significant management and non-management payroll titles within the department. If necessary, payroll titles should be aggregated to preserve the confidentiality of a specific employee's payroll.

Salaries and Wages includes the earnings associated with temporary employees when such expenses are processed through the property's payroll system.

*Service Charge Distribution.* Includes the cost of service charges paid through the payroll system for hotel employees.

*Contracted, Leased and Outsourced Labor.* Includes the gross cost of contracted, leased, and outsourced labor incurred when a property enters into an agreement with a third-party contractor to provide employees to fill positions that would normally be held by individuals paid on the regular payroll. In these situations, the property records or tracks the hours worked and pays the third-party contractor on an hourly or other agreed basis. A typical example is the use of individuals brought into the property to fill in for a shortage of Sales and Marketing staff.

Contracted, Leased and Outsourced Labor includes the gross cost associated with shared staffing arrangements when such arrangements are supported by formal agreements.

*Bonuses and Incentives.* Includes bonuses (contractual and discretionary), incentive pay, and other types of performance pay designed to drive revenue through sales, profit, or guest satisfaction.

*Total Salaries, Wages, Service Charges, Contracted Labor and Bonuses.* Calculated by summing Salaries and Wages, Service Charge Distribution, Contracted, Leased and Outsourced Labor, and Bonuses and Incentives.

*Payroll-Related Expenses.* Includes amounts paid for an employee for duties that relate to the operation of the property and amounts paid for an employee who works in a department other than his or her regular home department regardless of the duties being performed. Payroll-Related Expenses includes the following items:

- *Payroll Taxes.* Includes the employer share of contributions to national and state retirement, unemployment, disability and medical insurance programs, and other mandated payroll-related taxes or social insurance items. (See *Payroll-Related Expenses—Schedule 14.*)

- *Supplemental Pay.* Includes personal days, vacation pay, sick pay, holiday pay, jury duty pay, relocation pay, paid time off, and severance pay. (See *Payroll-Related Expenses—Schedule 14.*)

- *Employee Benefits.* Includes all other payroll-related expenses, such as employer-paid health insurance expenses, cost of meals furnished to employees, pension contributions, and union dues and fees. (See *Payroll-Related*

*Expenses — Schedule 14.*) The distribution of employee meal costs from *Staff Dining — Schedule 13* is charged to this line.

**Total Payroll-Related Expenses.** Calculated by summing Payroll Taxes, Supplemental Pay, and Employee Benefits.

*Note regarding shared staffing arrangements and cluster services:* Where reasonable and easily identifiable, labor costs related to shared staffing arrangements and cluster services should be charged to salaries and wages or payroll-related expenses.

## Total Labor Costs and Related Expenses

Total Labor Costs and Related Expenses is calculated by summing Total Salaries, Wages, Service Charges, Contracted Labor and Bonuses and Total Payroll-Related Expenses. The percentage for each labor cost component as well as Total Labor Costs and Related Expenses is calculated by dividing the line item amount by Total Operating Revenue for the entire property. Refer to Part III for recommended operating metrics that are pertinent to Labor Costs and Related Expenses.

## Other Expenses

This expense grouping includes the significant Sales and Marketing department expenses approved as Other Expenses in the *Uniform System.* Individual properties may delete irrelevant line items, but the *Uniform System* does not provide for the addition or substitution of other expense line items. Rather, properties may choose to develop a sub-account/sub-schedule to provide more detail related to a particular expense item. This sub-account/sub-schedule is then to be rolled into the appropriate line item listed below.

*Agency Fees.* Includes fees paid to advertising and/or public relations agencies.

*Cluster Services.* Includes allocation for costs shared between hotels in a limited geographic area (as opposed to nationally consolidated services such as Corporate Office Reimbursables). Where reasonable and easily identifiable, labor costs and related expenses should be charged to their respective line item and only other expenses are charged to Cluster Services. Where not practical, the fair allocation of the total cluster service expenses should be recognized here.

*Collateral Material.* Includes the cost of brochures, salespersons' kits, maps, floor plans, and similar materials used to describe the property's services.

*Complimentary Services and Gifts.* Includes the cost of providing gift items used in gratis presentations for promotional purposes to guests, prospective groups, and vendors associated with Sales and Marketing, such as VIP gifts, pens, golf balls, shirts, and key chains.

*Contract Services.* Includes expenses for activities performed for the Sales and Marketing department by outside contractors and professional service providers rather than hotel employees, unless identified in this department with a specific line item. Companies providing revenue management services and department-specific consulting services are typical examples. If supplies are purchased for contract companies to use, the supplies are charged to the appropriate supply account.

*Corporate Office Reimbursables.* Includes the allocations of salaries and expenses of corporate or management company Sales and Marketing department personnel billed to the property by the regional or corporate office or by the management company, consistent with any contractual arrangements. Travel expenses of such corporate or management company personnel that are incurred while visiting the property, including the costs of meals and other applicable services or amenities provided to corporate or management company staff while on business in the property for the benefit of the property, are also charged to this account.

*Decorations.* The cost of guest-facing holiday and special event decorations (inside and outside) is charged to this account. Department-specific decorations are charged to the appropriate department.

*Direct Mail.* Includes the cost of mailing lists, letter writing, postage, addressing envelopes or cards, and other work of this nature, including Internet e-mail blasts or other electronic versions of direct mail.

*Dues and Subscriptions.* Includes the cost of membership of the Sales and Marketing department, or of members of the staff when authorized to represent the Sales and Marketing department, in business or professional organizations. Dues and Subscriptions is also charged with the cost of subscriptions to newspapers, magazines, and books for use by the Sales and Marketing department staff.

*Entertainment—In-House.* Includes the food and beverage at cost, gratuities, service charges, and sales taxes (if applicable) consumed in the entertainment of guests, vendors, and business clients in the property's food and beverage facilities.

*Equipment Rental.* Includes the costs of renting any type of equipment that may be used either sporadically in the Sales and Marketing department or as a replacement for equipment out of service on a temporary basis. Equipment lease payments made under a qualified operating lease are charged to Other Property and Equipment under the Rent section of *Non-Operating Income and Expenses— Schedule 11.*

*Familiarization Trips.* Includes all costs associated with travel agents or meeting planners coming to a property for the purpose of familiarizing them with the property and gaining additional sales business from them. Rooms recorded as complimentary and food and beverage consumed at the property are recorded here at cost for familiarization (also called Fam or FAM) trips.

*Franchise and Affiliation Marketing.* Includes any costs paid to a franchise or affiliation entity for the purpose of promoting the brand on a national or regional basis. When the hotel operator or franchisor combines its reservations and marketing assessments, management should seek guidance from the hotel operator or franchisor regarding the percentage of the assessment attributable to reservations versus marketing activities. The assessment should then be allocated accordingly between the Rooms and Sales and Marketing departments, respectively. If management is unable to attain guidance from the hotel operator or franchisor, then the total assessment should be recorded to Franchise and Affiliation Marketing.

*Franchise and Affiliation Fees—Royalties.* Includes royalties for the licensing/branding/naming of the property itself. Fees paid for national advertising are charged to Franchise and Affiliation Marketing. Room reservation fees paid to the franchise company are charged to the Rooms department.

*In-House Graphics.* Includes the cost of directories, signs, brochures, and other costs associated with merchandising the services of the property on the property.

*Loyalty Programs.* Includes any costs associated with programs designed to build guest loyalty to the property or brand. Costs associated with cooperative loyalty programs, such as frequent flyer programs, are also charged to this account. Additionally, this account is charged with any fees associated with the administration of the property's loyalty or similar programs. The actual cost of executing the loyalty or similar programs, such as the charge based on revenue or sold room nights, is charged to this account. Reimbursement by brand programs to the property for discounted or free guest stays due to redemption of brand loyalty points/credits would be recognized as rooms revenue and not a credit to this account.

*Media.* Includes the cost of advertising on radio and television, including production costs, as well as advertising in newspapers, magazines, directories, and on the Internet (e.g., OTA and consortia ads). When such costs are significant, a property may break out the items in a series of sub-accounts, such as consumer media, newspapers, prep and production, radio, trade media, consortia, pay-per-click, and telephone directories, but the total of each of these items must be rolled into this line item.

*Miscellaneous.* Includes any expenses related to the Sales and Marketing department that do not apply to the other line items discussed in this section.

*Operating Supplies.* Includes the cost of items needed to operate the Sales and Marketing department that are not included in the descriptions of specific supply accounts. Examples are general office supplies, such as facsimile machines and calculators, and expendable office supplies, such as notepads, pens, pencils, and paper clips. Includes the cost of printed forms used in the Sales and Marketing department, whether they are purchased from an outside source or produced internally.

*Outside Sales Representation.* Includes the fees, commissions, and expenses paid to third parties, other than travel agents and meeting planners, whose services are retained for the purpose of selling and generating revenue for the property. Travel costs associated with this position would be recorded to the respective travel line items.

*Outside Services Market Research.* Includes the cost of any analysis prepared by independent research or consulting firms for the purpose of reviewing demographic characteristics, analyzing guest history, or providing market intelligence regarding bookings and reviews. Examples include Hotelligence, STR, PKF, Travel Click, monitoring of social media, and reader board services.

*Outside Signage.* Includes the cost of posters, billboards, reader boards, highway or directional signage, and other signs, including rental costs and service charges.

*Photography.* Includes the cost of photographs used in various types of promotional and publicity programs, including the cost of using professional models.

*Postage and Overnight Delivery Charges.* Includes the cost of stamps and express mail charges attributable to the Sales and Marketing department except those costs associated with direct mail campaigns.

*Promotion.* Includes the cost of goods and services provided to any individual or organization to promote the property in the community and the industry other than media advertising. Examples include entry fees to events held by civic groups to create a presence and awareness of the property, sponsoring gift certificates for non-profit and other organizations, participation in charity golf tournaments, and client appreciation parties. If food and beverage is involved, it is recorded here at the cost of the food and beverage items provided.

*Trade Shows.* Includes the cost of promoting the property at various trade shows, excluding travel expenses of attending representatives, but including the cost of the booth, registration fees, promotional logo items, and rental of exhibition space.

*Training.* Includes the costs, other than payroll cost, that can be directly attributed to the training of employees in the Sales and Marketing department. Examples include the costs of training materials, supplies, certification programs and instructor fees. The cost of employee wages incurred during training is charged to Salaries and Wages.

*Travel—Meals and Entertainment.* Includes the reimbursable cost of food, beverage and entertainment expenses incurred by employees of the Sales and Marketing department traveling on property business.

*Travel—Other.* Includes the cost of travel and reimbursable expenses (e.g., airfare car rental, hotel room and tax, guestroom Internet), other than food, beverage, and entertainment, incurred by employees of the Sales and Marketing department traveling on property business.

*Uniform Laundry.* Includes the cost of dry cleaning clothing worn by employees of the Sales and Marketing department, whether performed by an in-hotel facility or contracted to an outside company, when this service is offered as a benefit to Sales and Marketing department employees. Such employees generally do not wear property-provided uniforms.

*Website.* Includes the cost of website development and maintenance, including website registration fees, link costs, and the cost of producing a virtual tour, key word buys, content management, costs related to new media including social and mobile, search engine optimization, dynamic landing page management, hotel response costs to third-party consumer sites such as TripAdvisor, online marketing planning, and centralized labor or centrally managed costs associated with e-commerce that are distributed to the local property.

## Total Other Expenses

Total Other Expenses is calculated by summing all items listed under Other Expenses. The percentage for each line item expense as well as Total Other Expenses is calculated by dividing the line item amount by Total Operating Revenue for the entire property.

# Total Expenses

Total Expenses is calculated by adding Total Labor Costs and Related Expenses to Total Other Expenses. The percentage for Total Expenses is calculated by dividing Total Expenses by Total Operating Revenue for the entire property.

Total Expenses is the amount that appears on the Summary Operating Statement under Undistributed Operating Expenses—Sales and Marketing.

# PROPERTY OPERATION AND MAINTENANCE—SCHEDULE 8

| | PERIOD OF | | | | | |
|---|---|---|---|---|---|---|
| | CURRENT PERIOD | | | YEAR-TO-DATE | | |
| | ACTUAL | FORECAST/ BUDGET | PRIOR YEAR | ACTUAL | FORECAST/ BUDGET | PRIOR YEAR |
| | $   % | $   % | $   % | $   % | $   % | $   % |
| **EXPENSES** | | | | | | |
| Labor Costs and Related Expenses | | | | | | |
| Salaries, Wages, Service Charges, Contracted Labor and Bonuses | | | | | | |
| Salaries and Wages | | | | | | |
| Management | | | | | | |
| Non-Management | | | | | | |
| Sub-Total: Salaries and Wages | | | | | | |
| Service Charge Distribution | | | | | | |
| Contracted, Leased and Outsourced Labor | | | | | | |
| Bonuses and Incentives | | | | | | |
| Total Salaries, Wages, Service Charges, Contracted Labor and Bonuses | | | | | | |
| Payroll-Related Expenses | | | | | | |
| Payroll Taxes | | | | | | |
| Supplemental Pay | | | | | | |
| Employee Benefits | | | | | | |
| Total Payroll Related Expenses | | | | | | |
| Total Labor Costs and Related Expenses | | | | | | |
| Other Expenses | | | | | | |
| Building | | | | | | |
| Cluster Services | | | | | | |
| Contract Services | | | | | | |
| Corporate Office Reimbursables | | | | | | |
| Dues and Subscriptions | | | | | | |
| Electrical and Mechanical Equipment | | | | | | |
| Elevators and Escalators | | | | | | |
| Engineering Supplies | | | | | | |
| Entertainment—In-House | | | | | | |
| Equipment Rental | | | | | | |
| Floor Covering | | | | | | |
| Furniture and Equipment | | | | | | |
| Grounds Maintenance and Landscaping | | | | | | |
| Heating, Ventilation, and Air Conditioning Equipment | | | | | | |
| Kitchen Equipment | | | | | | |
| Laundry Equipment | | | | | | |
| Licenses and Permits | | | | | | |
| Life/Safety | | | | | | |
| Light Bulbs | | | | | | |
| Miscellaneous | | | | | | |
| Operating Supplies | | | | | | |
| Painting and Wallcovering | | | | | | |
| Plumbing | | | | | | |
| Swimming Pool | | | | | | |

**PROPERTY OPERATION AND MAINTENANCE—SCHEDULE 8** *(continued)*

| | PERIOD OF | | | | | |
|---|---|---|---|---|---|---|
| | CURRENT PERIOD | | | YEAR-TO-DATE | | |
| | ACTUAL | FORECAST/ BUDGET | PRIOR YEAR | ACTUAL | FORECAST/ BUDGET | PRIOR YEAR |
| | $    % | $    % | $    % | $    % | $    % | $    % |
| Training | | | | | | |
| Travel—Meals and Entertainment | | | | | | |
| Travel—Other | | | | | | |
| Uniform Costs | | | | | | |
| Uniform Laundry | | | | | | |
| Vehicle Repair | | | | | | |
| Waste Removal | | | | | | |
| Total Other Expenses | | | | | | |
| TOTAL EXPENSES | | | | | | |

*Property Operation and Maintenance—Schedule 8* reflects the proper format for a Property Operation and Maintenance department and designates the expense accounts that are approved as line items in the *Uniform System.* Individual properties may delete irrelevant line items, but the *Uniform System* does not provide for the addition or substitution of other revenue or expense line items. Rather, properties may choose to develop a sub-account/sub-schedule to provide more detail related to a particular expense item. This sub-account/sub-schedule is then to be rolled into the appropriate line item. Additionally, properties may choose to delete some of the columns or to show them in a different order and remain "in conformity with the *Uniform System.*"

Refer to Part III for operating ratios and statistics that are pertinent to the Property Operation and Maintenance department.

The line items for *Property Operation and Maintenance—Schedule 8* are defined in the following pages.

# Expenses

Property Operation and Maintenance expenses are separated into two major categories: Labor Costs and Related Expenses and Other Expenses.

## Labor Costs and Related Expenses

Labor Costs and Related Expenses includes all of the payroll expenses associated with Salaries, Wages, Service Charges, Contracted Labor, Bonuses, and Payroll-Related Expenses for employees and contractors. A list of the positions typically included in the Property Operation and Maintenance department is provided in the Department Payroll Titles section at the end of Part I.

*Salaries and Wages.* Includes the earnings paid to employees for duties that relate to the operation of the property, such as regular pay, overtime pay, and shift differential pay. If an employee works in a department other than his or her regular home department, his or her earnings must be charged as Salaries and Wages in that other department, regardless of the duties being performed. For example, if a Property Operations and Maintenance department employee regularly works as an engineer in the Property Operation and Maintenance department and temporarily works for the Food and Beverage department on a function, his or her earnings for the function are charged to Salaries and Wages in the Food and Beverage department, not to his or her home department.

Salaries and Wages should be delineated by significant management and non-management payroll titles within the department. If necessary, payroll titles should be aggregated to preserve the confidentiality of a specific employee's payroll.

Salaries and Wages includes the earnings associated with temporary employees when such expenses are processed through the property's payroll system.

*Service Charge Distribution.* Includes the cost of service charges paid through the payroll system for hotel employees.

*Contracted, Leased and Outsourced Labor.* Includes the gross cost of contracted, leased, and outsourced labor incurred when a property enters into an agreement with a third-party contractor to provide employees to fill positions that would normally be held by individuals paid on the regular payroll. In these situations, the property records or tracks the hours worked and pays the third-party contractor on an hourly or other agreed basis. A typical example is the use of individuals brought into the property to fill in for a shortage of engineering staff.

Contracted, Leased and Outsourced Labor includes the gross cost associated with shared staffing arrangements when such arrangements are supported by formal agreements.

*Bonuses and Incentives.* Includes bonuses (contractual and discretionary), incentive pay, and other types of performance pay designed to drive revenue through sales, profit, or guest satisfaction.

*Total Salaries, Wages, Service Charges, Contracted Labor and Bonuses.* Calculated by summing Salaries and Wages, Service Charge Distribution, Contracted, Leased and Outsourced Labor, and Bonuses and Incentives.

*Payroll-Related Expenses.* Includes amounts paid for an employee for duties that relate to the operation of the property and amounts paid for an employee who works in a department other than his or her regular home department regardless of the duties being performed. Payroll-Related Expenses includes the following items:

- *Payroll Taxes.* Includes the employer share of contributions to national and state retirement, unemployment, disability and medical insurance programs, and other mandated payroll-related taxes or social insurance items. (See *Payroll-Related Expenses—Schedule 14.*)

- *Supplemental Pay.* Includes personal days, vacation pay, sick pay, holiday pay, jury duty pay, relocation pay, paid time off, and severance pay. (See *Payroll-Related Expenses—Schedule 14.*)

- *Employee Benefits.* Includes all other payroll-related expenses, such as employer-paid health insurance expenses, cost of meals furnished to employees, pension contributions, and union dues and fees. (See *Payroll-Related Expenses—Schedule 14.*) The distribution of employee meal costs from *Staff Dining—Schedule 13* is charged to this line.

*Total Payroll-Related Expenses.* Calculated by summing Payroll Taxes, Supplemental Pay, and Employee Benefits.

*Note regarding shared staffing arrangements and cluster services:* Where reasonable and easily identifiable, labor costs related to shared staffing arrangements and cluster services should be charged to salaries and wages or payroll-related expenses.

## Total Labor Costs and Related Expenses

Total Labor Costs and Related Expenses is calculated by summing Total Salaries, Wages, Service Charges, Contracted Labor and Bonuses and Total Payroll-Related Expenses. The percentage for each labor cost component as well as Total Labor Costs and Related Expenses is calculated by dividing the line item amount by Total Operating Revenue for the entire property. Refer to Part III for recommended operating metrics that are pertinent to Labor Costs and Related Expenses.

## Other Expenses

This expense grouping includes the significant Property Operation and Maintenance department expenses approved as Other Expenses in the *Uniform System.* Individual properties may delete irrelevant line items, but the *Uniform System* does not provide for the addition or substitution of other expense line items. Rather, properties may choose to develop a sub-account/sub-schedule to provide more detail related to a particular expense item. This sub-account/sub-schedule is then to be rolled into the appropriate line item listed below.

*Building.* Includes any cost of material and contracts related to repairing and maintaining the building, both interior and exterior. The cost of locksets, as well as the cost associated with sign maintenance, is charged to this account unless the scope of work would dictate that it should be capitalized.

*Cluster Services.* Includes allocation for costs shared between hotels in a limited geographic area (as opposed to nationally consolidated services such as Corporate Office Reimbursables). Where reasonable and easily identifiable, labor costs and related expenses should be charged to their respective line item and only other expenses are charged to Cluster Services. Where not practical, the fair allocation of the total cluster service expenses should be recognized here.

*Contract Services.* Includes expenses for activities performed for the Property Operation and Maintenance department by outside contractors and professional service providers rather than by hotel employees, unless identified in this department with a specific line item. The cost of contracting outside companies for pest control or interior landscaping and department-specific consulting services are typical examples. If supplies are purchased for contract companies to use, the supplies are charged to the appropriate supply account.

*Corporate Office Reimbursables.* Includes the allocations of salaries and expenses of corporate or management company Property Operation and Maintenance department personnel billed to the property by the regional or corporate office or by the management company, consistent with any contractual arrangements. Travel expenses of such corporate or management company personnel that are incurred while visiting the property, including the costs of meals and other applicable services or amenities provided to corporate or management company staff while on business in the property for the benefit of the property, are also charged to this account.

*Dues and Subscriptions.* Includes the cost of membership of the Property Operation and Maintenance department, or of members of the staff when authorized to represent the Property Operation and Maintenance department, in business or professional organizations. Dues and Subscriptions is also charged with the cost of subscriptions to newspapers, magazines, and books for use by the Property Operation and Maintenance department staff.

*Electrical and Mechanical Equipment.* Includes the cost of materials and contracts related to repairing and maintaining general equipment not specifically identified elsewhere.

*Elevators and Escalators.* Includes the cost of materials and contracts related to repairing and maintaining elevators and escalators.

*Engineering Supplies.* Includes the costs related to any maintenance and chemical supplies and small tools used in the Property Operation and Maintenance department.

*Entertainment—In-House.* Includes the food and beverage at cost, gratuities, service charges, and sales taxes (if applicable) consumed in the entertainment of guests, vendors, and business clients in the property's food and beverage facilities.

*Equipment Rental.* Includes the costs of renting any type of equipment that may be used either sporadically in the Property Operations and Maintenance department or as a replacement for equipment out of service on a temporary basis. Equipment lease payments made under a qualified operating lease are charged to Other Property and Equipment under the Rent section of *Non-Operating Income and Expenses—Schedule 11.*

*Floor Covering.* Includes the cost of materials and contracts related to repairing floor covering throughout the building.

*Furniture and Equipment.* Includes the cost of repairing and replacing furniture and equipment not specifically addressed elsewhere. For example, the cost of contracts, materials and supplies such as textiles, fibers, lumber, metal parts, and glass related to the repair of furniture, including beds, tables, dressers, chairs, curtains and draperies, and other articles of similar nature is charged to this account, as is the cost of repairing guestroom televisions.

*Grounds Maintenance and Landscaping.* Includes the cost of supplies and contracts related to the maintenance of grounds, such as parking lot resealing and stripping and snow removal. For properties located in an area where snow removal tends to be a significant operating expense, a sub-account may be established for snow removal, with the total cost of that account rolled into Grounds Maintenance and Landscaping.

*Heating, Ventilation, and Air Conditioning Equipment.* Includes the cost of materials and contracts related to repairing and maintaining all heating, ventilation, and air conditioning equipment.

*Kitchen Equipment.* Includes the cost of materials and contracts related to repairing and maintaining kitchen equipment.

*Laundry Equipment.* Includes the cost of materials and contracts related to repairing and maintaining laundry equipment.

*Licenses and Permits.* Includes the cost of national and local jurisdiction licenses, including costs of inspections needed for licensing, for all activities of the Property Operation and Maintenance department.

*Life/Safety.* Includes the cost of regulatory inspection fees, certification tests, and materials and contracts to maintain fire control panels, tamper and flow switches, smoke detectors, sprinkler systems, and pull stations.

*Light Bulbs.* Includes the cost of replacement light bulbs.

*Miscellaneous.* Includes any expenses of the Property Operation and Maintenance department that do not apply to the other line items discussed in this section.

*Operating Supplies.* Includes the cost of items needed to operate the Property Operations and Maintenance department that are not included in the descriptions of specific accounts. An example would be general office supplies.

*Painting and Wallcovering.* Includes the cost of materials, supplies, and contracts related to painting and wallcovering throughout the property.

*Plumbing.* Includes the cost of repairing and maintaining plumbing equipment and facilities throughout the property, including kitchen and bathroom fixtures, supply lines, and drains, but excluding sprinkler systems.

*Swimming Pool.* Includes the cost of materials, supplies, pool chemicals, and contracts relating to the maintenance and repair of swimming pools when a separate Other Operated Department does not exist.

*Training.* Includes the costs, other than payroll cost, that can be directly attributed to the training of employees in the Property Operation and Maintenance department. Examples include the costs of training materials, supplies, certification programs and instructor fees. The cost of employee wages incurred during training is charged to Salaries and Wages.

*Travel—Meals and Entertainment.* Includes the reimbursable cost of food, beverage, and entertainment expenses incurred by employees of the Property Operation and Maintenance department traveling on property business.

*Travel—Other.* Includes the cost of travel and reimbursable expenses (e.g., airfare car rental, hotel room and tax, guestroom Internet, conference registration fees), other than food, beverage, and entertainment, incurred by employees of the Property Operation and Maintenance department traveling on property business.

*Uniform Costs.* Includes the cost of employee uniforms used in the Property Operations and Maintenance department, whether purchased or rented. Repair costs are also included in this line item. The cost of cleaning uniforms is charged to Uniform Laundry.

*Uniform Laundry.* Includes the cost of cleaning uniforms for employees of the Property Operation and Maintenance department, whether performed by an in-hotel facility or contracted to an outside company.

*Vehicle Repair.* Repairs and maintenance on hotel-owned or -leased vehicles. Costs associated with fuel and cleaning would stay within the department operating the vehicles.

*Waste Removal.* Includes the costs of removing trash, rubbish, and any other types of waste. Any costs associated with recycling of glass or other items as well as the rental charges for a trash container or compactor are also included in this line item.

## Total Other Expenses

Total Other Expenses is calculated by summing all items listed under Other Expenses. The percentage for each line item expense as well as Total Other Expenses is calculated by dividing the line item amount by Total Operating Revenue for the entire property.

# Total Expenses

Total Expenses is calculated by adding Total Labor Costs and Related Expenses to Total Other Expenses. The percentage for Total Expenses is calculated by dividing Total Expenses by Total Operating Revenue for the entire property.

Total Expenses is the amount that appears on the Summary Operating Statement under Undistributed Operating Expenses—Property Operation and Maintenance.

# UTILITIES—SCHEDULE 9

| | PERIOD OF | | | | | | | | | | | |
|---|---|---|---|---|---|---|---|---|---|---|---|---|
| | CURRENT PERIOD | | | | | | YEAR-TO-DATE | | | | | |
| | ACTUAL | | FORECAST/ BUDGET | | PRIOR YEAR | | ACTUAL | | FORECAST/ BUDGET | | PRIOR YEAR | |
| | $ | % | $ | % | $ | % | $ | % | $ | % | $ | % |
| **UTILITIES** | | | | | | | | | | | | |
| Electricity | | | | | | | | | | | | |
| Gas | | | | | | | | | | | | |
| Oil | | | | | | | | | | | | |
| Water/Sewer | | | | | | | | | | | | |
| Steam | | | | | | | | | | | | |
| Chilled Water | | | | | | | | | | | | |
| Other Fuels | | | | | | | | | | | | |
| Contract Services | | | | | | | | | | | | |
| **TOTAL EXPENSES** | | | | | | | | | | | | |

*Utilities—Schedule 9* reflects the proper format for a Utilities department and designates the expense accounts that are approved as line items in the *Uniform System*. Individual properties may delete irrelevant line items, but the *Uniform System* does not provide for the addition or substitution of other revenue or expense line items. Rather, properties may choose to develop a sub-account/sub-schedule to provide more detail related to a particular expense item. This sub-account/sub-schedule is then to be rolled into the appropriate line item. Additionally, properties may choose to delete some of the columns or to show them in a different order and remain "in conformity with the *Uniform System*."

Refer to Part III for operating ratios and statistics that are pertinent to the Utilities department.

# Expenses

## Electricity

The cost of electricity purchased from outside producers is charged to this account and would include taxes/assessments and any bulk/future purchase fees or allocations.

## Gas

The cost of gas purchased from outside producers is charged to this account and would include taxes/assessments and any bulk/future purchase fees or allocations.

## Oil

The cost of oil purchased from outside producers is charged to this account and would include taxes/assessments and any bulk/future purchase fees or allocations.

## Water/Sewer

The cost of water and sewer is charged to this account and would include taxes/assessments and water treatment/filtration.

If a property has a cogeneration or desalinization plant, a sub-schedule may be developed to provide more detail, but the sub-schedule total must roll up into this line item.

## Steam

The cost of steam purchased from outside producers is charged to this account and would include taxes/assessments and any bulk/future purchase fees or allocations.

## Chilled Water

The cost of chilled water and additives is charged to this account and would include taxes/assessments and any bulk/future purchase fees or allocations.

## Other Fuels

The cost of other fuels (for example, propane, kerosene, diesel, geothermal, solar, wind) purchased from outside producers is charged to this account and would include any taxes/assessments and any bulk/future purchase fees or allocations.

## Contract Services

This account includes services from firms that are engaged in energy audits, water reclamation, infrared detection for energy consumption, and other services provided with the goal of reducing energy consumption.

# Total Expenses

Total Expenses is calculated by summing all of the items listed under Utilities. The percentage for each line item expense as well as Total Expenses is calculated by dividing the line item amount by Total Operating Revenue for the entire property.

Total Expenses is the amount that appears on Summary Operating Statement under Undistributed Operating Expenses—Utilities.

# MANAGEMENT FEES—SCHEDULE 10

| | PERIOD OF | | | | | |
|---|---|---|---|---|---|---|
| | CURRENT PERIOD | | | YEAR-TO-DATE | | |
| | ACTUAL | FORECAST/ BUDGET | PRIOR YEAR | ACTUAL | FORECAST/ BUDGET | PRIOR YEAR |
| | $ \| % | $ \| % | $ \| % | $ \| % | $ \| % | $ \| % |
| MANAGEMENT FEES | | | | | | |
| Base Fee | | | | | | |
| Incentive Fees | | | | | | |
| TOTAL MANAGEMENT FEES | | | | | | |

*Management Fees—Schedule 10* reflects the proper format for reporting management fees and designates the expense accounts that are approved as line items in the *Uniform System*. Individual properties may delete irrelevant line items, but the *Uniform System* does not provide for the addition or substitution of other revenue or expense line items. Rather, properties may choose to develop a sub-account/ sub-schedule to provide more detail related to a particular expense item. This sub-account/sub-schedule is then to be rolled into the appropriate line item. Additionally, properties may choose to delete some of the columns or to show them in a different order and remain "in conformity with the *Uniform System*."

Refer to Part III for operating ratios and statistics that are pertinent to Management Fees.

## Base Fees

Management fees computed as a fixed amount or a percentage of revenues or profit are charged to this item.

## Incentive Fees

Management fees that are contingent upon achieving certain predefined levels of performance are charged to this item.

# Total Management Fees

Total Management Fees is the sum of Base Fees and Incentive Fees. The percentage for Total Management Fees is calculated by dividing Total Management Fees by Total Operating Revenue for the entire property.

Total Management Fees is the amount that appears on Summary Operating Statement under Management Fees.

# NON-OPERATING INCOME AND EXPENSES—SCHEDULE 11

| | PERIOD OF | | | | | |
| --- | --- | --- | --- | --- | --- | --- |
| | CURRENT PERIOD | | | YEAR-TO-DATE | | |
| | ACTUAL | FORECAST/ BUDGET | PRIOR YEAR | ACTUAL | FORECAST/ BUDGET | PRIOR YEAR |
| | $ \| % | $ \| % | $ \| % | $ \| % | $ \| % | $ \| % |
| INCOME | | | | | | |
| Cost Recovery Income | | | | | | |
| Interest Income | | | | | | |
| Other Income | | | | | | |
| TOTAL INCOME | | | | | | |
| RENT | | | | | | |
| Land and Buildings | | | | | | |
| Other Property and Equipment | | | | | | |
| TOTAL RENT | | | | | | |
| PROPERTY AND OTHER TAXES | | | | | | |
| Business and Occupation Taxes | | | | | | |
| Other Taxes and Assessments | | | | | | |
| Personal Property Taxes | | | | | | |
| Real Estate Taxes | | | | | | |
| TOTAL PROPERTY AND OTHER TAXES | | | | | | |
| INSURANCE | | | | | | |
| Building and Contents | | | | | | |
| Liability | | | | | | |
| Deductible | | | | | | |
| TOTAL INSURANCE | | | | | | |
| OTHER | | | | | | |
| Cost Recovery Expense | | | | | | |
| Gain/Loss on Fixed Assets | | | | | | |
| Owner Expenses | | | | | | |
| Unrealized Foreign Exchange Gains or Losses | | | | | | |
| TOTAL OTHER | | | | | | |
| TOTAL NON-OPERATING INCOME AND EXPENSES | | | | | | |

*Non-Operating Income and Expenses—Schedule 11* reflects the proper format for non-operating income and expenses and designates the income and expense accounts that are approved as line items in the *Uniform System*. Individual properties may delete irrelevant line items, but the *Uniform System* does not provide for the addition or substitution of other income or expense line items. Rather, properties may choose to develop a sub-account/sub-schedule to provide more detail related to a particular income or expense item. This sub-account/sub-schedule is then to be rolled into the appropriate line item. Additionally, properties may choose to delete some of the columns or to show them in a different order and remain "in conformity with the *Uniform System*."

Refer to Part III for operating ratios and statistics that are pertinent to non-operating income and expenses.

The line items for *Non-Operating Income and Expenses—Schedule 11* are defined in the following pages.

# Income

## Cost Recovery Income

Income collected from third parties for the recovery of common area maintenance (CAM) and out-of-pocket expenses, where the property does not earn a profit, is recorded here. GAAP requires the recording of revenue for cost recovery, where it would qualify as gross reporting under the gross versus net guidelines (see Part V), regardless of whether the property earns a profit or not. If the property does earn a profit on their cost recovery, it should be reported in *Minor Operated Departments—Sub-schedule 3-xx.*

## Interest Income

Interest income generated by funds deposited in reserve or restricted accounts that generate interest is recorded here.

## Other Income

Other income generated by the facility that is not associated with operations or managed by the operator (e.g., antenna, billboard and retail space in the building, CAM recovery for spaces directed and managed by the owner) is recorded here.

## Total Income

Total Income is calculated by summing all items listed under Income. The percentage for each line item expense as well as Total Income is calculated by dividing the dollar amount of that line item by Total Operating Revenue for the entire property.

Total Income is the amount that appears on Summary Operating Statement under Non-Operating Income and Expenses—Income.

*Note:* Since this income line is embedded in an expense category, be sure to record it in such a fashion that it offsets the non-operating expenses.

# Rent

The costs associated with the leasing and rental of property and equipment are charged to Rent. Rent expense includes operating leases, ground lease rent, and rentals of property and equipment, other than those rented for a specific function or event such as a specific banquet or New Year's Eve party. The rental of property or equipment for a specific event is generally short-term and the costs charged to the appropriate department. For example, tables and chairs rented for an outdoor wedding reception for a Food and Beverage department client are charged to the appropriate line item/account on *Food and Beverage—Schedule 2.* The costs associated with the following are examples of operating leases and rentals that are included in Rent: land and building leases, information systems and telecommunications or audiovisual equipment, vehicle leases, copiers, and leased or rented items other than those related to a specific function. Lease payments for property and equipment financed under a capital lease per GAAP definitions would not be expensed in this section, but instead should be treated as required according to GAAP.

### Land and Buildings

If the property is on a ground lease or is leased under an operating lease, this line item is charged with the lease payment base plus any participating rent. This would include property leases for a facility/complex in order to provide housing for employees. Any subsidies for the cost of renting the housing paid by employees would be credited to this account.

### Other Property and Equipment

Other rentals include any other major items (for example, vehicles, copy machines, and information or telecommunications equipment) which, had they not been rented, would be purchased and capitalized as property and equipment. Rent for off-site storage due to on-premises space limitations and managed by hotel staff would also be charged here. Rental of miscellaneous equipment (copiers, projectors, and sound equipment) for a specific function, such as a banquet or similar function, or merely to meet peak demand for a short-term period, is charged to the appropriate department and is not considered a rental expense chargeable to this line item.

### Total Rent

Total Rent is calculated by summing the items listed under Rent. The percentage for each line item expense as well as Total Rent is calculated by dividing the dollar amount of that line item by Total Operating Revenue for the entire property.

Total Rent is the amount that appears on Summary Operating Statement under Non-Operating Income and Expenses—Rent.

## Property and Other Taxes

### Business and Occupation Taxes

Taxes such as gross receipts tax on sale of rooms, food, and beverage that cannot be passed along to customers are charged to this line item.

### Other Taxes and Assessments

Any taxes or assessments other than income, payroll, or those listed above are charged to this line item and separately identified if material in a sub-schedule. Business Improvement District (BID) or assessments for public improvements are included in this category. This line also includes assessments by an entity (e.g., associations, non-government agencies) on an ongoing regular basis as part of a monthly or quarterly amount due. If there are clearly defined services in the assessment (e.g., snow or waste removal), then these individual costs should be recorded in the respective expense area of the Summary Operating Statement.

## Personal Property Taxes

Taxes on furnishings, fixtures, and equipment are charged to this line item.

## Real Estate Taxes

This account is charged with all taxes assessed against the real property by a government or public agency. This account also includes any professional fees incurred by the property in appealing a tax assessment. Refunds received from an overpayment of taxes are recorded to this account as a contra item.

## Total Property and Other Taxes

Total Property and Other Taxes is calculated by summing all items listed under Property and Other Taxes. The percentage for each line item expense as well as Total Property and Other Taxes is calculated by dividing the line item amount by Total Operating Revenue for the entire property.

Total Property and Other Taxes is the amount that appears on Summary Operating Statement under Non-Operating Income and Expenses—Property and Other Taxes.

# Insurance

## Building and Contents

The cost of insuring the property's business building and contents against damage or destruction by fire, weather, sprinkler leakage, terrorism, flood, boiler explosion, plate glass breakage, or any other cause is charged to this account, as are costs incurred for underinsurance, such as costs incurred as a result of coinsurance and legal or settlement costs.

## Liability

General insurance costs, including premiums relating to liability, including directors and officers coverage and miscellaneous professional liability coverage, employment practices liability insurance (EPLI), fidelity, umbrella, automobile, innkeepers, liquor, cyber and theft coverage, are charged to this account. Payroll-related insurance (workers' compensation) is included in Employee Benefits in the appropriate departmental schedule to which the associated payroll is charged. Premium adjustments resulting from the audit of underwriting assumptions submitted to insurance carriers are reported here, as are legal settlement costs.

## Deductible

This account includes amounts expended as a result of deductible provisions of insurance policies and self-insured retentions.

## Total Insurance

Total Insurance is calculated by summing all items listed under Insurance. The percentage for each line item expense as well as Total Insurance is calculated by dividing the dollar amount of that line item by Total Operating Revenue for the entire property.

Total Insurance is the amount that appears on Summary Operating Statement under Non-Operating Income and Expenses — Insurance.

# Other

## Cost Recovery Expense

Expenses that will be recovered by the property from a third party without profit are recorded here. Cost recovery income and cost recovery expense should net to zero.

## Gain/Loss on Fixed Assets

This represents the difference between the net book value of an asset and the amount received upon its disposal.

## Owner Expenses

Owner-directed expenses that are not associated with hotel operations (e.g., asset management fees, receiver fees, owner directed market studies or audits) are charged to this line item.

## Unrealized Foreign Exchange Gains or Losses

The foreign exchange gains or losses that occur when the foreign currency accounts on the Balance Sheet are revalued at the end of the accounting period are unrealized gains or losses. Unrealized gains and losses have no bearing on the normal and customary operation of the hotel and should be recorded here. When the assets or liabilities on the Balance Sheet are utilized in the operation of the hotel, any loss or gain on foreign exchange will be recorded in Administrative and General as those expenses are realized. Examples of accounts with unrealized foreign exchange gains and losses would be the revaluation of foreign currency bank accounts, FF&E reserve accounts, and foreign denominated debt.

## Total Other

Total Other is calculated by summing all items listed under Other. The percentage for each line item expense as well as Total Other is calculated by dividing the dollar amount of that line item by Total Operating Revenue for the entire property.

Total Other is the amount that appears on Summary Operating Statement under Non-Operating Income and Expenses — Other.

# Total Non-Operating Income and Expenses

Total Non-Operating Income and Expenses is the sum of the amounts shown for Rent, Property and Other Taxes, Insurance, and Other non-operating expenses offset by the non-operating Total Income amount. The percentage for Non-Operating

Income and Expenses is calculated by dividing Non-Operating Income and Expenses by Total Operating Revenue for the entire property.

Total Non-Operating Income and Expenses is the amount that appears on Summary Operating Statement under Total Non-Operating Income and Expenses.

# HOUSE LAUNDRY—SCHEDULE 12

| | PERIOD OF | | | | | |
| --- | --- | --- | --- | --- | --- | --- |
| | CURRENT PERIOD | | | YEAR-TO-DATE | | |
| | ACTUAL | FORECAST/ BUDGET | PRIOR YEAR | ACTUAL | FORECAST/ BUDGET | PRIOR YEAR |
| | $ \| % | $ \| % | $ \| % | $ \| % | $ \| % | $ \| % |
| **EXPENSES** | | | | | | |
| Labor Costs and Related Expenses | | | | | | |
| Salaries, Wages, Service Charges, Contracted Labor and Bonuses | | | | | | |
| Salaries and Wages | | | | | | |
| Management | | | | | | |
| Non-Management | | | | | | |
| Sub-Total: Salaries and Wages | | | | | | |
| Service Charge Distribution | | | | | | |
| Contracted, Leased and Outsourced Labor | | | | | | |
| Bonuses and Incentives | | | | | | |
| Total Salaries, Wages, Service Charges, Contracted Labor and Bonuses | | | | | | |
| Payroll-Related Expenses | | | | | | |
| Payroll Taxes | | | | | | |
| Supplemental Pay | | | | | | |
| Employee Benefits | | | | | | |
| Total Payroll Related Expenses | | | | | | |
| Total Labor Costs and Related Expenses | | | | | | |
| Other Expenses | | | | | | |
| Cleaning Supplies | | | | | | |
| Complimentary Services and Gifts | | | | | | |
| Contract Services | | | | | | |
| Corporate Office Reimbursables | | | | | | |
| Decorations | | | | | | |
| Dues and Subscriptions | | | | | | |
| Entertainment—In-House | | | | | | |
| Equipment Rental | | | | | | |
| Laundry and Dry Cleaning | | | | | | |
| Laundry Supplies | | | | | | |
| Licenses and Permits | | | | | | |
| Miscellaneous | | | | | | |
| Operating Supplies | | | | | | |
| Printing and Stationery | | | | | | |
| Training | | | | | | |
| Travel—Meals and Entertainment | | | | | | |
| Travel—Other | | | | | | |
| Uniform Costs | | | | | | |
| Uniform Laundry | | | | | | |
| Total Other Expenses | | | | | | |
| **TOTAL EXPENSES** | | | | | | |
| **CREDITS** | | | | | | |
| Cost of Guest and Outside Laundry | | | | | | |
| Concessionaires' Laundry | | | | | | |

**HOUSE LAUNDRY—SCHEDULE 12** *(continued)*

| | PERIOD OF | | | | | |
| --- | --- | --- | --- | --- | --- | --- |
| | CURRENT PERIOD | | | YEAR-TO-DATE | | |
| | ACTUAL | FORECAST/ BUDGET | PRIOR YEAR | ACTUAL | FORECAST/ BUDGET | PRIOR YEAR |
| | $ \| % | $ \| % | $ \| % | $ \| % | $ \| % | $ \| % |
| COST OF HOUSE LAUNDRY | | | | | | |
| ALLOCATIONS | | | | | | |
|   Allocation to Rooms | | | | | | |
|   Allocation to Food and Beverage | | | | | | |
|   Allocation to Department 1 | | | | | | |
|   Allocation to Department 2 | | | | | | |
|   - - - | | | | | | |
|   Allocation to Department x | | | | | | |
| TOTAL ALLOCATIONS | | | | | | |
| NET RECOVERY | | | | | | |

*House Laundry—Schedule 12* reflects the proper format for a House Laundry department and designates the expense accounts that are approved as line items in the *Uniform System*. Individual properties may delete irrelevant line items, but the *Uniform System* does not provide for the addition or substitution of other revenue or expense line items. Rather, properties may choose to develop a sub-account/sub-schedule to provide more detail related to a particular expense item. This sub-account/sub-schedule is then to be rolled into the appropriate line item. Additionally, properties may choose to delete some of the columns or to show them in a different order and remain "in conformity with the *Uniform System*."

Refer to Part III for operating ratios and statistics that are pertinent to the House Laundry department.

This schedule is allocated to various departments on an equitable basis.

The line items for *House Laundry—Schedule 12* are defined in the following pages.

# Expenses

House Laundry expenses are separated into two major categories: Labor Costs and Related Expenses and Other Expenses.

## Labor Costs and Related Expenses

Labor Costs and Related Expenses includes all of the payroll expenses associated with Salaries, Wages, Service Charges, Contracted Labor, Bonuses, and Payroll-Related Expenses for employees and contractors. A list of the positions typically included in the House Laundry department is provided in the Department Payroll Titles section at the end of Part I.

*Salaries and Wages.* Includes the earnings paid to employees for duties that relate to the operation of the property, such as regular pay, overtime pay, and shift differential pay. If an employee works in a department other than his or her regular home department, his or her earnings must be charged as Salaries and Wages in that other department, regardless of the duties being performed. For example, if a House Laundry department employee regularly works as an ironer in the House Laundry department and temporarily works for the Food and Beverage department on a function, his or her earnings for the function are charged to Salaries and Wages in the Food and Beverage department, not to his or her home department.

Salaries and Wages should be delineated by significant management and non-management payroll titles within the department. If necessary, payroll titles should be aggregated to preserve the confidentiality of a specific employee's payroll.

Salaries and Wages includes the earnings associated with temporary employees when such expenses are processed through the property's payroll system.

*Service Charge Distribution.* Includes the cost of service charges paid through the payroll system for hotel employees.

*Contracted, Leased and Outsourced Labor.* Includes the gross cost of contracted, leased, and outsourced labor incurred when a property enters into an agreement with a third-party contractor to provide employees to fill positions that would normally be held by individuals paid on the regular payroll. In these situations, the property records or tracks the hours worked and pays the third-party contractor on an hourly or other agreed basis. A typical example is the use of individuals brought into the property to fill in for a shortage of laundry staff.

Contracted, Leased and Outsourced Labor includes the gross cost associated with shared staffing arrangements when such arrangements are supported by formal agreements.

*Bonuses and Incentives.* Includes bonuses (contractual and discretionary), incentive pay, and other types of performance pay designed to drive revenue through sales, profit, or guest satisfaction.

*Total Salaries, Wages, Service Charges, Contracted Labor and Bonuses.* Calculated by summing Salaries and Wages, Service Charge Distribution, Contracted, Leased and Outsourced Labor, and Bonuses and Incentives.

*Payroll-Related Expenses.* Includes amounts paid for an employee for duties that relate to the operation of the property and amounts paid for an employee who works in a department other than his or her regular home department regardless of the duties being performed. Payroll-Related Expenses includes the following items:

- *Payroll Taxes.* Includes the employer share of contributions to national and state retirement, unemployment, disability and medical insurance programs, and other mandated payroll-related taxes or social insurance items. (See *Payroll-Related Expenses—Schedule 14.*)

- *Supplemental Pay.* Includes personal days, vacation pay, sick pay, holiday pay, jury duty pay, relocation pay, paid time off, and severance pay. (See *Payroll-Related Expenses—Schedule 14.*)

- *Employee Benefits.* Includes all other payroll-related expenses, such as employer-paid health insurance expenses, cost of meals furnished to employees, pension contributions, and union dues and fees. (See *Payroll-Related Expenses—Schedule 14.*) The distribution of employee meal costs from *Staff Dining—Schedule 13* is charged to this line.

   *Total Payroll-Related Expenses.* Calculated by summing Payroll Taxes, Supplemental Pay, and Employee Benefits.

   *Note regarding shared staffing arrangements and cluster services:* Where reasonable and easily identifiable, labor costs related to shared staffing arrangements and cluster services should be charged to salaries and wages or payroll-related expenses.

## Total Labor Costs and Related Expenses

Total Labor Costs and Related Expenses is calculated by summing Total Salaries, Wages, Service Charges, Contracted Labor and Bonuses and Total Payroll-Related Expenses. The percentage for each labor cost component as well as Total Labor Costs and Related Expenses is calculated by dividing the line item amount by Total Operating Revenue for the entire property. Refer to Part III for recommended operating metrics that are pertinent to Labor Costs and Related Expenses.

## Other Expenses

This expense grouping includes the significant House Laundry department expenses approved as Other Expenses in the *Uniform System.* Individual properties may delete irrelevant line items, but the *Uniform System* does not provide for the addition or substitution of other expense line items. Rather, properties may choose to develop a sub-account/sub-schedule to provide more detail related to a particular expense item. This sub-account/sub-schedule is then to be rolled into the appropriate line item listed below.

   *Cleaning Supplies.* Includes the cost of products used in cleansing, sweeping, polishing, waxing, and disinfecting areas associated with the House Laundry. The cost of materials and supplies used for laundering purposes is charged to Laundry Supplies.

   *Complimentary Services and Gifts.* Includes the cost of providing gift items used in gratis presentations for promotional purposes to guests and vendors of the House Laundry department and VIP gifts.

   *Contract Services.* Includes expenses for activities performed for the House Laundry department by outside companies rather than hotel employees. The cost of contracting outside companies to clean areas associated with the House Laundry department is an example. If supplies are purchased for contract companies to use, the supplies are charged to the appropriate supply account. The cost of contracts for the House Laundry department laundry and dry cleaning is charged to Laundry and Dry Cleaning.

   *Corporate Office Reimbursables.* Includes the allocations of salaries and expenses of corporate or management company House Laundry department personnel billed to the property by the regional or corporate office or by the management company. Travel expenses of such corporate or management company personnel that are incurred while visiting the property, including the costs of meals and other applicable services or amenities provided to corporate or management company staff while on business in the property for the benefit of the property, are also charged to this account.

*Decorations.* Includes the cost of decorative items used in House Laundry areas for holidays and special events.

*Dues and Subscriptions.* Includes the cost of membership of the House Laundry department, or of members of the staff when authorized to represent the House Laundry department, in business or professional organizations. Dues and Subscriptions is also charged with the cost of subscriptions to newspapers, magazines, and books for use by the House Laundry department staff.

*Entertainment—In-House.* Includes the food and beverage at cost, gratuities, service charges, and sales taxes (if applicable) consumed in the entertainment of guests, vendors, and business clients in the property's food and beverage facilities.

*Equipment Rental.* Includes the costs of renting any type of equipment that may be used either sporadically in the House Laundry department or as a replacement for equipment out of service on a temporary basis. Equipment lease payments made under a qualified operating lease are charged to Other Property and Equipment under the Rent section of *Non-Operating Income and Expenses—Schedule 11.*

*Laundry and Dry Cleaning.* Includes the cost of laundry and dry cleaning services applicable to the House Laundry department that are contracted to an outside company. When services are performed by an outside company, the amount charged to Laundry and Dry Cleaning is based on invoices sent by the outside laundry. The cost of cleaning employee uniforms is charged to Uniform Laundry.

*Laundry Supplies.* Includes the cost of supplies used for laundering and dry cleaning purposes.

*Licenses and Permits.* Includes the cost of national and local jurisdiction licenses, including costs of inspections needed for licensing, for all activities of the House Laundry department.

*Miscellaneous.* Includes any expenses of the House Laundry department that do not apply to the other line items discussed in this section.

*Operating Supplies.* Includes the cost of operating and general office supplies needed to operate the House Laundry department that are not included in the descriptions of specific supply accounts such as Cleaning Supplies, Laundry Supplies, or Printing and Stationery.

*Printing and Stationery.* Includes the cost of printed forms used in the House Laundry department, whether they are purchased from an outside source or produced internally.

*Training.* Includes the costs, other than time, that can be directly attributed to the training of employees in the House Laundry department. Examples include the costs of training materials, supplies, and instructor fees. The cost of employee wages incurred during training is charged to Salaries and Wages.

*Travel—Meals and Entertainment.* Includes the reimbursable cost of food and beverage expenses for travel and entertainment by employees of the House Laundry department traveling on property business.

*Travel—Other.* Includes the cost of travel and reimbursable expenses (e.g., airfare car rental, hotel room and tax, guestroom Internet, conference registration fees), other than food, beverage, and entertainment, by employees of the House Laundry department traveling on property business.

*Uniform Costs.* Includes the cost of employee uniforms used in the House Laundry department, whether purchased or rented. Repair costs are also included in this line item. The cost of cleaning uniforms is charged to Uniform Laundry.

*Uniform Laundry.* Includes the cost of cleaning uniforms for employees of the House Laundry department, whether performed by an in-hotel facility or contracted to an outside company.

## Total Other Expenses

Total Other Expenses is calculated by summing all items listed under Other Expenses. The percentage for each line item expense as well as Total Other Expenses is calculated by dividing the line item amount by Total Operating Revenue for the entire property.

# Total Expenses

Total Expenses is calculated by adding Total Labor Costs and Related Expenses to Total Other Expenses. The percentage for Total Expenses is calculated by dividing Total Expenses by Total Operating Revenue for the entire property.

# Credits

## Cost of Guest and Outside Laundry

Where no separate guest laundry is maintained, this line item is credited on an equitable basis to reflect the cost of processing guest laundry.

## Concessionaires' Laundry

Where laundering is done at cost for concessionaires such as spas or beauty salons or other related hotels, the proceeds received should be credited to the Credits account in order to offset departmental expenses.

Whenever laundering is done for third parties for the purpose of making a profit, the gross versus net principles should be applied. If reporting gross, the revenues and expenses should be recorded in Other Operated Departments, with a credit to the House Laundry department for the allocated expenses. If reporting net, the revenue should be reported on *Miscellaneous Income — Schedule 4.*

## Cost of House Laundry

Cost of House Laundry is Total Expenses less Credits.

## Allocations

Cost of House Laundry is allocated to the departments using an equitable basis reflecting usage, such as cost-per-pound, number of pieces cleaned, etc.

## Net Recovery

Cost of House Laundry less Total Allocations equals Net Recovery, which should always net to zero to reflect full allocation of this department.

# STAFF DINING—SCHEDULE 13

| | PERIOD OF | | | | | |
|---|---|---|---|---|---|---|
| | CURRENT PERIOD | | | YEAR-TO-DATE | | |
| | ACTUAL | FORECAST/ BUDGET | PRIOR YEAR | ACTUAL | FORECAST/ BUDGET | PRIOR YEAR |
| | $ \| % | $ \| % | $ \| % | $ \| % | $ \| % | $ \| % |
| **EXPENSES** | | | | | | |
| Cost of Food | | | | | | |
| Labor Costs and Related Expenses | | | | | | |
| Salaries, Wages, Service Charges, Contracted Labor and Bonuses | | | | | | |
| Salaries and Wages | | | | | | |
| Management | | | | | | |
| Non-Management | | | | | | |
| Kitchen | | | | | | |
| Service | | | | | | |
| Sub-Total: Salaries and Wages | | | | | | |
| Service Charge Distribution | | | | | | |
| Contracted, Leased and Outsourced Labor | | | | | | |
| Bonuses and Incentives | | | | | | |
| Total Salaries, Wages, Service Charges, Contracted Labor and Bonuses | | | | | | |
| Payroll-Related Expenses | | | | | | |
| Payroll Taxes | | | | | | |
| Supplemental Pay | | | | | | |
| Employee Benefits | | | | | | |
| Total Payroll-Related Expenses | | | | | | |
| Total Labor Costs and Related Expenses | | | | | | |
| Other Expenses | | | | | | |
| China | | | | | | |
| Cleaning Supplies | | | | | | |
| Contract Services | | | | | | |
| Corporate Office Reimbursables | | | | | | |
| Decorations | | | | | | |
| Dishwashing Supplies | | | | | | |
| Dues and Subscriptions | | | | | | |
| Entertainment—In-House | | | | | | |
| Equipment Rental | | | | | | |
| Flatware | | | | | | |
| Glassware | | | | | | |
| Ice | | | | | | |
| Kitchen Fuel | | | | | | |
| Kitchen Smallwares | | | | | | |
| Laundry and Dry Cleaning | | | | | | |
| Licenses and Permits | | | | | | |
| Linen | | | | | | |
| Miscellaneous | | | | | | |
| Operating Supplies | | | | | | |
| Paper and Plastics | | | | | | |
| Printing and Stationery | | | | | | |
| Training | | | | | | |

*(continued)*

### STAFF DINING—SCHEDULE 13 *(continued)*

| | PERIOD OF | | | | | |
|---|---|---|---|---|---|---|
| | CURRENT PERIOD | | | YEAR-TO-DATE | | |
| | ACTUAL | FORECAST/ BUDGET | PRIOR YEAR | ACTUAL | FORECAST/ BUDGET | PRIOR YEAR |
| | $ \| % | $ \| % | $ \| % | $ \| % | $ \| % | $ \| % |
| Travel—Meals and Entertainment | | | | | | |
| Travel—Other | | | | | | |
| Uniform Costs | | | | | | |
| Uniform Laundry | | | | | | |
| Utensils | | | | | | |
| Total Other Expenses | | | | | | |
| TOTAL EXPENSES | | | | | | |
| NET REVENUE | | | | | | |
| COST OF STAFF DINING | | | | | | |
| ALLOCATIONS | | | | | | |
| Allocation to Rooms | | | | | | |
| Allocation to Food and Beverage | | | | | | |
| Allocation to Department 1 | | | | | | |
| Allocation to Department 2 | | | | | | |
| - - - | | | | | | |
| Allocation to Department x | | | | | | |
| TOTAL ALLOCATIONS | | | | | | |
| NET RECOVERY | | | | | | |

*Staff Dining—Schedule 13* reflects the proper format for a Staff Dining department and designates the revenue and expense accounts that are approved as line items in the *Uniform System.* Individual properties may delete irrelevant line items, but the *Uniform System* does not provide for the addition or substitution of other revenue or expense line items. Rather, properties may choose to develop a sub-account/sub-schedule to provide more detail related to a particular revenue or expense item. This sub-account/sub-schedule is then to be rolled into the appropriate line item. Additionally, properties may choose to delete some of the columns or to show them in a different order and remain "in conformity with the *Uniform System.*"

Refer to Part III for operating ratios and statistics that are pertinent to the Staff Dining department.

This schedule is allocated to various departments on an equitable basis.

The line items for *Staff Dining—Schedule 13* are defined in the following pages.

## Expenses

Staff Dining department expenses are separated into three major categories: Cost of Food, Labor Costs and Related Expenses, and Other Expenses.

## Cost of Food

Cost of Food includes the cost of food items furnished for employee meals, whether consumed in a staff dining facility or in hotel food and beverage venues. Properties with staff dining facilities usually requisition the food items from either the storeroom or kitchen on a daily basis. Cost of Food is simply the cost of the products requisitioned each day, as evidenced on the respective vendor invoices, plus the cost of food consumed for on-duty meals consumed in food and beverage venues. The percentage for Cost of Food is calculated by dividing Cost of Food by Total Operating Revenue for the entire property.

## Labor Costs and Related Expenses

Labor Costs and Related Expenses includes all of the payroll expenses associated with Salaries, Wages, Service Charges, Contracted Labor, Bonuses, and Payroll-Related Expenses for employees and contractors. A list of the positions typically included in the Staff Dining department is provided in the Department Payroll Titles section at the end of Part I.

*Salaries and Wages.* Includes the earnings paid to employees for duties that relate to the operation of the property, such as regular pay, overtime pay, and shift differential pay. If an employee works in a department other than his or her regular home department, his or her earnings must be charged as Salaries and Wages in that other department, regardless of the duties being performed. For example, if a Staff Dining department employee regularly works as a cook in the Staff Dining department and temporarily works for the Food and Beverage department on a function, his or her earnings for the function are charged to Salaries and Wages in the Food and Beverage department, not to his or her home department.

Salaries and Wages should be delineated by significant management and non-management payroll titles within the department. If necessary, payroll titles should be aggregated to preserve the confidentiality of a specific employee's payroll.

Salaries and Wages includes the earnings associated with temporary employees when such expenses are processed through the property's payroll system.

*Service Charge Distribution.* Includes the cost of service charges paid through the payroll system for hotel employees.

*Contracted, Leased and Outsourced Labor.* Includes the gross cost of contracted, leased, and outsourced labor incurred when a property enters into an agreement with a third-party contractor to provide employees to fill positions that would normally be held by individuals paid on the regular payroll. In these situations, the property records or tracks the hours worked and pays the third-party contractor on an hourly or other agreed basis. A typical example is the use of individuals brought into the property to fill in for a shortage of Staff Dining service staff.

Contracted, Leased and Outsourced Labor includes the gross cost associated with shared staffing arrangements when such arrangements are supported by formal agreements.

*Bonuses and Incentives.* Includes bonuses (contractual and discretionary), incentive pay, and other types of performance pay designed to drive revenue through sales, profit, or guest satisfaction.

*Total Salaries, Wages, Service Charges, Contracted Labor and Bonuses.* Calculated by summing Salaries and Wages, Service Charge Distribution, Contracted, Leased and Outsourced Labor, and Bonuses and Incentives.

*Payroll-Related Expenses.* Includes amounts paid for an employee for duties that relate to the operation of the property and amounts paid for an employee who works in a department other than his or her regular home department regardless of the duties being performed. Payroll-Related Expenses includes the following items:

- *Payroll Taxes.* Includes the employer share of contributions to national and state retirement, unemployment, disability and medical insurance programs, and other mandated payroll-related taxes or social insurance items. (See *Payroll-Related Expenses—Schedule 14.*)

- *Supplemental Pay.* Includes personal days, vacation pay, sick pay, holiday pay, jury duty pay, relocation pay, paid time off, and severance pay. (See *Payroll-Related Expenses—Schedule 14.*)

- *Employee Benefits.* Includes all other payroll-related expenses, such as employer-paid health insurance expenses, cost of meals furnished to employees, pension contributions, and union dues and fees. (See *Payroll-Related Expenses—Schedule 14.*) The distribution of employee meal costs from *Staff Dining—Schedule 13* is charged to this line.

*Total Payroll-Related Expenses.* Calculated by summing Payroll Taxes, Supplemental Pay, and Employee Benefits.

*Note regarding shared staffing arrangements and cluster services:* Where reasonable and easily identifiable, labor costs related to shared staffing arrangements and cluster services should be charged to salaries and wages or payroll-related expenses.

## Total Labor Costs and Related Expenses

Total Labor Costs and Related Expenses is calculated by summing Total Salaries, Wages, Service Charges, Contracted Labor and Bonuses and Total Payroll-Related Expenses. The percentage for each labor cost component as well as Total Labor Costs and Related Expenses is calculated by dividing the line item amount by Total Operating Revenue for the entire property. Refer to Part III for recommended operating metrics that are pertinent to Labor Costs and Related Expenses.

## Other Expenses

This expense grouping includes the significant Staff Dining department expenses approved as Other Expenses in the *Uniform System.* Individual properties may delete irrelevant line items, but the *Uniform System* does not provide for the addition or substitution of other expense line items. Rather, properties may choose to develop a sub-account/sub-schedule to provide more detail related to a particular expense item. This sub-account/sub-schedule is then to be rolled into the appropriate line item listed below.

*China.* Includes the cost of purchased or rented plates, bowls, serving platters, etc., constructed from any material (ceramic, glass, metal, non-disposable plastic, etc.) and used in providing food service to employees, with the exception of non-alcoholic beverage items. The cost of containers for consumption of non-alcoholic beverages is charged to Glassware.

*Cleaning Supplies.* Includes the cost of products used in cleansing, sweeping, polishing, waxing, and disinfecting areas associated with the Staff Dining department.

*Contract Services.* Includes expenses for activities performed for the Staff Dining department by outside companies rather than hotel employees. The costs of contracting outside companies to clean carpets and rugs or to disinfect areas associated with the Staff Dining department are typical examples. Other examples include the cost of contracting outside companies to wash windows and degrease hoods. If supplies are purchased for contract companies to use, the supplies are charged to the appropriate supply account. The cost of contracts for the Staff Dining department laundry and dry cleaning is charged to Laundry and Dry Cleaning.

*Corporate Office Reimbursables.* Includes the allocations of salaries and expenses of corporate or management company Staff Dining department personnel billed to the property by the regional or corporate office or by the management company. Travel expenses of such corporate or management company personnel that are incurred while visiting the property, including the costs of meals and other applicable services or amenities provided to corporate or management company staff while on business in the property for the benefit of the property, are also charged to this account.

*Decorations.* Includes the cost of decorative items used in the Staff Dining areas for holidays and special events.

*Dishwashing Supplies.* Includes the cost of cleaning, rinsing, and soaking agents used specifically in washing china, glassware, flatware, and utensils in the Staff Dining department.

*Dues and Subscriptions.* Includes the cost of representation of the Staff Dining department, or of members of the staff when authorized to represent the Staff Dining department, in business or professional organizations. Dues and Subscriptions is also charged with the cost of subscriptions to newspapers, magazines, and books for use by the staff of the Staff Dining department.

*Entertainment—In-House.* Includes the food and beverage at cost, gratuities, service charges, and sales taxes (if applicable) consumed in the entertainment of guests, vendors, and business clients in the property's food and beverage facilities.

*Equipment Rental.* Includes the costs of renting any type of equipment that may be used either sporadically in the Staff Dining department or as a replacement for equipment out of service on a temporary basis. Equipment lease payments made under a qualified operating lease are charged to Other Property and Equipment under the Rent section of *Non-Operating Income and Expenses — Schedule 11.*

*Flatware.* Includes the cost of all flatware and serving pieces (serving spoons, cake knives, ladles, etc.), either purchased or rented, used in providing food service in the Staff Dining department.

*Glassware.* Includes the cost of purchased or rented containers constructed from any material (glass, ceramic, metal, non-disposable plastic) used in providing food service in the Staff Dining department.

*Ice.* Includes the cost of ice used in food service, storage, or preparation in the Staff Dining department.

*Kitchen Fuel.* Includes the cost of fuel used for cooking in the Staff Dining department.

*Kitchen Smallwares.* Includes the cost of all kitchen smallwares (pots, pans, and other small cooking apparatuses not included in Utensils), either purchased or rented, used in the preparation of food products in the Staff Dining department.

*Laundry and Dry Cleaning.* Includes the cost of laundry and dry cleaning services applicable to the Staff Dining department, whether the services are performed by an in-house facility or are contracted to an outside company. If the services are performed by an in-house laundry, an allocation from House Laundry is charged to Laundry and Dry Cleaning. If the services are performed by an outside company, the amount charged to Laundry and Dry Cleaning should be based on invoices sent by the outside laundry. The cost of cleaning employee uniforms is charged to Uniform Laundry.

*Licenses and Permits.* Includes the cost of national and local jurisdiction licenses, including costs of inspections needed for licensing, for all activities of the Staff Dining department.

*Linen.* Includes the cost, whether purchased or rented, of table cloths, napkins, table runners, and skirting used by the Staff Dining department.

*Miscellaneous.* Includes any expenses of the Staff Dining department that do not apply to the other line items discussed in this section.

*Operating Supplies.* Includes the cost of operating and general office supplies needed to operate the Staff Dining department that are not included in the descriptions of specific supply accounts such as Cleaning Supplies and Printing and Stationery.

*Paper and Plastics.* Includes the cost of paper supplies used by the Staff Dining department.

*Printing and Stationery.* Includes the cost of printed forms used in the Staff Dining department, whether they are purchased from an outside source or produced internally. Examples include placards identifying menu items.

*Training.* Includes the costs, other than time, that can be directly attributed to the training of employees in the Staff Dining department. Examples include the costs of training materials, supplies, and instructor fees. The cost of employee wages incurred during training is charged to Salaries and Wages.

*Travel—Meals and Entertainment.* Includes the reimbursable cost of food and beverage expenses for travel and entertainment by employees of the Staff Dining department traveling on property business.

*Travel—Other.* Includes the cost of travel and reimbursable expenses (e.g., airfare car rental, hotel room and tax, guestroom Internet, conference registration fees), other than food, beverage, and entertainment, by employees of the Staff Dining department traveling on property business.

*Uniform Costs.* Includes the cost of employee uniforms used in the Staff Dining department, whether purchased or rented. Repair costs are also included in this line item. The cost of cleaning uniforms is charged to Uniform Laundry.

*Uniform Laundry.* Includes the cost of cleaning uniforms for employees of the Staff Dining department, whether performed by an in-hotel facility or contracted to an outside company.

*Utensils.* Includes the cost of all tools needed in the process of food preparation in the Staff Dining department, such as butcher knives, spatulas, and whisks.

### Total Other Expenses

Total Other Expenses is calculated by summing all items listed under Other Expenses. The percentage for each line item expense as well as Total Other Expenses is calculated by dividing the line item amount by Total Operating Revenue for the entire property.

## Total Expenses

Total Expenses is calculated by adding Cost of Food, Total Labor Costs and Related Expenses, and Total Other Expenses. The percentage for Total Expenses is calculated by dividing Total Expenses by Total Operating Revenue for the entire property.

## Net Revenue

Net Revenue includes revenue derived from the sale of, or recovery from, employee meals, including sales of coffee, tea, milk, and soft drinks.

## Cost of Staff Dining

Cost of Staff Dining is Total Expenses less Net Revenue. Cost of Staff Dining is distributed to the various departments incurring a payroll expense on an equitable basis reflecting usage, such as number of employees fed, percentage of payroll, etc., and charged to Employee Benefits.

## Net Recovery

Cost of Staff Dining less Total Allocations equals Net Recovery, which should always net to zero to reflect full allocation of this department.

# PAYROLL-RELATED EXPENSES—SCHEDULE 14

| | PERIOD OF | | | | | |
| | CURRENT PERIOD | | | YEAR-TO-DATE | | |
| | ACTUAL | FORECAST/ BUDGET | PRIOR YEAR | ACTUAL | FORECAST/ BUDGET | PRIOR YEAR |
|---|---|---|---|---|---|---|
| | $ \| % | $ \| % | $ \| % | $ \| % | $ \| % | $ \| % |
| **PAYROLL TAXES** | | | | | | |
| National Disability Insurance | | | | | | |
| National Medical Insurance | | | | | | |
| National Retirement Contribution | | | | | | |
| National Unemployment Insurance | | | | | | |
| State Disability Insurance | | | | | | |
| State Medical Insurance | | | | | | |
| State Retirement Contribution | | | | | | |
| State Unemployment Insurance | | | | | | |
| **TOTAL PAYROLL TAXES** | | | | | | |
| **SUPPLEMENTAL PAY** | | | | | | |
| Other Pay | | | | | | |
| Personal Days | | | | | | |
| Severance Pay | | | | | | |
| Sick Pay | | | | | | |
| Holiday Pay | | | | | | |
| Vacation/Paid Time Off | | | | | | |
| **TOTAL SUPPLEMENTAL PAY** | | | | | | |
| **EMPLOYEE BENEFITS** | | | | | | |
| Automobile Allowance | | | | | | |
| Child Care | | | | | | |
| Contributory Savings Plan | | | | | | |
| Dental Insurance | | | | | | |
| Disability Insurance | | | | | | |
| Expat Benefits | | | | | | |
| Group Life Insurance | | | | | | |
| Health Insurance | | | | | | |
| Housing and Educational | | | | | | |
| Meals | | | | | | |
| Miscellaneous | | | | | | |
| Nonunion Insurance | | | | | | |
| Nonunion Pension | | | | | | |
| Profit Sharing | | | | | | |
| Public Subsidized Transportation | | | | | | |
| Stock Benefits | | | | | | |
| Stock Options | | | | | | |
| Union Insurance | | | | | | |
| Union Other | | | | | | |
| Union Pension | | | | | | |
| Workers' Compensation Insurance | | | | | | |
| **TOTAL EMPLOYEE BENEFITS** | | | | | | |
| **TOTAL PAYROLL-RELATED EXPENSES** | | | | | | |

Payroll systems in use today typically allow properties to charge payroll taxes and benefits directly to departments as salaries and wages are calculated, thus eliminating the need for allocation. *Payroll-Related Expenses—Schedule 14* illustrates a format for summarizing the total payroll taxes and employee benefits paid by a lodging property. Individual properties may delete irrelevant items, but the *Uniform System* does not permit combining or moving items between the two categories if the financial statements are to be "in conformity with the *Uniform System.*"

## Payroll Taxes

*National Disability Insurance.* Includes the employer share of contributions required by legislation to disability compensation programs administered by government agencies at the federal or national level.

*National Medical Insurance.* Includes the employer share of contributions required by legislation to government administered medical programs (e.g., Medicare, National Insurance System).

*National Retirement Contribution.* Includes the employer share of contributions required by legislation to retirement programs administered by government agencies at the federal or national level (e.g., Social Security portion of FICA, Canada Pension Plan, or National Insurance System).

*National Unemployment Insurance.* Includes the employer share of contributions required by legislation to unemployment compensation programs administered by government agencies at the federal or national level (e.g., FUTA, Canadian Employment Insurance, or National Insurance System).

*State Disability Insurance.* Includes the taxes or assessments imposed on employers by state or provincial agencies for employee disability benefits.

*State Medical Insurance.* Includes the employer share of contributions imposed by governmental agencies at the state or provincial level.

*State Retirement Contribution.* Includes the employer share of contributions required by legislation to retirement programs administered at the state or provincial level (e.g., Quebec Pension Plan).

*State Unemployment Insurance.* Includes the unemployment taxes imposed by governmental agencies at the state or provincial level.

## Supplemental Pay

*Other Pay.* Includes all other forms of supplemental pay not otherwise identified.

*Personal Days.* Includes the cost associated with paid personal days and paid jury duty for hotel employees.

*Severance Pay.* Includes the cost associated with pay in lieu of services for hotel employees that are discharged.

*Sick Pay.* Includes the cost associated with paid sick days for hotel employees.

*Holiday Pay.* Includes the cost associated with paid holidays for hotel employees.

*Vacation/Paid Time Off.* Includes the cost associated with paid vacation/PTO days for hotel employees.

## Employee Benefits

*Automobile Allowance.* Includes the cost of providing payment to employees for personally-owned vehicles and allowances for the use of an auto including lease payments made directly to the leasing company, but not travel reimbursements, which are recorded in the respective Travel—Other account.

*Child Care.* Includes the cost of child care for employees' children.

*Contributory Savings Plan.* Includes the employer's portion for any retirement matching programs offered to employees (e.g., 401(k), Registered Retirement Savings Plan). This line item also includes any administrative costs associated with these programs.

*Dental Insurance.* Includes the net employer cost of dental insurance coverage for employees.

*Disability Insurance.* Includes the insurance premium for employee disability insurance.

*Expat Benefits.* Includes the cost of benefits exclusively benefiting employees hired under an ex-patriot contract and would include such items as cost of living adjustments, education for family members, hardship premiums, tax equalization and transportation for home leave.

*Group Life Insurance.* ⊚⊚Includes the net employer cost for any group life insurance policy.

*Health Insurance.* Includes the net employer cost of health insurance coverage for employees.

*Housing and Educational.* Includes the cost associated with reimbursing some or all of the expenditures to employees for living off-property or sending themselves or family members to school.

*Meals.* Includes the cost of providing meals to employees consumed both in staff dining and those consumed in hotel venues less amounts charged to the employee.

*Miscellaneous.* Includes the cost of providing employees with benefits not included under other captions.

*Nonunion Insurance.* Includes the cost of accident and other insurance for employees not participating in a union fund.

*Nonunion Pension.* Includes the cost associated with nonunion pension plans.

*Profit Sharing.* Includes the employer's contribution to profit sharing plans.

*Public Subsidized Transportation.* Includes the cost to provide subsidized funding for public transportation to hotel employees.

*Stock Benefits.* Includes the cost (value) of company stock issued to employees as compensation.

*Stock Options.* Includes the cost related to the value of stock options issued to employees.

*Union Insurance.* Includes the employer's cost of union employees' benefit funds for insurance on life, health, accident, hospitalization, and other purposes.

*Union Other.* Includes dues, legal fund, and other contractual obligations of the employer for an employee union.

*Union Pension.* Includes the employer's portion of costs associated with union employees' pension benefit funds.

*Workers' Compensation Insurance.* Includes workers' compensation insurance premium and other associated costs.

# Departmental Payroll Titles

This section lists the typical job titles found in each of the departments of a lodging property. There may be variations in job titles based on an operator's or chain's own practices. Individual properties may choose to use the same names or different names for the positions, but the *Uniform System* does not allow properties to combine departments other than what has been described earlier in this guide and remain "in conformity with the *Uniform System*."

The relative operational and supervisory responsibilities of a position serve as the guiding principle for the assignment of the payroll titles to their respective departmental sub-categories. Managerial versus non-managerial designations assist in the analysis of payroll efficiency and productivity (see Part III).

In general, the payroll titles listed under "Management" reflect positions that typically manage and supervise other employees. These positions tend to be full-time and salaried.

The payroll titles listed under the non-management sub-categories normally do not supervise other employees. The hours worked by the non-management personnel may be subject to variation depending on levels of business. They are usually paid on an hourly, weekly, or monthly basis that is subject to overtime and not determined on an annual basis.

## Rooms

### Management

Rooms director, operations manager, front office manager, front desk manager, assistant front desk manager, night manager, director of guest services, guest services manager, chef concierge, executive housekeeper, director of housekeeping, housekeeping manager, director of reservations, reservations manager, transportation manager, club floor manager

### Front Office

Desk clerk, night desk clerk (former night auditor), bell captain, bell/luggage attendant, door attendant, dispatcher

### Guest Services

Concierge, guest services representative, activities attendant, guest services coordinator

### Housekeeping

Floor supervisor, room attendant, house attendant, public area attendant, turndown attendant, night attendant, sewing attendant, uniform room attendant

## Laundry

Housekeeping/linen runner, linen control supervisor, linen room attendant, uniform room attendant

## Reservations

Reservations agent, guest historian

## Transportation

Driver

## Complimentary Food and Beverage Club

Club floor attendant, breakfast attendant

# Food and Beverage

## Management—Service

Director of food and beverage, food and beverage manager, director of venues, restaurant manager, beverage manager, director of convention services, convention services manager

## Management—Kitchen

Executive chef, executive sous chef, sous chef, chef de cuisine, pastry chef, kitchen manager, executive steward, stewarding manager

## Banquet/Conference/Catering

Captain, bartender, server, busperson, porter, attendant, runner, houseperson

## Kitchen

Chef, garde manager, chef de partie, cook, pastry cook, butcher, baker, steward, cleaner

## Venues

Sommelier, maître d', host(ess), captain, bartender, server, busperson, porter, attendant, runner, cashier, houseperson

# Golf Course/Pro Shop

## Management

Director of golf course maintenance, director of golf, golf pro, golf pro shop manager, retail manager, golf course maintenance manager

## Golf Pros/Operations

Golf instructor, golf marshal, golf course attendant, caddy, golf ranger, golf pro assistant, instructor, starter

## Greens/Maintenance

Greens supervisor, greens keeper, gardener, general maintenance, driver, mechanic, golf cart maintenance, repair attendant, golf cart storage attendant

## Pro Shop

Golf cashier, locker room attendant, club storage attendant, golf pro shop cashier, golf pro shop attendant, sales clerk

# Health Club/Spa

## Management

Department manager/director, sales manager/director, retail manager/director, salon supervisor

## Attendant/Housekeeping

Attendant

## Fitness

Fitness consultant/technician, pool attendant/lifeguard (when operated by Health Club/Spa)

## Reception/Retail

Group activity coordinator, reception agent, sales associate

## Therapists/Technicians

Group activity coordinator, spa technicians, salon technicians

# Parking

## Management

Parking manager

## Non-Management

Valet/parking attendant, parking cashier

# Administrative and General

## Management

Managing director, general manager, resident manager, hotel manager, director of operations, quality assurance manager, controller, director of finance, assistant director of finance, assistant controller, accounting manager, credit manager, chief accountant, accounts receivable manager, financial analyst, audit manager, accounts payable manager, cost controller, profit improvement manager, director of purchasing, director of security, director of human resources, human resources manager, training director, benefits manager, employee relations manager, employment manager, package room manager, security manager

## Accounting

Accounts payable clerk, accounts receivable clerk, general cashier, paymaster, staff accountant, group billing clerk, accounting clerk

## General Support

Administrative assistant

## Human Resources

Human resources coordinator, benefits coordinator

## Purchasing and Receiving

Buyer, clerk, receiving agent, storekeeper, purchasing agent, purchasing coordinator, storeroom and receiving, general storeroom attendant, receiving clerk, package room attendant

## Security

Security officer

# Information and Telecommunications Systems

## Management

Director of information systems, MIS manager, systems manager, PBX manager

## Information Technology

Systems analyst, programmer, computer operator

## Telecommunications

PBX operator

# Sales and Marketing

## Management

Director of sales and marketing, director of marketing, director of sales, director of public relations, director of marketing communications, director of revenue optimization, director of catering, director of group sales, sales manager, public relations manager, pricing/revenue manager, catering sales manager, e-commerce manager, CRM (customer relationship management) manager

## Non-Management

Research analyst, sales assistant

# Property Operation and Maintenance

## Management

Director of engineering, chief engineer, engineering manager, environmental manager, energy manager

## Non-Management

Groundskeeper, equipment operator, heavy machine operator, general maintenance engineer, general maintenance laborer, carpenter, electrician, painter, plumber, engineer, engineering coordinator, mechanic, life guard (properties without Health Club/Spa)

# House Laundry

## Management

Laundry/valet manager

## Non-Management

Folder, press machine operator, ironer, finisher, washer, wringer, extractor, puller, tumbler, sorter, marker, checker, collection and delivery employee, linen attendant, chute attendant, sewing attendant, valet attendant

# Staff Dining

## Management

Staff dining manager

## Non-Management

Staff dining attendant, staff dining cook

# Part II
# Financial Statements

A complete set of financial statements includes a Balance Sheet, a Statement of Income, a Statement of Comprehensive Income, a Statement of Owners' Equity, a Statement of Cash Flows, and Notes to the Financial Statements that amplify the information presented in the basic statements. The Balance Sheet reflects the financial position of the business by detailing the assets, liabilities, and owners' equity as of a given date. The Statement of Income presents revenues and expenses associated with operations over a given period. The Statement of Comprehensive Income presents non-owner transactions that affect an entity's equity. (Note: Recent professional promulgations require entities to present net income and other comprehensive income in either a single continuous statement or in two separate, but consecutive, statements of net income and other comprehensive income as presented herein.) The Statement of Owners' Equity summarizes transactions, including owners' transactions, affecting equity over a given period. The Statement of Cash Flows presents information about the operating, investing, and financing activities that affected cash over a given period.

It should be noted that the financial statements discussed in Part II and the examples presented have been developed following accounting principles generally accepted in the United States of America (GAAP). There are comprehensive bases of accounting other than GAAP under which financial statements can be prepared, including the cash basis, income tax basis, and International Financial Reporting Standards (IFRS). IFRS is another set of accounting principles promulgated by the International Accounting Standards Board and is practiced, in some form, by most countries in the world. Such principles, as yet, have not been adopted in the United States. Therefore, this book does not address such standards.

While the usefulness of the other accounting bases is recognized, the principles and practices relating to the preparation of financial statements under these other bases are beyond the scope of this book.

Some of the major websites that detail the differences between GAAP and IFRS are as follows:

- The IFRS Foundation offers free access to the current year's consolidated unaccompanied [without implementation guidance and basis for conclusions] English language IFRS and official interpretations. This includes IFRS, International Accounting Standards (IAS), International Financial Reporting Interpretation Committee statements (IFRICs), and Standing Interpretations Committee standards (SICs). www.ifrs.org/IFRSs/Pages/IFRS.aspx

- The American Institute of Certified Public Accountants (AICPA) has a general IFRS resource page on their website: http://www.ifrs.com/index.html

- The AICPA also published *U.S. and International Accounting: Understanding the Differences.* www.ifrs.com/publications.html. There is a charge for this publication.

Should a question arise related to financial statement presentation, the principles of GAAP prevail.

# Section 1
# Balance Sheet

The Balance Sheet presents a listing of a business's assets and the claims to those assets, called liabilities and owners' equity, as of a given date. Assets represent those items owned by the business; liabilities represent the claims to the assets by outsiders, and owners' equity represents the claims of the owners to the assets.

The accounts appearing on the Balance Sheet may be arranged in either an account format or a report format. The account format of the Balance Sheet lists the asset accounts on the left side of the page and the liability and the owners' equity accounts on the right side of the page. The report format of the Balance Sheet lists assets, liabilities, and owners' equity in a single column. These arrangements allow the form of the Balance Sheet to reflect that either assets equal liabilities plus owners' equity or that assets minus liabilities equal owners' equity.

An illustration of the account format of the Balance Sheet follows. This illustration includes accounts applicable to many types of lodging properties. Each line item appearing on the Balance Sheet is explained in the pages that follow.

The number and types of accounts that appear on the Balance Sheet will vary according to the needs and requirements of the business. Accordingly, appropriate modification should be made to the suggested format to accommodate the individual requirements of the business, while remaining consistent with GAAP. It is important to remember, however, that similar items should be appropriately grouped and that all significant items should be reflected separately. Significant items are those that are considered material for financial statement purposes.

## BALANCE SHEET

### Assets

|  | Current Year | Prior Year |
|---|---|---|
| CURRENT ASSETS | | |
|    Cash and Cash Equivalents | | |
|       House Banks | $ | $ |
|       Demand Deposits | | |
|       Temporary Cash Investments | | |
|          Total Cash | | |
|    Restricted Cash | | |
|    Short-Term Investments | | |
|    Receivables | | |
|       Accounts Receivable | | |
|       Notes Receivable | | |
|       Current Maturities of Non-current Receivables | | |
|       Other | | |
|          Total Receivables | | |
|       Less Allowance for Doubtful Accounts | | |
|          Net Receivables | | |
|    Due To/From Owner, Management Company, | | |
|       or Related Party | | |
|    Inventories | | |
|    Operating Equipment | | |
|    Prepaid Expenses | | |
|    Deferred Income Taxes—Current | | |
|    Other | | |
|       Total Current Assets | | |
| NON-CURRENT RECEIVABLES, Net of Current Maturities | | |
| INVESTMENTS | | |
| PROPERTY AND EQUIPMENT | | |
|    Land | | |
|    Buildings | | |
|    Leaseholds and Leasehold Improvements | | |
|    Furnishings and Equipment | | |
|    Construction in Progress | | |
|       Total Property and Equipment | | |
|    Less Accumulated Depreciation and Amortization | | |
|       Net Property and Equipment | | |
| OTHER ASSETS | | |
|    Intangible Assets | | |
|    Cash Surrender Value of Life Insurance | | |
|    Deferred Charges | | |
|    Deferred Income Taxes—Non-current | | |
|    Operating Equipment | | |
|    Restricted Cash | | |
|    Preopening Expenses | | |
|    Other | | |
|       Total Other Assets | | |
| TOTAL ASSETS | $ | $ |

## BALANCE SHEET

### Liabilities and Owners' Equity

|  | Current Year | Prior Year |
|---|---|---|
| **CURRENT LIABILITIES** | | |
| Notes Payable | | |
|     Banks | $ | $ |
|     Others | | |
|         Total Notes Payable | | |
| Due To/From Owner, Management Company | | |
|   or Related Party | | |
| Accounts Payable | | |
| Accrued Expenses | | |
| Advance Deposits | | |
| Income Taxes Payable | | |
| Deferred Income Taxes—Current | | |
| Current Maturities of Long-Term Debt | | |
| Gift Certificates and Cards | | |
| Other | | |
|         Total Current Liabilities | | |
| | | |
| **LONG-TERM DEBT,** Net of Current Maturities | | |
|   Mortgage Notes, other notes, and similar liabilities | | |
|   Obligations Under Capital Leases | | |
|         Total Long-Term Debt | | |
| | | |
| **OTHER LONG-TERM LIABILITIES** | | |
| | | |
| **DEFERRED INCOME TAXES**—Non-current | | |
| | | |
| **COMMITMENTS AND CONTINGENCIES** | | |
| | | |
| **OWNERS' EQUITY**—one of the formats found on the next page | | |
| | | |
| **TOTAL LIABILITIES AND OWNERS' EQUITY** | $ | $ |

## Alternative Owners' Equity Presentations in the Balance Sheet

### CORPORATION
#### Stockholders' Equity

| | Current Year | Prior Year |
|---|---|---|
| ____% Cumulative Preferred Stock, $ ____ par value, authorized ____ shares; issued and outstanding ____ shares | $ | $ |
| Common Stock, $____ par value, authorized ____ shares; issued and outstanding ____ shares | | |
| Additional Paid-In Capital | | |
| Retained Earnings | | |
| Accumulated Other Comprehensive Income (Loss), Net of Income Tax | | |
| Less: Treasury Stock, ____ shares of Common Stock, at cost | | |
| Total Stockholders' Equity | $ | $ |

### PARTNERSHIP
#### Partners' Equity

| | Current Year | Prior Year |
|---|---|---|
| General Partners | $ | $ |
| Limited Partners | | |
| Accumulated Other Comprehensive Income (Loss), Net of Income Tax | | |
| Total Partners' Equity | $ | $ |

### LIMITED LIABILITY COMPANY

| | Current Year | Prior Year |
|---|---|---|
| Members' Equity | $ | $ |
| Accumulated Other Comprehensive Income (Loss), Net of Income Tax | | |
| Total Members' Equity | $ | $ |

### SOLE PROPRIETORSHIP

| | Current Year | Prior Year |
|---|---|---|
| Owner's Equity | $ | $ |
| Accumulated Other Comprehensive Income (Loss), Net of Income Tax | | |
| Total Owner's Equity | $ | $ |

# ASSETS

## Current Assets

This section of the Balance Sheet includes accounts that are to be converted to cash or used in operations within 12 months of the Balance Sheet date. Non-current assets (such as Non-current Receivables, Property and Equipment, and Other Assets) refer to accounts that are not expected to be converted to cash or used in operations within 12 months of the Balance Sheet date. The accounts appearing under the Current Assets section of the Balance Sheet are commonly listed in the order of their liquidity.

### Cash and Cash Equivalents

Cash and Cash Equivalents include Cash on Hand (House Banks), Demand Deposits, and Temporary Cash Investments. Temporary Cash Investments are those investments of a demand nature or that have maturities within 90 days at the time of purchase.

### Restricted Cash

Cash that is restricted should be separately classified as current or non-current based on the purpose of the restriction. If the purpose of the restriction is to pay for capital improvements, furniture and fixtures, or portions of the debt that would be classified as long term, the cash should be classified as long term. If the cash is restricted to pay portions of the debt that are classified as current or for current expenses such as real estate taxes, the cash should be classified as current.

### Short-Term Investments

Short-Term Investments are not Temporary Cash Investments, but are intended to be converted to cash or cash equivalents within a year. Short-Term Investments are, essentially, trading securities and are reflected at market value with the unrealized gain or loss recognized in the Statement of Income. The basis for valuation of such securities is disclosed in the Notes to the Financial Statements.

### Receivables

This line item groups Accounts Receivable and Notes Receivable. Based on the needs of the property, a supporting schedule may accompany the Balance Sheet, detailing significant items included within current receivables.

*Accounts Receivable.* Consists of the total amount due to the property from accounts carried in the guest and city ledgers. Accounts not expected to be collected within the next 12 months are included under Non-current Receivables. Significant credit balances are included in current liabilities under Advance Deposits or Other Liabilities, depending on the nature of the credit balance.

*Notes Receivable.* Includes notes that are expected to be collected within the next 12 months. Notes that are not expected to be collected within the next 12 months are included under Non-current Receivables.

*Current Maturities of Non-current Receivables.* Includes amounts that are expected to be collected within the next 12 months. Amounts that are not expected to be collected within the next 12 months are included under Non-current Receivables.

*Other.* Includes those receivables that are not either Accounts or Notes Receivable, such as Accrued Interest Receivables.

*Allowance for Doubtful Accounts.* Represents an allowance for the portion of current accounts and notes receivable estimated to be uncollectible. The allowance is based on historical experience, specific appraisal of individual accounts, or other accepted methods. Accounts that become uncollectible are charged to this account and recoveries of accounts previously written off are credited to it. The balance at the end of any period, however, represents the best estimate of the portion of accounts and notes receivable that will not be collected.

## Due To/From Owner, Management Company, or Related Party

Due to/from accounts contain the balances due to or from the owner, a management company, or other related entities for loans, advances for capital improvements, management fees, and other expenses or advances provided to a property. The accounts are classified as current or long term based on their payment terms. For example, if a management company has made advances for capital improvements that are being repaid over a period of years or are offset against future distributions, these amounts are reflected as long term. The various due to/from accounts are not offset against each other unless there is a legal right to offset them.

## Inventories

Inventories includes the cost of merchandise held for sale and the cost of supplies used in operating the property. The cost of merchandise held for sale includes such items as food, beverages, gift merchandise, and guest supplies. The cost of supplies used in operating the property includes such items as cleaning supplies and guest supplies. The basis for valuing inventory is disclosed in the Notes to the Financial Statements and, if individual inventory categories are significant, they are separately stated.

## Operating Equipment

Operating Equipment includes linen, china, glassware, silver, and uniforms. When a property purchases operating equipment items, it must determine the period of consumption and expense the purchase over that time period. If the estimated usage of the equipment is less than one year, the item is considered a current asset and expensed ratably to the appropriate department expense account over its estimated period of consumption, not to exceed 12 months. The reasonable useful life of linen, china, glassware, silver and uniforms is typically 12 months or less, and therefore should be expensed over this period to the department that has the benefit of the asset.

Operating equipment items with useful lives of more than one year are treated as long-term assets and recorded under Other Assets. Whether the items are categorized as current or long-term assets, operating equipment items are not depreciated, but are expensed to the appropriate department expense account. On a periodic basis, the property should verify the accuracy of the estimated consumption by taking a physical inventory of the operating equipment that remains unissued in the storeroom and comparing the value to the Balance Sheet value on the date of the inventory. Variances may result in an adjusting entry or a correction of the consumption estimate.

## Prepaid Expenses

Prepaid Expenses generally represents payments for items that will benefit future operating periods. Normally, the amounts are charged to operations based upon when the benefits are received. Examples include insurance, property taxes, rent, interest, maintenance, the unused net benefit under barter contracts, and other similar items.

## Deferred Income Taxes—Current

Deferred Income Taxes—Current represents the tax effects of temporary differences between the bases of current assets and current liabilities for financial and income tax reporting purposes. For example, only the direct write-off of a bad debt is deductible for tax purposes; therefore, a provision for an Allowance for Doubtful Accounts will result in a current deferred tax asset. Deferred Income Taxes—Current is presented as net current assets or net current liabilities as circumstances dictate. The deferred tax asset must be evaluated for realization and a valuation allowance established for any portion that is not to be realized.

## Other

Other current assets include items not shown elsewhere that are reasonably expected to be realized in cash or otherwise in the next 12 months. The category is normally used to capture minor items that are not separately disclosed.

## Non-current Receivables, Net of Current Maturities

Non-current Receivables represents accounts and notes that are not expected to be collected during the next 12 months. Amounts due from owners, officers, employees, and affiliated entities are shown separately, unless insignificant. If any Non-current Receivables are estimated to be uncollectible, an Allowance for Doubtful Non-current Receivables is established using procedures similar to those described under the caption Allowance for Doubtful Accounts.

## Investments

Investments generally includes debt or equity securities, whether or not they are traded in recognized markets, and ownership interests that are expected to be held on a long-term basis. Investments in marketable equity securities and debt securities, where there is not the intent and ability to hold such securities to maturity, are considered "available for sale" and are reflected at market value with unrealized gains and losses being shown, net of tax effects, as a separate component of equity. Investment in debt securities where there is the intent and ability to hold such securities to maturity are considered "held to maturity" and reflected at amortized cost. Investments in affiliated entities are shown separately, unless insignificant. Investments in entities over which the reporting entity has the ability to exercise significant influence (generally by ownership of more than 20 percent) are recorded using the equity method. The equity method requires the recording of the investor's share of the investee's operations in the Income Statement and an adjustment in the carrying value of the investment. The method of accounting for and the basis for valuing investments is dictated by GAAP and disclosed in the Notes to the Financial Statements.

## Property and Equipment

This grouping of accounts includes owned Land; Buildings; Furnishings and Equipment; the cost of Leaseholds and Leasehold Improvements; and Construction in Progress. It also includes similar assets held under capital leases. If material, assets held under capital leases are separately presented on the Balance Sheet or in the Notes to the Financial Statements.

Depreciation is a method of allocating the net cost (after reduction for expected salvage value) of the individual assets or classes of assets to operations over their anticipated useful lives. There are several different methods used for depreciation, including straight-line, declining balance, and other variants. Under GAAP, the straight-line method of depreciation is preferred. Declining balance is a method of depreciation usually used for tax depreciation. The number of years chosen for the life of an asset or class of assets also varies somewhat in practice for similar items; however, the methods and the lives used should result in a reasonable allocation of the cost of the assets to operations over their useful lives.

Amortization is a method of ratably charging off to income intangible assets with a life greater than one year.

The total Accumulated Depreciation and Amortization should appear as a separate line item. This amount is subtracted from the Total Property and Equipment line to arrive at the Net Property and Equipment line. The methods of depreciation and amortization used are identified in the Notes to the Financial Statements.

GAAP requires that a long-lived asset (group) be tested for impairment whenever events or changes in circumstances indicate that its carrying amount may not be recoverable. The recoverability test is based on the estimated future cash flows that are directly associated with, and that are expected to arise as a direct result of the use and eventual disposition of, the long-lived asset (group) that is being tested. GAAP pronouncements describe how the test is to be performed. An impairment loss is recognized only if the carrying amount of a long-lived asset (group) is not recoverable and is reflected as a loss on impairment (difference between the value and the cost) in the Income Statement. The carrying amount of the asset (group) is generally not recoverable when the sum of the cash flows expected to be generated from the use of a long-lived asset (group) and its value upon disposition (undiscounted and without interest charges) is less than the carrying amount of the asset (group). If the test is not met, impairment does not exist and, therefore, no loss is recognized, even if the net book value of the asset (group) exceeds its fair value.

If a lodging operation has property and equipment held for sale, the classification of the assets and the related operations should be reflected in accordance with GAAP.

# Other Assets

## Intangible Assets

Intangible assets are assets that lack physical substance. Many intangible assets are readily identifiable, such as patents, trademarks, customer lists, etc. Goodwill is an unidentifiable intangible asset.

Goodwill represents the excess of the purchase price over the fair value of the net assets acquired in the purchase of a business. Goodwill is evaluated periodically for impairment and an impairment loss recognized, if necessary, based on such evaluation.

Current GAAP literature provides guidelines on the amortization of all other intangible assets.

## Cash Surrender Value of Life Insurance

Some organizations purchase life insurance on the lives of key individuals. Many of these policies have a cash surrender value that is recorded as an asset and disclosed separately if significant. Changes in the amount of the Cash Surrender Value are reflected as adjustments to Insurance Expense.

## Deferred Charges

Deferred Charges typically relates to financing activities and represents direct costs of obtaining financing such as loan fees and bond issuance costs. Such costs are usually amortized over the life of the related financing. The method and period of amortization is disclosed in the Notes to the Financial Statements.

## Deferred Income Taxes—Non-current

Deferred Income Taxes—Non-current represents the tax effects of temporary differences between the bases of non-current assets and non-current liabilities for financial and income tax reporting purposes. For example, if a liability is accrued that will not be paid for an extended period and the expense is deductible only when paid for tax purposes, the accrual will result in a non-current deferred income tax asset. Deferred Income Taxes—Non-current is presented as net non-current assets or net non-current liabilities as circumstances dictate. The deferred tax asset must be evaluated for realization and a valuation allowance established for any portion that is more likely than not to be realized.

## Operating Equipment

Operating equipment includes linen, china, glassware, silver, and uniforms. When a property purchases operating equipment items, it must establish the period of consumption. If the period of consumption of the operating equipment items is expected to be less than one year, the items are classified as current assets. Whether the items are categorized as current or long-term assets, operating equipment items are not depreciated, but are expensed to the appropriate department expense account. Most purchases of operating equipment are expected to be consumed within a period of one year or less. However, if a property makes a bulk purchase of china, for example, and the expected usage period is greater than one year, the usage period is appropriately stated at the longer time period and the items are expensed to the appropriate department expense accounts. On a periodic basis, the property should verify the accuracy of the estimated consumption by taking a physical inventory of the operating equipment that remains unissued in the storeroom and comparing the value to the Balance Sheet value on the date of the inventory. Variances may result in an adjusting entry or a correction of the consumption estimate.

## Restricted Cash

Cash that is restricted should be separately classified as current or non-current based on the nature of the restriction. For example, if the restriction is to pay for capital improvements, furniture and fixtures, or portions of the debt that would be classified as long term, the cash should be classified as long term.

## Preopening Expenses

Costs of start-up activities are variously referred to in practice as preopening, pre-operating, organization, and start-up costs. Under GAAP, such costs are charged to operations as incurred.

## Other

Non-current items that cannot be included under other groupings, such as security deposits, initial franchise costs, and other miscellaneous or individually immaterial assets, are included under this caption. Restricted cash balances that are restricted to, for example, the acquisition of property and equipment (e.g., FF&E reserves) could also be included in this classification when such amounts are not material. The nature of these items, if material, is to be clearly indicated on the Balance Sheet or in the Notes to the Financial Statements. Amortization policies are also disclosed in the Notes to the Financial Statements.

# LIABILITIES
## Current Liabilities

### Notes Payable

Notes Payable includes short-term notes that are payable within the next 12 months, classified on the Balance Sheet as notes due to banks and notes due to other creditors.

### Due To/From Owner, Management Company, or Related Party

Due to/from accounts contain the balances due to or from the owner, a management company, or other related entities for loans, advances for capital improvements, management fees, and other expenses or advances provided to a property. The accounts are classified as current or long term based on their payment terms. For example, if a management company has made advances for capital improvements that are being repaid over a period of years or are offset against future distributions, these amounts are reflected as long term. The various due to/from accounts are not offset against each other unless there is a legal right to offset them.

### Accounts Payable

Accounts Payable represents amounts due to vendors. Amounts due to concessionaires for guest charges collected by the property may be included with Accounts Payable or shown separately.

### Accrued Expenses

Accrued Expenses represents expenses incurred, but not payable until after the Balance Sheet date. Each item of Accrued Expense, if material, is listed separately, either on the Balance Sheet or in the Notes to the Financial Statements. Examples include salaries and wages and related benefits, vacation pay, interest, management fees, rent, taxes other than on income, and utilities.

### Advance Deposits

Advance Deposits represents amounts received that are to be applied as part of the payment for future sales of rooms, food and beverage, or other goods and services.

### Income Taxes Payable

Income Taxes Payable represents the estimated obligations for income taxes.

### Deferred Income Taxes—Current

Deferred Income Taxes—Current represents the tax effects of temporary differences between the bases of current assets and current liabilities for financial and income tax reporting purposes. For example, revenue recognized in the financial statements before it is taxable will result in Deferred Income Taxes—Current if it will be taxable in the next year. Deferred Income Taxes—Current is presented as net current assets or net current liabilities as circumstances dictate.

### Current Maturities of Long-Term Debt

Current Maturities of Long-Term Debt includes the principal payments of mortgage notes, other notes, and similar liabilities, and the installments on capital leases due within the next 12 months.

### Gift Certificates and Cards

Gift Certificates and Cards includes unredeemed amounts recognized as a liability by the issuing entity, whether that be the hotel or the corporate office. As the certificates and cards are redeemed, the appropriate revenue is recognized and the liability is reduced.

### Other

Current liabilities not included under other captions are shown here. The category is normally used to capture minor items that are not separately disclosed. Examples include the unearned portion of amounts received or charged to non-guests for the use of recreational facilities, unclaimed wages, and the net liability under barter contracts.

## Long-Term Debt

This category includes mortgage notes, other notes, and similar liabilities and obligations under capital leases that are not payable during the next 12 months.

### Mortgage Notes, Other Notes, and Similar Liabilities

For this caption, the following information is disclosed either on the Balance Sheet or in the Notes to the Financial Statements:

- Interest rates
- Payment or sinking fund requirements
- Maturity dates
- Collateralization and assets pledged
- Financial restrictive covenants
- Payment and sinking fund payments required for each of the five years subsequent to the Balance Sheet date

### Obligations Under Capital Leases

For Obligations Under Capital Leases, disclosure is made with regard to the future minimum lease payments for each of the five years subsequent to the Balance Sheet date and the total future minimum lease obligations, with a deduction for the imputed interest necessary to reduce the net minimum lease payments to present value.

## Other Long-Term Liabilities

Long-term liabilities that do not require satisfaction within a year and are not included under other captions are included here. Examples include deferred compensation, deferred management fees, tenants' lease deposits, and accrued obligations for pension and other post-employment benefits. The nature of these items, if material, should be clearly indicated on the Balance Sheet or in the Notes to the Financial Statements.

## Deferred Income Taxes—Non-current

Deferred Income Taxes—Non-current represents the tax effects of temporary differences between the bases of non-current assets and non-current liabilities for financial and income tax reporting purposes. For example, the use of accelerated depreciation for tax purposes and straight-line depreciation for financial reporting purposes will result in non-current deferred income taxes. Deferred Income Taxes—Non-current is presented as net non-current assets or net non-current liabilities as circumstances dictate.

## Commitments and Contingencies

The Commitments and Contingencies caption is indicated on the Balance Sheet only to bring the reader's attention to such items. No dollar amounts are shown on the Balance Sheet. Adequate disclosure of all significant commitments and contingencies is made in the Notes to the Financial Statements. Examples include commitments for purchase contracts, employment contracts, long-term leases, management agreements, contingencies for pending or threatened litigation, and certain guarantees of indebtedness of others.

## OWNERS' EQUITY

The Owners' Equity section of the Balance Sheet is presented differently for corporations, partnerships, limited liability companies, and sole proprietorships, depending upon the type of equity ownership. Balance Sheet presentation formats are shown earlier in this section. Examples of detailed presentations of Statements of Owners' Equity are shown in Section 4.

## Corporation

### Stockholders' Equity

*Capital Stock.* Capital Stock denotes the shares of ownership of a corporation that have been authorized by its articles of incorporation. The most prevalent classes of Capital Stock are Preferred and Common Stock. The par or stated value and the number of shares authorized and issued for each class of stock is presented on the Balance Sheet. Changes during the period should be shown in the Statement of Stockholders' Equity.

*Additional Paid-In Capital.* Additional Paid-In Capital includes cash, property, and other capital contributed to a corporation by its shareholders in excess of the stated or par value of Capital Stock. Changes during the period are shown in the Statement of Stockholders' Equity.

*Retained Earnings.* Retained Earnings represents the accumulated Net Income not distributed as dividends but retained in the business. Changes during the period are shown in the Statement of Stockholders' Equity. Negative retained earnings are generally referred to as deficits.

*Treasury Stock.* Treasury Stock represents the cost of the company's stock acquired by the company and not retired, and is reflected as a reduction in total Stockholders' Equity. Changes during the period are shown in the Statement of Stockholders' Equity.

# Partnership

## Partners' Equity

Partners' Equity represents the net equity of the partners in the partnership and is classified where appropriate as general and limited partners' equity. Changes during the period are shown in the Statement of Partners' Equity.

*Contributions.* Contributions include the amount of any additional assets that the partners invested in the business during the period just ended.

*Withdrawals.* Withdrawals include the amount of any assets that are taken out of the business and distributed to the partners during the period just ended.

# Limited Liability Company

## Members' Equity

Members' Equity represents the net equity of the members in the limited liability company. Changes during the period are shown in the Statement of Members' Equity.

*Contributions.* Contributions include the amount of any additional assets that the members invested in the business during the period just ended.

*Withdrawals.* Withdrawals include the amount of any assets that are taken out of the business and distributed to the members during the period just ended.

# Sole Proprietorship

## Owner's Equity

The Owner's Equity of a sole proprietorship is similar to the equity of a partnership except that it represents the interest of one individual as opposed to a number of partners. Changes during the period should be shown in the Statement of Owner's Equity.

*Contributions.* Contributions include the amount of any additional assets that the owner invested in the business during the period just ended.

*Withdrawals.* Withdrawals include the amount of any assets that are taken out of the business and distributed to the owner during the period just ended.

## Comprehensive Income (Loss)

Comprehensive Income refers to net income plus "other comprehensive income," which includes certain revenues, expenses, gains, and losses that are reported as separate components of equity instead of net income. Other comprehensive income currently includes:

- Unrealized gains and losses on available-for-sale marketable securities.

- Unrealized gains and losses that result from a transfer of a debt security to the available-for-sale category from the held-to-maturity category.

- Foreign currency translation adjustments.

- Gains and losses on foreign currency transactions that are designed and are effective as economic hedges on a net investment in a foreign entity.

- A change in the fair value of a derivative instrument that qualifies as the hedging instrument in a cash flow derivative.

- Gains and losses on inter-company foreign currency transactions that are of a long-term investment nature when the entities to the transaction are consolidated, combined, or accounted for under the equity method.

- Minimum pension liability adjustments.

# Section 2
# Statement of Income

The Statement of Income reflects the results of operations for a period of time. The time covered by this statement usually ends at the Balance Sheet date. When the statement reflects a net loss, the title is generally changed to a Statement of Operations.

Hospitality organizations prepare income statements for both external users (e.g., potential investors, creditors, and owners not active in managing the business) and internal users (i.e., managers of the business). These statements differ in the amount of information presented. The statement presented to external users is typically relatively brief, providing only summary detail about the results of operations.

A sample GAAP income statement for external users follows. The degree of detail presented in the statement is somewhat discretionary, although captions for revenue, expenses, interest, depreciation, and income taxes are included unless the amounts are insignificant. To the extent that any individual revenue or expense item is significant, separate disclosures are made.

A format useful for analytical users such as managers operating the property, asset managers, and similarly involved parties is presented and discussed in Part I as the Summary Operating Statement.

**STATEMENT OF INCOME**

|  | Period | |
| --- | --- | --- |
|  | **Current Year** | **Prior Year** |
| **REVENUE** | | |
| Rooms | $ | $ |
| Food and Beverage | | |
| Other Operated Departments | | |
| Miscellaneous Income* | | |
| Total Revenue | | |
| **EXPENSES** | | |
| Rooms | | |
| Food and Beverage | | |
| Other Operated Departments | | |
| Administrative and General | | |
| Information and Telecommunications Systems | | |
| Sales and Marketing | | |
| Property Operation and Maintenance | | |
| Utilities | | |
| Management Fees | | |
| Non-Operating Expenses | | |
| Interest Expense | | |
| Depreciation and Amortization | | |
| Loss or (Gain) on the Disposition of Assets | | |
| Total Expenses | | |
| **INCOME BEFORE INCOME TAXES** | | |
| **INCOME TAXES** | | |
| Current | | |
| Deferred | | |
| Total Income Taxes | | |
| **NET INCOME** | $ | $ |

*For the Statement of Income, Miscellaneous Income includes non-operating income. This differs from Miscellaneous Income on the Summary Operating Statements.

# Section 3
# Statement of Comprehensive Income

The Statement of Comprehensive Income reflects non-owner activity that affects the entity's equity. The time period for this Statement follows the Statement of Income.

### STATEMENT OF COMPREHENSIVE INCOME

|  | Current Year | Prior Year |
|---|---|---|
| NET INCOME | $ | $ |
| | | |
| OTHER COMPREHENSIVE INCOME, BEFORE TAX | | |
| Unrealized gains on available-for-sale marketable securities | | |
| Unrealized gains for the period | | |
| Less: Reclassification adjustment included in net income | | |
| Unrealized gains on available-for-sale securities | | |
| Foreign currency translation adjustments | | |
| Minimum pension liability adjustments | | |
| | | |
| OTHER COMPREHENSIVE INCOME, BEFORE INCOME TAX | | |
| Income tax benefit (expense) related to items of other comprehensive income | | |
| | | |
| OTHER COMPREHENSIVE INCOME (LOSS), NET OF INCOME TAX | | |
| | | |
| COMPREHENSIVE INCOME | $ | $ |

# Section 4
# Statement of Owners' Equity

A separate Statement of Owners' Equity should be presented if there is significant activity in the accounts during the period. If net income or loss is the only change to the equity accounts in the period, it is permissible to reconcile the change in retained earnings at the bottom of the Statement of Income and exclude presentation of the separate owners' equity statement. The format of the owners' equity statement will depend on the type of entity. The following pages show examples of the type of presentation for corporations, partnerships, limited liability companies, and sole proprietorships.

# STATEMENT OF STOCKHOLDERS' EQUITY

| | Preferred Stock | | Common Stock | | Additional Paid-in Capital | Retained Earnings | Treasury Stock | | Accumulated Other Comprehensive Income (Loss), Net of Income Taxes | Total Stockholders' Equity |
| | Number of Shares Outstanding | Amount | Number of Shares Outstanding | Amount | | | Number of Shares | Amount | | |
|---|---|---|---|---|---|---|---|---|---|---|
| **BALANCE AT BEGINNING OF PRIOR YEAR** | | $ | | $ | $ | $ | | $ | $ | $ |
| Add (Deduct) | | | | | | | | | | |
| Net Income | | | | | | | | | | |
| Dividends Declared | | | | | | | | | | |
| Change in Unrealized Gains (Losses) | | | | | | | | | | |
| Net Proceeds from Sale of Stock | | | | | | | | | | |
| Treasury Stock Acquired | | | | | | | | | | |
| Other | | | | | | | | | | |
| **BALANCE AT END OF PRIOR YEAR** | | $ | | $ | $ | $ | | $ | $ | $ |
| Add (Deduct) | | | | | | | | | | |
| Net Income | | | | | | | | | | |
| Dividends Declared | | | | | | | | | | |
| Change in Unrealized Gains (Losses) | | | | | | | | | | |
| Net Proceeds from Sale of Stock | | | | | | | | | | |
| Treasury Stock Acquired | | | | | | | | | | |
| Other | | | | | | | | | | |
| **BALANCE AT END OF CURRENT YEAR** | | $ | | $ | $ | $ | | $ | $ | $ |

Cumulative foreign currency translation adjustments should also be reflected in this statement.

## STATEMENT OF PARTNERS' EQUITY

| | General Partners | Limited Partners | Accumulated Other Comprehensive Income (Loss), Net of Income Taxes | Total |
|---|---|---|---|---|
| BALANCE AT BEGINNING OF PRIOR YEAR | $ | $ | $ | $ |
| Add (Deduct) | | | | |
| Net Income | | | | |
| Contributions | | | | |
| Change in Unrealized Gains (Losses) | | | | |
| Withdrawals | | | | |
| Other | | | | |
| BALANCE AT END OF PRIOR YEAR | $ | $ | $ | $ |
| Add (Deduct) | | | | |
| Net Income | | | | |
| Contributions | | | | |
| Change in Unrealized Gains (Losses) | | | | |
| Withdrawals | | | | |
| Other | | | | |
| BALANCE AT END OF CURRENT YEAR | $ | $ | $ | $ |

Cumulative foreign currency translation adjustments should also be reflected in this statement.

## STATEMENT OF MEMBERS' EQUITY

|  | Members | Accumulated Other Comprehensive Income (Loss), Net of Income Taxes | Total |
|---|---|---|---|
| **BALANCE AT BEGINNING OF PRIOR YEAR** | $ | $ | $ |
| Add (Deduct) |  |  |  |
| Net Income |  |  |  |
| Contributions |  |  |  |
| Change in Unrealized Gains (Losses) |  |  |  |
| Withdrawals |  |  |  |
| Other |  |  |  |
| **BALANCE AT END OF PRIOR YEAR** | $ | $ | $ |
| Add (Deduct) |  |  |  |
| Net Income |  |  |  |
| Contributions |  |  |  |
| Change in Unrealized Gains (Losses) |  |  |  |
| Withdrawals |  |  |  |
| Other |  |  |  |
| **BALANCE AT END OF CURRENT YEAR** | $ | $ | $ |

Cumulative foreign currency translation adjustments should also be reflected in this statement.

## STATEMENT OF OWNER'S EQUITY

| | Owner | Accumulated Other Comprehensive Income (Loss), Net of Income Taxes | Total |
|---|---|---|---|
| **BALANCE AT BEGINNING OF PRIOR YEAR** | $ | $ | $ |
| Add (Deduct) | | | |
|     Net Income | | | |
|     Contributions | | | |
|     Change in Unrealized Gains (Losses) | | | |
|     Withdrawals | | | |
|     Other | | | |
| **BALANCE AT END OF PRIOR YEAR** | $ | $ | $ |
| Add (Deduct) | | | |
|     Net Income | | | |
|     Contributions | | | |
|     Change in Unrealized Gains (Losses) | | | |
|     Withdrawals | | | |
|     Other | | | |
| **BALANCE AT END OF CURRENT YEAR** | $ | $ | $ |

Cumulative foreign currency translation adjustments should also be reflected in this statement.

# Section 5
# Statement of Cash Flows

The Statement of Cash Flows summarizes the change in Cash and Temporary Cash Investments over the same period of time as that covered by the Statement of Income. Temporary Cash Investments are readily convertible investments with a maturity of less than three months at the time of purchase. The change in Cash and Temporary Cash Investments is classified as being derived from three activities: operating, investing, and financing.

Cash flows from operating activities represent the amount of cash generated by property operations. Operating activities include transactions involving acquiring, selling, and delivering goods for sale, as well as providing services. Cash flows from operating activities for a property include cash collected from customers, cash paid to employees and other suppliers, interest paid and received, taxes paid, and other operating payments and receipts. Cash from operating activities measures the amount that net income would have been if the cash method were used for measuring revenues and expenses.

Cash flows from investing activities represent changes in cash arising from transactions related to asset accounts that do not affect operations. Transactions include acquisition and disposal of property and facilities as well as the purchase and sale of investments, whether they are current or non-current.

Cash flows from financing activities represent cash changes related to liability and equity accounts that do not affect operations. These include obtaining and repaying debt (whether current or non-current), issuing and repurchasing stock, and dividend payments.

Cash flows from operating activities can be computed using either the direct or indirect method. The direct method identifies the operating cash receipts and cash disbursements. The indirect method determines the cash from operations by adjusting net income for non-cash items. The indirect method is useful for identifying why net income differs from cash from operating activities. The direct method is easier to interpret, as it specifically identifies the cash inflows and outflows from operations.

If the direct method of presentation is used, a summarized reconciliation of the significant items constituting the difference between net income and cash flows from operating activities should also be presented.

While the Statement of Cash Flows summarizes all significant sources and uses of cash, there is also a requirement to disclose significant non-cash investing and financing activities. This information is generally presented in narrative form immediately below the Statement. Items that should be disclosed include the purchase of capital assets by incurring debt or through capital lease transactions. Transactions involving the sale of assets where the seller provides financing is another example requiring disclosure.

## Direct Method

### Statement of Cash Flows

| | Period | |
|---|---|---|
| | **Current Year** | **Prior Year** |
| **CASH FLOWS FROM OPERATING ACTIVITIES** | | |
| Guest Receipts | $ | $ |
| Other Receipts | | |
| Payroll Disbursements | | |
| Other Operating Disbursements | | |
| Interest Paid | | |
| Income Taxes Paid | | |
| **Net Cash Provided By (Used In) Operating Activities** | | |
| **CASH FLOWS FROM INVESTING ACTIVITIES** | | |
| Capital Expenditures | | |
| Decrease (Increase) in Restricted Cash | | |
| Proceeds from Asset Dispositions | | |
| Proceeds from Sale of Investments | | |
| Purchases of Investments | | |
| **Net Cash Provided By (Used In) Investing Activities** | | |
| **CASH FLOWS FROM FINANCING ACTIVITIES** | | |
| Proceeds from Debt or Equity Financing | | |
| Debt Repayments | | |
| Dividends Paid | | |
| Distribution to Owners/Partners | | |
| **Net Cash Provided By (Used In) Financing Activities** | | |
| **INCREASE (DECREASE) IN CASH AND TEMPORARY CASH INVESTMENTS** | | |
| **CASH AND TEMPORARY CASH INVESTMENTS, BEGINNING OF PERIOD** | | |
| **CASH AND TEMPORARY CASH INVESTMENTS, END OF PERIOD** | $ | $ |

**SUPPLEMENTAL INFORMATION RELATED TO NONCASH INVESTING AND FINANCING ACTIVITIES**
(DISCLOSE SIGNIFICANT ITEMS SEPARATELY.)

# Indirect Method

## Statement of Cash Flows

|  | Period | |
|  | Current Year | Prior Year |
| --- | --- | --- |

**CASH FLOWS FROM OPERATING ACTIVITIES**
Net Income $ $
Adjustments to Reconcile Net Income
    To Cash Provided By (Used In) Operating Activities:
Depreciation and Amortization
Loss (Gain) on Sale of Property and Equipment
Deferred Taxes
Decrease (Increase) in Accounts Receivable
Decrease (Increase) in Inventory
Decrease (Increase) in Prepaids
Increase (Decrease) in Payables
Increase (Decrease) in Accruals
    **Net Cash Provided By (Used In) Operating
    Activities**

**CASH FLOWS FROM INVESTING ACTIVITIES**
Capital Expenditures
Decrease (Increase) in Restricted Cash
Proceeds from Asset Dispositions
Proceeds from Sale of Investments
Purchases of Investments
    **Net Cash Provided By (Used In) Investing
    Activities**

**CASH FLOWS FROM FINANCING ACTIVITIES**
Proceeds from Debt or Equity Financing
Debt Repayments
Dividends Paid
Distribution to Owners/Partners
    **Net Cash Provided By (Used In) Financing
    Activities**

**INCREASE (DECREASE) IN CASH AND TEMPORARY
  CASH INVESTMENTS**

**CASH AND TEMPORARY CASH INVESTMENTS, BEGINNING
  OF PERIOD**

**CASH AND TEMPORARY CASH INVESTMENTS, END OF PERIOD** $ $

**CASH PAID FOR INTEREST**

**CASH PAID FOR INCOME TAXES**

**SUPPLEMENTAL INFORMATION RELATED TO NONCASH INVESTING AND FINANCING ACTIVITIES
  (DISCLOSE SIGNIFICANT ITEMS SEPARATELY)**

## Cash Flows from Operating Activities

### Guest Receipts

Guest Receipts includes all receipts from guest-related activities including those applicable to unearned income.

### Other Receipts

Other Receipts includes proceeds from transactions other than with guests; for example, from casual sales of furnishings, salvage, interest and dividends received, and other activities.

### Payroll Disbursements

Payroll Disbursements includes salary and wage payments as well as related payments for employee benefits.

### Other Operating Disbursements

Other Operating Disbursements includes payments for food and beverage, other merchandise and supplies, energy, rent, taxes other than income, franchise and other management fees, and other expenditures incurred by operations.

### Interest Paid

Interest Paid includes cash payments to lenders and other creditors for interest. The amount should be shown net of interest capitalized.

### Income Taxes Paid

Income Taxes Paid includes all payments for taxes based on income. It does not include amounts paid for sales or occupancy taxes.

## Cash Flows from Investing Activities

### Capital Expenditures

Capital Expenditures represents payments to purchase property, buildings, equipment, and other productive assets. These payments include interest payments capitalized as part of the cost of those assets. A separate disclosure may be appropriate for the portion of the capital expenditures that results in an increase in the revenue-generating capacity of the lodging property. Separating cash payments that represent an increase in revenue-generating capacity from cash payments that are required to maintain operating capacity is helpful in enabling users to determine whether the lodging property is investing adequately in the maintenance of its operating capacity.

## Decrease (Increase) in Restricted Cash

The change in the non-current restricted cash is included in this item. The change represents the difference between the additional cash set aside or restricted and the use of those funds for the restricted purpose.

## Proceeds from Asset Dispositions

The Proceeds from Asset Dispositions, reduced by selling cost payments, are included in this item. This item should not include any amount of the sales consideration that has been financed by the seller.

## Proceeds from Sale of Investments

The net Proceeds from the Sale of Investments, after deduction of selling expenses, should be included in this item.

## Purchases of Investments

The purchase price paid for investments, including the transaction costs paid, should be included in this item.

## Cash Flows from Financing Activities

## Proceeds from Debt or Equity Financing

The net proceeds after deduction of transaction costs should be included in this item. Separate captions are shown if amounts are significant. This item includes long- and short-term financing.

## Debt Repayments

Aggregate principal repayments on indebtedness should be included in this item.

## Dividends and Distributions Paid

The amount of Dividends Paid to owners should be included. Other distributions to owners should be included, with appropriate modification of the caption if the entity is not a corporation.

# Section 6
# Notes to the Financial Statements

In order for a financial presentation to be complete, the financial statements are accompanied by explanatory notes. The notes should describe all significant accounting policies followed by the organization. Commonly required disclosures include, but are not limited to, policies regarding the following:

- Description of business
- Earnings per share
- Stock-based compensation
- Basis of consolidation
- Use of estimates
- Cash and temporary cash investments
- Inventory methods and valuation
- Accounting for investments, including the valuation of marketable securities
- Property, plant, and equipment
- Depreciation and amortization policies
- Intangibles—Goodwill
- Accounting for deferred charges
- Advertising costs
- Accounting for pensions
- Revenue recognition
- Accounting for income taxes
- Fair value of financial instruments
- Capitalization
- Lease disclosure
- Computation of net income (loss) per share (only public companies)
- Foreign currency translation
- Concentration of credit risk

Disclosure of accounting policy–related footnotes should be followed by such additional notes as are necessary to provide for full disclosure of all significant events or conditions reflected in the financial statements (including adequate disclosure of all significant commitments and contingencies mentioned on the

Balance Sheet), or as otherwise required by the rules of professional accounting or regulatory organizations. Typical events and conditions that are disclosed in the notes accompanying financial statements include the following:

- Changes in accounting methods
- Long-term debt agreements
- Pension and/or profit-sharing plans
- Other post-retirement and post-employment benefits
- Income taxes
- Long-term contracts
- Extraordinary items of income or expense
- Significant long-term commitments, including leases
- Foreign operations
- Related-party transactions
- Contingent liabilities, including pending litigation
- Subsequent events
- Stockholders' equity transactions
- Financial instruments (including derivatives)
- Impairment or disposal of long-lived assets
- Restructuring costs
- Extinguishment of debt
- Discontinued operations
- Business combinations
- Accumulated other comprehensive income (loss)
- Business segment information (public companies only)
- Quarterly financial information (public companies only)
- Organization (geographic and nature of business)
- Major customers

# Part III
# Financial Ratios and
# Operating Metrics

The use of financial ratios and operating metrics as a basis of comparison, measurement, and communication is prevalent within the lodging industry. The usefulness of these tools is predicated on a commonality of definition and understanding. The various financial ratios and operating metrics that can be developed and be useful are numerous. The intent of this section is to provide a consistent, uniform definition of basic lodging industry financial ratios and operating metrics. This section includes only those financial ratios and operating metrics that are in widespread general use within the industry. It is not intended to be a complete listing and definition of all possible relevant financial ratios and operating metrics.

# Ratio Analysis

Financial statements issued by lodging properties contain a large amount of information. A thorough analysis of this information requires more than simply reading the reported figures and other disclosures. Users of financial statements need to be able to interpret the reported results, and make them yield information that reveals aspects of the property's financial situation or operation that could otherwise go unnoticed. This is accomplished through analysis of financial ratios and operating metrics, which compares related facts and figures reported in the financial statements and supporting operating schedules.

A ratio gives mathematical expression to a relationship between two figures, and is calculated by dividing one figure by the other. Ratios are meaningful only when compared to useful criteria. Useful criteria with which to compare the results of ratio analysis include:

- Other properties and industry averages
- The corresponding ratio calculated for a prior period
- Planned (budgeted) ratio goals

Ratio analysis can be extremely useful. However, ratios are only indicators; they do not resolve problems or actually reveal what the problems may be. At best, when ratios vary significantly from past periods, budgeted standards, or industry averages, they indicate that problems may exist. When problems appear to exist, analysis and investigation is necessary to determine the appropriate corrective actions.

## Comparisons to Other Properties and Industry Averages

The comparison of financial performance measurements to other properties and industry averages can be valuable. However, care must be used when comparing the performance of one hotel's operation to the average performance of the industry at large, a competitive set of properties, or a comparable group or type of properties. Consider the following points:

- The data should be used as a benchmark to measure the performance of the subject hotel against properties of similar size, age, location, revenue mix, chain-segment, ownership structure, management, facilities and services offered, amenities offered, etc. Careful consideration should be given to the comparability of these criteria and the degree to which the criteria influence each revenue and expense item.

- Variances from the average should be used as an indication of the need for further investigation. There may be perfectly valid reasons why a particular hotel should be achieving a performance level above or below the industry-wide, competitive set, or comparable group average.

- The data presented are averages, not standards. You may wish to exceed the average profit and income levels and achieve lower expense ratios.

## Comparisons to Prior Periods or Budgets

While comparison to industry-wide, competitive set, or comparable property statistics has some use for general benchmarking of a property, an internal analysis of a hotel's operation from period to period or against planned goals (as expressed in the budget) is an invaluable practice. This discipline can provide insight to answer such questions as:

- How have revenues and expenses changed from period to period?

- What has been the correlation between movements in revenues, expenses, and rooms occupied?

- Which departments are ahead of or behind budget?

- Which departments are operating efficiently or inefficiently?

- Was the budget realistic?

Note that during the initial year of implementation of this *Uniform System,* comparisons to prior performance may be distorted if the historical data cannot be adjusted to conform to the Eleventh Revised Edition.

## Methods of Analysis—Fixed vs. Variable

There are various ways to analyze ratios and compare statistics. The proper method used is often dictated by the fixed or variable nature of the revenue or expense item.

### Fixed

In general, fixed revenues and expenses are those that are set by contractual agreement or established by third parties for periods of time, typically one year. The volume of business has little effect on the amount paid for these expense items or the revenues received. Examples of fixed expenses are property/liability insurance, property taxes, base annual salaries, and dues and subscriptions. Examples of fixed revenue could be rental payments from a restaurant or retail operation leasing space from the property.

### Variable

Variable revenues and expenses are those that are driven by the volume of business at the hotel. In the lodging industry, volume of business is predominantly measured by the number of rooms occupied, as well as number of food and beverage customers served. Variable expenses are closely tied to the number of rooms occupied and would include housekeeping costs, complimentary breakfast expense, laundry, and guest supplies. Rooms and food revenue are two examples of revenues that vary with the number of rooms occupied.

Some expenses vary directly with changes in revenue. Franchise fees, management fees, and credit card commissions are examples of expenses that frequently vary with changes in revenue.

### Semi-Variable

There are some revenue and expense items that have both fixed and variable components to them. For instance, Rooms departmental labor costs typically have a fixed component (management salaries) and a variable component (room attendant wages).

## Methods of Calculation and Comparison

The most common calculations made to analyze lodging data are as follows:

- Per occupied room
- Per available room
- Percentage of revenue
- Total dollars

Since the volume of rooms occupied most frequently drives *variable* revenues and expenses, these line items are most frequently analyzed on a per-occupied-room basis. On the other hand, *fixed* expenses are typically examined on a per-available-room or total dollar basis. Analysis of both fixed and variable expenses as a percentage of revenue can be valuable. Each method will provide the analyst with a different perspective. Often, multiple methods are necessary to gain a comprehensive picture of a property's performance.

When making industry-wide, competitive property, or comparable property comparisons, total dollar comparisons should not be used. Instead, measurements need to be scaled to account for differences in room counts. Therefore, fixed revenue and expense comparisons among properties are frequently made on a dollar-per-available-room basis. Measurements calculated on a dollar-per-occupied-room or percentage-of-revenue basis are already proportioned for comparable comparative analysis.

## Operating Metrics

Operating metrics assist owners and management in analyzing the operations of a lodging property. These operating metrics relate expenses to business volume and/or revenue and are useful for control purposes when the results are compared to budgeted or planned goals, as well as other properties and industry averages. Significant variations between actual results and budgeted results, planned goals, or other properties and industry averages may indicate the need for further investigation and analysis to determine underlying causes and appropriate corrective action.

Caution should be used when using operating ratios for comparison across competitive sets or comparable property groups. Several factors influence the relative market position of one property compared to another.

Operating metrics may be prepared at a variety of frequencies depending on user requirements. Some operating metrics are prepared and separately reported on a daily or weekly basis, with additional reporting provided with monthly financial reporting.

*Note for mixed-ownership hotels:* For lodging properties that include units owned by third parties, it is appropriate to develop a supplemental schedule of ratios and statistics that includes the performance of these units. The performance measurements that would be affected are identified in the Definitions section of Part III by two asterisks (**).

The following discussions present operating metrics for each operating department and select undistributed departments. After that, labor metrics that can be applied to all departments in a hotel are presented.

For each department we also provide recommended tables that present the key operating metrics for that department. The Financial Management Committee believes these metrics are critical to understand the performance of each department. Other pertinent metrics should be added as needed.

## Rooms Department Operating Metrics

The following tables are recommended for the presentation of key Rooms department operating metrics. After the tables, formulas are provided for select ratios, along with descriptions of their potential use.

| | Current Month | | | YTD | | |
|---|---|---|---|---|---|---|
| | Actual | Variance to Budget | Variance to Prior Year | Actual | Variance to Budget | Variance to Prior Year |
| Rooms Operating Metrics: Revenue Mix, % | | | | | | |
| Transient Rooms | | | | | | |
| -Retail | | | | | | |
| -Discount | | | | | | |
| -Negotiated | | | | | | |
| -Qualified | | | | | | |
| -Wholesale | | | | | | |
| Total Transient | | | | | | |
| Group Rooms | | | | | | |
| -Corporate | | | | | | |
| -Association/Convention | | | | | | |
| -Government | | | | | | |

*(continued)*

|  | Current Month | | | YTD | | |
|---|---|---|---|---|---|---|
|  | Actual | Variance to Budget | Variance to Prior Year | Actual | Variance to Budget | Variance to Prior Year |
| -Tour Wholesalers |  |  |  |  |  |  |
| -SMERF |  |  |  |  |  |  |
| Total Group Rooms |  |  |  |  |  |  |
| Contract Rooms |  |  |  |  |  |  |
| Other Rooms Revenue |  |  |  |  |  |  |
| Less: Allowances |  |  |  |  |  |  |
| Total Rooms Revenue Mix |  |  |  |  |  |  |
| **Rooms Operating Metrics: Average Daily Rate** | | | | | | |
| Transient Rooms |  |  |  |  |  |  |
| -Retail |  |  |  |  |  |  |
| -Discount |  |  |  |  |  |  |
| -Negotiated |  |  |  |  |  |  |
| -Qualified |  |  |  |  |  |  |
| -Wholesale |  |  |  |  |  |  |
| Total Transient |  |  |  |  |  |  |
| Group Rooms |  |  |  |  |  |  |
| -Corporate |  |  |  |  |  |  |
| -Association/Convention |  |  |  |  |  |  |
| -Government |  |  |  |  |  |  |
| -Tour Wholesalers |  |  |  |  |  |  |
| -SMERF |  |  |  |  |  |  |
| Total Group Rooms |  |  |  |  |  |  |
| Contract Rooms |  |  |  |  |  |  |
| Total ADR (inclusive of Other Rooms Rev. & Net of Allowances) |  |  |  |  |  |  |
| **Rooms Operating Metrics: Room Inventory** | | | | | | |
| 1.  Total Room Inventory  (Total Keys in Property) |  |  |  |  |  |  |
| 2.  Seasonally Closed Rooms |  |  |  |  |  |  |
| 3.  Extended Closed Rooms |  |  |  |  |  |  |
| 4.  Rooms for Permanent House Use |  |  |  |  |  |  |
| 5.  Total Rooms Not Available for Sale (2 + 3 + 4) |  |  |  |  |  |  |
| 6.  Rooms Available (1 - 5) |  |  |  |  |  |  |
| **Room Occupancy Statistics** | | | | | | |
| 7.  Transient Rooms |  |  |  |  |  |  |
| -Retail |  |  |  |  |  |  |
| -Discount |  |  |  |  |  |  |
| -Negotiated |  |  |  |  |  |  |
| -Qualified |  |  |  |  |  |  |
| -Wholesale |  |  |  |  |  |  |
| Total Transient |  |  |  |  |  |  |
| 8.  Group Rooms |  |  |  |  |  |  |
| -Corporate |  |  |  |  |  |  |
| -Association/Convention |  |  |  |  |  |  |
| -Government |  |  |  |  |  |  |
| -Tour Wholesalers |  |  |  |  |  |  |
| -SMERF |  |  |  |  |  |  |
| Total Group Rooms |  |  |  |  |  |  |
| 9.  Contract Rooms |  |  |  |  |  |  |
| 10.  Rooms Sold |  |  |  |  |  |  |

| | Current Month | | | YTD | | |
|---|---|---|---|---|---|---|
| | Actual | Variance to Budget | Variance to Prior Year | Actual | Variance to Budget | Variance to Prior Year |
| 12. Complimentary Rooms | | | | | | |
| 13. Rooms Occupied | | | | | | |
| 14. Vacant Rooms | | | | | | |
| 6. Rooms Available | | | | | | |
| | | | | | | |
| 11. Occupancy % (10/6) | | | | | | |
| **Number of Guests** | | | | | | |
| 19. Transient | | | | | | |
| 20. Group | | | | | | |
| 21. Contract | | | | | | |
| 22. Complimentary | | | | | | |
| 23. Total Guests | | | | | | |
| **Per Available Room Statistics** | | | | | | |
| Revenue per Available Room | | | | | | |
| Labor Costs and Related Expenses | | | | | | |
| Other Expenses | | | | | | |
| Rooms Department Profit per Available Room | | | | | | |
| **Per Occupied Room Statistics** | | | | | | |
| Average Daily Rate | | | | | | |
| | | | | | | |
| Total Labor Costs and Related Expenses per Occupied Room | | | | | | |
| | | | | | | |
| *Other Expenses* | | | | | | |
| Cleaning Supplies | | | | | | |
| Cluster Services | | | | | | |
| Commissions | | | | | | |
| Commissions and Fees Group | | | | | | |
| Complimentary Food & Beverage | | | | | | |
| Complimentary In-Room Media/Entertainment | | | | | | |
| Complimentary Services and Gifts | | | | | | |
| Contract Services | | | | | | |
| Corporate Office Reimbursables | | | | | | |
| Decoration | | | | | | |
| Dues and Subscriptions | | | | | | |
| Entertainment—In House | | | | | | |
| Equipment Rental | | | | | | |
| Guest Relocation | | | | | | |
| Guest Supplies | | | | | | |
| Guest Transportation | | | | | | |
| Laundry and Dry Cleaning | | | | | | |
| Licenses and Permits | | | | | | |
| Linen | | | | | | |
| Miscellaneous | | | | | | |
| Operating Supplies | | | | | | |
| Postage and Overnight Delivery Charges | | | | | | |
| Printing and Stationery | | | | | | |
| Reservations | | | | | | |
| Royalty Fees | | | | | | |

*(continued)*

| | Current Month | | | YTD | | |
|---|---|---|---|---|---|---|
| | Actual | Variance to Budget | Variance to Prior Year | Actual | Variance to Budget | Variance to Prior Year |
| Training | | | | | | |
| Travel Meals and Entertainment | | | | | | |
| Travel Other | | | | | | |
| Uniform Cost | | | | | | |
| Uniform Laundry | | | | | | |
| Total Expenses per Occupied Room | | | | | | |
| Rooms Department Profit per Occupied  Room | | | | | | |

The room segmentation presented in *Rooms—Schedule 1* is the preferred method of reporting rooms revenue. With the development of the revenue management discipline and the evolution of the Internet and other technologies, the relevant means of reporting and reviewing rooms revenue is constantly changing. At the time of the writing of this book, one prominent approach to viewing rooms revenue is to track and analyze it by booking channel or source. Therefore, it is recommended, but not required, that rooms revenue be reported by booking channel as supplemental information.

### Average Daily Rate

Although room rates may vary seasonally, by market segment, or by room type within a property, most lodging properties calculate an overall average room rate, referred to as the average daily rate (ADR). The ADR reveals the average rate charged per sold room and is calculated by dividing total rooms revenue for a period by the number of rooms sold during that period. Rooms sold includes rooms sold on a paid basis, as well as rooms sold without charge in connection with a promotion or contract. Complimentary rooms are not included in the denominator of the ADR calculation. The ADR is calculated as follows:

$$\text{ADR} \quad = \quad \frac{\text{Total Rooms Revenue}}{\text{Rooms Sold}}$$

### ADR per Revenue Segment

For analytical purposes, many lodging properties calculate an ADR for each revenue segment (transient, group, and contract). The ADR for a revenue segment reveals the average rate charged per sold room and is calculated by dividing rooms revenue for a specific revenue segment for a period by the number of rooms sold to guests in that revenue segment during that period. Rooms sold by revenue segment includes rooms sold on a paid basis, as well as rooms sold without charge in connection with a promotion or contract. Complimentary rooms are not included in the denominator of the ADR per revenue segment calculation. The ADR for a revenue segment is calculated as follows:

$$\frac{\text{Average Room Rate}}{\text{per Revenue Segment}} \quad = \quad \frac{\text{Gross Room Revenue for Revenue Segment}}{\text{Rooms Sold to that Revenue Segment}}$$

## Rooms Revenue per Available Room

Rooms revenue per available room (RevPAR) measures the rooms revenue yield a property achieves relative to the rooms available in the property for a period. RevPAR includes the influence of two factors—occupancy and ADR. RevPAR can be used as a way to compare rooms revenue results with prior period results or to compare actual to budgeted results. In addition, since the rooms revenue is scaled by the number of rooms at the property, it can be used as one comparison of the rooms revenue yield of a property to its competitors or comparable properties. RevPAR is calculated as follows:

$$\text{RevPAR} = \frac{\text{Total Rooms Revenue}}{\text{Rooms Available}}$$

## Total Operating Revenue per Available Room

Total operating revenue per available room (Total RevPAR) measures the total operating revenue yield a property achieves relative to the rooms available in the property for a period. Total RevPAR can be used as one measure of total operating revenue change from prior period results or to compare actual to budgeted results. Since the total operating revenue is scaled by the number of rooms at the property, it can be used as one comparison of the revenue yield of a property to its competitors or comparable properties. For properties with significant revenue sources other than rooms revenue, this may be a better indicator of revenue yield or growth than RevPAR. Total RevPAR is calculated as follows:

$$\text{Total RevPAR} = \frac{\text{Total Operating Revenue}}{\text{Rooms Available}}$$

# Room Statistics and Occupancy Ratios

Lodging properties usually supplement the rooms operation information reported on the Summary Operating Statement and Statement of Income with occupancy ratio results. Occupancy ratios measure the success of the rooms operation in selling the primary product of the property. In order to calculate basic occupancy ratios, various rooms statistics must be kept during the period.

The following is a list with definitions of several common rooms statistics and occupancy ratios. Note that the term "room nights" can be substituted for the word "rooms" in the following measurements and ratio definitions.

(1)    Total Room Inventory
        Rooms Not Available for Sale:
(2)        Seasonally Closed Rooms
(3)        Extended Closed Rooms
(4)        Rooms for Permanent House Use
(5)    Total Rooms Not Available for Sale
(6)    Rooms Available
        Number of Rooms Sold:*
(7)        Transient Rooms Sold
(8)        Group Rooms Sold
(9)        Contract Rooms Sold

| | |
|---|---|
| (10) | Rooms Sold |
| (11) | Occupancy % |
| (12) | Complimentary Rooms Occupied |
| (13) | Rooms Occupied |
| (14) | Vacant Rooms |
| | Occupancy %: |
| (15) | Transient % |
| (16) | Group % |
| (17) | Contract % |
| (18) | Complimentary % |
| | Number of Guests: |
| (19) | Transient |
| (20) | Group |
| (21) | Contract |
| (22) | Complimentary |
| (23) | Total Guests |
| (24) | Arrivals |
| (25) | Average Length of Stay |

*See *Rooms—Schedule 1* for definitions of types of guests by revenue category.

## DEFINITIONS:

(1) **Total Room Inventory**

Total number of guestrooms (keys) in a property whether available for sale or not. Included are (5) Total Rooms Not Available for Sale, (13) Rooms Occupied, and (14) Vacant Rooms.

(2) **Seasonally Closed Rooms**

When all operations of a hotel are closed for a minimum of 30 consecutive days due to seasonal demand patterns, then the rooms for this period should be removed from the annual salable inventory. The hotel must be consistently closed year-to-year.

(3) **Extended Closed Rooms**

Those rooms removed from salable inventory for a period of six consecutive months or more. Examples include rooms that are damaged due to a hurricane, earthquake, or fire, where there is intent to return the rooms to salable inventory.

(4) **Rooms for Permanent House Use**

Those rooms removed from salable inventory for a minimum of six consecutive months for use by a hotel employee (e.g., manager's apartment).

(5) **Total Rooms Not Available for Sale**

Total of rooms that are (2) Seasonally Closed, (3) Extended Closed, or used for (4) Permanent House Use.

(6) **Rooms Available\*\***

Total Room Inventory (1) less (5) Total Rooms Not Available for Sale.

(7) **Transient Rooms Sold**

Total rooms sold to guests on an individual basis. Included are rooms sold on a paid basis, as well as rooms sold on a gratis basis in connection with a promotion or contract.

(8)    **Group Rooms Sold**

Total rooms sold to guests as part of a group (10 rooms or more). Included are rooms sold on a paid basis, as well as rooms sold on a gratis basis in connection with a promotion or contract.

(9)    **Contract Rooms Sold**

Total rooms sold to guests as part of a special contract, generally of a longer-term nature (i.e., multiple weeks or months). Included are rooms sold on a paid basis, as well as rooms sold on a gratis basis in connection with a promotion or contract.

(10)    **Rooms Sold**

Total rooms sold to (7) Transient, (8) Group and (9) Contract guests.

(12)    **Complimentary Rooms Occupied**

Free rooms provided to any guest, often for marketing purposes, but not related to an existing contractual relationship. Examples of complimentary rooms include rooms provided on a gratis basis to owners, employees, people on familiarization tours, friends, and family. Also included are rooms used by the hotel on a short-term basis (e.g., employee relocation, manager-on-duty, etc.).

Not classified as complimentary rooms are rooms provided due to a trade-out arrangement, rooms provided in connection with a promotion (e.g., stay two nights, get one free), or rooms provided as part of a group contract (e.g., book 50 rooms, get one free). These rooms should be classified as one of the revenue categories (transient, group, or contract).

(13)    **Rooms Occupied\*\***

Total rooms sold to (7) Transient, (8) Group, and (9) Contract guests and occupied by (12) Complimentary guests.

(14)    **Vacant Rooms**

Rooms Available (6) less (13) Rooms Occupied. Vacant rooms can be classified into the following sub-categories:

*Rooms Out-of-Order:* Those rooms removed from salable inventory for a period of less than six consecutive months due to renovation or a temporary fault or problem rendering them inadequate for occupancy.

*Temporary Closed Rooms:* Those rooms removed from salable inventory on a discretionary basis for a period of less than six consecutive months.

*Rooms Unoccupied:* Those rooms available for sale, but not occupied by a paying or complimentary guest.

(19)    **Number of Guests—Transient**

Total guests traveling as individuals.

(20)    **Number of Guests—Group**

Total guests traveling as part of a group.

(21)    **Number of Guests—Contract**

Total guests who occupy their room through a special contract.

(22)    **Number of Guests—Complimentary**

Total persons staying on a complimentary basis as described in #12 above.

(23)     **Total Guests**
         Total (19) Transient, (20) Group, (21) Contract, and (22) Complimentary guests.

(24)     **Arrivals**
         Number of room check-ins, both paying and complimentary.

### FORMULAS:

(11)   Occupancy %   $= \dfrac{(10) \quad \text{Rooms Sold}}{(6) \quad \text{Rooms Available}} \times 100$

(15)   Occupancy % Transient   $= \dfrac{(7) \quad \text{Transient Rooms Sold}}{(6) \quad \text{Rooms Available}} \times 100$

(16)   Occupancy % Group   $= \dfrac{(8) \quad \text{Group Rooms Sold}}{(6) \quad \text{Rooms Available}} \times 100$

(17)   Occupancy % Contract   $= \dfrac{(9) \quad \text{Contract Rooms Sold}}{(6) \quad \text{Rooms Available}} \times 100$

(18)   Occupancy % Complimentary   $= \dfrac{(12) \ \text{Complimentary Rooms Occupied}}{(6) \quad \text{Rooms Available}} \times 100$

(25)   Average Length of Stay   $= \dfrac{(13) \quad \text{Rooms Occupied}}{(24) \quad \text{Arrivals}} \times 100$

**\*\*Note for lodging properties with mixed-ownership units:** When a lodging property includes rooms owned by parties other than the owner of the hotel, it is appropriate to develop a supplemental schedule of ratios and statistics that includes the performance of such elements. The ratios and statistics in this schedule can be used when providing data to independent industry reporting agencies in order to reflect the performance of the entire property.

The measurements that are affected include rooms available, rooms sold, and room revenue. These measurements are used to calculate occupancy, ADR, and RevPAR. When preparing the ratios and statistics in the supplemental schedule, note the following guidance:

- *Rooms Available:* third-party-owned units under the control of hotel management for the purpose of renting to guests other than the unit owners should be added to the Rooms Available of the hotel.

- *Rooms Sold:* third-party-owned units that are rented to guests other than the unit owners should be added to the Rooms Sold of the hotel.

- *Rooms Revenue:* revenue earned for the rental of third-party-owned units to guests other than the unit owners should be added to rooms revenue as defined in the discussion of Schedule 1.

# Food and Beverage Department Operating Metrics

The following tables are recommended for the presentation of key food and beverage department operating metrics. The tables are followed by definitions of terminology as used in this section. See Schedule 2 for additional definitions. The discussion continues with metrics developed by the AH&LA Food and Beverage Council in 2012 for the purpose of benchmarking hotel food and beverage operations. Finally, formulas are provided for select ratios, along with descriptions of their potential use.

| | Current Month | | | YTD | | |
|---|---|---|---|---|---|---|
| | Actual | Variance to Budget | Variance to Prior Year | Actual | Variance to Budget | Variance to Prior Year |
| **Food and Beverage Operating Metrics: Revenue Mix, %** | | | | | | |
| F&B Venue Revenue | | | | | | |
| Catering and Banquets Revenue | | | | | | |
| In-Room Dining Revenue | | | | | | |
| Audiovisual | | | | | | |
| Function Room Rental Revenue | | | | | | |
| Other | | | | | | |
| Total | | | | | | |
| **Food and Beverage Operating Metrics: Average Check, $** | | | | | | |
| Food | | | | | | |
| Beverage | | | | | | |
| Food and Beverage | | | | | | |
| Food and Beverage Venues | | | | | | |
| Banquet/Conference/Catering | | | | | | |
| In-Room Dining | | | | | | |
| Other | | | | | | |
| Total | | | | | | |
| **Food and Beverage Operating Metrics: Cost of Food Sales, %** | | | | | | |
| Food and Beverage Venues | | | | | | |
| Banquet/Conference/Catering | | | | | | |
| In-Room Dining | | | | | | |
| Total | | | | | | |
| **Food and Beverage Operating Metrics: Cost of Beverage Sales, %** | | | | | | |
| Food and Beverage Venues | | | | | | |
| Banquet/Conference/Catering | | | | | | |
| In-Room Dining | | | | | | |
| Total | | | | | | |
| **Food and Beverage Operating Metrics: Inventory Turns** | | | | | | |
| Inventory Turns | | | | | | |
| Liquor | | | | | | |
| Wine | | | | | | |
| Bottled Beer | | | | | | |
| Draft Beer | | | | | | |
| Number of Days of Inventory on Hand | | | | | | |

*(continued)*

| | Current Month | | | YTD | | |
|---|---|---|---|---|---|---|
| | Actual | Variance to Budget | Variance to Prior Year | Actual | Variance to Budget | Variance to Prior Year |
| **Revenue: Food and Beverage Venues** | | | | | | |
| F&B Venue Revenue per Available Seat, $ | | | | | | |
| F&B Venue Revenue per Customer, $ | | | | | | |
| **Revenue: Catering and Banquets** | | | | | | |
| Catering and Banquet Revenue per Group Room Sold, $ | | | | | | |
| Catering and Banquet Revenue per Square Foot (Meter) of Function Space, $ | | | | | | |
| **Revenue: Function Room Rentals** | | | | | | |
| Function Room Rental Revenue per Group Room Sold, $ | | | | | | |
| Function Room Rental Revenue per Square Foot (Meter) of Function Space, $ | | | | | | |
| **Revenue: Audiovisual Revenue** | | | | | | |
| Audiovisual Revenue per Group Room Sold, $ | | | | | | |
| Audiovisual Revenue per Square Foot (Meter) of Function Space, $ | | | | | | |
| Audiovisual Revenue Cost of Sales, % | | | | | | |
| **Revenue: In-Room Dining** | | | | | | |
| In-Room Dining Revenue per Rooms Sold, $ | | | | | | |
| **Revenue: Total F&B Revenue** | | | | | | |
| Total F&B Revenue per Available Room, $ | | | | | | |

## Definitions

*Venue.* An individual food and beverage facility in a hotel, usually a restaurant or lounge. Banquet rooms, guestrooms, group functions outside the property, and the front desk are not considered food and beverage venues.

*Number of Available Seats.* The total number of available seats in a food and beverage venue for the purpose of consuming food and beverage items. The number should be based on how the venue is set up during normal operations. Outdoor seating is not included unless it is available year-round; temporary seating is not included.

*Number of Available Seats per Venue.* The number of available seats in a particular venue.

*Function Space.* Space between four walls used for meal functions and meeting room sets. Outdoor space is not included.

*Customer.* One person served in a food and beverage venue or function space.

*Total Customers.* Total number of customers who are served in a food and beverage venue or function space.

# FOOD AND BEVERAGE VENUES—REVENUE AND DEPARTMENTAL PROFIT STATISTICS

| Venue Name | Number of Seats | Revenue Per Available Seat, $ | | | | | | Departmental Profit Per Available Seat, $ | | | | | |
|---|---|---|---|---|---|---|---|---|---|---|---|---|---|
| | | Current Month | | | YTD | | | Current Month | | | YTD | | |
| | | Actual, $ | Variance to Budget, $ | Variance to Prior Year, $ | Actual, $ | Variance to Budget, $ | Variance to Prior Year, $ | Actual, $ | Variance to Budget, $ | Variance to Prior Year, $ | Actual, $ | Variance to Budget, $ | Variance to Prior Year, $ |
| Venue # 1 | | | | | | | | | | | | | |
| Venue # 2 | | | | | | | | | | | | | |
| Venue # 3 | | | | | | | | | | | | | |
| Total | | | | | | | | | | | | | |

# FOOD AND BEVERAGE VENUES—COST STATISTICS

| Venue Name | Number of Seats | Cost of Food Sales, % | | | | | | Cost of Beverage Sales, % | | | | | |
|---|---|---|---|---|---|---|---|---|---|---|---|---|---|
| | | Current Month | | | YTD | | | Current Month | | | YTD | | |
| | | Actual, % | Variance to Budget, PPT* | Variance to Prior Year, PPT* | Actual, % | Variance to Budget, PPT* | Variance to Prior Year, PPT* | Actual, % | Variance to Budget, PPT* | Variance to Prior Year, PPT* | Actual, % | Variance to Budget, PPT* | Variance to Prior Year, PPT* |
| Venue # 1 | | | | | | | | | | | | | |
| Venue # 2 | | | | | | | | | | | | | |
| Venue # 3 | | | | | | | | | | | | | |
| Total | | | | | | | | | | | | | |

* Percentage Point

# FOOD AND BEVERAGE VENUES—MEAL PERIOD STATISTICS

| Venue Name | Number of Seats | Meal Period | Number of Customers | | | | | | Average Check, $ | | | | | | |
| | | | Current Month | | | YTD | | | Current Month | | | YTD | | | |
| | | | Actual | Variance to Budget | Variance to Prior Year | Actual | Variance to Budget | Variance to Prior Year | Actual, $ | Variance to Budget, $ | Variance to Prior Year, $ | Actual, $ | Variance to Budget, $ | Variance to Prior Year, $ |
|---|---|---|---|---|---|---|---|---|---|---|---|---|---|---|
| Venue # 1 | | Breakfast | | | | | | | | | | | | |
| | | Lunch | | | | | | | | | | | | |
| | | Dinner | | | | | | | | | | | | |
| | | Other | | | | | | | | | | | | |
| | | **Total** | | | | | | | | | | | | |
| Venue # 2 | | Breakfast | | | | | | | | | | | | |
| | | Lunch | | | | | | | | | | | | |
| | | Dinner | | | | | | | | | | | | |
| | | Other | | | | | | | | | | | | |
| | | **Total** | | | | | | | | | | | | |
| Venue # 3 | | Breakfast | | | | | | | | | | | | |
| | | Lunch | | | | | | | | | | | | |
| | | Dinner | | | | | | | | | | | | |
| | | Other | | | | | | | | | | | | |
| | | **Total** | | | | | | | | | | | | |
| Total Restaurant Facilities | | Breakfast | | | | | | | | | | | | |
| | | Lunch | | | | | | | | | | | | |
| | | Dinner | | | | | | | | | | | | |
| | | Other | | | | | | | | | | | | |
| | | **Total** | | | | | | | | | | | | |

*Average Customer Value.* Venue Food Revenue and Venue Beverage Revenue divided by the Total Customers served in the venue. This can be further determined by meal period.

*Meal Period.* Breakfast, lunch, or dinner, defined by time of day.

*Total Customers per Meal Period by Venue.* Number of customers during a specific meal period in an individual venue.

*F&B Venue Revenue.* The total of Venue Food Revenue, Venue Beverage Revenue, Cover Charges, Surcharges and Service Charges, and Miscellaneous Other Revenue for a specific venue.

*Catering and Banquets Revenue.* The total of Banquet/Conference/ Catering Food Revenue, Banquet/Conference/Catering Beverage Revenue, Audiovisual, Function Room Rental and Setup Charges, Surcharges and Service Charges, and Miscellaneous Other Revenue generated in a hotel's function space.

*In-Room Dining Revenue.* The total of In-Room Dining Food Revenue, In-Room Dining Beverage Revenue, and Surcharges and Service Charges for food and beverages delivered to guests in their guestrooms.

*Function Room Rental Revenue.* The equivalent of Function Room Rentals and Setup Charges on Schedule 2.

*Total F&B Revenue.* The sum of Total Food Revenue, Total Beverage Revenue, and Total Other Revenue. This is the equivalent of Total Revenue on Schedule 2.

## AH&LA Food and Beverage Council Metrics

### Catering/Banquet Revenue per Square Foot (Meter) of Function Space

This is the total of Catering and Banquets Revenue divided by the total amount of Function Space measured in square feet or square meters. This comparison helps determine how effectively the sales staff is driving revenues for this specialized space.

$$\frac{\text{Catering and Banquet Revenue}}{\text{per Square ft./m}} = \frac{\text{Catering and Banquets Revenue}}{\text{Square ft./m of Function Space}}$$

### F&B Venue Revenue per Available Seat

This metric measures the F&B Venue Revenue yield a food and beverage venue achieves relative to the seats available in the venue for a period. This can be used when comparing the yield of one venue with a competitor or comparable venue.

$$\frac{\text{F\&B Venue Revenue}}{\text{per Available Seat}} = \frac{\text{F\&B Venue Revenue}}{\text{Number of Available Seats}}$$

### F&B Venue Revenue per Customer

This operating metric reveals the amount of the average food and beverage check per customer and is calculated by dividing F&B Venue Revenue by the number of customers. This analysis is typically carried out for each meal period and each venue.

$$\text{F\&B Venue Revenue per Customer} = \frac{\text{F\&B Venue Revenue}}{\text{Number of Customers}}$$

### In-Room Dining Revenue per Occupied Room

This operating metric reveals the amount of the in-room dining check per occupied room and is calculated by dividing In-Room Dining Revenue by the total number of rooms sold. This analysis is typically carried out for each meal period.

$$\frac{\text{In-Room Dining Revenue}}{\text{per Occupied Room}} = \frac{\text{In-Room Dining Revenue}}{\text{Rooms Sold}}$$

### Total F&B Revenue per Available Room

This metric measures the Total F&B Revenue yield a hotel achieves relative to the number of available rooms at a property. This can be used when comparing the yield of one hotel with a competitor or comparable hotel.

$$\text{Total F\&B Revenue per Available Room} = \frac{\text{Total F\&B Revenue}}{\text{Rooms Available}}$$

## Additional Food and Beverage Metrics

### Revenue Mix

This ratio is calculated based on the revenue received by the venues, catering and banquets, in-room dining, audiovisual, and function room rentals as percentages of Total F&B Revenue. It is useful to understand how food and beverage revenues are derived when evaluating the performance of the operation. For the complete revenue mix, perform the following calculation for each revenue reference.

$$\text{Revenue Mix Percentage} = \frac{\text{F\&B Venue Revenue (or other revenue reference)}}{\text{Total F\&B Revenue}} \times 100$$

### Average Food Check

This operating ratio reveals the amount of the average food check per customer and is calculated by dividing Total Food Revenue by the number of customers. This analysis is typically carried out for each meal period and each venue.

$$\text{Average Food Check} = \frac{\text{Total Food Revenue}}{\text{Number of Customers}}$$

### Average Beverage Check

This operating ratio reveals the amount of the average beverage check per customer and is calculated by dividing Total Beverage Revenue by the number of customers. This analysis is typically carried out for each meal period and each venue.

$$\text{Average Beverage Check} = \frac{\text{Total Beverage Revenue}}{\text{Number of Customers}}$$

## Average Food Check per Meal Period by Venue (or Banquet)

This operating ratio reveals the amount of the average food check per meal period by venue (or catering/banquet function) and is calculated by dividing the Total Food Revenue per meal period per venue (or catering/banquet function) by the number of customers served in that venue (or catering/banquet function) during that meal period.

$$\text{Average Food Check per Meal Period by Venue (or Banquet)} = \frac{\text{Total Food Revenue per Meal Period per Venue (or Catering/Banquet Function)}}{\text{Number of Customers Served during that Meal Period in that Venue (or Catering/Banquet Function)}}$$

## Average Beverage Check per Meal Period by Venue (or Banquet)

This operating ratio reveals the amount of the average beverage check per meal period by venue (or catering/banquet function) and is calculated by dividing the total beverage revenue per meal period per venue (or catering/banquet function) by the number of customers served in that venue (or catering/banquet function) during that meal period.

$$\text{Average Beverage Check per Meal Period by Venue (or Banquet)} = \frac{\text{Total Beverage Revenue per Meal Period per Venue (or Catering/Banquet Function)}}{\text{Number of Customers Served during that Meal Period in that Venue (or Catering/Banquet Function)}}$$

## Food Cost Percentage

This measure evaluates if a venue or the catering/banquet department has issues with portion size, waste, theft, or other problems in controlling costs of food. Hotel managers should compare their actual cost percentages to their budgeted or potential cost percentages. Potential cost percentages are determined by taking into account an operation's selling prices, purchasing costs, and sales mix. When calculating a potential food cost percentage, the desired portion size needs to be considered as well as the expected waste. Food cost percentage is calculated by dividing the cost of food sales by total food revenue over the time period being measured.

$$\text{Food Cost Percentage} = \frac{\text{Cost of Food Sales}}{\text{Total Food Revenue}} \times 100$$

## Beverage Cost Percentage

This measure evaluates if a venue or the catering/banquet department has issues with pouring controls, waste, theft or other problems in controlling cost of beverage. Hotel managers should compare their actual cost percentages to their budgeted or potential cost percentages. Potential cost percentages are determined by taking into account an operation's selling prices, purchasing costs, and sales mix. When calculating a potential liquor cost percentage, the desired liquor shot size needs to be considered. When determining potential draft beer cost percentages, the sales mix of each draft beer container used (mugs, glasses, pitchers) has to be figured into the calculation. Beverage cost percentage is calculated by dividing the cost of beverage sales by total beverage revenue over the time period being measured.

$$\text{Beverage Cost Percentage} = \frac{\text{Cost of Beverage Sales}}{\text{Total Beverage Revenue}} \times 100$$

### Cost per Customer

This ratio measures a variable cost that is influenced by food and beverage volume. For example, labor cost and related expenses for a venue may be measured by cost per customer.

$$\text{Total Labor Cost and Related Expenses per Customer} = \frac{\text{Total Labor Costs and Related Expenses}}{\text{Number of Customers}}$$

### Audiovisual Cost of Sales Percentage

This represents equipment rental or any other costs associated with the cost of providing audiovisual services to customers. The cost of sales should be shown as a percentage of audiovisual revenue and is calculated by dividing audiovisual cost by audiovisual revenue.

$$\text{Audiovisual Cost of Sales Percentage} = \frac{\text{Audiovisual Cost}}{\text{Audiovisual Revenue}} \times 100$$

### Catering and Banquet Revenue per Group Room Night Sold

This is the total of catering and banquet revenue divided by the total number of group rooms nights sold. This comparison helps determine how effectively the sales staff is driving these incremental revenues from group customers.

$$\text{Catering and Banquet Revenue per Group Room Night Sold} = \frac{\text{Catering and Banquet Revenue}}{\text{Group Room Nights Sold}}$$

### Function Room Rental Revenue per Square Foot (Meter) of Function Space

This is the total of function room rental revenue divided by the total amount of function space measured in square feet or square meters. This comparison helps determine how effectively the sales staff is driving these incremental revenues for this specialized space.

$$\text{Function Room Rental Revenue per Square Foot (Meter)} = \frac{\text{Function Room Rental Revenue}}{\text{Square ft./m of Function Space}}$$

## Function Room Rental Revenue per Group Room Night Sold

This is the total of function room rental revenue divided by the total number of group rooms sold. This comparison helps determine how effectively the sales staff is driving these incremental revenues from group customers.

$$\text{Function Space Rental Revenue per Group Room Night Sold} = \frac{\text{Function Room Rental Revenue}}{\text{Group Room Nights Sold}}$$

## Audiovisual Revenue per Group Room Night Sold

This is the total of audiovisual revenue divided by the total number of group rooms sold. This comparison helps determine how effectively the sales staff is driving these incremental revenues from group customers.

$$\text{Audiovisual Revenue per Group Room Night Sold} = \frac{\text{Audiovisual Revenue}}{\text{Group Room Nights Sold}}$$

## Audiovisual Revenue per Square Foot (Meter) of Function Space

This is the total of audiovisual revenues divided by the total amount of function space measured in square feet or square meters. This comparison helps determine how effectively the sales staff is driving these incremental revenues for this specialized space.

$$\text{Audiovisual Revenue per Square Foot (Meter)} = \frac{\text{Audiovisual revenue}}{\text{Square ft./m of Function Space}}$$

## Departmental (Venue) Profit per Available Seat

This measures the departmental profit yield a food and beverage venue achieves relative to the seats available in the venue for a period. This can be used when comparing the yield of one venue with a competitor or comparable venue.

$$\text{Departmental (Venue) Profit per Available Seat} = \frac{\text{Food and Beverage Departmental (Venue) Profit}}{\text{Number of Available Seats}}$$

# Golf Course and Pro Shop Metrics

The ensuing table is recommended for the presentation of key metrics Golf Course and Pro Shop department metrics. Following the table, formulas are provided for select ratios, along with descriptions of their potential use.

|  | Current Month | | | YTD | | |
|---|---|---|---|---|---|---|
|  | Actual | Variance to Budget | Variance to Prior Year | Actual | Variance to Budget | Variance to Prior Year |
| **Golf/Pro Shop Operating Metrics: Revenue Generated per Round** | | | | | | |
| Average Greens Fee per round* | | | | | | |
| Merchandise/clothing revenue per round | | | | | | |
| Other revenue per round | | | | | | |
| Total Golf & Pro Shop Revenue per round | | | | | | |
| **Golf/Pro Shop Operating Metrics: Golf Rounds per Occupied Room Night** | | | | | | |
| Golf rounds per occupied room night | | | | | | |
| **Golf/Pro Shop Operating Metrics: Golf Rounds by Category of Guest** | | | | | | |
| Member | | | | | | |
| Member-guest | | | | | | |
| Resort | | | | | | |
| Outside (non-member or non-guest) | | | | | | |
| Employee | | | | | | |
| Total Golf Rounds Played | | | | | | |

\* Additional detail can be provided by individual category, including member, member-guest, resort, outside, and employee.

## Average Greens Fee per Round

This operating ratio reveals the average greens fee generated per round of golf played and is calculated by dividing total greens fee by the total number of golf rounds played.

$$\text{Average Greens Fee per Round} \ = \ \frac{\text{Greens Fees}}{\text{Number of Rounds Played}}$$

Additional detail can be provided by individual category such as by member, member guest, resort, and outside (non-member or non-resort).

## Merchandise/Clothing Revenue per Round

This operating ratio reveals the average merchandise generated by the golf and pro shop per round of golf played.

$$\frac{\text{Merchandise/Clothing}}{\text{Revenue per Round}} = \frac{\text{Merchandise Revenue} + \text{Clothing Revenue}}{\text{Number of Rounds Played}}$$

## Total Golf and Pro Shop Revenues per Round

This operating ratio reveals the average total golf revenue generated by the overall golf department, which takes into consideration greens fees, merchandise revenue, clothing revenue and other golf revenues.

$$\frac{\text{Total Golf Revenues}}{\text{per Round}} = \frac{\text{Greens Fees} + \text{Merchandise Revenue} + \text{Clothing Revenue} + \text{Other Revenue}}{\text{Number of Rounds Played}}$$

## Golf Rounds per Occupied Room Night

This operating metric tracks the number of golf rounds generated per occupied room night, which reveals the overall usage of the hotel's golf operations.

$$\text{Golf Rounds per Occupied Room Night} = \frac{\text{Number of Rounds Played}}{\text{Total Occupied Room Nights}}$$

## Golf Rounds by Category of User

This operating metric tracks users of the golf course by type. It is useful to know how many golf rounds are played by members, member-guests, hotel/resort guests, outside (non-member or non-resort) users, and employees.

# Health Club/Spa Metrics

The following tables are recommended for the presentation of key health club/spa metrics. After the tables, formulas are provided for select ratios, along with descriptions of their potential use.

| | Current Month | | | YTD | | |
|---|---|---|---|---|---|---|
| | Actual | Variance to Budget | Variance to Prior Year | Actual | Variance to Budget | Variance to Prior Year |
| **Health Club/Spa Operating Metrics: Revenue Mix, % of Department Revenue by Source** | | | | | | |
| Massage and Body Treatment | | | | | | |
| Skin Care | | | | | | |
| Hair Care | | | | | | |
| Nail Care | | | | | | |
| Fitness | | | | | | |
| Health and Wellness | | | | | | |
| Membership Fee | | | | | | |
| Retail | | | | | | |
| Other | | | | | | |
| Total | | | | | | |
| **Health Club/Spa Operating Metrics: Revenue per Square Feet (Meter)** | | | | | | |
| Treatment Revenue (massage and body treatment, skin care) | | | | | | |
| Salon Revenue (hair care, nail care) | | | | | | |
| Health and Wellness | | | | | | |
| Membership Fee | | | | | | |
| Retail | | | | | | |
| Other | | | | | | |
| Total | | | | | | |
| **Health Club/Spa Operating Metrics: Revenue per Occupied Guestroom** | | | | | | |
| Treatment Revenue (massage and body treatment, skin care) | | | | | | |
| Salon Revenue (hair care, nail care) | | | | | | |
| Health and Wellness | | | | | | |
| Membership Fee | | | | | | |
| Retail | | | | | | |
| Other | | | | | | |
| Total | | | | | | |

*(continued)*

| | Current Month | | | YTD | | |
|---|---|---|---|---|---|---|
| | Actual | Variance to Budget | Variance to Prior Year | Actual | Variance to Budget | Variance to Prior Year |
| **Health Club/Spa Operating Metrics: Treatment Revenue per Treatment Room** | | | | | | |
| Massage and Body Treatment | | | | | | |
| Skin Care | | | | | | |
| Total | | | | | | |
| **Health Club/Spa Operating Metrics: Treatment Revenue per Number of Treatments** | | | | | | |
| Massage and Body Treatment | | | | | | |
| Skin Care | | | | | | |
| Total | | | | | | |
| **Health Club/Spa Operating Metrics: Salon Revenue per Salon Station** | | | | | | |
| Hair Care | | | | | | |
| Nail Care | | | | | | |
| Total | | | | | | |
| **Health Club/Spa Operating Metrics: Expenses, % of Department Revenue** | | | | | | |
| Salaries and Wages | | | | | | |
| Payroll-Related Expenses | | | | | | |
| Cost of Sales | | | | | | |
| Ambience and Decoration | | | | | | |
| Athletic and Health and Beauty Supplies | | | | | | |
| Equipment Rental, Cleaning Supplies, Swimming Pool, Printing and Stationary, and Operating Supplies | | | | | | |
| Linen and Laundry and Dry Cleaning | | | | | | |
| Uniform Laundry and Costs | | | | | | |
| Travel—Meals and Entertainment and Other, Entertainment—In-House | | | | | | |
| Royalty and Management Fees | | | | | | |
| Cluster Services, Contract Services, and Corporate Office Reimbursables | | | | | | |
| Complimentary Services and Gifts, Dues and Subscriptions, Licenses and Permits, Training, and Miscellaneous | | | | | | |
| Total | | | | | | |
| **Health Club/Spa Operating Metrics: Guest Mix Percentages** | | | | | | |
| Local Guests | | | | | | |
| Hotel Guests | | | | | | |
| Total | | | | | | |
| **Health Club/Spa Operating Metrics: Treatment Analysis** | | | | | | |
| Treatments per Treatment Room | | | | | | |
| Treatments per Hour | | | | | | |

## Spa Revenue and Expenses per Square Foot (Meter)

Since the spa department is a specialized form of retail, revenue and expenses are frequently measured on a per-square-foot or per-square-meter basis. Space used includes indoor treatment rooms, outdoor treatment space, salon space, retail space, fitness center/studio, indoor pool/whirlpool/sauna/stream (if operated by health club/spa), indoor whirlpool, locker rooms, and waiting rooms. This metric can be applied to any specific revenue source (i.e., massage and body treatment, retail, fitness, etc.) within the spa department and its corresponding space usage.

$$\frac{\text{Spa Revenue (Expenses)}}{\text{per Square Foot/Meter}} = \frac{\text{Spa Revenue (Expenses)}}{\text{Square ft./m of Space Used}}$$

## Treatment Revenue and Expenses per Treatment Room

Treatment revenue/expenses per treatment room (where massage, facials and other body work services are performed) provides a measure of utilization and profitability of this specialized space.

$$\text{Treatment Revenue (Expenses) per Treatment Room} = \frac{\text{Treatment Revenue (Expenses)}}{\text{Number of Treatment Rooms}}$$

## Salon Revenue and Expenses per Salon Station

Salon revenue/expenses per salon station (where manicures, pedicures, and hair styling are performed) provides a measure of utilization and profitability of this specialized space.

$$\text{Salon Revenue (Expenses) per Salon Station} = \frac{\text{Salon Revenue (Expenses)}}{\text{Number of Salon Stations}}$$

## Treatment Revenue and Expenses per Treatment

Treatment revenue/expenses per treatment provides a measure of utilization and profitability for the various forms of treatments provided.

$$\text{Treatment Revenue (Expenses) per Treatment} = \frac{\text{Treatment Revenue (Expenses)}}{\text{Number of Treatments}}$$

## Treatment Revenue and Expenses as Percentage of Departmental Revenue

Looking at treatment revenue/expenses as percentages of departmental revenue provides a measure of revenue mix and profitability for the various forms of treatments provided.

$$\frac{\text{Treatment Revenue (Expenses) as a}}{\text{Percentage of Department Revenue}} = \frac{\text{Treatment Revenue (Expenses)}}{\text{Departmental Revenue}} \times 100$$

## Spa Revenue per Occupied Guestroom

Spa revenue per occupied guestroom measures the ability of the spa department to capture revenue from guests of the hotel.

$$\text{Spa Revenue per Occupied Guestroom} = \frac{\text{Spa Revenue}}{\text{Occupied Guestrooms}}$$

## Percentage of Hotel Guests vs. Local Guests

These measures provide spa management with information on the source of their customers.

$$\text{Percentage of Local Guests} \ = \ \frac{\text{Number of Local Spa Guests}}{\text{Total Number of Spa Guests}} \ \times \ 100$$

$$\text{Percentage of Hotel Guests} \ = \ \frac{\text{Number of Hotel Spa Guests}}{\text{Total Number of Spa Guests}} \ \times \ 100$$

### Treatments per Treatment Room

Treatments per treatment room provides a measure of utilization of this specialized space.

$$\text{Number of Treatments per Treatment Room} \ = \ \frac{\text{Number of Treatments}}{\text{Number of Treatment Rooms}}$$

### Treatments per Hour

Treatments per hour provides a measure of utilization and efficiency of this specialized space and the staff.

$$\text{Number of Treatments per Hour} \ = \ \frac{\text{Total Treatments}}{\text{Total Hours of Operation}}$$

## Parking Metrics

The following table is recommended for the presentation of key financial and operating metrics for parking. After the table, formulas are provided for select ratios, along with descriptions of their potential use.

| | Current Month | | | YTD | | |
|---|---|---|---|---|---|---|
| | Actual | Variance to Budget | Variance to Prior Year | Actual | Variance to Budget | Variance to Prior Year |
| **Parking Financial Metrics** | | | | | | |
| Total Parking RevPAR | | | | | | |
| Total Parking RevPOR | | | | | | |
| Total Parking RevPAS | | | | | | |
| Overnight Parking RevPAR | | | | | | |
| Overnight Parking RevPOR | | | | | | |
| Parking Profit PAR | | | | | | |
| Parking Profit POR | | | | | | |
| Parking Profit Margin | | | | | | |
| **Parking Operating Metrics** | | | | | | |
| Drive-In Capture | | | | | | |
| Overnight Drive-In Capture | | | | | | |
| Daily Parking Capture | | | | | | |
| Valet Parking Capture | | | | | | |
| Overnight Valet Parking Capture | | | | | | |

## Parking Revenue per Available Room

Parking revenue per available room (Parking RevPAR) provides a measure of parking revenue yield from all customers relative to the size of the property. It is useful for comparison to hotels with different room counts.

$$\text{Parking RevPAR} \quad = \quad \frac{\text{Parking Revenue}}{\text{Rooms Available}}$$

## Parking Revenue per Occupied Room

Parking revenue per occupied room (Parking RevPOR) provides a measure of parking revenue productivity (for all customers) relative to the number of rooms occupied at the property.

$$\text{Parking RevPOR} \quad = \quad \frac{\text{Parking Revenue}}{\text{Rooms Occupied}}$$

## Parking Revenue per Available Space

Parking revenue per available space (Parking RevPAS) provides a measure of parking revenue productivity relative to the number of parking spaces at the hotel.

$$\text{Parking RevPAS} \quad = \quad \frac{\text{Parking Revenue}}{\text{Available Spaces}}$$

## Overnight Parking Revenue per Available Room

Overnight parking revenue per available room (O/N Parking RevPAR) provides a measure of parking revenue yield based solely on the revenue generated from overnight hotel guests. It is useful for comparison to hotels with different room counts.

$$\text{O/N Parking RevPAR} \quad = \quad \frac{\text{O/N Parking Revenue}}{\text{Rooms Available}}$$

## Overnight Parking Revenue per Occupied Room

Overnight parking revenue per occupied room (O/N Parking RevPOR) provides a measure of parking revenue productivity based solely on the revenue generated from overnight hotel guests.

$$\text{O/N Parking RevPOR} \quad = \quad \frac{\text{O/N Parking Revenue}}{\text{Rooms Occupied}}$$

## Parking Profits per Available Room

Parking profits per available room provides a measure of parking profit yield relative to the size of the property. It is useful for comparison to hotels with different room counts.

$$\text{Parking Profits per Available Room} \quad = \quad \frac{\text{Parking Profits}}{\text{Rooms Available}}$$

## Parking Profits per Occupied Room

Parking profits per occupied room provides a measure of parking profitability relative to the number of rooms occupied at the property.

$$\text{Parking Profits per Occupied Room} = \frac{\text{Parking Profits}}{\text{Rooms Occupied}}$$

## Parking Department Profit Margin

The parking department profit margin measures management's ability to produce profits by generating revenues and controlling departmental expenses.

$$\text{Parking Department Profit Margin} = \frac{\text{Parking Profit}}{\text{Parking Revenue}} \times 100$$

## Drive-In Capture

Drive-in capture measures the utilization of the parking lot by all customers.

$$\text{Drive-In Capture} = \frac{\text{Number of Parked Cars}}{\text{Rooms Occupied}} \times 100$$

## Overnight Drive-In Capture

Overnight drive-in capture measures the utilization of the parking lot solely by overnight guests.

$$\text{Overnight Drive-In Capture} = \frac{\text{Number of Overnight Parked Cars}}{\text{Rooms Occupied}} \times 100$$

## Daily Parking Capture

Daily parking capture measures the utilization of the parking lot by day-use customers.

$$\text{Daily Parking Capture} = \frac{\text{Number of Daily Cars (Number of Local Meeting/Catering/Venue Customers)}}{\text{Total Number of Cars}} \times 100$$

## Valet Parking Capture

Valet parking capture measures the utilization of the parking lot by valet customers.

$$\text{Valet Parking Capture} = \frac{\text{Number of Valet Cars}}{\text{Total Number of Cars}} \times 100$$

## Overnight Valet Parking Capture

Overnight valet parking capture measures the utilization of the parking lot by overnight guests using the valet parking service.

$$\text{Overnight Valet Parking Capture} = \frac{\text{Number of Overnight Valet Cars}}{\text{Total Number of Valet Cars}}$$

# Utilities and Refuse/Waste Metrics

Hotel utilities, refuse, and waste are the subject of increased scrutiny because of rising commodity rates and the emerging global focus on ecological sustainability for existing hospitality assets. By applying basic financial and operating ratios to their utility costs for usage and waste, hotel owners and operators can evaluate and monitor performance trends over time. Tracking utility and energy usage will help the hotel improve energy efficiency and energy management, which will lead to reductions in energy usage, waste, and greenhouse gas emissions.

The following discussion provides broad monitoring and benchmarking ratios to track regarding the hotel's utilities usage, waste, and overall energy efficiency. Reviewing these metrics for each property on a rolling basis will allow a hotel to identify fluctuations or deviations in usage and efficiency. Identified variations can signal overuse, rapidly increasing commodity rates, inefficacies, or other indicators that warrant a more detailed review of utility consumption and pricing.

Caution should be used when using these ratios for comparison across competitive sets or comparable property groups. Numerous factors combine to influence actual utility consumption, including building configuration and equipment, climate and weather, occupancy levels, and more. To compare utility consumption and efficiency among diverging types of properties, a more detailed, engineering-based analysis of energy use intensity (units of energy per square foot or meter), water use intensity (units of water per occupied room), and waste generation/diversion is encouraged.

The following table is recommended for the presentation of key utilities metrics. The table is followed by definitions of terminology as used in this section. Finally, formulas are provided for several ratios.

| Utility | Per Available Room | Per Occupied Room | Per Total Overnight Guest | Per Square Feet (Meters) |
|---|---|---|---|---|
| Electrical—kWh (hps) | | | | |
| Gas—Therms | | | | |
| Steam—Mlb (Kgs) | | | | |
| Water/Sewer—Gallons (Liters) | | | | |
| Chilled Water—Ton (Metric Ton) | | | | |
| Total Energy Cost | | | | |
| Total Utility Cost | | | | |

## Definitions

*Kilowatt Hour.* A unit of energy or work equal to 1,000 watt-hours or 3.6 megajoules (where 1 joule equals 1 watt per second). The kilowatt hour (kWh) is commonly used to measure electric energy.

*Therm.* A unit of heat energy equal to 100,000 British thermal units (BTU); 1 BTU is the heat required to raise the temperature of one pound of water by 1 degree Fahrenheit or 0.56 degree Celsius. Stating the energy content of various fuels in BTU allows for accurate comparisons between fuels. Natural gas in the U.S. is measured by volume in cubic feet rather than by energy content. The therm can be used to measure natural gas usage and to convert the volume of gas used to its heat equivalent: 1 therm = 96.7 cubic feet of natural gas or 29.3 kilowatt hours.

*Mlb.* This represents a traditional unit of mass for steam equivalent to 1,000 pounds.

*Ton Hour.* A unit of weight or volume used to measure chilled water. Chilled water is typically used in HVAC units.

- 1 Ton = 2,000lbs (907kg) in U.S.
- 1 Ton = 2,240lbs (1,016kg) in U.K.
- 1 Ton = 2,204lbs (1,000kg) in International System of Units
- 1 Ton Hour of cooling capacity = 12,000 BTU/hour or 3.5169 kWh (where 3,412 BTU/hour = 1 kWh).

## Electric Consumption (kWh and Horsepower)

$$\text{kWh (hps) per Available Room} = \frac{\text{Kilowatt Hours (Horsepower)}}{\text{Rooms Available}}$$

$$\text{kWh (hps) per Occupied Room} = \frac{\text{Kilowatt Hours (Horsepower)}}{\text{Rooms Occupied}}$$

$$\text{kWh (hps) per Overnight Guest} = \frac{\text{Kilowatt Hours (Horsepower)}}{\text{Total Overnight Guests}}$$

$$\text{kWh per Square Foot or Meter} = \frac{\text{Kilowatt Hours}}{\text{Total Square Feet/Meters}}$$

## Gas Consumption

$$\text{Therms per Available Room} = \frac{\text{Number of Therms}}{\text{Rooms Available}}$$

$$\text{Therms per Occupied Room} = \frac{\text{Number of Therms}}{\text{Rooms Occupied}}$$

$$\text{Therms per Overnight Guest} = \frac{\text{Number of Therms}}{\text{Number of Overnight Guests}}$$

$$\text{Therms per Square Foot/Meter} = \frac{\text{Number of Therms}}{\text{Total Square Feet/Meters}}$$

## Steam Consumption

$$\text{Mlb (Kgs) per Available Room} = \frac{\text{Thousand Pounds (Kilograms)}}{\text{Rooms Available}}$$

$$\text{Mlb (Kgs) per Occupied Room} = \frac{\text{Thousand Pounds (Kilograms)}}{\text{Rooms Occupied}}$$

$$\text{Mlb (Kgs) per Overnight Guest} = \frac{\text{Thousand Pounds (Kilograms)}}{\text{Number of Overnight Guests}}$$

$$\text{Mlb (Kgs) per Square Foot/Meter} = \frac{\text{Thousand Pounds (Kilograms)}}{\text{Total Square Feet/Meters}}$$

## Water/Sewer Consumption

$$\text{Gallons (Liters)/Available Room} = \frac{\text{Gallons (Liters)}}{\text{Rooms Available}}$$

$$\text{Gallons (Liters)/Occupied Room} = \frac{\text{Gallons (Liters)}}{\text{Rooms Occupied}}$$

$$\text{Gallons (Liters)/Overnight Guest} = \frac{\text{Gallons (Liters)}}{\text{Number of Overnight Guests}}$$

## Chilled Water

$$\text{Ton (Metric Ton) Hours per Available Room} = \frac{\text{Tons (Metric Tons)}}{\text{Rooms Available}}$$

$$\text{Ton (Metric Ton) Hours per Occupied Room} = \frac{\text{Tons (Metric Tons)}}{\text{Rooms Occupied}}$$

$$\text{Ton (Metric Ton) Hours per Overnight Guest} = \frac{\text{Tons (Metric Tons)}}{\text{Number of Overnight Guests}}$$

## Total Energy Cost (Electricity, Gas, Oil, Steam, Other Fuels)

$$\text{Total Energy Cost per Available Room} = \frac{\text{Total Energy Cost}}{\text{Rooms Available}}$$

$$\text{Total Energy Cost per Occupied Room} = \frac{\text{Total Energy Cost}}{\text{Rooms Occupied}}$$

$$\text{Total Energy Cost per Overnight Guest} = \frac{\text{Total Energy Cost}}{\text{Number of Overnight Guests}}$$

$$\text{Total Energy Cost per Square Foot/Meter} = \frac{\text{Total Energy Cost}}{\text{Total Square Feet/Meters}}$$

## Total Utility Cost (Energy, Water/Sewer, and Chilled Water)

$$\text{Total Utility Cost PAR} = \frac{\text{Total Utility Cost}}{\text{Rooms Available}}$$

$$\text{Total Utility Cost POR} = \frac{\text{Total Utility Cost}}{\text{Rooms Occupied}}$$

$$\begin{array}{c}\text{Total Utility Cost} \\ \text{per Overnight Guest}\end{array} = \frac{\text{Total Utility Cost}}{\text{Number of Overnight Guests}}$$

$$\begin{array}{c}\text{Total Utility Cost} \\ \text{per Square Foot/Meter}\end{array} = \frac{\text{Total Utility Cost}}{\text{Total Square Feet/Meters}}$$

$$\begin{array}{c}\text{Total Utility Cost as a Percentage} \\ \text{of Total Operating Revenue}\end{array} = \frac{\text{Total Utility Cost}}{\text{Total Operating Revenue}}$$

## Sustainability and Environmental Impact

As with other industries, hotels are being asked by a variety of stakeholders, including meeting planners, corporate and leisure customers, investors, and municipalities, to quantify the environmental impact of a guest's stay, as well as the overall environmental impact of the hotel. While this *Uniform System* does not attempt to provide the detailed calculations to determine the carbon footprint or greenhouse gas emissions generated by the hotel, it does provide a general framework to measure a hotel's energy usage, water usage, and waste production in a consistent manner to evaluate performance trends over time. Several metrics and ratios appear are identified in the Utilities and Refuse/Water Metrics section immediately preceding this section.

A starting point is to monitor and track the components necessary to understand a hotel's environmental impact. Metrics such as energy consumption per occupied room, water consumption per occupied room, and waste production per occupied room are important components of understanding and reducing a hotel's utilities cost and environmental impact.

Caution should be exercised when using metrics and ratios for comparison across competitive sets or comparable property groups. Numerous factors combine to influence actual utility consumption, including building configuration and equipment, climate and weather, occupancy levels, and more. To compare utility consumption and efficiency among diverging types of properties, a more detailed analysis of energy use intensity, water use intensity, and waste generation/diversion will be required.

## Labor Cost Metrics

Labor cost represents the largest operating cost for hotels due to the labor-intensive nature of hotel operations. Given the high correlation of labor cost with total operating revenues, a hotel's profitability can rise and fall with labor cost. Therefore, it is important to track and monitor this operating cost in order to manage employee productivity and labor inefficiencies and to respond to business cycle changes. This section focuses on the many statistics and ratios used to monitor and evaluate labor performance in a hotel. These ratios represent the commonly used labor statistics and can be applied to both operating and undistributed departments.

The following tables are recommended for the presentation of key labor metrics. After the table, formulas are provided for select ratios, along with descriptions of their potential use.

**Note:** If necessary, the presentation of payroll titles in a table should be aggregated to preserve the confidentiality of a specific employee's payroll.

### Consolidated Payroll Cost Stastics

| Rooms Salaries & Wages | Dollars | | | | Hours | | | |
|---|---|---|---|---|---|---|---|---|
| | POR | PAR | % Rev | Avg. Wage | Hours | POR | PAR | # FTE |
| Management | | | | | | | | |
| Non-Management: Front Office | | | | | | | | |
| Non-Management: Guest Services | | | | | | | | |
| Non-Management: Housekeeping | | | | | | | | |
| Non-Management: Laundry | | | | | | | | |
| Non-Management: Reservations | | | | | | | | |
| Non-Management: Transportation | | | | | | | | |
| Non-Management: Complimentary F&B | | | | | | | | |
| *Total Rooms Salaries & Wages* | | | | | | | | |
| Service Charge Distribution | | | | | | | | |
| Contracted, Leased or Oursourced Labor | | | | | | | | |
| Bonuses and Incentives | | | | | | | | |
| Payroll-Related Expenses | | | | | | | | |
| *Total Rooms Labor Costs and Related Expenses* | | | | | | | | |

| Food & Beverage Salaries & Wages | Dollars | | | | Hours | | | |
|---|---|---|---|---|---|---|---|---|
| | Per Cust.* | PAR | % Rev | Avg. Wage | Hours | Per Cust. | PAR | # FTE |
| Management: Venue #1 Service | | | | | | | | |
| Non-Management: Venue #1 Service | | | | | | | | |
| Management: Venue #2 Service | | | | | | | | |
| Non-Management:Venue #2 Service | | | | | | | | |
| Management: Banquets, Conference, & Catering Service | | | | | | | | |
| Non-Management: Banquets, Conference, & Catering Service | | | | | | | | |
| Management: In-Room Dining Front of House | | | | | | | | |
| Non-Management: In-Room Dining Front of House | | | | | | | | |
| Management: Kitchen | | | | | | | | |
| Non-Management: Kitchen | | | | | | | | |
| *Total F&B Salaries & Wages* | | | | | | | | |
| Service Charge Distribution | | | | | | | | |
| Contracted, Leased or Oursourced Labor | | | | | | | | |
| Bonuses and Incentives | | | | | | | | |
| Payroll-Related Expenses | | | | | | | | |
| *Total F&B Labor Costs and Related Expenses* | | | | | | | | |

*\* One customer served in a food and beverage venue or function space.*

*(continued)*

### Consolidated Payroll Cost Stastics *(continued)*

| Golf & Pro Shop Salaries & Wages | Dollars | | | | Hours | | | |
|---|---|---|---|---|---|---|---|---|
| | Per Round | PAR | % Rev | Avg. Wage | Hours | Per Round | PAR | # FTE |
| Management | | | | | | | | |
| Non-Management: Golf Pros & Operations | | | | | | | | |
| Non-Management: Greens & Maintenance | | | | | | | | |
| Non-Management: Pro Shop | | | | | | | | |
| *Total Golf & Pro Shop Salaries & Wages* | | | | | | | | |
| Service Charge Distribution | | | | | | | | |
| Contracted, Leased or Oursourced Labor | | | | | | | | |
| Bonuses and Incentives | | | | | | | | |
| Payroll-Related Expenses | | | | | | | | |
| TOTAL GOLF & PRO SHOP LABOR COSTS AND RELATED EXPENSES | | | | | | | | |

| Health Club & Spa Salaries & Wages | Dollars | | | | Hours | | | |
|---|---|---|---|---|---|---|---|---|
| | Per Total or Respective Treatments* | PAR | % Rev | Avg. Wage | Hours | Per Service | PAR | # FTE |
| Management | | | | | | | | |
| Non-Management: Attendant / Housekeeping | | | | | | | | |
| Non-Management: Fitness | | | | | | | | |
| Non-Management: Reception & Retail | | | | | | | | |
| Non-Management: Spa Therapists & Technicians | | | | | | | | |
| *Total Health Club & Spa Salaries & Wages* | | | | | | | | |
| Service Charge Distribution | | | | | | | | |
| Contracted, Leased or Oursourced Labor | | | | | | | | |
| Bonuses and Incentives | | | | | | | | |
| Payroll-Related Expenses | | | | | | | | |
| *Total Health Club & Spa Labor Costs and Related Expenses* | | | | | | | | |

*\* Include massage, body treatments, salon service, fitness session, etc..*

| Parking Salaries & Wages | Dollars | | | | Hours | | | |
|---|---|---|---|---|---|---|---|---|
| | POR | PAR | % Rev | Avg. Wage | Hours | POR | PAR | # FTE |
| Management | | | | | | | | |
| Non-Management | | | | | | | | |
| *Total Parking Salaries & Wages* | | | | | | | | |
| Service Charge Distribution | | | | | | | | |
| Contracted, Leased or Oursourced Labor | | | | | | | | |
| Bonuses and Incentives | | | | | | | | |
| Payroll-Related Expenses | | | | | | | | |
| *Total Parking Labor Costs and Related Expenses* | | | | | | | | |

## Consolidated Payroll Cost Stastics *(continued)*

| Other Operated Department Salaries & Wages | Dollars | | | | Hours | | | |
|---|---|---|---|---|---|---|---|---|
| | POR | PAR | % Rev | Avg. Wage | Hours | POR | PAR | # FTE |
| Management | | | | | | | | |
| Non-Management | | | | | | | | |
| *Total Other Operated Departments Salaries & Wages* | | | | | | | | |
| Service Charge Distribution | | | | | | | | |
| Contracted, Leased or Oursourced Labor | | | | | | | | |
| Bonuses and Incentives | | | | | | | | |
| Payroll-Related Expenses | | | | | | | | |
| *Total Other Operated Depts. Labor Costs and Related Expenses* | | | | | | | | |

| Administrative & General Salaries & Wages | Dollars | | | | Hours | | | |
|---|---|---|---|---|---|---|---|---|
| | POR | PAR | % Rev | Avg. Wage | Hours | POR | PAR | # FTE |
| Management | | | | | | | | |
| Non-Management: Accounting | | | | | | | | |
| Non-Management: General Support | | | | | | | | |
| Non-Management: Human Resources | | | | | | | | |
| Non-Management: Purchasing & Receiving | | | | | | | | |
| Non-Management: Security | | | | | | | | |
| *Total A&G Salaries & Wages* | | | | | | | | |
| Service Charge Distribution | | | | | | | | |
| Contracted, Leased or Oursourced Labor | | | | | | | | |
| Bonuses and Incentives | | | | | | | | |
| Payroll-Related Expenses | | | | | | | | |
| *Total A&G Labor Costs and Related Expenses* | | | | | | | | |

| IT & Telecom Salaries & Wages | Dollars | | | | Hours | | | |
|---|---|---|---|---|---|---|---|---|
| | POR | PAR | % Rev | Avg. Wage | Hours | POR | PAR | # FTE |
| Management | | | | | | | | |
| Non-Management: IT | | | | | | | | |
| Non-Management: Telecom | | | | | | | | |
| *Total IT & Telecom Salaries & Wages* | | | | | | | | |
| Service Charge Distribution | | | | | | | | |
| Contracted, Leased or Oursourced Labor | | | | | | | | |
| Bonuses and Incentives | | | | | | | | |
| Payroll-Related Expenses | | | | | | | | |
| *Total IT & Telecom Labor Costs and Related Expenses* | | | | | | | | |

*(continued)*

### Consolidated Payroll Cost Stastics *(continued)*

| Sales & Marketing Salaries & Wages | Dollars | | | | Hours | | | |
|---|---|---|---|---|---|---|---|---|
| | POR | PAR | % Rev | Avg. Wage | Hours | POR | PAR | # FTE |
| Management | | | | | | | | |
| Non-Management | | | | | | | | |
| *Total Sales & Marketing Salaries & Wages* | | | | | | | | |
| Service Charge Distribution | | | | | | | | |
| Contracted, Leased or Oursourced Labor | | | | | | | | |
| Bonuses and Incentives | | | | | | | | |
| Payroll-Related Expenses | | | | | | | | |
| *Total Sales & Marketing Labor Costs and Related Expenses* | | | | | | | | |

| Property Operations & Maintenance Salaries & Wages | Dollars | | | | Hours | | | |
|---|---|---|---|---|---|---|---|---|
| | POR | PAR | % Rev | Avg. Wage | Hours | POR | PAR | # FTE |
| Management | | | | | | | | |
| Non-Management | | | | | | | | |
| *Total Property Operations & Maintenance Salaries & Wages* | | | | | | | | |
| Service Charge Distribution | | | | | | | | |
| Contracted, Leased or Oursourced Labor | | | | | | | | |
| Bonuses and Incentives | | | | | | | | |
| Payroll-Related Expenses | | | | | | | | |
| *Total Property Operations & Maintenance Labor Costs and Related Expenses* | | | | | | | | |

| House Laundry Salaries & Wages | Dollars | | | | Hours | | | |
|---|---|---|---|---|---|---|---|---|
| | POR | PAR | % Rev | Avg. Wage | Hours | POR | PAR | # FTE |
| Management | | | | | | | | |
| Non-Management | | | | | | | | |
| *Total House Laundry Salaries & Wages* | | | | | | | | |
| Service Charge Distribution | | | | | | | | |
| Contracted, Leased or Oursourced Labor | | | | | | | | |
| Bonuses and Incentives | | | | | | | | |
| Payroll-Related Expenses | | | | | | | | |
| *Total House Laundry Labor Costs and Related Expenses* | | | | | | | | |

| Staff Dining Salaries & Wages | Dollars | | | | Hours | | | |
|---|---|---|---|---|---|---|---|---|
| | POR | PAR | % Rev | Avg. Wage | Hours | Per Customer | PAR | # FTE |
| Management | | | | | | | | |
| Non-Management | | | | | | | | |
| *Total Staff Dining Salaries & Wages* | | | | | | | | |
| Service Charge Distribution | | | | | | | | |
| Contracted, Leased or Oursourced Labor | | | | | | | | |

**Consolidated Payroll Cost Stastics** *(continued)*

| | | | |
|---|---|---|---|
| Bonuses and Incentives | | | |
| Payroll-Related Expenses | | | |
| *Total Staff Dining Labor Costs and Related Expenses* | | | |

| | Dollars | | | | Hours | | | |
|---|---|---|---|---|---|---|---|---|
| TOTAL SALARIES / WAGES / HOURS | POR | PAR | % Rev | Avg. Wage | Hours | POR | PAR | # FTE |
| *Total Hotel* | | | | | | | | |

| | Dollars | | | |
|---|---|---|---|---|
| PAYROLL-RELATED EXPENSE | POR | PAR | % Rev | Avg. Wage |
| Payroll Taxes | | | | |
| Supplemental Pay | | | | |
| Employee Benefits | | | | |
| *Total Hotel Payroll-Related Expense* | | | | |

| | Dollars | | | |
|---|---|---|---|---|
| BONUSES & INCENTIVES | POR | PAR | % Rev | Avg. Wage |
| Rooms | | | | |
| Food & Beverage | | | | |
| Golf & Pro Shop | | | | |
| Health Club & Spa | | | | |
| Parking | | | | |
| Other Operated Departments | | | | |
| Administrative & General | | | | |
| IT & Telecom | | | | |
| Sales & Marketing | | | | |
| Property Operations & Maintenance | | | | |
| House Laundry | | | | |
| Staff Dining | | | | |
| *Total Bonuses & Incentives* | | | | |

| | Dollars | | | | Hours | | | |
|---|---|---|---|---|---|---|---|---|
| TOTAL PAYROLL AND RELATED EXPENSES | POR | PAR | % Rev | Avg. Wage | Hours | POR | PAR | # FTE |
| *Total Hotel* | | | | | | | | |

## Salaries and Wages Cost Percentage

The total salaries and wages cost includes the salaries and wages paid out to hotel employees for all departments and operational areas of the property. A total hotel salaries and wages percentage is calculated by dividing total for employees salaries and wages expense by total operating revenue. For control purposes, payroll cost percentages also should be calculated and analyzed for each department and operational area of the property. The payroll cost percentage is calculated as follows:

$$\text{Salaries and Wages Cost Percentage} = \frac{\text{Total (or Department) Salaries and Wages}}{\text{Total Operating (or Department) Revenue}} \times 100$$

## Salaries and Wages Cost per Available or Occupied Room

An alternative method to measure salaries and wages is on a dollar per available room (PAR) basis or dollar per occupied room (POR) basis. For those departments having labor requirements that are significantly influenced by the number of rooms occupied (e.g., rooms), labor cost per occupied room is one measure of labor efficiency. For departments having labor requirements that are not significantly influenced by the number of rooms occupied (e.g., undistributed), labor cost per available room is one measure of labor efficiency. The salaries and wages cost ratio is calculated as follows:

$$\frac{\text{Salaries and Wages per}}{\text{Available (Occupied) Room}} = \frac{\text{Total (or Department) Salaries and Wages}}{\text{Rooms Available (Occupied)}}$$

## Salaries and Wages Cost per Customer/Round/Service

For operated departments having labor requirements that are not necessarily influenced by the number of rooms occupied (e.g., food and beverage, golf and pro shop), salary and wage cost compared with a relevant variable component is a measure of labor efficiency. For example, in food and beverage, the variable component is the number of customers served, while in the golf and pro shop, the variable measure is the number of golf rounds played. The salaries and wages cost ratio is calculated as follows:

$$\frac{\text{Salaries and Wages per}}{\text{Customer/Round/Service}} = \frac{\text{Total (or Department) Salaries and Wages}}{\text{Total Customers/Rounds/Services}}$$

## Total Labor Costs and Related Expenses Percentage

Total Labor Costs and Related Expenses includes the total salaries and wages and payroll and related expenses for all departments and operational areas of the property. A total hotel labor costs and related expenses percentage is calculated by dividing Total Labor Costs and Related Expenses by Total Operating (or Department) Revenue. The labor costs and related expense percentage is calculated as follows:

$$\frac{\text{Labor Costs and Related}}{\text{Expenses Percentage}} = \frac{\begin{array}{c}\text{Total (Department)}\\\text{Labor Costs and Related Expenses}\end{array}}{\text{Total Operating (Department) Revenue}} \times 100$$

## Hours Worked

The following ratios are based on hours worked. Hours worked is the total number of hours worked by employees during the period. This total does not include annual leave, unworked public holidays, sick days, days in lieu, etc.

## Hours Worked per Available or Occupied Room

In order to analyze labor productivity, it is necessary to strip out salary differences and consider only the hours worked and this is done by measuring on a hour per available room basis (PAR) or hour per occupied room basis (POR). For those departments whose labor requirements are significantly influenced by the number of rooms occupied (e.g., rooms), hours per occupied room is one measure of labor efficiency. For departments whose labor requirements are not significantly influenced by the number of rooms occupied (e.g., undistributed), hours per available room is one measure of labor efficiency. The productivity ratio is calculated as follows:

$$\frac{\text{Hours Worked per}}{\text{Available (Occupied) Room}} = \frac{\text{Total (or Department) Hours Worked}}{\text{Rooms Available (Occupied)}}$$

## Hours Worked per Customer/Round/Service

For operational departments whose labor requirements are not necessarily influenced by the number of rooms occupied (e.g. Food & Beverage, Golf & Pro Shop), hours worked per the relevant variable component is a measure of labor efficiency. For example, in Food & Beverage, the variable component of the operations are the number of Customers served while in the Golf & Pro Shop the variable measure would be the number of golf rounds played. The productivity ratio is calculated as follows:

$$\frac{\text{Hours Worked per}}{\text{Customer/Round/Service}} = \frac{\text{Total (or Department) Hours Worked}}{\text{Total Customers/Rounds/Services}}$$

## Full-Time Equivalent (FTE)

One way to express the number of hours worked is to use a measure known as the full-time equivalent (FTE). This measure states the total number of hours worked (including overtime) by all employees (including part-time) as the equivalent number of full-time employees. An FTE is the number of hours that a full-time employee would work over a standard work week (e.g., 40 hours in the U.S.) or other period. FTEs are based on hours worked only and do not include annual leave, public holidays, sick days, days in lieu, etc. The FTE is calculated as follows:

$$\text{FTE} = \frac{\text{Total (or Department) Number of Hours Worked}}{\dfrac{\text{Number of Hours in}}{\text{Standard Work Week}} \times \dfrac{\text{Number of Days in Period}}{7}}$$

## Average Wage

Certain drivers, including geographical location, employee tenure, and labor negotiations, can influence a hotel's payroll cost with no relation to productivity. The effects of these drivers can be observed in the average wage of all hotel employees. The average wage is calculated as follows:

$$\text{Average Wage} = \frac{\text{Total (or Department) Salaries and Wages}}{\text{Total Employee Hours Worked}}$$

# ——————— Financial Ratios ———————

Financial statistics quantify many aspects of a hotel's financial statements and are an important part of the comprehensive analysis used to evaluate the overall financial condition of a hotel. Financial statistics are categorized according to the financial area of the hotel measured, including liquidity, solvency, activity, and profitability. The following sections discuss useful ratios that should be part of the overall comprehensive analysis of the hotel's financial condition. This ratios may be benchmarked against prior reporting periods, comparable hotels, and budgeted targets.

The sources of the financial statistics are derived from the hotel's balance sheet, income statement and statement of cash flows. Employing this broad set of financial statements gives greater value to the hotel's financial analysis and improved insight to the overall health of the hotel's financial status.

## Liquidity Ratios

Liquidity ratios measure an operation's ability to meet its current, short-term obligations. Owners and stockholders often prefer relatively low current ratios because investments in many current assets may be less productive than investments in non-current assets. Creditors, on the other hand, normally prefer relatively high current ratios because this gives them assurance that the lodging property will be able to meet its short-term obligations. Management must try to satisfy both owners and creditors while maintaining adequate working capital and sufficient liquidity to ensure the smooth operation of the property.

### Current Ratio

The most common liquidity ratio is the current ratio, which is the ratio of total current assets to total current liabilities:

$$\text{Current Ratio} \ = \ \frac{\text{Current Assets}}{\text{Current Liabilities}}$$

This ratio reveals the amount of current assets for every dollar of current liabilities.

### Acid-Test Ratio

The acid-test ratio measures a property's liquidity by considering only "quick assets"—current assets minus inventories and prepaid expenses:

$$\text{Acid-Test Ratio} \ = \ \frac{\text{Quick Assets}}{\text{Current Liabilities}}$$

This ratio reveals the amount of quick assets for every dollar of current liabilities. This is often a more stringent measure of a property's liquidity because it may take several months for many properties to convert their inventories to cash.

## Accounts Receivable Turnover

Accounts receivable can be the largest current asset of lodging properties because credit is often extended to guests. Therefore, any examination of a property's liquidity must consider how quickly accounts receivable are converted to cash. This is determined by the accounts receivable turnover ratio, which divides total operating revenue by the average accounts receivable. A refinement of this ratio uses only charge sales in the numerator; however, quite often charge sales figures are unavailable. Regardless of whether total operating revenue or charge sales are used as the numerator, the calculation should be consistent from period to period.

To calculate the accounts receivable turnover, it is first necessary to determine the average accounts receivable. This is accomplished by adding accounts receivable at the beginning and end of the period and then dividing that figure by two. The average accounts receivable figure is then divided into the total operating revenue for the period:

$$\text{Accounts Receivable Turnover} = \frac{\text{Total Operating Revenue}}{\text{Average Accounts Receivable}}$$

## Average Collection Period

This ratio reveals the number of days required to collect the average accounts receivable. The average collection period is calculated by dividing the number of days in the year by the accounts receivable turnover:

$$\text{Average Collection Period} = \frac{\text{Days in Year}}{\text{Accounts Receivable Turnover}}$$

# Solvency Ratios

Solvency ratios measure the degree of debt financing used by the lodging property. These ratios reflect the ability of the property to meet its long-term obligations. Owners view solvency ratios as a measure of their financial leverage, and often prefer relatively low solvency ratios because their leverage increases as debt is used in place of equity dollars to increase the return on equity dollars already invested. Creditors, on the other hand, prefer relatively high solvency ratios because they reveal an equity cushion available to absorb any operating losses. Management is again caught in the middle, trying to satisfy owners by financing assets with debt so as to maximize return on investments and trying to satisfy creditors by not unduly jeopardizing the property's ability to meet its long-term obligations.

## Solvency Ratio

A lodging operation is solvent when its assets are greater than its liabilities. The solvency ratio compares total assets to total liabilities:

$$\text{Solvency Ratio} = \frac{\text{Total Assets}}{\text{Total Liabilities}}$$

This ratio reveals the amount of assets for every dollar of liabilities.

## Debt Yield Ratio

The debt yield ratio is an important indicator for lenders interested in knowing the size of loan to lend to an owner relative to the size of the hotel's EBITDA (earnings before interest, taxes, depreciation and amortization). Alternatively, it shows the cash-on-cash return on the loan to the lender:

$$\text{Debt Yield Ratio} = \frac{\text{EBITDA - Replacement Reserve}}{\text{Total Debt}} \times 100$$

## Debt-Equity Ratio

One of the most common solvency ratios is the debt-equity ratio, which compares the total debt of the operation to the total investment in the operation by the owners:

$$\text{Debt-Equity Ratio} = \frac{\text{Total Liabilities}}{\text{Total Owners' Equity}}$$

This ratio reveals the amount owed to creditors for every dollar of owners' equity.

## Debt Service Coverage Ratio

This ratio measures the extent to which a hotel generates sufficient EBITDA to cover its debt obligations (interest and/or principal payments):

$$\frac{\text{Debt Service}}{\text{Coverage Ratio}} = \frac{\text{EBITDA}}{\text{Interest Expense + Principal Expense}}$$

# Activity Ratios

It is management's responsibility to generate earnings for owners while providing products and services to guests. Activity ratios measure the effectiveness with which management uses the resources of the property.

## Inventory Turnover

This ratio measures the number of times inventory turns over during the period. Generally, the greater the number of times the better, because inventories can be expensive to maintain. Inventory turnovers are usually calculated separately for food items and beverage items. To calculate inventory turnover, it is first necessary to determine the average inventory. This is accomplished by adding inventory at the beginning and end of the period and then dividing that figure by two. An example of an inventory turnover ratio is the food inventory turnover ratio, calculated as follows:

$$\text{Food Inventory Turnover} = \frac{\text{Cost of Food Sales}}{\text{Average Food Inventory}}$$

# Profitability Ratios

Profitability ratios allow management and owners to compare their profit performance to other competitive and/or comparable properties, to themselves over time, or to budget. Profitability ratios reflect the overall effectiveness of management in producing the bottom line figure expected by owners and creditors. Owners invest in lodging properties in order to increase their wealth through dividends and through increases in the value of the property. Dividends and values are highly dependent upon the present and future profits generated by the operation. Since future profits may be required to repay lenders, creditors normally perceive dealings with the more profitable businesses in their communities to be less risky.

Caution should be used when using profitability ratios for comparison across competitive sets or comparable property groups. Several factors influence the relative profitability of one type of hotel (e.g., convention versus limited service) or individual hotel compared to another or within its competitive set or comparable group.

## Gross Operating Profit per Available Room (GOPAR)

GOPAR measures management's ability to produce profits by generating sales and controlling the operating expenses over which they have the most direct control. GOPAR is calculated by dividing gross operating profit by the rooms available in the hotel:

$$\text{GOPAR} = \frac{\text{Gross Operating Profit}}{\text{Number of Rooms Available}}$$

GOPAR is somewhat useful in relating gross operating profits, on a proportional basis, across properties within a competitive set or comparable property groups. Because GOPAR is calculated before any deduction for management fees, this ratio can be used to compare comparable properties that are operated by a third-party management company with owner-operated properties.

## Gross Operating Profit Margin Ratio

This ratio is another measure of management's overall ability to produce profits by generating sales and controlling the operating expenses over which they have the most direct control. It is calculated by dividing gross operating profit by total operating revenue:

$$\text{GOP Margin Ratio} = \frac{\text{Gross Operating Profit}}{\text{Total Operating Revenue}}$$

Because gross operating profit is calculated before any deduction for management fees, this ratio can be used to compare comparable properties that are operated by a third-party management company with owner-operated properties. Care should be taken in comparing only gross operating profit margins among comparable properties as the revenue mix achieved can significantly influence these margins.

## Income Before Non-Operating Income and Expenses per Available Room

This ratio measures management's ability to produce profits by generating sales and controlling all departmental costs, undistributed expenses, and management fees. It is calculated by dividing income before non-operating income and expenses by the rooms available in the hotel:

$$\text{Income Before Non-Operating Income and Expenses per Available Room} = \frac{\text{Income Before Non-Operating Income and Expenses}}{\text{Rooms Available}}$$

## Income Before Non-Operating Income and Expenses Margin Ratio

This ratio measures management's overall ability to produce profits by generating sales and controlling all departmental costs, undistributed expenses, and management fees. It is calculated by dividing income before non-operating income and expenses by total operating revenue:

$$\text{Income Before Non-Operating Income and Expenses Margin Ratio} = \frac{\text{Income Before Non-Operating Income and Expenses}}{\text{Total Operating Revenue}}$$

## EBITDA per Available Room

This ratio measures management's ability to produce profits by generating sales and controlling all departmental costs, undistributed expenses, management fees, property taxes, insurance, and rent. Care should be taken in comparing EBITDA among comparable properties, since not all hotels have ground, building, or major equipment leases. This ratio is calculated by dividing EBITDA by the rooms available in the hotel:

$$\text{EBITDA per Available Room} = \frac{\text{EBITDA}}{\text{Rooms Available}}$$

## EBITDA Margin Ratio

This ratio measures management's overall ability to produce profits by generating sales and controlling all departmental costs, undistributed expenses, management fees, and non-operating income and expenses. Care should be taken in comparing only EBITDA margins among comparable properties, since not all hotels have ground, building, or major equipment leases. This ratio is calculated by dividing EBITDA by total operating revenue:

$$\text{EBITDA Margin Ratio} = \frac{\text{EBITDA}}{\text{Total Operating Revenue}}$$

## Flow Through/Flex Ratios

The term "flow through" is used when revenues increase relative to budget or the previous year and can be defined as the percentage of incremental profit that "flows" to the bottom-line from each incremental dollar of topline revenue. The term "flex" is used when revenues decrease relative to budget or the previous year and can be defined as the amount of profit that is "flexed" or saved as revenue declines.

Flow through and flex can be calculated for individual departments as well as on the GOP, EBITDA before Non-Operating Income and Expenses, and EBITDA levels. Both ratios can be calculated based on actual results relative to budget, actual results relative to the previous last year, or budget projections relative to the previous year.

The following formulas present flow through and flex, comparing actual to budgeted results, for each scenario of revenue and GOP changes:

**GOP Flow Through: Revenues Increase and Profits Increase**

$$\frac{\text{Actual GOP - Budgeted GOP}}{\text{Actual Revenue - Budgeted Revenue}}$$

**GOP Flow Through: Revenue Increase and Profits Decrease**

$$\frac{\text{Actual GOP - Budgeted GOP}}{\text{Actual Revenue - Budgeted Revenue}}$$

**GOP Flex: Revenues Decrease and Profits Decrease**

$$1 - \frac{\text{Actual GOP - Budgeted GOP}}{\text{Actual Revenue - Budgeted Revenue}}$$

**GOP Flex: Revenues Decrease and Profits Increase**

$$1 - \frac{\text{Actual GOP - Budgeted GOP}}{\text{Actual Revenue - Budgeted Revenue}}$$

## Cash on Cash Return

This calculation is one method of estimating return on investment. Cash on cash return is determined by dividing the EBITDA less debt service by the average owners' equity for a period of time. Average owners' equity is calculated by totaling owners' equity at the beginning and end of the period and then dividing that figure by two. Cash on cash return is calculated as follows:

$$\text{Cash on Cash Return} = \frac{\text{EBITDA - Debt Service}}{\text{Average Owners' Equity}}$$

Note that owners, lenders, and analysts on specific investments frequently use other ratios and calculations, such as internal rate of return.

# Part IV
# Revenue and Expense Guide

This Revenue and Expense Guide is designed to help members of the lodging industry classify, in accordance with the *Uniform System of Accounts for the Lodging Industry,* the numerous revenue and expense items encountered in their daily work. It serves as a ready reference for accounting and non-accounting staff, indicating the proper department and line item/account for recording each expense item.

This Revenue and Expense Guide is not intended to be a complete and comprehensive list of all items that can be recorded in a property. The intention is to present a representative list that is large enough to allow a user either to find the classification of an item or to find examples that will assist in classifying the item if it is not in the guide. The guide does not deal with the question of when to capitalize versus when to expense. Generally Accepted Accounting Principles must be used to make this decision, as well as the "materiality" policies of the owner and/ or management entity. One of the most common examples of how this decision affects the departmental statements is with the recording of an expenditure made to repair property or equipment. Many properties make this decision based on the size of the expenditure when, in general, the expenditure should be capitalized only if it materially extends the life of the item being repaired or materially increases its value.

This guide is organized into two groups: a Revenue Guide and an Expense Guide. Each group is further organized into two sections showing items alphabetically by item and by department. Each section has three columns. In Section One of each guide, the items to be recorded are presented alphabetically in the first column. The second column designates the department or schedule, and the third column indicates the specific line item or account name to be used. In Section Two of each guide, the department or schedule appears in the first column. The second column lists the specific line items or account names of the relevant department or schedule. Column three presents various items that apply to the second column's line item. In the Expense Guide, Section Two begins with a listing of expense items that can apply to multiple departments/schedules and then continues with an alphabetical listing of individual departments/schedules.

Many expense items are shown to be charged to Multiple Departments. This was done to eliminate unnecessary repetition when a given item could apply to the same line item or account in several departments, depending on its actual use. When looking up an item by department or schedule, remember to check under Multiple Departments when an expected item does not appear under a specific department.

With the exception of the Multiple Departments category in the Expense Dictionary, all department and account names used in these dictionaries match those presented in the various sections of the *Uniform System of Accounts for the Lodging Industry.*

Many items are listed under different names so that the user can more easily find an item based on what he/she may perceive as the correct item name. In the case of hotels that operate under a specific brand, users should consult their brand's standards to ensure consistency of classification. Finally, the user of the Revenue and Expense Guide should refer to account definitions in the individual departments of the *Uniform System of Accounts for the Lodging Industry* in order to make classification decisions whenever an item being researched is not found in the Guide.

Because of space considerations, the Revenue and Expense Guide makes use of several abbreviations. The Key to Abbreviations explains all but the most basic abbreviations used.

## KEY TO ABBREVIATIONS

| Abbreviation | Department/Function/Item |
|---|---|
| A&G | Administrative and General |
| B&O | Business and Occupation |
| Banq./Conf./Catering | Banquet/Conference/Catering |
| Bev. | Beverage |
| Cent. Acct. | Centralized Accounting |
| Cost of Merch. Sales | Cost of Merchandise Sales |
| Cur. | Currency |
| Dept. | Department |
| Elec. & Mech. | Electrical and Mechanical Equipment |
| Exch | Exchange |
| Fam Trips | Familiarization Trips |
| F&B | Food and Beverage |
| Grounds M&L | Grounds Maintenance and Landscaping |
| HVAC | Heating, Ventilation, and Air Conditioning |
| Info & Telecom | Information and Telecommunication Systems |
| Minor Oper. Dept. | Minor Operated Department |
| Misc. | Miscellaneous |
| Mult. Depts. | Multiple Departments |
| Non Op. I&E | Non-Operating Income and Expenses |
| P&ODC | Postage and Overnight Delivery Charges |
| Payroll-Rel. Exp. | Payroll-Related Expenses |
| POM | Property Operation and Maintenance |
| Rev. | Revenue |
| Travel—Meals & Enter. | Travel—Meals and Entertainment |
| Vehicle Rep. & Maint. | Vehicle Repairs and Maintenance |

# Revenue Guide
## Section One: Sorted by Item

| Item Name | Department/ Schedule | Account Name |
|---|---|---|
| Accessory sales | Health Club/Spa | Retail Rev. |
| Antenna lease income | Non Op. I&E | Other Income |
| Apparel sales | F&B | Misc. Other Rev. |
| Apparel sales | Health Club/Spa | Retail Rev. |
| Association/convention | Rooms | Association/Convention |
| ATM commission income | Misc. Income | Commissions |

| Item Name | Department/Schedule | Account Name |
|---|---|---|
| Attrition fees | Misc. Income | Attrition Fees |
| Audiovisual services | F&B | Audiovisual |
| Bag storage fees | Golf/Pro Shop | Storage Fee Rev. |
| Banq./conf./catering business services | F&B | Misc. Other Rev. |
| Banq./conf./catering Internet access fee | F&B | Audiovisual |
| Banq./conf./catering recoverable supplies | F&B | Misc. Other Rev. |
| Beer—bottle | F&B | Banq./Conf./Catering Bev. Rev. |
| Beer—bottle | F&B | In-Room Beverage Rev. |
| Beer—bottle | F&B | Mini-Bar Beverage Rev. |
| Beer—bottle | F&B | Outlet Beverage Rev. |
| Beer—draught | F&B | Banq./Conf./Catering Bev. Rev. |
| Beer—draught | F&B | Outlet Beverage Rev. |
| Beverage allowances | F&B | Allowances |
| Billboard or building wall rent | Non Op. I&E | Other Income |
| Body treatment | Health Club/Spa | Massage and Body Treatment Rev. |
| Business interruption insurance proceeds | Misc. Income | Proceeds from Business Interruption Insurance |
| Cancellation fees | Misc. Income | Cancellations Fees |
| Cash discounts earned | Misc. Income | Cash Discounts Earned |
| China and glassware (sold in F&B) | F&B | Misc. Other Rev. |
| Clothing cost of sales | Golf/Pro Shop | Cost of Clothing Sales |
| Clothing sales | Golf/Pro Shop | Clothing Rev. |
| Concessions | Misc. Income | Space Rental & Concessions |
| Contract corrections (e.g., error in posting such as posting incorrect rate) | Rooms | Contract Rooms Rev. |
| Cooler/cider | F&B | Banq./Conf./Catering Bev. Rev. |
| Cooler/cider | F&B | In-Room Beverage Rev. |
| Cooler/cider | F&B | Outlet Beverage Rev. |
| Corkage | F&B | Banquet/Conference/Catering Beverage Rev. |
| Corkage | F&B | Outlet Beverage Rev. |
| Corporate | Rooms | Corporate |
| Cover charges | F&B | Cover Charges |
| Daily facility fees | Health Club/Spa | Membership Fee Rev. |
| Day use | Rooms | Other Rooms Rev. |
| Discount (advance purchase, loyalty redemption, packages, promotions, OTA opaque) | Rooms | Discount |
| Domiciled airline crews | Rooms | Contract Rooms Rev. |
| Early departure fees | Rooms | Other Rooms Rev. |
| Exercise class | Health Club/Spa | Fitness Rev. |

| Item Name | Department/ Schedule | Account Name |
|---|---|---|
| Facial treatment | Health Club/Spa | Skin Care Rev. |
| Fitness evaluation | Health Club/Spa | Fitness Rev. |
| Food allowances | F&B | Allowances |
| Food sales | F&B | Outlet Food Rev. |
| Food sales | F&B | Banq./Conf./Catering Food Rev. |
| Food sales | F&B | In-Room Dining Food Rev. |
| Food sales | F&B | Mini-Bar Food Rev. |
| Function room rentals | F&B | Function Room Rentals and Setup Charges |
| Function room set-up charges | F&B | Function Room Rentals and Setup Charges |
| Golf allowances | Golf/Pro Shop | Allowances |
| Golf cart rentals | Golf/Pro Shop | Golf Cart Rental Rev. |
| Golf equipment rentals | Golf/Pro Shop | Golf Equipment Rental Rev. |
| Golf lessons | Golf/Pro Shop | Lesson Fee Rev. |
| Golf maintenance charges | Golf/Pro Shop | Golf Club Maintenance Rev. |
| Golf membership fees | Golf/Pro Shop | Membership Fee Rev. |
| Government | Rooms | Government |
| Greens fees | Golf/Pro Shop | Greens Fee Rev. |
| Group corrections (e.g., error in posting such as posting incorrect rate) | Rooms | Group Rooms Rev.— (relevant account) |
| Guest dry cleaning revenue—partially serviced by the hotel | Minor Oper. Dept. | Guest Laundry Rev. |
| Guest fax revenue | Minor Oper. Dept. | Guest Communications |
| Guest fees | Health Club/Spa | Membership Fee Rev. |
| Guest foreign currency exchange gains (losses) | Misc. Income | Guest Foreign Currency Exchange Gains (Losses) |
| Guest laundry revenue—partially serviced by the hotel | Minor Oper. Dept. | Guest Laundry Rev. |
| Guest room internet revenue | Minor Oper. Dept. | Guest Communications |
| Guest room telephone revenue | Minor Oper. Dept. | Guest Communications |
| Hair chemical treatment | Health Club/Spa | Hair Care Rev. |
| Hair coloring | Health Club/Spa | Hair Care Rev. |
| Hair-cut and styling | Health Club/Spa | Hair Care Rev. |
| Hair shampoo revenue | Health Club/Spa | Hair Care Rev. |
| Initiation fees | Health Club/Spa | Membership Fee Rev. |
| In-room movie rentals | Minor Oper. Dept. | In-Room Movie Rentals |
| In-room refrigerator rental | Misc. Income | Other |
| In-room safes | Misc. Income | Other |
| In-room video game commissions (outside tv entertainment service agreement) | Misc. Income | Commissions |
| Interest income—reserve accounts | Non Op. I&E | Interest Income |

| Item Name | Department/ Schedule | Account Name |
|---|---|---|
| Interest income—restricted accounts | Non Op. I&E | Interest Income |
| Interest income from bank accounts and note receivable | Misc. Income | Interest Income |
| Kiosk sales operated by the front desk personnel | Minor Oper. Dept. | Retail Kiosk Sales |
| Late check-out fees | Rooms | Other Rooms Rev. |
| Laundry commissions received (outside concessionaire) | Misc. Income | Guest Laundry & Dry Cleaning (Net) |
| Liquor | F&B | Banq./Conf./Catering Bev. Rev. |
| Liquor | F&B | In-Room Beverage Rev. |
| Liquor | F&B | Mini-Bar Beverage Rev. |
| Liquor | F&B | Outlet Beverage Rev. |
| Liquor—bottle | F&B | In-Room Beverage Rev. |
| Locker rentals | Golf/Pro Shop | Storage Fee Rev. |
| Logo merchandise (sold in F&B) | F&B | Misc. Other Rev. |
| Mandatory pool towel charge | Health Club/Spa | Other Rev. |
| Mandatory service charge | Health Club/Spa | Other Rev. |
| Massage | Health Club/Spa | Massage and Body Treatment Rev. |
| Medically supervised services | Health Club/Spa | Health and Wellness Rev. |
| Membership dues | Health Club/Spa | Membership Fee Rev. |
| Merchandise cost of sales | Golf/Pro Shop | Cost of Merchandise Sales |
| Merchandise sales | Golf/Pro Shop | Merchandise Rev. |
| Miscellaneous other F&B revenue | F&B | Misc. Other Rev. |
| Negotiated (special corporate) | Rooms | Negotiated |
| Non-alcoholic beverage sales | F&B | Banq./Conf./Catering Food Rev. |
| Non-alcoholic beverage sales | F&B | In-Room Dining Food Rev. |
| Non-alcoholic beverage sales | F&B | Mini-Bar Food Rev. |
| Non-alcoholic beverage sales | F&B | Outlet Food Rev. |
| No-shows | Rooms | Other Rooms Rev. |
| Nutrition classes | Health Club/Spa | Health and Wellness Rev. |
| Occasional food and beverage revenue— limited service hotels | Minor Oper. Dept. | Occasional Food and Beverage Rev. |
| Off-premises beer | F&B | Outlet Beverage Rev. |
| Off-premises cooler/cider | F&B | Outlet Beverage Rev. |
| Off-premises liquor | F&B | Outlet Beverage Rev. |
| Off-premises wine | F&B | Outlet Beverage Rev. |
| On-demand music commissions (outside tv entertainment service agreement) | Misc. Income | Commissions |
| Ongoing corporate training seminars | Rooms | Contract Rooms Rev. |
| Other beverage revenue | F&B | Other Beverage Rev. |
| Other food revenue | F&B | Other Food Rev. |

| Item Name | Department/ Schedule | Account Name |
|---|---|---|
| Other parking revenue (in-house or outside contractor) | Parking | Other Rev. |
| Other revenue | Golf/Pro Shop | Other Rev. |
| Package breakage | Misc. Income | Breakage |
| Parking commissions (self/valet/other with an outside concessionaire) | Misc. Income | Commissions |
| Parking garage allowances | Parking | Allowances |
| Pay-per-view commissions (outside tv entertainment service agreement) | Misc. Income | Commissions |
| Personal training | Health Club/Spa | Fitness Rev. |
| Practice range balls | Golf/Pro Shop | Practice Range Fee Rev. |
| Product sales | Health Club/Spa | Retail Rev. |
| Qualified (senior citizen, AAA, government, employee rate) | Rooms | Qualified |
| Rental of rollaway beds and cribs | Rooms | Other Rooms Rev. |
| Resort fees | Misc. Income | Resort Fees |
| Retail (non-discounted, non-qualified rates) | Rooms | Retail |
| Room upsell charges (e.g., ocean view, high floor, etc.) | Rooms | Other Rooms Rev. |
| Safety deposit boxes | Misc. Income | Other |
| Self-parking revenue (in-house or outside contractor) | Parking | Self-Parking Rev. |
| Service charges | F&B | Surcharges and Service Charges |
| Service charges | Rooms | Other Rooms Rev. |
| Service problems/failures | Rooms | Allowances |
| SMERF (social, military, educational, religious, fraternal) | Rooms | SMERF |
| Space license rent | Misc. Income | Space Rental & Concessions |
| Space rent | Misc. Income | Space Rental & Concessions |
| Spiritual guidance | Health Club/Spa | Health and Wellness Rev. |
| Tobacco sales | F&B | Misc. Other Rev. |
| Tour/wholesaler group | Rooms | Tour/Wholesalers |
| Tournament fees | Golf/Pro Shop | Tournament Fee Rev. |
| Transient corrections (e.g., error in posting such as posting incorrect rate) | Rooms | Transient Rooms Rev.— (relevant account) |
| TV on demand commissions (outside TV entertainment service agreement) | Misc. Income | Commissions |
| Valet parking revenue (in-house or outside contractor) | Parking | Valet Parking Rev. |
| Vending machine income—hotel operated | Minor Oper. Dept. | Vending Rev. |
| Video game income—hotel operated | Minor Oper. Dept. | Video Game Sales |

| Item Name | Department/ Schedule | Account Name |
|-----------|---------------------|--------------|
| Waxing services | Health Club/Spa | Skin Care Rev. |
| Wellness consultations | Health Club/Spa | Health and Wellness Rev. |
| Wholesalers | Rooms | Wholesale |
| Wine | F&B | Mini-Bar Beverage Rev. |
| Wine—bottle | F&B | Banq./Conf./Catering Bev. Rev. |
| Wine—bottle | F&B | In-Room Beverage Rev. |
| Wine—bottle | F&B | Outlet Beverage Rev. |
| Wine—glass | F&B | Banq./Conf./Catering Bev. Rev. |
| Wine—glass | F&B | In-Room Beverage Rev. |
| Wine—glass | F&B | Outlet Beverage Rev. |

# Revenue Guide
## Section Two: Sorted by Department/Schedule and Account Name

| Department/ Schedule | Account Name | Item Name |
|---------------------|--------------|-----------|
| F&B | Allowances | Beverage allowances |
| F&B | Allowances | Food allowances |
| F&B | Audiovisual | Audiovisual services |
| F&B | Audiovisual | Banq./conf./catering internet access fee |
| F&B | Banq./Conf./Catering Bev. Rev. | Beer—bottle |
| F&B | Banq./Conf./Catering Bev. Rev. | Beer—draught |
| F&B | Banq./Conf./Catering Bev. Rev. | Cooler/cider |
| F&B | Banq./Conf./Catering Bev. Rev. | Corkage |
| F&B | Banq./Conf./Catering Bev. Rev. | Liquor |
| F&B | Banq./Conf./Catering Bev. Rev. | Wine—bottle |
| F&B | Banq./Conf./Catering Bev. Rev. | Wine—glass |
| F&B | Banq./Conf./Catering Food Rev. | Food sales |
| F&B | Banq./Conf./Catering Food Rev. | Non-alcoholic beverage sales |
| F&B | Cover Charges | Cover charges |
| F&B | Function Room Rentals and Setup Charges | Function room rentals |
| F&B | Function Room Rentals and Setup Charges | Function room setup charges |
| F&B | In-Room Dining Beverage Revenue | Beer—bottle |
| F&B | In-Room Dining Beverage Revenue | Cooler/cider |
| F&B | In-Room Dining Beverage Revenue | Liquor |
| F&B | In-Room Dining Beverage Revenue | Liquor—bottle |
| F&B | In-Room Dining Beverage Revenue | Wine—bottle |
| F&B | In-Room Dining Beverage Revenue | Wine—glass |

| Department/ Schedule | Account Name | Item Name |
|---|---|---|
| F&B | In-Room Dining Food Revenue | Food sales |
| F&B | In-Room Dining Food Revenue | Non-alcoholic beverage sales |
| F&B | Mini-Bar Beverage Revenue | Beer—bottle |
| F&B | Mini-Bar Beverage Revenue | Liquor |
| F&B | Mini-Bar Beverage Revenue | Wine |
| F&B | Mini-Bar Food Revenue | Food sales |
| F&B | Mini-Bar Food Revenue | Non-alcoholic beverage sales |
| F&B | Miscellaneous Other Revenue | Apparel (sold in F&B) |
| F&B | Miscellaneous Other Revenue | Banq./conf./catering business services |
| F&B | Miscellaneous Other Revenue | Banq./conf./catering recoverable supplies |
| F&B | Miscellaneous Other Revenue | China and glassware (for sale in F&B) |
| F&B | Miscellaneous Other Revenue | Logo merchandise (for sale in F&B) |
| F&B | Miscellaneous Other Revenue | Miscellaneous other revenue |
| F&B | Miscellaneous Other Revenue | Tobacco sales |
| F&B | Other Beverage Revenue | Other beverage revenue |
| F&B | Other Food Revenue | Other food revenue |
| F&B | Surcharges and Service Charges | Service charges |
| F&B | Venue Beverage Revenue | Beer—bottle |
| F&B | Venue Beverage Revenue | Beer—draught |
| F&B | Venue Beverage Revenue | Cooler/cider |
| F&B | Venue Beverage Revenue | Corkage |
| F&B | Venue Beverage Revenue | Liquor |
| F&B | Venue Beverage Revenue | Off-premises beer |
| F&B | Venue Beverage Revenue | Off-premises cooler/cider |
| F&B | Venue Beverage Revenue | Off-premises liquor |
| F&B | Venue Beverage Revenue | Off-premises wine |
| F&B | Venue Beverage Revenue | Wine—bottle |
| F&B | Venue Beverage Revenue | Wine—glass |
| F&B | Venue Food Revenue | Food sales |
| F&B | Venue Food Revenue | Non-alcoholic beverage sales |
| Golf/Pro Shop | Allowances | Golf allowances |
| Golf/Pro Shop | Clothing Revenue | Clothing sales |
| Golf/Pro Shop | Cost of Clothing Sales | Clothing cost of sales |
| Golf/Pro Shop | Cost of Merchandise Sales | Merchandise cost of sales |
| Golf/Pro Shop | Golf Cart Rental Revenue | Golf cart rentals |
| Golf/Pro Shop | Golf Club Maintenance Revenue | Golf maintenance charges |
| Golf/Pro Shop | Golf Equipment Rental Revenue | Golf equipment rentals |

| Department/ Schedule | Account Name | Item Name |
|---|---|---|
| Golf/Pro Shop | Greens Fee Revenue | Greens fees |
| Golf/Pro Shop | Lesson Fee Revenue | Golf lessons |
| Golf/Pro Shop | Membership Fee Revenue | Golf membership fees |
| Golf/Pro Shop | Merchandise Revenue | Merchandise sales |
| Golf/Pro Shop | Other Revenue | Other revenue |
| Golf/Pro Shop | Practice Range Fee Revenue | Practice range balls |
| Golf/Pro Shop | Storage Fee Revenue | Bag storage fees |
| Golf/Pro Shop | Storage Fee Revenue | Locker rentals |
| Golf/Pro Shop | Tournament Fee Revenue | Tournament fees |
| Health Club/Spa | Fitness Revenue | Exercise class |
| Health Club/Spa | Fitness Revenue | Fitness evaluation |
| Health Club/Spa | Fitness Revenue | Personal training |
| Health Club/Spa | Hair Care Revenue | Hair chemical treatment |
| Health Club/Spa | Hair Care Revenue | Hair coloring |
| Health Club/Spa | Hair Care Revenue | Hair-cut and styling |
| Health Club/Spa | Hair Care Revenue | Hair shampoo revenue |
| Health Club/Spa | Health and Wellness Revenue | Medically supervised services |
| Health Club/Spa | Health and Wellness Revenue | Nutrition classes |
| Health Club/Spa | Health and Wellness Revenue | Spiritual guidance |
| Health Club/Spa | Health and Wellness Revenue | Wellness consultations |
| Health Club/Spa | Massage and Body Treatment Revenue | Body treatment |
| Health Club/Spa | Massage and Body Treatment Revenue | Massage |
| Health Club/Spa | Membership Fee Revenue | Daily facility fees |
| Health Club/Spa | Membership Fee Revenue | Guest fees |
| Health Club/Spa | Membership Fee Revenue | Initiation fees |
| Health Club/Spa | Membership Fee Revenue | Membership dues |
| Health Club/Spa | Other Revenue | Mandatory pool towel charge |
| Health Club/Spa | Other Revenue | Mandatory service charge |
| Health Club/Spa | Retail Revenue | Accessory sales |
| Health Club/Spa | Retail Revenue | Apparel sales |
| Health Club/Spa | Retail Revenue | Product sales |
| Health Club/Spa | Skin Care Revenue | Facial treatment |
| Health Club/Spa | Skin Care Revenue | Waxing services |
| Minor Oper. Dept. | Guest Communications | Guest fax revenue |
| Minor Oper. Dept. | Guest Communications | Guest room internet revenue |
| Minor Oper. Dept. | Guest Communications | Guest room telephone revenue |
| Minor Oper. Dept. | Guest Laundry Revenue | Guest dry cleaning revenue— partially serviced by the hotel |
| Minor Oper. Dept. | Guest Laundry Revenue | Guest laundry revenue— partially serviced by the hotel |

| Department/<br>Schedule | Account Name | Item Name |
|---|---|---|
| Minor Oper. Dept. | In-Room Movie Rentals | In-room movie rentals |
| Minor Oper. Dept. | Occasional Food and Beverage Revenue | Occasional food and beverage revenue—limited service hotels |
| Minor Oper. Dept. | Retail Kiosk Sales | Kiosk sales operated by the front desk personnel |
| Minor Oper. Dept. | Vending Revenue | Vending machine income—hotel operated |
| Minor Oper. Dept. | Video Game Sales | Video game income—hotel operated |
| Misc. Income | Attrition Fees | Attrition fees |
| Misc. Income | Cancellations Fees | Cancellation fees |
| Misc. Income | Cash Discounts Earned | Cash discounts earned |
| Misc. Income | Commissions | ATM commission income |
| Misc. Income | Commissions | In-room video game commissions (outside TV entertainment service agreement) |
| Misc. Income | Commissions | On-demand music commissions (outside TV entertainment service agreement) |
| Misc. Income | Commissions | Parking commissions (self/valet/other with an outside concessionaire) |
| Misc. Income | Commissions | Pay-per-view commissions (outside TV entertainment service agreement) |
| Misc. Income | Commissions | TV on demand commissions (outside TV entertainment service agreement) |
| Misc. Income | Guest Foreign Cur. Exch. Gains (Losses) | Guest foreign currency exchange gains (losses) |
| Misc. Income | Guest Laundry & Dry Cleaning | Laundry commissions received (outside concessionaire) |
| Misc. Income | Interest Income | Interest income from bank accounts and note receivable |
| Misc. Income | Other | In-room refrigerator rental |
| Misc. Income | Other | In-room safes |
| Misc. Income | Other | Safety deposit boxes |
| Misc. Income | Package Breakage | Package breakage |
| Misc. Income | Proceeds from Business Interruption Insurance | Business interruption insurance proceeds |
| Misc. Income | Resort Fees | Resort fees |
| Misc. Income | Space Rental and Concessions | Concessions |
| Misc. Income | Space Rental and Concessions | Space license rent |
| Misc. Income | Space Rental and Concessions | Space rent |

| Department/Schedule | Account Name | Item Name |
|---|---|---|
| Non Op. I&E | Interest Income | Interest income—reserve accounts |
| Non Op. I&E | Interest Income | Interest income—restricted accounts |
| Non Op. I&E | Other Income | Antenna lease income |
| Non Op. I&E | Other Income | Billboard or building wall rent |
| Parking | Allowances | Parking garage allowances |
| Parking | Other Revenue | Other parking revenue (in-house or outside contractor) |
| Parking | Self-Parking Revenue | Self-parking revenue (in-house or outside contractor) |
| Parking | Valet Parking Revenue | Valet parking revenue (in-house or outside contractor) |
| Rooms | Allowances | Service problems/failures |
| Rooms | Association/convention | Association/convention |
| Rooms | Contract Rooms Revenue | Contract corrections (e.g., error in posting such as posting incorrect rate) |
| Rooms | Contract Rooms Revenue | Domiciled airline crews |
| Rooms | Contract Rooms Revenue | Ongoing corporate training seminars |
| Rooms | Corporate | Corporate |
| Rooms | Discount | Discount (advance purchase, loyalty redemption, packages, promotions, OTA opaque) |
| Rooms | Government | Government |
| Rooms | Group Rooms Revenue—(relevant account) | Group corrections (e.g., error in posting such as posting incorrect rate) |
| Rooms | Negotiated | Negotiated (special corporate) |
| Rooms | Other Rooms Revenue | Day use |
| Rooms | Other Rooms Revenue | Early departure fees |
| Rooms | Other Rooms Revenue | Late check-out fees |
| Rooms | Other Rooms Revenue | No-shows |
| Rooms | Other Rooms Revenue | Rental of rollaway beds and cribs |
| Rooms | Other Rooms Revenue | Room upsell charges (e.g., ocean view, high floor, etc.) |
| Rooms | Other Rooms Revenue | Service charges |
| Rooms | Qualified | Qualified (senior citizen, AAA, government, employee rate) |
| Rooms | Retail | Retail (non-discounted, non-qualified rates) |
| Rooms | SMERF | SMERF (social, military, educational, religious, fraternal) |
| Rooms | Tour/Wholesalers | Tour/wholesaler group |

| Department/ Schedule | Account Name | Item Name |
|---|---|---|
| Rooms | Transient Rooms Revenue—(relevant account) | Transient corrections (e.g., error in posting such as posting incorrect rate) |
| Rooms | Wholesalers | Wholesalers |

# Expense Guide
## Section One: Sorted by Item

| Item Name | Department/ Schedule | Account Name |
|---|---|---|
| Accessories (for sale in health club/spa) | Health Club/Spa | Cost of Sales |
| Accident insurance for non-union employees | Payroll-Rel. Exp. | Nonunion Insurance |
| Accountant's fees, consulting | A&G | Professional Fees |
| Accounting fees—centralized (management company) | A&G | Cent. Acct. Charges |
| Accounting fees—centralized (owner) | A&G | Cent. Acct. Charges |
| Accounting hardware, small value purchases | Info & Telecom | A&G |
| Accounting software licenses, support and maintenance fees | Info & Telecom | A&G |
| Acids | Mult. Depts. | Cleaning Supplies |
| Ad design and creative | Sales/Marketing | Media |
| ADA compliance items—not capitalized | POM | Life/Safety |
| Adapter plug, electrical | Mult. Depts. | Operating Supplies |
| Adding machine tape | Mult. Depts. | Operating Supplies |
| Adding machines | Mult. Depts. | Operating Supplies |
| Address list maintenance/purchase/rental | Sales/Marketing | Direct Mail |
| Adhesive, stair tread | POM | Floor Covering |
| Adhesive tape | Mult. Depts. | Operating Supplies |
| Administrative fees for contributory savings plans | Payroll-Rel. Exp. | Contributory Savings Plan |
| Advertising agency fees | Sales/Marketing | Agency Fees |
| Advertising assessments | Sales/Marketing | Franchise and Affiliation Marketing |
| Advertising—direct mail | Sales/Marketing | Direct Mail |
| Advertising—directories | Sales/Marketing | Media |
| Advertising—Internet incl. OTA | Sales/Marketing | Media |
| Advertising—magazines | Sales/Marketing | Media |
| Advertising—newspapers | Sales/Marketing | Media |
| Advertising—outdoor | Sales/Marketing | Outside Signage |
| Advertising production—magazines | Sales/Marketing | Media |
| Advertising production—miscellaneous | Sales/Marketing | Media |
| Advertising production—newspaper | Sales/Marketing | Media |

| Item Name | Department/ Schedule | Account Name |
|---|---|---|
| Advertising production—TV and radio | Sales/Marketing | Media |
| Advertising—radio | Sales/Marketing | Media |
| Advertising—recruiting | A&G | Human Resources |
| Advertising signs—interior | Sales/Marketing | In-House Graphics |
| Affiliation advertising fee | Sales/Marketing | Franchise and Affiliation Marketing |
| Affiliation marketing fee | Sales/Marketing | Franchise and Affiliation Marketing |
| Afghans, guestroom | Rooms | Operating Supplies |
| Aftershave lotion | Rooms | Guest Supplies |
| Air deodorizing accessories/systems | Mult. Depts. | Operating Supplies |
| Air filters | POM | HVAC Equipment |
| Air freshener | Mult. Depts. | Cleaning Supplies |
| Airfare | Mult. Depts. | Travel—Other |
| Airfare—corporate—sales and marketing | Sales/Marketing | Corporate Office Reimbursables |
| Airline loyalty program fees | Sales/Marketing | Loyalty Programs |
| Airport van maintenance | Rooms | Guest Transportation |
| Alarm systems repairs | POM | Life/Safety |
| Alcohol (cleaning) | Mult. Depts. | Cleaning Supplies |
| All-purpose cleaner | Mult. Depts. | Cleaning Supplies |
| Aluminum foil | F&B | Paper and Plastics |
| Aluminum trays | F&B | China |
| Amenities, gifts | Mult. Depts. | Complimentary Services/ Gifts |
| Amenities, guest | Rooms | Guest Supplies |
| Amenity baskets/containers (not reusable) | Rooms | Guest Supplies |
| Amenity baskets/containers (reusable) | Rooms | Operating Supplies |
| Ammonia | Mult. Depts. | Cleaning Supplies |
| Annual report fee | A&G | Licenses and Permits |
| Answering machines | Mult. Depts. | Operating Supplies |
| Antacid (for use by guests in rooms) | Rooms | Guest Supplies |
| Anti-fatigue mats | Mult. Depts. | Operating Supplies |
| Apparel (for sale in F&B) | F&B | Misc. Cost (of Other Rev.) |
| Apparel (for sale in health club/spa) | Health Club/Spa | Cost of Sales |
| Aprons | Mult. Depts. | Uniform Costs |
| Aquarium, guestroom or lobby | Rooms | Operating Supplies |
| Aquarium supplies, guestroom or lobby | Rooms | Operating Supplies |
| Armored transport fee | A&G | Security |
| Aromatherapy oils (health club/spa) | Health Club/Spa | Ambience |
| Artificial plant cleaner | Mult. Depts. | Cleaning Supplies |

| Item Name | Department/Schedule | Account Name |
| --- | --- | --- |
| Artwork | Mult. Depts. | Operating Supplies |
| Ash cans | Mult. Depts. | Operating Supplies |
| Ashtrays | Mult. Depts. | Operating Supplies |
| Ashtrays, aluminum, glass | F&B | China |
| Aspirin (for use by guests in rooms) | Rooms | Guest Supplies |
| Asset manager fees | Non Op. I&E | Owner Expenses |
| Association assessment—general. (Not if defined: e.g., snow removal) | Non Op. I&E | Other Taxes and Assessments |
| Association dues—sales and marketing staff | Sales/Marketing | Dues and Subscriptions |
| Attorney's fees/expenses—real estate taxes | Non Op. I&E | Real Estate Taxes |
| Audiovisual equipment rent (charged to customer) | F&B | Audiovisual Cost |
| Audit fees, public accountants | A&G | Audit Charges |
| Auto fuel costs (guest transport) | Rooms | Guest Transportation |
| Auto/truck repair—property use | POM | Vehicle Repairs |
| Awards—employees | A&G | Human Resources |
| Awning repairs | POM | Building |
| Bad debt allowance | A&G | Provision for Doubtful Accounts |
| Baggage tags (gratis) | Rooms | Guest Supplies |
| Bags—beverage glass covers, guestroom | Rooms | Operating Supplies |
| Bags, paper leftover | F&B | Paper and Plastics |
| Bags, pastry | F&B | Utensils |
| Baked goods | F&B | Cost of Food Sales |
| Ball washers, golf course | Golf/Pro Shop | Operating Supplies |
| Band-aids | Mult. Depts. | Operating Supplies |
| Bank checks, charges | A&G | Bank Charges |
| Bank related fees and costs | A&G | Bank Charges |
| Banners, golf tournament | Golf/Pro Shop | Tournament Expenses |
| Banquet space map and floor plans | Sales/Marketing | Collateral Material |
| Banquet/conference/catering recoverable supplies | F&B | Misc. Cost (of Other Rev.) |
| Bar fruit and garnish | F&B | Cost of Beverage Sales |
| Bar mats | F&B | Operating Supplies |
| Bar supplies—consumable | F&B | Cost of Beverage Sales |
| Barter/contra agreement | Sales/Marketing | Media |
| Baskets, amenity | Rooms | Operating Supplies |
| Baskets, urinal | Mult. Depts. | Operating Supplies |
| Baskets, waste liners | Mult. Depts. | Operating Supplies |
| Baskets, welcome | Rooms | Complimentary Services/Gifts |
| Baskets, wine (for gratis presentations)—not reusable | Mult. Depts. | Complimentary Services/Gifts |

| Item Name | Department/Schedule | Account Name |
|---|---|---|
| Baskets, wine (for gratis presentations)— reusable .. | Mult. Depts. ......... | Operating Supplies |
| Bath gel ................................................................. | Rooms .................... | Guest Supplies |
| Bath mats (health club/spa) ....................................... | Health Club/Spa.... | Linen |
| Bath salts.................................................................. | Rooms .................... | Guest Supplies |
| Bath sheets................................................................ | Rooms .................... | Guest Supplies |
| Bath soap .................................................................. | Rooms .................... | Guest Supplies |
| Bath tissue ................................................................ | Rooms .................... | Guest Supplies |
| Bath towels (all sizes) ................................................ | Rooms .................... | Linen |
| Bathing cap................................................................ | Rooms .................... | Guest Supplies |
| Bathing suits, disposable............................................. | Rooms .................... | Guest Supplies |
| Bathmats ................................................................... | Rooms .................... | Linen |
| Bathrobes (health club/spa) ........................................ | Health Club/Spa.... | Linen |
| Bathroom cleaner ....................................................... | Mult. Depts. ......... | Cleaning Supplies |
| Bathroom scale .......................................................... | Rooms .................... | Operating Supplies |
| Bathroom throw rugs .................................................. | Rooms .................... | Linen |
| Bathtub safety mats.................................................... | Rooms .................... | Operating Supplies |
| Bathtub safety strips ................................................... | Rooms .................... | Operating Supplies |
| Batteries ................................................................... | Mult. Depts. ......... | Operating Supplies |
| Beaters...................................................................... | F&B ....................... | Utensils |
| Bed pads ................................................................... | Rooms .................... | Linen |
| Bed ruffles ................................................................ | Rooms .................... | Linen |
| Bed skirts.................................................................. | Rooms .................... | Linen |
| Bedspreads................................................................ | Rooms .................... | Linen |
| Beeper rental ............................................................. | Mult. Depts. ......... | Equipment Rental |
| Beer—bottle............................................................... | F&B....................... | Cost of Beverage Sales |
| Beer coil cleaning (outside service) ............................ | F&B ....................... | Contract Services |
| Beer—draught ............................................................ | F&B....................... | Cost of Beverage Sales |
| Beverage assessment (this is not other tax and assessment) ....................................................... | F&B....................... | Cost of Beverage Sales |
| Beverage lists ............................................................ | F&B ....................... | Menus and Beverage Lists |
| Beverages for fam trip attendees................................. | Sales/Marketing..... | Familiarization Trips |
| Billboards ................................................................. | Sales/Marketing..... | Outside Signage |
| Binder clips ............................................................... | Mult. Depts. ......... | Operating Supplies |
| Binders...................................................................... | Mult. Depts. ......... | Operating Supplies |
| Blackout drapes.......................................................... | Rooms .................... | Operating Supplies |
| Blanket covers............................................................ | Rooms .................... | Linen |
| Blankets, guestroom ................................................... | Rooms .................... | Linen |
| Blankets (health club/spa)........................................... | Health Club/Spa.... | Linen |
| Bleach....................................................................... | Mult. Depts. ......... | Cleaning Supplies |
| Bleach packets........................................................... | Mult. Depts. ......... | Cleaning Supplies |

| Item Name | Department/ Schedule | Account Name |
|---|---|---|
| Blenders, bar | F&B | Utensils |
| Blouses | Mult. Depts. | Uniform Costs |
| Body lotion | Rooms | Guest Supplies |
| Boiler repairs | POM | HVAC Equipment |
| Book matches (guest) | Mult. Depts. | Operating Supplies |
| Books, golf (for sale) | Golf/Pro Shop | Cost of Merch. Sales |
| Books, in-room guest reading | Rooms | Operating Supplies |
| Books, outlet reservations log | F&B | Operating Supplies |
| Books, technical | Mult. Depts. | Training |
| Booths at trade shows | Sales/Marketing | Trade Shows |
| Boots | Mult. Depts. | Uniform Costs |
| Bottle openers | F&B | Utensils |
| Bottle openers, guestroom | Rooms | Operating Supplies |
| Bottle warmers | Rooms | Operating Supplies |
| Bottled water (gratis in rooms) | Rooms | Guest Supplies |
| Bowls, mixing/preparation (all sizes and materials) | F&B | China |
| Bowls, serving (all sizes and materials) | F&B | China |
| Boxes, carry out | F&B | Paper and Plastics |
| Boxes, pastry | F&B | Paper and Plastics |
| Braille signs | Rooms | Operating Supplies |
| Brand meetings fee | Sales/Marketing | Travel—Other |
| Brochures | Sales/Marketing | Collateral Material |
| Brooms | Mult. Depts. | Cleaning Supplies |
| Brushes | Mult. Depts. | Cleaning Supplies |
| Buckets, mop | Mult. Depts. | Cleaning Supplies |
| Bug traps | Mult. Depts. | Cleaning Supplies |
| Building lease, base rent | Non Op. I&E | Land and Buildings |
| Building lease, participating rent (based on operating results) | Non Op. I&E | Land and Buildings |
| Building repairs | POM | Building |
| Bumpers, bed | Rooms | Linen |
| Bumpers, crib | Rooms | Linen |
| Bunting | Rooms | Linen |
| Business cards | Mult. Depts. | Printing and Stationery |
| Business improvement district (bid) assessment or tax | Non Op. I&E | Real Estate Taxes |
| Business licenses, general | A&G | Licenses and Permits |
| Business taxes that cannot be passed on to the customer (non-revenue-generating department) | Non Op. I&E | B&O Taxes |
| Butane fuel | F&B | Kitchen Fuel |

| Item Name | Department/ Schedule | Account Name |
|---|---|---|
| Butter dishes (all materials) | F&B | China |
| Buttons (for use by guests in rooms) | Rooms | Guest Supplies |
| Cable guide cover | Rooms | Printing and Stationery |
| Cable television service | Rooms | Complimentary In-Room/ Media Entertainment |
| Caddy service | Golf/Pro Shop | Contract Services |
| Calculators | Mult. Depts. | Operating Supplies |
| Calendars and diaries | Mult. Depts. | Operating Supplies |
| Call accounting system lease (non-capital) | Non Op. I&E | Other Property & Equipment |
| Call accounting system software lease (non-capital) | Non Op. I&E | Other Property & Equipment |
| Cameras, security | Info & Telecom | A&G |
| Can openers | F&B | Utensils |
| Can openers | Rooms | Operating Supplies |
| Candle holders, tabletop | F&B | Operating Supplies |
| Candles | Mult. Depts. | Operating Supplies |
| Candlesticks | Mult. Depts. | Operating Supplies |
| Candy dishes, guestroom (gratis candy for customers) | Rooms | Operating Supplies |
| Candy (gratis) | Rooms | Guest Supplies |
| Canned food | F&B | Cost of Food Sales |
| Canopies, bed | Rooms | Operating Supplies |
| Cappuccino machines | Rooms | Operating Supplies |
| Caps | Mult. Depts. | Uniform Costs |
| Car rental | Mult. Depts. | Travel—Other |
| Car rental—corporate—sales and marketing | Sales/Marketing | Corporate Office Reimbursables |
| Car rental loyalty program fees | Sales/Marketing | Loyalty Programs |
| Car washing (rooms vans, carts, limos) | Rooms | Guest Transportation |
| Carafes | F&B | Glassware |
| Carafes, guestroom | Rooms | Operating Supplies |
| Cardboard boxes | F&B | Paper and Plastics |
| Carpet cleaner chemical | Mult. Depts. | Cleaning Supplies |
| Carpet cleaner equipment | Rooms | Cleaning Supplies |
| Carpet cleaning services | Mult. Depts. | Contract Services |
| Carpet cleaning supplies | Mult. Depts. | Cleaning Supplies |
| Carpet repairs | POM | Floor Covering |
| Carpet shampoo | Mult. Depts. | Cleaning Supplies |
| Carpet shampoo machines | Mult. Depts. | Cleaning Supplies |
| Carpet sweepers | Mult. Depts. | Cleaning Supplies |
| Carpet/rug cleaning (outside service) | Mult. Depts. | Contract Services |

| Item Name | Department/ Schedule | Account Name |
|---|---|---|
| Carry out containers | F&B | Paper and Plastics |
| Cart name plates, golf tournament | Golf/Pro Shop | Tournament Expenses |
| Carts, fuel costs (guest transport) | Rooms | Guest Transportation |
| Carts, housekeeper | Rooms | Operating Supplies |
| Carts, laundry | Rooms | Operating Supplies |
| Cash boxes | A&G | Operating Supplies |
| Cash overages and shortages | A&G | Cash Overages/Shortages |
| Cashier envelopes | Mult. Depts. | Operating Supplies |
| Cashier forms | Mult. Depts. | Operating Supplies |
| Casseroles | F&B | China |
| CD-ROM, writable | Mult. Depts. | Operating Supplies |
| Ceiling fan repairs | POM | HVAC Equipment |
| Ceiling, wall and floor repairs | POM | Building |
| Cell phone chargers | Rooms | Guest Supplies |
| Cell phone equipment | Info & Telecom | Cost of Cell Phones |
| Cellophane tape | Mult. Depts. | Operating Supplies |
| Cellophane wrap | F&B | Paper and Plastics |
| Central plant costs | POM | HVAC Equipment |
| Chafing dishes | F&B | Utensils |
| Chamber of commerce dues | Sales/Marketing | Dues and Subscriptions |
| Chamber of commerce events/registration | Sales/Marketing | Travel—Other |
| Chamois | Mult. Depts. | Cleaning Supplies |
| Charcoal, cooking | F&B | Kitchen Fuel |
| Charge vouchers | Mult. Depts. | Printing and Stationery |
| Charitable contributions | A&G | Donations |
| Charity events (fees, donations, registrations) | Sales/Marketing | Promotion |
| Check presenters | F&B | Operating Supplies |
| Check verification | A&G | Credit and Collection |
| Check writer machines | A&G | Operating Supplies |
| Check/folio/statement presentation folders | Mult. Depts. | Printing and Stationery |
| Check-out folders | Rooms | Printing and Stationery |
| Check-out notices | Rooms | Printing and Stationery |
| Cheese baskets, gratis | Mult. Depts. | Complimentary Services/Gifts |
| Chef hats | F&B | Paper and Plastics |
| Chemicals, cooling tower | POM | HVAC Equipment |
| Chemicals, fire extinguishers | POM | Life/Safety |
| China | F&B | China |
| China and glassware (for sale in F&B) | F&B | Misc. Cost (of Other Rev.) |
| China, guestroom | Rooms | Operating Supplies |
| China rental | F&B | China |

| Item Name | Department/ Schedule | Account Name |
|---|---|---|
| Christmas decorations (inside and outside, visible to guests) | Sales/Marketing | Decorations |
| Christmas gifts—employees | A&G | Human Resources |
| Cigar cost | F&B | Misc. Cost (of Other Rev.) |
| Claim/litigation settlement costs, contract disputes | A&G | Settlement Costs |
| Claim/litigation settlement costs, EEOC | A&G | Settlement Costs |
| Claim/litigation settlement costs, non-insured | A&G | Settlement Costs |
| Cleaner, concrete (parking garage) | Parking | Cleaning Supplies |
| Cleaning beer coils (outside service) | F&B | Contract Services |
| Cleaning chemicals | Mult. Depts. | Cleaning Supplies |
| Cleaning cloths, compounds, fluids, rags, sponges | Mult. Depts. | Cleaning Supplies |
| Cleaning supplies | F&B | Cleaning Supplies |
| Cleansers (non-dishwashing) | Mult. Depts. | Cleaning Supplies |
| Cleansing powder | Mult. Depts. | Cleaning Supplies |
| Client gifts | Sales/Marketing | Promotion |
| Clipboards | Mult. Depts. | Operating Supplies |
| Clock radios for guestrooms | Rooms | Operating Supplies |
| Clock/DVD players, Blu-ray, Apple TV for guestrooms | Rooms | Operating Supplies |
| Clocks for guestrooms | Rooms | Operating Supplies |
| Closet rod | Rooms | Operating Supplies |
| Closet sachets | Rooms | Operating Supplies |
| Clothes brushes | Rooms | Operating Supplies |
| Clothing, golf (for sale) | Golf/Pro Shop | Cost of Clothing Sales |
| Clothing hangers (health club/spa) | Health Club/Spa | Operating Supplies |
| Cluster accounting office costs | A&G | Cluster Services |
| Cluster allocation from brand or management (no breakdown) | Sales/Marketing | Cluster Services |
| Cluster allocation from brand or management (payroll) | Sales/Marketing | Salaries and Wages |
| C02 for soft drink mix | F&B | Cost of Beverage Sales |
| C02 for soft drink mix | F&B | Cost of Food Sales |
| Coasters | Rooms | Operating Supplies |
| Coats | Mult. Depts. | Uniform Costs |
| Cocktail picks | F&B | Paper and Plastics |
| Coffee filters | F&B | Paper and Plastics |
| Coffee filters | Rooms | Guest Supplies |
| Coffee for use by guests in rooms | Rooms | Guest Supplies |
| Coffee mugs | Rooms | Operating Supplies |
| Coffee pots for use by guests in rooms | Rooms | Operating Supplies |
| Coffee pots (glass, plastic, silver) | F&B | China |

| Item Name | Department/Schedule | Account Name |
|---|---|---|
| Coffee urn | F&B | Utensils |
| Coffee/tea | F&B | Cost of Food Sales |
| Cogeneration of water | Utilities | Water/Sewer |
| Coin drawers | Mult. Depts. | Operating Supplies |
| Coin handling equipment | A&G | Operating Supplies |
| Coin wrappers | A&G | Operating Supplies |
| Coin/currency bag seals | A&G | Operating Supplies |
| Coin/currency equipment | A&G | Operating Supplies |
| Colanders | F&B | Utensils |
| Collection fees | A&G | Credit and Collection |
| Combs | Rooms | Guest Supplies |
| Comforters | Rooms | Linen |
| Comment card processing (outside service) | Mult. Depts. | Contract Services |
| Comment cards | Mult. Depts. | Printing and Stationery |
| Commissions, meeting planners | Rooms | Commissions and Fees—Group |
| Commissions, rental agents | A&G | Professional Fees |
| Commissions, travel agent (food and beverage exclusively) | F&B | Commissions |
| Commissions, travel agent (rooms) | Rooms | Commissions |
| Company issued stock to employees | Payroll-Rel. Exp. | Stock Benefits |
| Complimentary beverage | Mult. Depts. | Complimentary Services/Gifts |
| Complimentary beverages for guests (health club/spa) | Health Club/Spa | Complimentary Services/Gifts |
| Complimentary cotton swabs and cotton balls for guest use (health club/spa) | Health Club/Spa | Complimentary Services/Gifts |
| Complimentary food | Mult. Depts. | Complimentary Services/Gifts |
| Complimentary parking | Mult. Depts. | Complimentary Services/Gifts |
| Complimentary razors for guest use (health club/spa) | Health Club/Spa | Complimentary Services/Gifts |
| Complimentary snacks for guests (health club/spa) | Health Club/Spa | Complimentary Services/Gifts |
| Complimentary soap and shampoo for guest use (health club/spa) | Health Club/Spa | Complimentary Services/Gifts |
| Computer books | Info & Telecom | Other Equipment |
| Computer discs | Mult. Depts. | Operating Supplies |
| Computer forms—commercial, printed | Mult. Depts. | Printing and Stationery |
| Computer hardware lease (non-capital) | Non Op. I&E | Other Property & Equipment |
| Computer keyboards | Info & Telecom | Hardware |
| Computer manuals, commercial | Info & Telecom | Operating Supplies |
| Computer manuals, printed | Info & Telecom | Operating Supplies |

| Item Name | Department/Schedule | Account Name |
|---|---|---|
| Computer monitors | Info & Telecom | Hardware |
| Computer monitors, guestrooms | Rooms | Operating Supplies |
| Computer mouse | Info & Telecom | Hardware |
| Computer printer paper | Info & Telecom | Operating Supplies |
| Computer software lease (non-capital) | Non Op. I&E | Other Property & Equipment |
| Computer supplies and accessories | Info & Telecom | Operating Supplies |
| Conditioner, hair | Rooms | Guest Supplies |
| Conference registration | Sales/Marketing | Travel—Other |
| Consortia ads | Sales/Marketing | Media |
| Consultant fees | Mult. Depts. | Contract Services |
| Consultant fees, market research | Sales/Marketing | Outside Services Market Research |
| Consultant fees, professional | A&G | Professional Fees |
| Consultant fees—real estate property taxes | Non Op. I&E | Real Estate Taxes |
| Consultant fees (shared savings plans) | Utilities | Gas |
| Containers, amenity | Rooms | Operating Supplies |
| Contract cleaning—awning, floors, fumigation, windows | Mult. Depts. | Contract Services |
| Contract cleaning, kitchen hoods | F&B | Contract Services |
| Convention bureau dues | Sales/Marketing | Dues and Subscriptions |
| Cookie cutters | F&B | Utensils |
| Cookie wrappings, guestroom | Rooms | Guest Supplies |
| Cookies, guestroom | Rooms | Guest Supplies |
| Cooking utensils | F&B | Utensils |
| Cooler/cider | F&B | Cost of Beverage Sales |
| Cooling system repairs | POM | HVAC Equipment |
| Cooling tower repairs | POM | HVAC Equipment |
| Cooperative marketing charges | Sales/Marketing | Franchise and Affiliation Marketing |
| Copier lease (non-capital) | Non Op. I&E | Other Property and Equipment |
| Copier paper | Mult. Depts. | Operating Supplies |
| Copier rental—temporary | A&G | Equipment Rental |
| Copier rental/lease | Mult. Depts. | Equipment Rental |
| Copier toner | Mult. Depts. | Operating Supplies |
| Copy writing for advertising | Sales/Marketing | Media |
| Copy writing for direct mail | Sales/Marketing | Direct Mail |
| Copying service | Mult. Depts. | Printing and Stationery |
| Cords | Rooms | Operating Supplies |
| Cords, drapery | Rooms | Operating Supplies |
| Corkscrews | F&B | Utensils |

| Item Name | Department/ Schedule | Account Name |
|---|---|---|
| Corkscrews for use by guests in rooms | Rooms | Operating Supplies |
| Corporate office reimbursables | F&B | Corporate Office Reimbursables |
| Correction fluid/tape | A&G | Operating Supplies |
| Cosmetics | Rooms | Guest Supplies |
| Cost of cell phone plans | Info & Telecom | Cost of Cell Phones |
| Cost of complimentary Internet—function room | Info & Telecom | Cost of Internet Services |
| Cost of complimentary Internet—guest room | Info & Telecom | Cost of Internet Services |
| Cost of complimentary local telephone call— guest room | Info & Telecom | Cost of Local Calls |
| Cost of complimentary long distance telephone call—guest room | Info & Telecom | Cost of Long Distance Calls |
| Cost of fax—guest room | Minor Oper. Dept. | Guest Communications |
| Cost of Internet—function room | F&B | Audiovisual Cost |
| Cost of Internet—guest room | Minor Oper. Dept. | Guest Communications |
| Cost of living adjustments (COLA) | Payroll-Rel. Exp. | Expat Benefits |
| Cost of local calls, admin. and guest | Info & Telecom | Cost of Local Calls |
| Cost of long distance calls, admin. and guest | Info & Telecom | Cost of Long Distance Calls |
| Cost of telephone call—guest room | Minor Oper. Dept. | Guest Communications |
| Cots | Rooms | Operating Supplies |
| Cotton balls | Rooms | Guest Supplies |
| Coupons | Sales/Marketing | Collateral Material |
| Court/legal fees—other than collections | A&G | Legal Services |
| Covers, toilet seats | Rooms | Operating Supplies |
| CPR kits | Mult. Depts. | Operating Supplies |
| CPU stands | Info & Telecom | Hardware |
| Creamer packets | Rooms | Guest Supplies |
| Creamers | F&B | China |
| Creams, body/face (rooms) | Rooms | Guest Supplies |
| Credit card commissions | A&G | Credit Card Commissions |
| Credit reports | A&G | Credit and Collection |
| Credit service expense | A&G | Credit and Collection |
| Crib bumper pads | Rooms | Operating Supplies |
| Crib covers | Rooms | Operating Supplies |
| Crib mattresses | Rooms | Operating Supplies |
| Cribs | Rooms | Operating Supplies |
| Crocks (all materials) | F&B | China |
| Cups, china, for use by guests in rooms | Rooms | Operating Supplies |
| Cups, disposable, for use by guests in rooms | Rooms | Guest Supplies |
| Cups, drinking (non-coffee, all sizes & materials) | F&B | Glassware |

| Item Name | Department/ Schedule | Account Name |
|---|---|---|
| Cups, paper/plastic | F&B | Paper and Plastics |
| Cups/saucers, cappuccino | F&B | China |
| Cups/saucers, coffee | F&B | China |
| Cups/saucers, espresso | F&B | China |
| Currency bill straps | A&G | Operating Supplies |
| Curtain holdbacks | Mult. Depts. | Operating Supplies |
| Curtain hooks | Mult. Depts. | Operating Supplies |
| Curtain rods | Mult. Depts. | Operating Supplies |
| Curtain stackbacks | Mult. Depts. | Operating Supplies |
| Curtains | Mult. Depts. | Operating Supplies |
| Curtains, dry cleaning | Mult. Depts. | Laundry and Dry Cleaning |
| Customer parking paid to third party | Parking | Contract Services |
| Customer research/survey—outside service | Sales/Marketing | Outside Services Market Research |
| Cut flowers | Mult. Depts. | Decorations |
| Cutting boards | F&B | Utensils |
| Dairy products | F&B | Cost of Food Sales |
| Dance floor rental (one time event) | F&B | Equipment Rental |
| Data binders and accessories | Mult. Depts. | Operating Supplies |
| Data cartridges and tapes | Info & Telecom | Operating Supplies |
| Data processing supplies | Info & Telecom | Operating Supplies |
| Database purchase | Sales/Marketing | Direct Mail |
| Decorations, holiday and special occasion | Mult. Depts. | Decorations |
| Decorations—inside—special events | Sales/Marketing | Decorations |
| Defibrillator | Mult. Depts. | Operating Supplies |
| Degreaser | Mult. Depts. | Cleaning Supplies |
| Dental floss | Rooms | Guest Supplies |
| Dental kit | Rooms | Guest Supplies |
| Deodorant | Rooms | Guest Supplies |
| Deodorizers | Rooms | Cleaning Supplies |
| Desalinization of water | Utilities | Water/Sewer |
| Desk accessories | Mult. Depts. | Operating Supplies |
| Desk caddies | Mult. Depts. | Operating Supplies |
| Desk pad and holder | Mult. Depts. | Operating Supplies |
| Desk pads (employee) | A&G | Operating Supplies |
| Detective service | A&G | Security |
| Detergent for use by guests in rooms | Rooms | Guest Supplies |
| Detergents (dish) | F&B | Dishwashing Supplies |
| Diffusers (health club/spa) | Health Club/Spa | Ambience |
| Direct mail expenses—outside service | Sales/Marketing | Direct Mail |

| Item Name | Department/Schedule | Account Name |
|---|---|---|
| Directional signs (outside) | Sales/Marketing | Outside Signage |
| Directory advertising | Sales/Marketing | Media |
| Directory listing | Sales/Marketing | Media |
| Dish drainer, guestroom | Rooms | Operating Supplies |
| Dish soap for use by guests in rooms | Rooms | Guest Supplies |
| Dishcloths, guestroom | Rooms | Operating Supplies |
| Dishes for use by guests in rooms | Rooms | Operating Supplies |
| Dishwasher soap for use by guests in rooms | Rooms | Guest Supplies |
| Dishwashing soaps and rinsing agents | F&B | Dishwashing Supplies |
| Disinfectants | Mult. Depts. | Cleaning Supplies |
| Diskettes | Info & Telecom | Other Equipment |
| Dispensers, bath tissue | Rooms | Operating Supplies |
| Dispensers, lotion | Rooms | Operating Supplies |
| Dispensers, soap | Rooms | Operating Supplies |
| Do not disturb cards | Rooms | Operating Supplies |
| Document destruction fees | A&G | Contract Services |
| Doilies, guestroom | Rooms | Operating Supplies |
| Doilies, paper | F&B | Paper and Plastics |
| Domain name registration | Sales/Marketing | Website |
| Donations | Sales/Marketing | Promotion |
| Door viewer | Rooms | Operating Supplies |
| Doormats | Rooms | Operating Supplies |
| Doorstop | Rooms | Operating Supplies |
| Double-stick tape | Mult. Depts. | Operating Supplies |
| Draperies, dry cleaning | Mult. Depts. | Laundry and Dry Cleaning |
| Drapery baton | Mult. Depts. | Operating Supplies |
| Drapery cords | Mult. Depts. | Operating Supplies |
| Drapery liners | Mult. Depts. | Operating Supplies |
| Drapes | Mult. Depts. | Operating Supplies |
| Drapes, blackout | Mult. Depts. | Operating Supplies |
| Dresses | Mult. Depts. | Uniform Costs |
| Drug testing of employees | A&G | Human Resources |
| Dry cleaning bags for use by guests in rooms | Rooms | Guest Supplies |
| Dry cleaning costs, non-guest (in-house laundry) | Mult. Depts. | Laundry and Dry Cleaning |
| Dry cleaning services, non-guest (outside laundry) | Mult. Depts. | Laundry and Dry Cleaning |
| Dry goods (flour, pasta, etc.) | F&B | Cost of Food Sales |
| Dry ice | F&B | Ice |
| Dryers, hair | Rooms | Operating Supplies |
| Duct tape | Mult. Depts. | Operating Supplies |
| Dues, associations (marketing) | Sales/Marketing | Dues and Subscriptions |

| Item Name | Department/ Schedule | Account Name |
|---|---|---|
| Dues—hotel associations (non-marketing) | A&G | Dues and Subscriptions |
| Dues—professional associations (non-marketing) | A&G | Dues and Subscriptions |
| Dust cloths | Mult. Depts. | Cleaning Supplies |
| Dust mop | Mult. Depts. | Cleaning Supplies |
| Dusters | Mult. Depts. | Cleaning Supplies |
| Dusting mitts | Mult. Depts. | Cleaning Supplies |
| Dustpan brushes | Mult. Depts. | Cleaning Supplies |
| Dustpans | Mult. Depts. | Cleaning Supplies |
| Duvet covers | Rooms | Linen |
| Duvets | Rooms | Linen |
| DVD player, guestrooms | Rooms | Operating Supplies |
| Easels (charged to customer) | F&B | Audiovisual Cost |
| Educational activities for employees | Mult. Depts. | Training |
| Educational assistance | Mult. Depts. | Training |
| Educational books/pamphlets for employees | Mult. Depts. | Training |
| Educational cost of non-ex-pat family members | Payroll-Rel. Exp. | Housing and Educational |
| Eggs | F&B | Cost of Food Sales |
| EIFS repair | POM | Building |
| Electric bulbs—all | POM | Light Bulbs |
| Electric sub-meters maintenance | POM | Elec. & Mech. |
| Electric supplies | POM | Elec. & Mech. |
| Electrical adapters | Mult. Depts. | Operating Supplies |
| Electrical hookup (charged to customer) | F&B | Misc. Cost (of Other Rev.) |
| Electrical repairs | POM | Elec. & Mech. |
| Electricity | Utilities | Electricity |
| Elevator and escalator repairs | POM | Elevators and Escalators |
| Elixirs (health club/spa) | Health Club/Spa | Health and Beauty Products |
| Email blasts | Sales/Marketing | Direct Mail |
| Emergency equipment and supplies | POM | Life/Safety |
| Emergency exit instruction card | Rooms | Operating Supplies |
| Emergency exit signs repairs | POM | Life/Safety |
| Emery boards | Rooms | Guest Supplies |
| Employee auto leases | Payroll-Rel. Exp. | Automobile Allowance |
| Employee child care | Payroll-Rel. Exp. | Child Care |
| Employee housing—employee reimbursement (contra) | Non Op. I&E | Land and Buildings |
| Employee housing—property lease | Non Op. I&E | Land and Buildings |
| Employee meal food cost credit | F&B | Cost of Food Sales |
| Employee meals from cafeteria | Payroll-Rel. Exp. | Meals |
| Employee meals in hotel restaurants at cost | Payroll-Rel. Exp. | Meals |

| Item Name | Department/ Schedule | Account Name |
|---|---|---|
| Employee pins | Mult. Depts. | Operating Supplies |
| Employer 401(k) contributions | Payroll-Rel. Exp. | Contributory Savings Plan |
| Employer cost for non-union pension plans | Payroll-Rel. Exp. | Nonunion Pension |
| Employer cost of dental insurance | Payroll-Rel. Exp. | Dental Insurance |
| Employer cost of disability insurance | Payroll-Rel. Exp. | Disability Insurance |
| Employer cost of profit sharing plan | Payroll-Rel. Exp. | Profit Sharing |
| Employer registered retirement savings plan contributions | Payroll-Rel. Exp. | Contributory Savings Plan |
| Employer share of a national retirement program | Payroll-Rel. Exp. | National Retirement Contribution |
| Employer share of a state retirement program | Payroll-Rel. Exp. | State Retirement Contribution |
| Employer share of Canadian employment insurance | Payroll-Rel. Exp. | National Unemployment Insurance |
| Employer share of employee health insurance | Payroll-Rel. Exp. | Health Insurance |
| Employer share of federal unemployment compensation | Payroll-Rel. Exp. | National Unemployment Insurance |
| Employer share of governmental medical program | Payroll-Rel. Exp. | National Medical Insurance |
| Employer share of group life insurance | Payroll-Rel. Exp. | Group Life Insurance |
| Employer share of insurance administered by national insurance system | Payroll-Rel. Exp. | National Medical Insurance |
| Employer share of Medicare (FICA) | Payroll-Rel. Exp. | National Medical Insurance |
| Employer share of national disability insurance program | Payroll-Rel. Exp. | National Disability Insurance |
| Employer share of Quebec pension plan | Payroll-Rel. Exp. | State Retirement Contribution |
| Employer share of retirement administered by national insurance system | Payroll-Rel. Exp. | National Retirement Contribution |
| Employer share of social security Canadian pension plan | Payroll-Rel. Exp. | National Retirement Contribution |
| Employer share of Social Security (FICA) | Payroll-Rel. Exp. | National Retirement Contribution |
| Employer share of unemployment administered by national insurance system | Payroll-Rel. Exp. | National Unemployment Insurance |
| Employer share of union employees insurance | Payroll-Rel. Exp. | Union Insurance |
| Employer share of union employees pension plan | Payroll-Rel. Exp. | Union Pension |
| Energy management hardware, small value purchases | Info & Telecom | Energy Management |
| Energy management software licenses, support and maintenance fees | Info & Telecom | Energy Management |
| Entertainment of non-employees in-house | Mult. Depts. | Entertainment—In-House |
| Entertainment, outside—employee | Mult. Depts. | Travel—Meals & Enter. |

| Item Name | Department/ Schedule | Account Name |
|---|---|---|
| Entertainment while traveling | Sales/Marketing | Travel—Meals & Enter. |
| Envelopes | Mult. Depts. | Printing and Stationery |
| Envelopes—cashier | Mult. Depts. | Printing and Stationery |
| Equipment instructions (health club/spa) | Health Club/Spa | Printing and Stationery |
| Erasers | Mult. Depts. | Operating Supplies |
| Espresso maker for use by guests in rooms | Rooms | Operating Supplies |
| Espresso pods for use by guests in rooms | Rooms | Guest Supplies |
| Ethernet cables | Info & Telecom | Hardware |
| Exchange on bank checks and currency | A&G | Bank Charges |
| Expert witness costs | A&G | Legal Services |
| Express delivery charges | A&G | P&ODC |
| Express mail/UPS (non-marketing) | A&G | P&ODC |
| Extension cords | Mult. Depts. | Operating Supplies |
| Extermination services | POM | Contract Services |
| Face cream (health club/spa) | Health Club/Spa | Health and Beauty Products |
| Facial tissue | Rooms | Guest Supplies |
| Facial tissue box cover | Rooms | Operating Supplies |
| Familiarization (fam) tour expenses | Sales/Marketing | Familiarization Trips |
| Fans, paper (for use by guests in rooms) | Rooms | Guest Supplies |
| Fans, portable | Mult. Depts. | Operating Supplies |
| Fax machine supplies and accessories | A&G | Operating Supplies |
| Feather duster | Mult. Depts. | Cleaning Supplies |
| Federal unemployment tax | Mult. Depts. | Payroll Taxes |
| Fees, attorney, for collections | A&G | Credit and Collection |
| Fees, collection | A&G | Credit and Collection |
| Fees, medical | A&G | Human Resources |
| Fees, stock transfer agents | A&G | Professional Fees |
| Fees, transfer | A&G | Professional Fees |
| Fees, trustees (handling bond, etc.) | A&G | Professional Fees |
| Fences and bridges maintenance | Golf/Pro Shop | Grounds M&L |
| Fertilizer | POM | Grounds M&L |
| Fertilizers, golf course | Golf/Pro Shop | Grounds M&L |
| File folders | Mult. Depts. | Operating Supplies |
| Film, camera | Mult. Depts. | Operating Supplies |
| Film purchase and developing | A&G | Operating Supplies |
| Filter paper | F&B | Paper and Plastics |
| Filters, coffee | Rooms | Guest Supplies |
| Filters, vacuum | Mult. Depts. | Cleaning Supplies |
| Fines (health, safety, etc.) | Mult. Depts. | Miscellaneous |
| Fingernail file | Rooms | Guest Supplies |

| Item Name | Department/ Schedule | Account Name |
|---|---|---|
| Fire alarm service—third party | POM | Life/Safety |
| Fire alarm system repairs (smoke, heat, strobe, attenuators, etc.) | POM | Life/Safety |
| Fireplace lighter | Mult. Depts. | Operating Supplies |
| Fireplace screen | Mult. Depts. | Operating Supplies |
| Fireplace tools | Mult. Depts. | Operating Supplies |
| Fire-starter packets for use by guests in rooms | Rooms | Guest Supplies |
| Firewood | Mult. Depts. | Operating Supplies |
| First aid kits/supplies | Mult. Depts. | Operating Supplies |
| Fish | F&B | Cost of Food Sales |
| Fitness class supplies (health club/spa) | Health Club/Spa | Athletic Supplies |
| Flag pins, golf | Golf/Pro Shop | Operating Supplies |
| Flags | Mult. Depts. | Operating Supplies |
| Flashlights | Mult. Depts. | Operating Supplies |
| Flatware cleaner | F&B | Dishwashing Supplies |
| Flatware for use by guests in rooms | Rooms | Operating Supplies |
| Flatware (includes silver, stainless) | F&B | Flatware |
| Flatware rental | F&B | Flatware |
| Flip charts (charged to customers) | F&B | Audiovisual Cost |
| Floor plans | Mult. Depts. | Printing and Stationery |
| Floor polish | Mult. Depts. | Cleaning Supplies |
| Floor refinishing | POM | Floor Covering |
| Floor soap | Mult. Depts. | Cleaning Supplies |
| Floor wax | Mult. Depts. | Cleaning Supplies |
| Floral arrangements | Mult. Depts. | Decorations |
| Flower purchases | POM | Grounds M&L |
| Flower vases, glass (tabletop) | F&B | Decorations |
| Flowers, banquet tables | F&B | Decorations |
| Flowers, fresh and artificial | Mult. Depts. | Decorations |
| Flowers, golf course | Golf/Pro Shop | Grounds M&L |
| Flowers (tabletop) | F&B | Decorations |
| Fly strips | Mult. Depts. | Cleaning Supplies |
| Fly swatters | Mult. Depts. | Cleaning Supplies |
| Flyers | Sales/Marketing | Collateral Material |
| Foam insulated cups | F&B | Paper and Plastics |
| Foil wrapping | F&B | Paper and Plastics |
| Folios | Rooms | Printing and Stationery |
| Food and beverage software licenses, support and maintenance fees | Info & Telecom | Food and Beverage |
| Food and beverage systems hardware, small value purchases | Info & Telecom | Food and Beverage |

| Item Name | Department/ Schedule | Account Name |
|---|---|---|
| Food processor | F&B | Utensils |
| Food warmer fuel | F&B | Kitchen Fuel |
| Foreign exchange gain or loss related to FF&E reserve accounts | Non Op. I&E | Unrealized Foreign Exch. Gains or Losses |
| Foreign exchange gain or loss related to foreign currency account | Non Op. I&E | Unrealized Foreign Exch. Gains or Losses |
| Foreign exchange gain or loss related to foreign denominated debt | Non Op. I&E | Unrealized Foreign Exch. Gains or Losses |
| Forks, kitchen | F&B | Utensils |
| Forms, general | Mult. Depts. | Printing and Stationery |
| Forms, printed | Mult. Depts. | Printing and Stationery |
| Fountain pens for use by guests in rooms | Rooms | Guest Supplies |
| Frames, art | Mult. Depts. | Operating Supplies |
| Franchise advertising fee | Sales/Marketing | Franchise and Affiliation Marketing |
| Franchise fee (chain royalty) | Sales/Marketing | Franchise and Affiliation Fees—Royalties |
| Franchise marketing fee | Sales/Marketing | Franchise and Affiliation Marketing |
| Franchise royalty | Sales/Marketing | Franchise and Affiliation Fees—Royalties |
| Freight and shipping charged to banquet customer | F&B | Misc. Cost (of Other Rev.) |
| Freight charges (non-marketing) | A&G | P&ODC |
| Frequent car rental fees | Sales/Marketing | Loyalty Programs |
| Frequent flyer fees | Sales/Marketing | Loyalty Programs |
| Frequent guest fees | Sales/Marketing | Loyalty Programs |
| Fruit | F&B | Cost of Food Sales |
| Fruit baskets gratis to customers | Mult. Depts. | Complimentary Services/Gifts |
| Fuel costs, auto (guest transport) | Rooms | Guest Transportation |
| Fuel costs, cart (guest transport) | Rooms | Guest Transportation |
| Fuel, kitchen | F&B | Kitchen Fuel |
| Fumigation | POM | Contract Services |
| Fumigators, kitchen/restaurant | F&B | Contract Services |
| Furniture polish | Mult. Depts. | Cleaning Supplies |
| Furniture refinishing | POM | Furniture and Equipment |
| Furniture repairs | POM | Furniture and Equipment |
| Furniture wax | Mult. Depts. | Cleaning Supplies |
| FUTA | Payroll-Rel. Exp. | National Unemployment Insurance |
| Garage licenses | Parking | Licenses and Permits |
| Garbage bags | Mult. Depts. | Operating Supplies |
| Garbage can liners | Mult. Depts. | Operating Supplies |

| Item Name | Department/ Schedule | Account Name |
|---|---|---|
| Garbage cans | Mult. Depts. | Operating Supplies |
| Gas for beer lines | F&B | Cost of Beverage Sales |
| Gas (for utility use) | Utilities | Gas |
| Gasoline and lubricants, golf cart | Golf/Pro Shop | Gasoline and Lubricants |
| Gasoline and lubricants, mowers (golf course) | Golf/Pro Shop | Gasoline and Lubricants |
| Gasoline and lubricants, tractors/trucks (golf course) | Golf/Pro Shop | Gasoline and Lubricants |
| Gasoline for food delivery vehicle | F&B | Operating Supplies |
| Gasoline—motor vehicles (company and employee use) | Mult. Depts. | Operating Supplies |
| General insurance—legal settlement costs or audit adjustments | Non Op. I&E | Liability |
| Generator rentals (property power back-up) | POM | Equipment Rental |
| Generator repairs | POM | Elec. & Mech. |
| Geothermal power | Utilities | Other Fuels |
| Gideon Bibles | Rooms | Operating Supplies |
| Gift certificates donated | Sales/Marketing | Promotion |
| Gifts to customers | Mult. Depts. | Complimentary Services/Gifts |
| Glass bags | Rooms | Operating Supplies |
| Glass bowls | F&B | China |
| Glass cleaner | Mult. Depts. | Cleaning Supplies |
| Glass covers | Rooms | Operating Supplies |
| Glass dishes | F&B | China |
| Glass racks | F&B | Operating Supplies |
| Glasses, drinking (alcoholic beverage/all sizes and materials) | F&B | Glassware |
| Glasses, drinking (non-alcoholic/all sizes and materials) | F&B | Glassware |
| Glassware (all types) for use by guests in rooms | Rooms | Operating Supplies |
| Glassware rental | F&B | Glassware |
| Gloves, golf (for sale) | Golf/Pro Shop | Cost of Merch. Sales |
| Gloves, rubber | Mult. Depts. | Cleaning Supplies |
| Glue | Mult. Depts. | Operating Supplies |
| Goldfish | Mult. Depts. | Operating Supplies |
| Golf bags (for rental) | Golf/Pro Shop | Operating Supplies |
| Golf bags (for sale) | Golf/Pro Shop | Cost of Merch. Sales |
| Golf balls (for sale) | Golf/Pro Shop | Cost of Merch. Sales |
| Golf balls (practice range) | Golf/Pro Shop | Operating Supplies |
| Golf cart batteries | Golf/Pro Shop | Vehicle Rep. & Maint. |
| Golf cart rental | Golf/Pro Shop | Equipment Rental |
| Golf cart repairs and maintenance | Golf/Pro Shop | Vehicle Rep. & Maint. |
| Golf clubs (for rental) | Golf/Pro Shop | Operating Supplies |

| Item Name | Department/Schedule | Account Name |
|---|---|---|
| Golf clubs (for sale) | Golf/Pro Shop | Cost of Merch. Sales |
| Golf course software licenses, support and maintenance fees | Info & Telecom | Golf |
| Gratis food, bar | F&B | Complimentary Services/Gifts |
| Gross receipts taxes not paid by customers—state/county/city | Non Op. I&E | B&O Taxes |
| Guest checks | F&B | Printing and Stationery |
| Guest comment cards | Mult. Depts. | Printing and Stationery |
| Guest dry cleaning expenses—partially serviced by the hotel | Minor Oper. Dept. | Guest Laundry Revenue |
| Guest guide | Rooms | Printing and Stationery |
| Guest laundry expenses—partially serviced by the hotel | Minor Oper. Dept. | Guest Laundry Revenue |
| Guest loyalty fees | Sales/Marketing | Loyalty Programs |
| Guest questionnaire forms | Mult. Depts. | Printing and Stationery |
| Guest relocation due to lack of room availability | Rooms | Guest Relocation |
| Guest suggestion forms | Mult. Depts. | Printing and Stationery |
| Guest surveys (outside service) | Sales/Marketing | Contract Services |
| Guest transportation service contracts | Rooms | Guest Transportation |
| Guest treatment forms (health club/spa) | Health Club/Spa | Printing and Stationery |
| Gum remover | Mult. Depts. | Cleaning Supplies |
| Hair dryers | Rooms | Operating Supplies |
| Hair nets for food service employees | F&B | Operating Supplies |
| Hair nets for use by guests in rooms | Rooms | Guest Supplies |
| Hair pins for use by guests in rooms | Rooms | Guest Supplies |
| Hair shampoo (health club/spa) | Health Club/Spa | Health and Beauty Products |
| Hair spray for use by guests in rooms | Rooms | Guest Supplies |
| Hairbrushes for use by guests in rooms | Rooms | Guest Supplies |
| Hand lotion | Rooms | Guest Supplies |
| Hand sanitizer | Rooms | Guest Supplies |
| Hand soap for use by guests in rooms | Rooms | Guest Supplies |
| Hand towels | Rooms | Linen |
| Hangers (all types) | Rooms | Operating Supplies |
| Hardship premiums for ex-pats | Payroll-Rel. Exp. | Expat Benefits |
| Hats | Mult. Depts. | Uniform Costs |
| Hazardous materials remediation | POM | Life/Safety |
| Health club/spa hardware, small value purchases | Info & Telecom | Health Club/Spa |
| Health club/spa software licenses, support and maintenance fees | Info & Telecom | Health Club/Spa |
| Health permits | F&B | Licenses and Permits |

| Item Name | Department/Schedule | Account Name |
|---|---|---|
| Help wanted ads | A&G | Human Resources |
| High chairs | Mult. Depts. | Operating Supplies |
| Highway signs | Sales/Marketing | Outside Signage |
| Hole punch | Mult. Depts. | Operating Supplies |
| Holiday decorations (inside and outside, visible to guests) | Sales/Marketing | Decorations |
| Holiday pay | Mult. Depts. | Supplemental Pay |
| Holiday/special event decorations for A&G areas | A&G | Decorations |
| Hooks, coat | Mult. Depts. | Operating Supplies |
| Hooks, door | Mult. Depts. | Operating Supplies |
| Hot chocolate packets for use by guests in rooms | Rooms | Guest Supplies |
| Hotel association dues (non-marketing) | A&G | Dues and Subscriptions |
| Hotel maps | Rooms | Printing and Stationery |
| Hotel sales and marketing association dues | Sales/Marketing | Dues and Subscriptions |
| Hotelligence fee | Sales/Marketing | Outside Services Market Research |
| Housekeeper carts | Rooms | Operating Supplies |
| Housekeeping reports | Rooms | Printing and Stationery |
| Housing and educational | Mult. Depts. | Employee Benefits |
| Human resources hardware, small value purchases | Info & Telecom | Human Resources |
| Human resources software licenses, support and maintenance fees | Info & Telecom | Human Resources |
| Humidifier | Rooms | Operating Supplies |
| HVAC systems repairs | POM | HVAC Equipment |
| Ice buckets and liners | F&B | Operating Supplies |
| Ice buckets and liners | Rooms | Operating Supplies |
| Ice carvings/sculpture | F&B | Decorations |
| Ice consumption | F&B | Ice |
| Ice tongs | F&B | Utensils |
| Ice tongs for use by guests in rooms | Rooms | Operating Supplies |
| Inflatable beds | Rooms | Operating Supplies |
| Information and telecommunication hardware maintenance non-system specific | Info & Telecom | Contract Services |
| In-house newsletter (for employees) | A&G | Human Resources |
| Ink | Mult. Depts. | Operating Supplies |
| Ink cartridges | Mult. Depts. | Operating Supplies |
| Innkeepers liability card frames | Rooms | Operating Supplies |
| Innkeepers liability cards | Rooms | Printing and Stationery |
| In-room dining breakfast cards | F&B | Menus and Beverage Lists |
| In-room guest account services (check-out) | Rooms | Contract Services |
| In-room movie rental expenses—hotel operated | Minor Oper. Dept. | In-Room Movie Rentals |

| Item Name | Department/ Schedule | Account Name |
|---|---|---|
| Insecticides | Mult. Depts. | Cleaning Supplies |
| Insecticides, golf course | Golf/Pro Shop | Grounds M&L |
| Inspection fees—boilers, elevators, escalators, life/safety | POM | Licenses and Permits |
| Inspection fees for licensing | Mult. Depts. | Licenses and Permits |
| Instructor fees, training | A&G | Training |
| Instructor fees, training | Mult. Depts. | Training |
| Insurance deductibles—property | Non Op. I&E | Deductible |
| Insurance deductibles—general liability | Non Op. I&E | Deductible |
| Insurance deductibles—liability/burglary, theft, umbrella, fidelity, auto, innkeeper, liquor, cyber | Non Op. I&E | Deductible |
| Insurance expense, automobile | Non Op. I&E | Liability |
| Insurance expense, boiler explosion | Non Op. I&E | Building and Contents |
| Insurance expense, building | Non Op. I&E | Building and Contents |
| Insurance expense, burglary | Non Op. I&E | Liability |
| Insurance expense, business interruption | Non Op. I&E | Building and Contents |
| Insurance expense, cyber | Non Op. I&E | Liability |
| Insurance expense, director and officer coverage | Non Op. I&E | Liability |
| Insurance expense, earthquake | Non Op. I&E | Building and Contents |
| Insurance expense, EPLI | Non Op. I&E | Liability |
| Insurance expense, fidelity | Non Op. I&E | Liability |
| Insurance expense, fire | Non Op. I&E | Building and Contents |
| Insurance expense, flood | Non Op. I&E | Building and Contents |
| Insurance expense, furnishings and equipment | Non Op. I&E | Building and Contents |
| Insurance expense, guest liability | Non Op. I&E | Liability |
| Insurance expense, innkeepers | Non Op. I&E | Liability |
| Insurance expense, liability | Non Op. I&E | Liability |
| Insurance expense, liquor | Non Op. I&E | Liability |
| Insurance expense, property | Non Op. I&E | Building and Contents |
| Insurance expense, terrorism | Non Op. I&E | Building and Contents |
| Insurance expense, theft | Non Op. I&E | Liability |
| Insurance expense, tornado | Non Op. I&E | Building and Contents |
| Insurance expense, umbrella | Non Op. I&E | Liability |
| Insurance expense, weather | Non Op. I&E | Building and Contents |
| Insurance—legal or settlement expenses | Non Op. I&E | Building and Contents |
| Internal audit expense | A&G | Audit Charges |
| Internal audit fees (chain properties) | A&G | Audit Charges |
| Internet access charges | Info & Telecom | Cost of Internet Services |
| Internet advertising | Sales/Marketing | Media |
| Internet equipment not subject to capitalization | Info & Telecom | Cost of Internet Services |

| Item Name | Department/Schedule | Account Name |
|---|---|---|
| Internet review monitoring fees | Sales/Marketing | Outside Services Market Research |
| Internet web page, reservations | Rooms | Reservations |
| Interview expenses | A&G | Human Resources |
| Investigation of employees (including background checks) | A&G | Human Resources |
| Iron | Rooms | Operating Supplies |
| Ironing board covers | Rooms | Operating Supplies |
| Ironing board holders | Rooms | Operating Supplies |
| Ironing boards | Rooms | Operating Supplies |
| Irrigation system repairs | POM | Grounds M&L |
| Jackets | Mult. Depts. | Uniform Costs |
| Juice | F&B | Cost of Food Sales |
| Juices for cocktail mix | F&B | Cost of Beverage Sales |
| Jumpers | Mult. Depts. | Uniform Costs |
| Key blank, key cards (non-guestroom) and key machine repairs | POM | Building |
| Key cards | Rooms | Operating Supplies |
| Key chain coils | Mult. Depts. | Operating Supplies |
| Key chain reels | Mult. Depts. | Operating Supplies |
| Key lock box | Mult. Depts. | Operating Supplies |
| Key rings | Mult. Depts. | Operating Supplies |
| Key tags | Mult. Depts. | Operating Supplies |
| Key word buys | Sales/Marketing | Website |
| Keyboard drawers | Mult. Depts. | Operating Supplies |
| Keyboards, computer | Info & Telecom | Hardware |
| Keys, safe deposit box | Rooms | Operating Supplies |
| Kiosk cost of sales operated by the front desk personnel | Minor Oper. Dept. | Retail Kiosk Sales |
| Kitchen equipment repairs | POM | Kitchen Equipment |
| Kitchen hood cleaning | F&B | Contract Services |
| Kitchen smallwares | F&B | Kitchen Smallwares |
| Knife sharpening | F&B | Contract Services |
| Knives, kitchen | F&B | Utensils |
| Label maker | Mult. Depts. | Operating Supplies |
| Label maker supplies | Mult. Depts. | Operating Supplies |
| Ladles, kitchen | F&B | Utensils |
| Lampshades | Mult. Depts. | Operating Supplies |
| LAN/WAN e-mail hardware, small value purchases | Info & Telecom | Information Security |
| LAN/WAN e-mail software licenses, support and maintenance fees | Info & Telecom | Information Systems |

| Item Name | Department/ Schedule | Account Name |
|---|---|---|
| Land lease | Non Op. I&E | Land and Buildings |
| Landscaping service (indoor and outdoor) | POM | Grounds M&L |
| Laptop computers | Info & Telecom | Hardware |
| Laundry bags (cloth) for use by guests in rooms | Rooms | Operating Supplies |
| Laundry bags (disposable) for use by guests in rooms | Rooms | Guest Supplies |
| Laundry costs, non-guest (in-house laundry) | Mult. Depts. | Laundry and Dry Cleaning |
| Laundry equipment repairs | POM | Laundry Equipment |
| Laundry services, non-guest (outside laundry) | Mult. Depts. | Laundry and Dry Cleaning |
| Legal fees for acquiring visas for ex-pats | A&G | Legal Services |
| Legal fees/expenses for collections | A&G | Credit and Collection |
| Legal fees/expenses—real estate taxes | Non Op. I&E | Real Estate Taxes |
| Legal retainer | A&G | Legal Services |
| Lemon oil | Mult. Depts. | Cleaning Supplies |
| Letters for bulletin/sign boards | A&G | Operating Supplies |
| Licenses, beverage | F&B | Licenses and Permits |
| Licenses, building | POM | Licenses and Permits |
| Licenses, cabaret | F&B | Licenses and Permits |
| Licenses, canopy | POM | Licenses and Permits |
| Licenses, checkrooms | F&B | Licenses and Permits |
| Licenses, elevators | POM | Licenses and Permits |
| Licenses, engineering | POM | Licenses and Permits |
| Licenses, health permit | F&B | Licenses and Permits |
| Licenses, locksmith | POM | Licenses and Permits |
| Licenses, music copyright | F&B | Licenses and Permits |
| Licenses, public assembly | F&B | Licenses and Permits |
| Licenses, sidewalk | POM | Licenses and Permits |
| Licenses, temporary space liquor | F&B | Licenses and Permits |
| Life preserver (health club/spa operated) | Health Club/Spa | Swimming Pool |
| Limousine—employee use | A&G | Staff Transportation |
| Limousine services, guest (no charge) | Rooms | Guest Transportation |
| Linen cleaning (all types) | F&B | Laundry and Dry Cleaning |
| Linen napkins | F&B | Linen |
| Linen rental | Mult. Depts. | Linen |
| Linen rental (all types) | F&B | Linen |
| Linen tablecloth | F&B | Linen |
| Liners, drapery | Mult. Depts. | Operating Supplies |
| Liners, paper | F&B | Paper and Plastics |
| Lint brush | Mult. Depts. | Cleaning Supplies |
| Lint remover | Mult. Depts. | Cleaning Supplies |
| Liquid soap for use by guests in rooms | Rooms | Guest Supplies |

| Item Name | Department/ Schedule | Account Name |
|---|---|---|
| Liquor | F&B | Cost of Beverage Sales |
| Liquor—bottle | F&B | Cost of Beverage Sales |
| Literature—educational for employees | A&G | Training |
| Lock repairs/service | POM | Building |
| Lodging of employees | A&G | Human Resources |
| Log books | Mult. Depts. | Operating Supplies |
| Logo merchandise (for sale in F&B) | F&B | Misc. Cost (of Other Rev.) |
| Logoed items for marketing | Sales/Marketing | Complimentary Services/Gifts |
| Lost and damaged articles—guest non-insured | A&G | Loss and Damage |
| Lotions (health club/spa) | Health Club/Spa | Health and Beauty Products |
| Luggage racks | Rooms | Operating Supplies |
| Luggage tags for use by guests in rooms | Rooms | Guest Supplies |
| Lye | Mult. Depts. | Cleaning Supplies |
| Machine stands | A&G | Operating Supplies |
| Magazine advertising | Sales/Marketing | Media |
| Magazine subscriptions | Mult. Depts. | Dues and Subscriptions |
| Magazines for use by guests in rooms | Rooms | Guest Supplies |
| Magazines, golf (for sale) | Golf/Pro Shop | Cost of Merch. Sales |
| Magazines, golf (for staff use) | Golf/Pro Shop | Dues and Subscriptions |
| Magazines—trade (non-marketing) | A&G | Dues and Subscriptions |
| Mail bags | A&G | Operating Supplies |
| Mail chute rentals | A&G | Operating Supplies |
| Mailing lists | Sales/Marketing | Direct Mail |
| Maintenance contracts, elevators and escalators | POM | Elevators and Escalators |
| Maintenance request forms | POM | Miscellaneous |
| Makeup mirror | Rooms | Operating Supplies |
| Makeup remover for use by guests in rooms | Rooms | Guest Supplies |
| Management company expenses (travel, entertainment, etc.) | Mult. Depts. | Corporate Office Reimbursables |
| Management fees | F&B | Management Fees |
| Management fees—specific department | Mult. Depts. | Management Fees |
| Manuals, instructional/training | Mult. Depts. | Training |
| Manuals, service (instructional materials) | POM | Operating Supplies |
| Maps | Rooms | Printing and Stationery |
| Markers (flip chart) | F&B | Operating Supplies |
| Market studies or audits—owner directed | Non Op. I&E | Owner Expenses |
| Marketing assessments | Sales/Marketing | Franchise and Affiliation Marketing |
| Marking ink | Mult. Depts. | Operating Supplies |
| Massage oils (health club/spa) | Health Club/Spa | Health and Beauty Products |

| Item Name | Department/ Schedule | Account Name |
|---|---|---|
| Matches, customer use | Mult. Depts. | Operating Supplies |
| Mats, floor | Mult. Depts. | Operating Supplies |
| Mats, floor | POM | Operating Supplies |
| Mats, rubber (bar) | F&B | Operating Supplies |
| Mattress cover | Rooms | Linen |
| Mattress pad | Rooms | Linen |
| Mattress protectors | Rooms | Operating Supplies |
| Mattress, crib | Rooms | Operating Supplies |
| Meals | Sales/Marketing | Travel—Meals & Enter. |
| Meals and entertainment, outside | Mult. Depts. | Travel—Meals & Enter. |
| Meals, business expense | Mult. Depts. | Travel—Meals & Enter. |
| Meals—corporate—sales and marketing | Sales/Marketing | Corporate Office Reimbursables |
| Meals for fam trip attendees | Sales/Marketing | Familiarization Trips |
| Meals, musicians and entertainers | F&B | Music and Entertainment |
| Meat | F&B | Cost of Food Sales |
| Mechanical, electrical or other recurring contracted service | POM | Contract Services |
| Medical supplies and drugs for employees | A&G | Human Resources |
| Medical supplies for employees | A&G | Human Resources |
| Meeting guides advertising | Sales/Marketing | Media |
| Meeting guides listing | Sales/Marketing | Media |
| Meeting space map and floor plans | Sales/Marketing | Collateral Material |
| Membership dues—associations (marketing) | Sales/Marketing | Dues and Subscriptions |
| Membership dues—associations (non-marketing) | A&G | Dues and Subscriptions |
| Membership fees—professional organizations | Mult. Depts. | Dues and Subscriptions |
| Memo pads | Mult. Depts. | Operating Supplies |
| Menu covers (food or beverage) | F&B | Menus and Beverage Lists |
| Menu design (food or beverage) | F&B | Menus and Beverage Lists |
| Menu printing (food or beverage) | F&B | Menus and Beverage Lists |
| Microwave, guestroom | Rooms | Operating Supplies |
| Mileage reimbursement | Mult. Depts. | Travel—Other |
| Mini-blinds | Mult. Depts. | Operating Supplies |
| Mints, guest (restaurant) | F&B | Complimentary Services/Gifts |
| Misc. banquet equipment rental (for a function or to meet peak demand) | F&B | Equipment Rental |
| Miscellaneous | F&B | Miscellaneous |
| Mixing bowls | F&B | Utensils |
| Mixing cans, bar | F&B | Utensils |
| Model fees | Sales/Marketing | Photography |

| Item Name | Department/ Schedule | Account Name |
|---|---|---|
| Modem lines | Info & Telecom | Telecommunications |
| Modems | Info & Telecom | Hardware |
| Molds | F&B | Utensils |
| Mop buckets | Mult. Depts. | Cleaning Supplies |
| Mop handles | Mult. Depts. | Cleaning Supplies |
| Mop wringers | Mult. Depts. | Cleaning Supplies |
| Mops | Mult. Depts. | Cleaning Supplies |
| Motor repairs (other than vehicles) | POM | Elec. & Mech. |
| Mouse, computer | Mult. Depts. | Operating Supplies |
| Mouse pads | Mult. Depts. | Operating Supplies |
| Mouse traps | Rooms | Operating Supplies |
| Mouthwash for use by guests in rooms | Rooms | Guest Supplies |
| Mowers, tractors, and trucks maintenance—golf | Golf/Pro Shop | Grounds M&L |
| Mugs, coffee, for use by guests in rooms | Rooms | Operating Supplies |
| Music, live musicians | F&B | Music and Entertainment |
| Music, mechanical | F&B | Music and Entertainment |
| Music on hold service | Info & Telecom | Telecommunications |
| Nail polish (health club/spa) | Health Club/Spa | Health and Beauty Products |
| Nail polish remover for use by guests in rooms | Rooms | Guest Supplies |
| Name badges | Mult. Depts. | Operating Supplies |
| Napkins, cocktail | F&B | Paper and Plastics |
| Napkins, paper | F&B | Paper and Plastics |
| Napkins (paper/cloth) for use by guests in rooms | Rooms | Operating Supplies |
| Newsletter production | Sales/Marketing | Direct Mail |
| Newspaper advertising | Sales/Marketing | Media |
| Newspaper bags for use by guests in rooms | Rooms | Guest Supplies |
| Newspaper subscriptions | Sales/Marketing | Dues and Subscriptions |
| Newspapers | Rooms | Complimentary Services/Gifts |
| Night lights | Rooms | Operating Supplies |
| Non-capitalized gym equipment (health club/spa) | Health Club/Spa | Athletic Supplies |
| Notary fees | A&G | Professional Fees |
| Notary fees, collection of accounts | A&G | Credit and Collection |
| Occasional food and beverage expenses— limited-service hotels | Minor Oper. Dept. | Occasional Food and Bev. Rev. |
| Office supplies, general | Mult. Depts. | Operating Supplies |
| Off-premises beer | F&B | Cost of Beverage Sales |
| Off-premises cooler/cider | F&B | Cost of Beverage Sales |
| Off-premises liquor | F&B | Cost of Beverage Sales |
| Off-premises wine | F&B | Cost of Beverage Sales |
| Off-property housing costs for non-ex-pat employees | Payroll-Rel. Exp. | Housing and Educational |

| Item Name | Department/Schedule | Account Name |
|---|---|---|
| Off-site storage rent | Non Op. I&E | Other Property and Equipment |
| Oil (for utility use) | Utilities | Oil |
| Online travel agency (OTA) ads | Sales/Marketing | Media |
| Orientation expenses | Mult. Depts. | Training |
| Outdoor advertising | Sales/Marketing | Outside Signage |
| Outlet safety plugs | Mult. Depts. | Operating Supplies |
| Overalls | Mult. Depts. | Uniform Costs |
| Overdraft fees | A&G | Bank Charges |
| Overnight delivery (marketing) | Sales/Marketing | P&ODC |
| Overnight delivery (non-marketing) | A&G | P&ODC |
| Owners' expenses (travel, entertainment, etc.) | A&G | Corporate Office Reimbursables |
| Oxalic acid | Mult. Depts. | Cleaning Supplies |
| Packing tape | Mult. Depts. | Operating Supplies |
| Paid time off | Mult. Depts. | Supplemental Pay |
| Pails | Mult. Depts. | Cleaning Supplies |
| Pain relievers | Mult. Depts. | Operating Supplies |
| Paint and ancillary chemicals | POM | Painting and Wallcovering |
| Paint brushes/rollers/sprayers and other supplies | POM | Painting and Wallcovering |
| Paint sprayer rental | POM | Equipment Rental |
| Painting, contracted | POM | Painting and Wallcovering |
| Pamphlets, educational/instructional (for employees) | Mult. Depts. | Training |
| Pans, baking, broiling, frying | F&B | Utensils |
| Pants | Mult. Depts. | Uniform Costs |
| Paper clips | Mult. Depts. | Operating Supplies |
| Paper, copier | Mult. Depts. | Operating Supplies |
| Paper liners | Mult. Depts. | Operating Supplies |
| Paper towel holders, guestroom | Rooms | Operating Supplies |
| Paper towels, guestroom | Rooms | Operating Supplies |
| Paper tray liners, rooms | Rooms | Operating Supplies |
| Parchment | Mult. Depts. | Operating Supplies |
| Parking, gate tickets | Parking | Printing and Stationery |
| Parking, gratis F&B guest | F&B | Complimentary Services/Gifts |
| Parking lot repair | POM | Building |
| Parking permit cards | Mult. Depts. | Printing and Stationery |
| Parking violation stickers | Mult. Depts. | Printing and Stationery |
| Paste | Mult. Depts. | Operating Supplies |
| Payroll, 401(k) costs | Mult. Depts. | Employee Benefits |
| Payroll, accounting clerk | A&G | Salaries and Wages |

| Item Name | Department/ Schedule | Account Name |
|---|---|---|
| Payroll, administrative | A&G | Salaries and Wages |
| Payroll, automobile | Mult. Depts. | Employee Benefits |
| Payroll, baker | F&B | Salaries and Wages |
| Payroll, banquet/conference/catering attendant | F&B | Salaries and Wages |
| Payroll, banquet/conference/catering houseperson | F&B | Salaries and Wages |
| Payroll, banquet/conference/catering porter | F&B | Salaries and Wages |
| Payroll, banquet/conference/catering runner | F&B | Salaries and Wages |
| Payroll, banquet/conference/catering server | F&B | Salaries and Wages |
| Payroll, bartender | F&B | Salaries and Wages |
| Payroll, bell service | Rooms | Salaries and Wages |
| Payroll, beverage manager | F&B | Salaries and Wages |
| Payroll, bonus pay (discretionary) | Mult. Depts. | Supplemental Pay |
| Payroll, bonus pay (performance-based) | Mult. Depts. | Bonuses and Incentives |
| Payroll, breakfast attendant | Rooms | Salaries and Wages |
| Payroll, butcher | F&B | Salaries and Wages |
| Payroll, chef de partie | F&B | Salaries and Wages |
| Payroll, chief engineer | POM | Salaries and Wages |
| Payroll, child care, employee | Mult. Depts. | Employee Benefits |
| Payroll, city head tax | Mult. Depts. | Payroll Taxes |
| Payroll, cleaner | F&B | Salaries and Wages |
| Payroll, club floor attendant | Rooms | Salaries and Wages |
| Payroll, concierge | Rooms | Salaries and Wages |
| Payroll, conference/event services manager | F&B | Salaries and Wages |
| Payroll, controller | A&G | Salaries and Wages |
| Payroll, cook | F&B | Salaries and Wages |
| Payroll, dental insurance | Mult. Depts. | Employee Benefits |
| Payroll, desk clerk | Rooms | Salaries and Wages |
| Payroll, director of finance | A&G | Salaries and Wages |
| Payroll, director of food and beverage | F&B | Salaries and Wages |
| Payroll, director of human resources | A&G | Salaries and Wages |
| Payroll, director of IT | Info & Telecom | Salaries and Wages |
| Payroll, director of operations | A&G | Salaries and Wages |
| Payroll, director of outlets | F&B | Salaries and Wages |
| Payroll, director of reservations | Rooms | Salaries and Wages |
| Payroll, disability insurance | Mult. Depts. | Employee Benefits |
| Payroll, dishwasher | F&B | Salaries and Wages |
| Payroll, door attendant | Rooms | Salaries and Wages |
| Payroll, engineer | POM | Salaries and Wages |
| Payroll, executive chef | F&B | Salaries and Wages |
| Payroll, executive sous chef | F&B | Salaries and Wages |

| Item Name | Department/ Schedule | Account Name |
|---|---|---|
| Payroll, food and beverage manager | F&B | Salaries and Wages |
| Payroll, front office manager | Rooms | Salaries and Wages |
| Payroll, parking manager | Parking | Salaries and Wages |
| Payroll, general manager | A&G | Salaries and Wages |
| Payroll, golf hourly | Golf/Pro Shop | Salaries and Wages |
| Payroll, golf management | Golf/Pro Shop | Salaries and Wages |
| Payroll, group life insurance | Mult. Depts. | Employee Benefits |
| Payroll, guest services | Rooms | Salaries and Wages |
| Payroll, health club hourly | Health Club/Spa | Salaries and Wages |
| Payroll, health club management | Health Club/Spa | Salaries and Wages |
| Payroll, health insurance | Mult. Depts. | Employee Benefits |
| Payroll, host(ess) | F&B | Salaries and Wages |
| Payroll, hourly wages | Mult. Depts. | Salaries and Wages |
| Payroll, housekeeping attendant | Rooms | Salaries and Wages |
| Payroll, housekeeping director/manager | Rooms | Salaries and Wages |
| Payroll, incentive pay (discretionary) | Mult. Depts. | Supplemental Pay |
| Payroll, incentive pay (performance-based) | Mult. Depts. | Bonuses and Incentives |
| Payroll, informations technology | A&G | Salaries and Wages |
| Payroll, in-room dining server | F&B | Salaries and Wages |
| Payroll, jury duty pay | Mult. Depts. | Supplemental Pay |
| Payroll, kitchen manager | F&B | Salaries and Wages |
| Payroll, kitchen steward | F&B | Salaries and Wages |
| Payroll, laundry attendant | Mult. Depts. | Salaries and Wages |
| Payroll, laundry manager | Mult. Depts. | Salaries and Wages |
| Payroll, leased labor | Mult. Depts. | Salaries and Wages |
| Payroll, long-term disability | Mult. Depts. | Employee Benefits |
| Payroll, maître d' | F&B | Salaries and Wages |
| Payroll, meals (cost allocation from staff dining) | Mult. Depts. | Employee Benefits |
| Payroll, miscellaneous | A&G | Salaries and Wages |
| Payroll, national retirement contribution tax (Social Security) | Mult. Depts. | Payroll Taxes |
| Payroll, national unemployment tax (FUTA) | Mult. Depts. | Payroll Taxes |
| Payroll, night manager | Rooms | Salaries and Wages |
| Payroll, outlet attendant | F&B | Salaries and Wages |
| Payroll, outlet busperson | F&B | Salaries and Wages |
| Payroll, outlet cashier | F&B | Salaries and Wages |
| Payroll, outlet houseperson | F&B | Salaries and Wages |
| Payroll, outlet porter | F&B | Salaries and Wages |
| Payroll, outlet runner | F&B | Salaries and Wages |
| Payroll, outlet server | F&B | Salaries and Wages |

| Item Name | Department/ Schedule | Account Name |
|---|---|---|
| Payroll, pension costs | Mult. Depts. | Employee Benefits |
| Payroll, personal days | Mult. Depts. | Supplemental Pay |
| Payroll—plumber, HVAC, electrical, painter, gardener, or other specialized trade | POM | Salaries and Wages |
| Payroll, processing fees | A&G | Payroll Processing |
| Payroll, profit sharing | Mult. Depts. | Employee Benefits |
| Payroll, purchasing clerk | A&G | Salaries and Wages |
| Payroll, purchasing manager | A&G | Salaries and Wages |
| Payroll, receiving clerk | A&G | Salaries and Wages |
| Payroll, relocation pay | Mult. Depts. | Supplemental Pay |
| Payroll, reservations agent | Rooms | Salaries and Wages |
| Payroll, restaurant manager | F&B | Salaries and Wages |
| Payroll, room director | Rooms | Salaries and Wages |
| Payroll, salaried wages | Mult. Depts. | Salaries and Wages |
| Payroll, security director | A&G | Salaries and Wages |
| Payroll, security officer | A&G | Salaries and Wages |
| Payroll, service captain | F&B | Salaries and Wages |
| Payroll, service charges | Mult. Depts. | Salaries and Wages |
| Payroll, severance pay | Mult. Depts. | Supplemental Pay |
| Payroll, sick pay | Mult. Depts. | Supplemental Pay |
| Payroll, sommelier | F&B | Salaries and Wages |
| Payroll, spa hourly | Health Club/Spa | Salaries and Wages |
| Payroll, spa management | Health Club/Spa | Salaries and Wages |
| Payroll, staff dining attendant | Mult. Depts. | Salaries and Wages |
| Payroll, staff dining manager | Mult. Depts. | Salaries and Wages |
| Payroll, state disability insurance | Mult. Depts. | Payroll Taxes |
| Payroll, state unemployment tax | Mult. Depts. | Payroll Taxes |
| Payroll, statutory holiday pay | Mult. Depts. | Supplemental Pay |
| Payroll, stewarding manager | F&B | Salaries and Wages |
| Payroll, storeroom clerk | A&G | Salaries and Wages |
| Payroll, swimming pool attendant (health club/spa operated) | Health Club/Spa | Salaries and Wages |
| Payroll, swimming pool attendant (no health club/spa) | POM | Salaries and Wages |
| Payroll, transportation driver | Rooms | Salaries and Wages |
| Payroll, union insurance | Mult. Depts. | Employee Benefits |
| Payroll, union other | Mult. Depts. | Employee Benefits |
| Payroll, union pension | Mult. Depts. | Employee Benefits |
| Payroll, vacation pay | Mult. Depts. | Supplemental Pay |
| Payroll, valet/parking attendant | Parking | Salaries and Wages |

| Item Name | Department/ Schedule | Account Name |
|---|---|---|
| Payroll, valet/parking cashier | Parking | Salaries and Wages |
| Payroll, workers' compensation insurance | Mult. Depts. | Employee Benefits |
| PCI compliance costs | Info & Telecom | Information Systems |
| Pencil holders | Mult. Depts. | Operating Supplies |
| Pencil sharpeners | Mult. Depts. | Operating Supplies |
| Pencils | Mult. Depts. | Operating Supplies |
| Pens | Mult. Depts. | Operating Supplies |
| Personal computer lease (non-capital) | Non Op. I&E | Other Property and Equipment |
| Personal property tax refunds (contra)— state/county/city | Non Op. I&E | Personal Property Taxes |
| Personal property taxes—state/county/city | Non Op. I&E | Personal Property Taxes |
| Personnel forms, general | A&G | Human Resources |
| Pest control, golf course | Golf/Pro Shop | Contract Services |
| Pest control services | POM | Contract Services |
| Pest control supplies (in-house use) | POM | Engineering Supplies |
| Phone books for guestrooms | Rooms | Operating Supplies |
| Photos | Sales/Marketing | Photography |
| Physicians' fees—employees (non-workers' compensation) | A&G | Human Resources |
| Piano rental (lounge/restaurant entertainment) | F&B | Music and Entertainment |
| Piano tuning | F&B | Contract Services |
| Pillow cases | Rooms | Linen |
| Pillow mints | Rooms | Guest Supplies |
| Pillow shams | Rooms | Linen |
| Pillows, down, foam, polyester, neck, decorative throw | Rooms | Linen |
| Pins—employee, safety, stick, straight | Mult. Depts. | Operating Supplies |
| Pitchers, guestrooms | Rooms | Operating Supplies |
| Pitchers, water | F&B | China |
| Placards | Mult. Depts. | Operating Supplies |
| Placemats, guestrooms | Rooms | Operating Supplies |
| Plant and tree purchases (indoor and outdoor) | POM | Grounds M&L |
| Plant and tree rentals | POM | Grounds M&L |
| Plant services (watering, etc.) | POM | Contract Services |
| Plants | Mult. Depts. | Operating Supplies |
| Plants and shrubs, golf course | Golf/Pro Shop | Grounds M&L |
| Plastic flatware | F&B | Paper and Plastics |
| Plastic food storage containers | F&B | Paper and Plastics |
| Plastic spray bottles | Mult. Depts. | Cleaning Supplies |
| Plastic wrap | F&B | Paper and Plastics |

| Item Name | Department/ Schedule | Account Name |
|---|---|---|
| Plate cover, dome | F&B | Utensils |
| Plates, all sizes and materials (except paper/plastic) | F&B | China |
| Plates, paper/plastic | F&B | Paper and Plastics |
| Platform lift/cherry picker rental | POM | Equipment Rental |
| Platters, serving | F&B | China |
| Playing cards for use by guests in rooms | Rooms | Guest Supplies |
| Playpens | Rooms | Operating Supplies |
| Plumbing fixture repair parts | POM | Plumbing |
| Plumbing system repair parts | POM | Plumbing |
| Plungers, toilet | Rooms | Operating Supplies |
| PMS hardware lease (non-capital) | Non Op. I&E | Other Property and Equipment |
| PMS software lease (non-capital) | Non Op. I&E | Other Property and Equipment |
| Pocket thermometers | F&B | Utensils |
| Polish | Mult. Depts. | Cleaning Supplies |
| Pool chemicals (health club/spa operated) | Health Club/Spa | Swimming Pool |
| Pool safety equipment (health club/spa operated) | Health Club/Spa | Swimming Pool |
| Pool toys (health club/spa operated) | Health Club/Spa | Swimming Pool |
| Portable fans | Mult. Depts. | Operating Supplies |
| Portable sanitary facilities, golf tournament | Golf/Pro Shop | Tournament Expenses |
| Portable steam cleaners | Mult. Depts. | Operating Supplies |
| POS hardware lease (non-capital) | Non Op. I&E | Other Property and Equipment |
| POS software lease (non-capital) | Non Op. I&E | Other Property and Equipment |
| POS supplies | F&B | Printing and Stationery |
| Post office box rental | A&G | P&ODC |
| Postage and overnight delivery charges | Mult. Depts. | P&ODC |
| Postage for direct mail | Sales/Marketing | Direct Mail |
| Postage (marketing) | Sales/Marketing | P&ODC |
| Postage meter rentals (marketing) | Sales/Marketing | P&ODC |
| Postage meter rentals (non-marketing) | A&G | P&ODC |
| Postage (non-marketing) | A&G | P&ODC |
| Postcards | Sales/Marketing | Collateral Material |
| Postcards for use by guests in rooms | Rooms | Guest Supplies |
| Poster board | Mult. Depts. | Operating Supplies |
| Posters | Sales/Marketing | In-House Graphics |
| Posters, safety | A&G | Human Resources |
| Post-it notes | Mult. Depts. | Operating Supplies |
| Potholder, guestroom | Rooms | Operating Supplies |

| Item Name | Department/Schedule | Account Name |
|---|---|---|
| Potholder mitt, guestroom | Rooms | Operating Supplies |
| Pots | F&B | Utensils |
| Pour spouts, liquor | F&B | Utensils |
| PPC fees | Sales/Marketing | Website |
| Presentation binders | A&G | Operating Supplies |
| Presto logs, guestroom | Rooms | Operating Supplies |
| Preventive maintenance hardware, small value purchases | Info & Telecom | POM |
| Preventive maintenance software licenses, support and maintenance fees | Info & Telecom | POM |
| Printed forms | Mult. Depts. | Printing and Stationery |
| Printer paper | Mult. Depts. | Printing and Stationery |
| Printer supplies and accessories | Mult. Depts. | Operating Supplies |
| Printing calculator | Mult. Depts. | Operating Supplies |
| Prizes, employee | A&G | Human Resources |
| Prizes, golf tournament | Golf/Pro Shop | Tournament Expenses |
| Production—magazines | Sales/Marketing | Media |
| Production—newspapers | Sales/Marketing | Media |
| Production—other | Sales/Marketing | Media |
| Production—TV | Sales/Marketing | Media |
| Professional dues (marketing) | Sales/Marketing | Dues and Subscriptions |
| Professional dues (non-marketing) | A&G | Dues and Subscriptions |
| Professional fees | A&G | Professional Fees |
| Promotional gifts | Sales/Marketing | Complimentary Services/Gifts |
| Promotional signs, interior | Sales/Marketing | In-House Graphics |
| Propane, cooking and preparation | F&B | Kitchen Fuel |
| Propane (for utility use) | Utilities | Other Fuels |
| Property management system hardware, small value purchases | Info & Telecom | Rooms |
| Property management system software license, support and maintenance fees | Info & Telecom | Rooms |
| Props, banquets | F&B | Operating Supplies |
| Protective service | A&G | Security |
| Provision for doubtful accounts | A&G | Provision for Doubtful Accounts |
| Public address system repairs | POM | Elec. & Mech. |
| Public area cleaning service, lobby/guestroom corridors | Rooms | Contract Services |
| Public area cleaning service, restaurant/banquet foyers | F&B | Contract Services |
| Public relations | Sales/Marketing | Agency Fees |

| Item Name | Department/ Schedule | Account Name |
|---|---|---|
| Public restroom cleaning service | F&B | Contract Services |
| Publications, house (for employees) | Mult. Depts. | Training |
| Pull carts, golf (for rental) | Golf/Pro Shop | Operating Supplies |
| Pull carts, golf (for sale) | Golf/Pro Shop | Cost of Merch. Sales |
| Purchasing service fees | Mult. Depts. | Contract Services |
| Q-tips | Mult. Depts. | Operating Supplies |
| Quilt | Rooms | Linen |
| Quilt rack | Rooms | Operating Supplies |
| Rack cards | Sales/Marketing | Collateral Material |
| Radio advertising | Sales/Marketing | Media |
| Radios, guestroom | Rooms | Operating Supplies |
| Rags, cleaning | Mult. Depts. | Cleaning Supplies |
| Ramekins (all materials) | F&B | China |
| Razors for use by guests in rooms | Rooms | Guest Supplies |
| Reader board service fee | Sales/Marketing | Outside Services Market Research |
| Real property tax refunds (contra)— state/county/city | Non Op. I&E | Real Estate Taxes |
| Real property taxes—state/county/city | Non Op. I&E | Real Estate Taxes |
| Receiver fees | Non Op. I&E | Owner Expenses |
| Record books | Mult. Depts. | Operating Supplies |
| Recorders, mini/micro cassette and accessories | Mult. Depts. | Operating Supplies |
| Recruiter fees | A&G | Human Resources |
| Recycle bins | Mult. Depts. | Operating Supplies |
| Reference checking, employee | A&G | Human Resources |
| Referral programs | Sales/Marketing | Loyalty Programs |
| Refuse/compactor container charges | POM | Waste Removal |
| Relocation costs | A&G | Human Resources |
| Rent, temporary parking space | Parking | Rent |
| Repairs and maintenance, golf cart paths | Golf/Pro Shop | Grounds M&L |
| Repairs, uniforms | Mult. Depts. | Uniform Costs |
| Report covers | A&G | Operating Supplies |
| Reports | Mult. Depts. | Operating Supplies |
| Representation firms | Sales/Marketing | Outside Sales Representation |
| Reputation management fee | Sales/Marketing | Outside Services Market Research |
| Reseeding golf course | Golf/Pro Shop | Grounds M&L |
| Reservation books | F&B | Operating Supplies |
| Reservation fees | F&B | Reservation Fees |
| Reservation fees (chain assessment) | Rooms | Reservations |
| Reservation fees (GDS) | Rooms | Reservations |

| Item Name | Department/ Schedule | Account Name |
|---|---|---|
| Reservation fees (OTA) | Rooms | Reservations |
| Reservation telephone expense | Rooms | Reservations |
| Reservation website building and maintenance | Rooms | Reservations |
| Revenue management fee (third party) | Sales/Marketing | Contract Services |
| Revenue optimization fee (third party) | Sales/Marketing | Contract Services |
| Review monitoring fees | Sales/Marketing | Outside Services Market Research |
| Ribbons—typewriter, calculator, cash register | Mult. Depts. | Operating Supplies |
| Ring binders | A&G | Operating Supplies |
| Road signs | Sales/Marketing | Outside Signage |
| Robes | Rooms | Linen |
| Rollaway beds | Rooms | Operating Supplies |
| Roller shades | Mult. Depts. | Operating Supplies |
| Roman shades | Mult. Depts. | Operating Supplies |
| Room attendant reports | Rooms | Printing and Stationery |
| Room charges, travel | Mult. Depts. | Travel—Other |
| Room costs, musicians and entertainers | F&B | Music and Entertainment |
| Room directories | Rooms | Printing and Stationery |
| Room directory binders | Rooms | Printing and Stationery |
| Room rack forms | Rooms | Printing and Stationery |
| Royalties for use of third-party brand name | Mult. Depts. | Royalty Fees |
| Royalty fee—franchise or affiliation | Sales/Marketing | Franchise and Affiliation Fees—Royalties |
| Royalty fees | F&B | Royalty Fees |
| Rubber bands | Mult. Depts. | Operating Supplies |
| Rubber boots, kitchen | F&B | Operating Supplies |
| Rubber cement | Mult. Depts. | Operating Supplies |
| Rubber gloves | Mult. Depts. | Cleaning Supplies |
| Rubber sheets | Rooms | Linen |
| Rubber stamps | Mult. Depts. | Operating Supplies |
| Rubber tub mat | Rooms | Operating Supplies |
| Rug cleaners | Mult. Depts. | Cleaning Supplies |
| Rug cleaning services | Mult. Depts. | Contract Services |
| Rugs, bathroom | Rooms | Linen |
| Rugs, throw | Mult. Depts. | Operating Supplies |
| Rulers | Mult. Depts. | Operating Supplies |
| Safe deposit box keys | Rooms | Operating Supplies |
| Safe deposit box rentals (off-site) | A&G | Security |
| Safe deposit record cards | Rooms | Printing and Stationery |
| Safety glasses | Mult. Depts. | Operating Supplies |

| Item Name | Department/ Schedule | Account Name |
|---|---|---|
| Safety pins | Mult. Depts. | Operating Supplies |
| Salad bowls | F&B | China |
| Sales and marketing hardware, small value purchases | Info & Telecom | Sales and Marketing |
| Sales and marketing software licenses, support and maintenance fees | Info & Telecom | Sales and Marketing |
| Sales and occupancy taxes not paid by customers | Non Op. I&E | B&O Taxes |
| Sales initiated client amenities | Sales/Marketing | Complimentary Services/Gifts |
| Sales kits | Sales/Marketing | Collateral Material |
| Salt and pepper shakers | F&B | China |
| Sand, cinders, and top dressing, golf course | Golf/Pro Shop | Grounds M&L |
| Sanitary pads/tampons | Rooms | Guest Supplies |
| Satellite television service | Rooms | Complimentary In-Room/ Media Entertainment |
| Sauce boats (all materials) | F&B | China |
| Scissors | Mult. Depts. | Operating Supplies |
| Scissors, kitchen | F&B | Utensils |
| Scoreboard rental, golf tournament | Golf/Pro Shop | Tournament Expenses |
| Scorecards, golf | Golf/Pro Shop | Printing and Stationery |
| Scouring pads | F&B | Dishwashing Supplies |
| Scrapers, cleaning | Mult. Depts. | Cleaning Supplies |
| Scrapers, dish | F&B | Dishwashing Supplies |
| Scrub brushes | Mult. Depts. | Cleaning Supplies |
| Search engine optimization costs | Sales/Marketing | Website |
| Security, contracted | A&G | Security |
| Security, golf tournament | Golf/Pro Shop | Tournament Expenses |
| Security hardware, small value purchases | Info & Telecom | A&G |
| Security system licenses, support and maintenance fees | Info & Telecom | A&G |
| Seeds, golf course | Golf/Pro Shop | Grounds M&L |
| Self-insurance retention | Non Op. I&E | Deductible |
| SEO costs | Sales/Marketing | Website |
| Service manuals (employee) | Mult. Depts. | Training |
| Serving spoons for use by guests in rooms | Rooms | Guest Supplies |
| Serving utensils | F&B | Flatware |
| Sewer | Utilities | Water/Sewer |
| Sewing kits for use by guests in rooms | Rooms | Guest Supplies |
| Shakers, bar | F&B | Utensils |
| Shampoo, carpet | Mult. Depts. | Cleaning Supplies |
| Shampoo for use by guests in rooms | Rooms | Guest Supplies |
| Shams | Rooms | Linen |

| Item Name | Department/ Schedule | Account Name |
|---|---|---|
| Shaving cream/gel for use by guests in rooms | Rooms | Guest Supplies |
| Shaving mirror, guestroom | Rooms | Operating Supplies |
| Sheers | Rooms | Operating Supplies |
| Sheet music | F&B | Music and Entertainment |
| Sheets, fitted | Rooms | Linen |
| Sheets, flat | Rooms | Linen |
| Shelf paper | Mult. Depts. | Operating Supplies |
| Shipping supplies | Mult. Depts. | Operating Supplies |
| Shipping tags | Mult. Depts. | Operating Supplies |
| Shirts | Mult. Depts. | Uniform Costs |
| Shoe brushes for use by guests in rooms | Rooms | Guest Supplies |
| Shoe mitts for use by guests in rooms | Rooms | Guest Supplies |
| Shoe polish for use by guests in rooms | Rooms | Guest Supplies |
| Shoes | Mult. Depts. | Uniform Costs |
| Shoes, golf (for rent) | Golf/Pro Shop | Operating Supplies |
| Shoes, golf (for sale) | Golf/Pro Shop | Cost of Merch. Sales |
| Shopping service | Mult. Depts. | Contract Services |
| Shopping services (bar spotters) | F&B | Contract Services |
| Shorts | Mult. Depts. | Uniform Costs |
| Shot glasses, bar | F&B | Glassware |
| Shower caps for use by guests in rooms | Rooms | Guest Supplies |
| Shower curtain liners | Rooms | Operating Supplies |
| Shower curtain rings | Rooms | Operating Supplies |
| Shower curtains | Rooms | Operating Supplies |
| Shower slippers | Rooms | Operating Supplies |
| Sign repairs | POM | Building |
| Signage, golf maintenance | Golf/Pro Shop | Grounds M&L |
| Signs (inside) | Sales/Marketing | In-House Graphics |
| Signs (outside) | Sales/Marketing | Outside Signage |
| Signs and banners | Mult. Depts. | Operating Supplies |
| Silver polish | F&B | Dishwashing Supplies |
| Silverware for use by guests in rooms | Rooms | Guest Supplies |
| Skirts | Mult. Depts. | Uniform Costs |
| Slippers for use by guests in rooms | Rooms | Operating Supplies |
| Slippers (health club/spa) | Health Club/Spa | Linen |
| Smocks | Mult. Depts. | Uniform Costs |
| Smoking urn sand stamp | Mult. Depts. | Operating Supplies |
| Sneeze guards | F&B | Operating Supplies |
| Snow removal service | POM | Grounds M&L |
| Soap and soap dishes, guestroom | Rooms | Guest Supplies |

| Item Name | Department/ Schedule | Account Name |
| --- | --- | --- |
| Soap scum remover, guestroom | Rooms | Cleaning Supplies |
| Soaps, cleaning | Mult. Depts. | Cleaning Supplies |
| Social activities, employees | A&G | Human Resources |
| Social media monitoring service | Sales/Marketing | Outside Services Market Research |
| Socks | Mult. Depts. | Uniform Costs |
| Soda for use by guests in rooms | Rooms | Guest Supplies |
| Soft drink syrup or premix | F&B | Cost of Food Sales |
| Soft drinks for bar mix | F&B | Cost of Beverage Sales |
| Software application upgrades | Info & Telecom | System Expenses |
| Software, golf tournament | Golf/Pro Shop | Tournament Expenses |
| Solar power | Utilities | Other Fuels |
| Soufflé dishes (all materials) | F&B | China |
| Sound system repairs | POM | Elec. & Mech. |
| Spa music | Health Club/Spa | Ambience |
| Spa products (for sale in health club/spa) | Health Club/Spa | Cost of Sales |
| Spatulas, kitchen | F&B | Utensils |
| Speaker fees, training | Mult. Depts. | Training |
| Speakers, stereo, guestroom | Rooms | Operating Supplies |
| Sponges | Mult. Depts. | Cleaning Supplies |
| Sponges, dishwashing | F&B | Dishwashing Supplies |
| Sponsorships | Sales/Marketing | Promotion |
| Spoons for use by guests in rooms | Rooms | Operating Supplies |
| Spoons, mixing | F&B | Utensils |
| Sports activities and equipment, employees | A&G | Human Resources |
| Spray bottle | Mult. Depts. | Cleaning Supplies |
| Squeegees | Mult. Depts. | Cleaning Supplies |
| Stain remover | Mult. Depts. | Cleaning Supplies |
| Stain remover packets | Mult. Depts. | Cleaning Supplies |
| Stain spotter | Mult. Depts. | Cleaning Supplies |
| Stainless steel cleaner | Mult. Depts. | Cleaning Supplies |
| Stamp pads | Mult. Depts. | Operating Supplies |
| Stamp pads (ink) | Mult. Depts. | Operating Supplies |
| Stamps (marketing) | Sales/Marketing | P&ODC |
| Stamps, rubber | Mult. Depts. | Operating Supplies |
| Staplers | Mult. Depts. | Operating Supplies |
| Staples | Mult. Depts. | Operating Supplies |
| STAR Report fee | Sales/Marketing | Outside Services Market Research |
| State disability insurance | Payroll-Rel. Exp. | State Disability Insurance |

| Item Name | Department/Schedule | Account Name |
|---|---|---|
| State medical insurance | Payroll-Rel. Exp. | State Medical Insurance |
| State unemployment insurance | Payroll-Rel. Exp. | State Unemployment Insurance |
| Stationery | Mult. Depts. | Printing and Stationery |
| Stationery for use by guests in rooms | Rooms | Guest Supplies |
| Stationery portfolio | Rooms | Operating Supplies |
| Steak markers | F&B | Operating Supplies |
| Steam (for utility use) | Utilities | Steam |
| Steel wool | F&B | Dishwashing Supplies |
| Stencils | Mult. Depts. | Operating Supplies |
| Sterno for food warming | F&B | Kitchen Fuel |
| Stir sticks, cocktail | F&B | Paper and Plastics |
| Stir sticks for use by guests in rooms | Rooms | Guest Supplies |
| Stirrers, beverage | F&B | Utensils |
| Stock benefits | Mult. Depts. | Employee Benefits |
| Stock options | Mult. Depts. | Employee Benefits |
| Stock transfer agents, fees | A&G | Professional Fees |
| Stop payment charges | A&G | Bank Charges |
| Stoppers, bottle (bar) | F&B | Utensils |
| Storage files | A&G | Operating Supplies |
| Storage of equipment/records (off-site) | A&G | Contract Services |
| STR fee | Sales/Marketing | Outside Services Market Research |
| Strainers, bar | F&B | Utensils |
| Strainers, guestroom | Rooms | Operating Supplies |
| Straws, cocktail | F&B | Paper and Plastics |
| Straws, soft drink | F&B | Paper and Plastics |
| Styrofoam cups | F&B | Paper and Plastics |
| Subscription TV channels (e.g., HBO) | Rooms | Complimentary In-Room/Media Entertainment |
| Subscriptions (marketing) | Sales/Marketing | Dues and Subscriptions |
| Subscriptions—trade (non-marketing) | A&G | Dues and Subscriptions |
| Subsidized public transportation for employees | Payroll-Rel. Exp. | Public Subsidized Transportation |
| Sugar caddy, guestroom | Rooms | Operating Supplies |
| Sugar holders | F&B | China |
| Sugar packets for use by guests in rooms | Rooms | Guest Supplies |
| Suggestion awards, employees | A&G | Human Resources |
| Suits | Mult. Depts. | Uniform Costs |
| Surge protectors | Mult. Depts. | Operating Supplies |
| Survey—meeting planner | Sales/Marketing | Contract Services |

| Item Name | Department/ Schedule | Account Name |
|---|---|---|
| Sweetener packets for use by guests in rooms | Rooms | Guest Supplies |
| Swimming pool/spa parts, repairs, and chemicals/ maintenance (no health club/spa) | POM | Swimming Pool |
| Swimsuit bags for use by guests in rooms | Rooms | Guest Supplies |
| Switchboard repairs | Info & Telecom | Telecommunications |
| Swizzle sticks for use by guests in rooms | Rooms | Guest Supplies |
| T-1 | Info & Telecom | Telecommunications |
| Table and chair rental (banquets, charged to customer) | F&B | Misc. Cost (of Other Rev.) |
| Table and chair rental (one time event) | F&B | Equipment Rental |
| Table and chair rental (short term or for one time event) | F&B | Equipment Rental |
| Table linen and chair cover rental (banquets, charged to custmer) | F&B | Misc. Cost (of Other Rev.) |
| Table pads | F&B | Operating Supplies |
| Table pads, guestroom | Rooms | Operating Supplies |
| Table protectors, guestroom | Rooms | Operating Supplies |
| Table rental (banquet not charged to customer) | F&B | Banquet Expense |
| Table runners, linen | F&B | Linen |
| Table skirt clips | F&B | Linen |
| Table skirts, linen | F&B | Linen |
| Table tent cards, guestroom | Rooms | Operating Supplies |
| Table tents | F&B | Printing and Stationery |
| Table top promotion printing | Sales/Marketing | In-House Graphics |
| Table undercloth, linen | F&B | Linen |
| Tablecloths, guestroom | Rooms | Operating Supplies |
| Tablecloths, linen | F&B | Linen |
| Tablecloths, paper/plastic | F&B | Paper and Plastics |
| Tags, baggage (gratis) | Rooms | Guest Supplies |
| Tape, adhesive | Mult. Depts. | Operating Supplies |
| Tape, carpet | POM | Floor Covering |
| Tape holder | Mult. Depts. | Operating Supplies |
| Tape, Scotch | Mult. Depts. | Operating Supplies |
| Tax equalization payments for ex-pats | Payroll-Rel. Exp. | Expat Benefits |
| Taxi fare | Mult. Depts. | Travel—Other |
| Tea bags for use by guests in rooms | Rooms | Guest Supplies |
| Teapots and lids (all materials) | F&B | China |
| Teapots, guestroom | Rooms | Operating Supplies |
| Technical books and publications, maintenance | POM | Operating Supplies |
| Telecommunication software license, support and maintenance fees | Info & Telecom | Telecommunications |
| Telecommunications equipment maintenance | Info & Telecom | Other Equipment |

| Item Name | Department/<br>Schedule | Account Name |
|---|---|---|
| Telephone access charges | Info & Telecom | Cost of Local Calls |
| Telephone access charges | Info & Telecom | Cost of Long Distance Calls |
| Telephone cords | Info & Telecom | Other Equipment |
| Telephone directories for departmental use | Sales/Marketing | Operating Supplies |
| Telephone directories for guestrooms | Rooms | Operating Supplies |
| Telephone directory advertising | Sales/Marketing | Media |
| Telephone directory covers and holders | Mult. Depts. | Operating Supplies |
| Telephone face plate | Info & Telecom | Other Equipment |
| Telephone hardware lease (non-capital) | Non Op. I&E | Other Property and Equipment |
| Telephone headsets | Info & Telecom | Other Equipment |
| Telephone message cards | Rooms | Printing and Stationery |
| Telephone message pads | Rooms | Guest Supplies |
| Telephone software lease (non-capital) | Non Op. I&E | Other Property and Equipment |
| Telephone switch lease (non-capital) | Non Op. I&E | Other Property and Equipment |
| Telephone usage fees | Info & Telecom | Cost of Local Calls |
| Telephone usage fees | Info & Telecom | Cost of Long Distance Calls |
| Telephone utility taxes | Info & Telecom | Cost of Local Calls |
| Telephone utility taxes | Info & Telecom | Cost of Long Distance Calls |
| Television ad | Sales/Marketing | Media |
| Television remote | Rooms | Operating Supplies |
| Television repairs | POM | Furniture and Equipment |
| Temporary housing, employee | A&G | Human Resources |
| Tent rental (banquets, charged to customer) | F&B | Misc. Cost (of Other Rev.) |
| Tent rental for parties/banquets (not charged to customer) | F&B | Banquet Expense |
| Third-party outsourcing | A&G | Contract Services |
| Thread for use by guests in rooms | Rooms | Guest Supplies |
| Throw, guestroom | Rooms | Operating Supplies |
| Ties | Mult. Depts. | Uniform Costs |
| Tile cleaner | Mult. Depts. | Cleaning Supplies |
| Tile repairs (floor) | POM | Floor Covering |
| Timeclocks | Info & Telecom | Human Resources |
| Tissue box covers, guestroom | Rooms | Operating Supplies |
| Tissue for use by guests in rooms | Rooms | Guest Supplies |
| Tobacco cost | F&B | Misc. Cost (of Other Rev.) |
| Toilet brushes | Mult. Depts. | Cleaning Supplies |
| Toilet paper (health club/spa) | Health Club/Spa | Operating Supplies |
| Toilet tissue | Rooms | Guest Supplies |

| Item Name | Department/ Schedule | Account Name |
|---|---|---|
| Tolls, highway | Mult. Depts. | Travel—Other |
| Toner for copiers | A&G | Operating Supplies |
| Tongs, cooking | F&B | Utensils |
| Tongs, serving | F&B | Flatware |
| Tonics (health club/spa) | Health Club/Spa | Health and Beauty Products |
| Tools | POM | Engineering Supplies |
| Toothbrush holders, guestroom | Rooms | Operating Supplies |
| Toothbrushes for use by guests in rooms | Rooms | Guest Supplies |
| Toothpaste for use by guests in rooms | Rooms | Guest Supplies |
| Toothpicks | F&B | Paper and Plastics |
| Toothpicks for use by guests in rooms | Rooms | Guest Supplies |
| Topsoil for golf course | Golf/Pro Shop | Grounds M&L |
| Total quality management | A&G | Human Resources |
| Tourist board/bureau fees | Sales/Marketing | Dues and Subscriptions |
| Tourist guide ad | Sales/Marketing | Media |
| Tourist guide listing | Sales/Marketing | Media |
| Towelettes for use by guests in rooms | Rooms | Guest Supplies |
| Towels, bar | F&B | Linen |
| Towels, bar (guestroom) | Rooms | Linen |
| Towels, bath (all sizes) | Rooms | Linen |
| Towels, cleaning rags | Mult. Depts. | Cleaning Supplies |
| Towels, hand | Rooms | Linen |
| Towels (health club/spa) | Health Club/Spa | Linen |
| Towels, paper | Mult. Depts. | Cleaning Supplies |
| Toys for use by guests in rooms | Rooms | Operating Supplies |
| Trade publication subscriptions (marketing) | Sales/Marketing | Dues and Subscriptions |
| Trade show booth construction | Sales/Marketing | Trade Shows |
| Trade show promotional items | Sales/Marketing | Trade Shows |
| Trade show registration | Sales/Marketing | Trade Shows |
| Training | F&B | Training |
| Training program costs | Mult. Depts. | Training |
| Transfer fees, licenses | Mult. Depts. | Licenses and Permits |
| Transportation charged to customer, banquets | F&B | Misc. Cost (of Other Rev.) |
| Transportation costs for home leave for ex-pats | Payroll-Rel. Exp. | Expat Benefits |
| Transportation of employees | A&G | Staff Transportation |
| Trash can liners | Mult. Depts. | Operating Supplies |
| Trash cans/receptacles | Mult. Depts. | Operating Supplies |
| Trash compactor lease (non-capital) | Non Op. I&E | Other Property and Equipment |
| Travel click fee | Sales/Marketing | Outside Services Market Research |

| Item Name | Department/ Schedule | Account Name |
|---|---|---|
| Travel—corporate—sales and marketing | Sales/Marketing | Corporate Office Reimbursables |
| Travel expenses (food/beverage) | Mult. Depts. | Travel—Meals & Enter. |
| Travel expenses (non-food/beverage) | Mult. Depts. | Travel—Other |
| Travel meals | Mult. Depts. | Travel—Meals & Enter. |
| Travel—other | F&B | Travel—Other |
| Tray jacks | F&B | Operating Supplies |
| Tray liners | F&B | Operating Supplies |
| Trays, guestroom | Rooms | Operating Supplies |
| Trays, serving (all materials) | F&B | Operating Supplies |
| Tree purchases | POM | Grounds M&L |
| Tree removal and trimming service, golf course | Golf/Pro Shop | Contract Services |
| Trigger sprayer bottles | Mult. Depts. | Cleaning Supplies |
| Trousers | Mult. Depts. | Uniform Costs |
| Truck rental (food delivery) | F&B | Equipment Rental |
| Trunk line charges | Info & Telecom | Cost of Local Calls |
| Trunk line charges | Info & Telecom | Cost of Long Distance Calls |
| T-shirts | Mult. Depts. | Uniform Costs |
| Tubes, pastry | F&B | Utensils |
| Tuition cost for family members of ex-pats | Payroll-Rel. Exp. | Expat Benefits |
| Tumblers, guestroom | Rooms | Operating Supplies |
| TV advertising | Sales/Marketing | Media |
| *TV Guides*, guestroom | Rooms | Operating Supplies |
| Tweezers for use by guests in rooms | Rooms | Guest Supplies |
| Umbrellas | Mult. Depts. | Operating Supplies |
| Uncollectible accounts | A&G | Provision for Doubtful Accounts |
| Underinsured losses, liability | Non Op. I&E | Liability |
| Underinsured losses, property | Non Op. I&E | Building and Contents |
| Uniform | F&B | Uniform Costs |
| Uniform cleaning | Mult. Depts. | Uniform Laundry |
| Uniform cleaning allowance | Mult. Depts. | Uniform Laundry |
| Uniform laundry | F&B | Uniform Laundry |
| Uniform repair | Mult. Depts. | Uniform Costs |
| Union dues | Payroll-Rel. Exp. | Union Other |
| Union legal fund | Payroll-Rel. Exp. | Union Other |
| Upholstery cleaner | Mult. Depts. | Cleaning Supplies |
| Upholstery repairs | POM | Furniture and Equipment |
| Urinal baskets | Mult. Depts. | Operating Supplies |
| Utensils, kitchen | F&B | Utensils |

| Item Name | Department/ Schedule | Account Name |
|---|---|---|
| Vacuum accessories | Mult. Depts. | Cleaning Supplies |
| Vacuum belts | Mult. Depts. | Cleaning Supplies |
| Vacuum cleaner accessories | Mult. Depts. | Cleaning Supplies |
| Vacuum cleaners | Mult. Depts. | Cleaning Supplies |
| Vacuum filters | Mult. Depts. | Cleaning Supplies |
| Vacuums—canister, portable, upright | Mult. Depts. | Cleaning Supplies |
| Vases (tabletop) | F&B | Operating Supplies |
| Vegetables | F&B | Cost of Food Sales |
| Vehicle lease (non-capital) | Non Op. I&E | Other Property and Equipment |
| Vehicle parts and supplies—not capitalized | POM | Operating Supplies |
| Vending machine expenses—hotel operated | Minor Oper. Dept. | Vending Revenue |
| Video camera | Mult. Depts. | Operating Supplies |
| Video check-out service | Rooms | Contract Services |
| Video comment card service | Rooms | Contract Services |
| Video game expenses—hotel operated | Minor Oper. Dept. | Video Game Sales |
| Video—welcome channel | Sales/Marketing | Media |
| Videotapes, training/safety | Mult. Depts. | Training |
| VIP guest gifts | Mult. Depts. | Complimentary Services/Gifts |
| Virtual tour production | Sales/Marketing | Website |
| Visa costs for an ex-pat employee | A&G | Human Resources |
| Visitors bureau dues | Sales/Marketing | Dues and Subscriptions |
| Visitors bureau events/registration | Sales/Marketing | Travel—Other |
| Visitors guide ad | Sales/Marketing | Media |
| Visitors guide listing | Sales/Marketing | Media |
| Visual planners | Mult. Depts. | Operating Supplies |
| VoIP | Info & Telecom | Telecommunications |
| Walks, relocation of guest due to lack of room availability | Rooms | Guest Relocation |
| Wall covering repairs, minor replacements | POM | Painting and Decorating |
| Want ads (help wanted) | A&G | Human Resources |
| Washcloths | Rooms | Linen |
| Waste, garbage, debris, and recycling removal | POM | Waste Removal |
| Waste receptacles | Mult. Depts. | Operating Supplies |
| Wastebaskets | Mult. Depts. | Operating Supplies |
| Wastebaskets (employee) | Mult. Depts. | Operating Supplies |
| Wastewater surcharge | Utilities | Water/Sewer |
| Water and drainage systems maintenance, golf course | Golf/Pro Shop | Irrigation |
| Water conservation cards | Rooms | Printing and Stationery |

| Item Name | Department/ Schedule | Account Name |
|---|---|---|
| Water controllers, computerized water systems, golf course | Golf/Pro Shop | Irrigation |
| Water for golf course | Golf/Pro Shop | Water |
| Water other than for golf course | Utilities | Water/Sewer |
| Water pitchers, guestroom | Rooms | Operating Supplies |
| Waxed paper | F&B | Paper and Plastics |
| Waxes | Mult. Depts. | Cleaning Supplies |
| Website design and maintenance | Sales/Marketing | Website |
| Website development | Sales/Marketing | Website |
| Weight scale (health club/spa) | Health Club/Spa | Operating Supplies |
| Welcome baskets, guestroom | Rooms | Complimentary Services/Gifts |
| Wet floor signs | Mult. Depts. | Operating Supplies |
| Wind power | Utilities | Other Fuels |
| Window cleaning services | Mult. Depts. | Contract Services |
| Window repair (glass screen, lock, mechanism, framing, etc.) | POM | Building |
| Window shade and treatment repairs | POM | Building |
| Wine—bottle | F&B | Cost of Beverage Sales |
| Wine cellar supplies | F&B | Operating Supplies |
| Wine—glass | F&B | Cost of Beverage Sales |
| Wine lists | F&B | Menus and Beverage Lists |
| Wireless cards | Info & Telecom | Other Equipment |
| Woolite packets | Mult. Depts. | Cleaning Supplies |
| Workers' compensation insurance premium | Payroll-Rel. Exp. | Workers' Compensation Insurance |
| Wrapping paper | Mult. Depts. | Operating Supplies |
| Writing supplies | Mult. Depts. | Operating Supplies |
| Yellow Pages ad | Sales/Marketing | Media |

# Expense Guide
## Section Two: Sorted by Department/Schedule and Account Name

| Department/ Schedule | Account Name | Item Name |
|---|---|---|
| Mult. Depts. | Bonuses and Incentives | Payroll, bonus pay (performance-based) |
| Mult. Depts. | Bonuses and Incentives | Payroll, incentive pay (performance-based) |
| Mult. Depts. | Cleaning Supplies | Acids |

| Department/<br>Schedule | Account Name | Item Name |
|---|---|---|
| Mult. Depts. | Cleaning Supplies | Air freshener |
| Mult. Depts. | Cleaning Supplies | Alcohol (cleaning) |
| Mult. Depts. | Cleaning Supplies | All-purpose cleaner |
| Mult. Depts. | Cleaning Supplies | Ammonia |
| Mult. Depts. | Cleaning Supplies | Artificial plant cleaner |
| Mult. Depts. | Cleaning Supplies | Bathroom cleaner |
| Mult. Depts. | Cleaning Supplies | Bleach |
| Mult. Depts. | Cleaning Supplies | Bleach packets |
| Mult. Depts. | Cleaning Supplies | Brooms |
| Mult. Depts. | Cleaning Supplies | Brushes |
| Mult. Depts. | Cleaning Supplies | Buckets, mop |
| Mult. Depts. | Cleaning Supplies | Bug traps |
| Mult. Depts. | Cleaning Supplies | Carpet cleaner chemical |
| Mult. Depts. | Cleaning Supplies | Carpet cleaning supplies |
| Mult. Depts. | Cleaning Supplies | Carpet shampoo |
| Mult. Depts. | Cleaning Supplies | Carpet shampoo machines |
| Mult. Depts. | Cleaning Supplies | Carpet sweepers |
| Mult. Depts. | Cleaning Supplies | Chamois |
| Mult. Depts. | Cleaning Supplies | Cleaning chemicals |
| Mult. Depts. | Cleaning Supplies | Cleaning cloths, compounds, fluids, rags, sponges |
| Mult. Depts. | Cleaning Supplies | Cleansers (non-dishwashing) |
| Mult. Depts. | Cleaning Supplies | Cleansing powder |
| Mult. Depts. | Cleaning Supplies | Degreaser |
| Mult. Depts. | Cleaning Supplies | Disinfectants |
| Mult. Depts. | Cleaning Supplies | Dust cloths |
| Mult. Depts. | Cleaning Supplies | Dust mop |
| Mult. Depts. | Cleaning Supplies | Dusters |
| Mult. Depts. | Cleaning Supplies | Dusting mitts |
| Mult. Depts. | Cleaning Supplies | Dustpan brushes |
| Mult. Depts. | Cleaning Supplies | Dustpans |
| Mult. Depts. | Cleaning Supplies | Feather duster |
| Mult. Depts. | Cleaning Supplies | Filters, vacuum |
| Mult. Depts. | Cleaning Supplies | Floor polish |
| Mult. Depts. | Cleaning Supplies | Floor soap |
| Mult. Depts. | Cleaning Supplies | Floor wax |
| Mult. Depts. | Cleaning Supplies | Fly strips |
| Mult. Depts. | Cleaning Supplies | Fly swatters |
| Mult. Depts. | Cleaning Supplies | Furniture polish |
| Mult. Depts. | Cleaning Supplies | Furniture wax |

| Department/Schedule | Account Name | Item Name |
|---|---|---|
| Mult. Depts. | Cleaning Supplies | Glass cleaner |
| Mult. Depts. | Cleaning Supplies | Gloves, rubber |
| Mult. Depts. | Cleaning Supplies | Gum remover |
| Mult. Depts. | Cleaning Supplies | Insecticides |
| Mult. Depts. | Cleaning Supplies | Lemon oil |
| Mult. Depts. | Cleaning Supplies | Lint brush |
| Mult. Depts. | Cleaning Supplies | Lint remover |
| Mult. Depts. | Cleaning Supplies | Lye |
| Mult. Depts. | Cleaning Supplies | Mop buckets |
| Mult. Depts. | Cleaning Supplies | Mop handles |
| Mult. Depts. | Cleaning Supplies | Mop wringers |
| Mult. Depts. | Cleaning Supplies | Mops |
| Mult. Depts. | Cleaning Supplies | Oxalic acid |
| Mult. Depts. | Cleaning Supplies | Pails |
| Mult. Depts. | Cleaning Supplies | Plastic spray bottles |
| Mult. Depts. | Cleaning Supplies | Polish |
| Mult. Depts. | Cleaning Supplies | Rags, cleaning |
| Mult. Depts. | Cleaning Supplies | Rubber gloves |
| Mult. Depts. | Cleaning Supplies | Rug cleaners |
| Mult. Depts. | Cleaning Supplies | Scrapers, cleaning |
| Mult. Depts. | Cleaning Supplies | Scrub brushes |
| Mult. Depts. | Cleaning Supplies | Shampoo, carpet |
| Mult. Depts. | Cleaning Supplies | Soaps, cleaning |
| Mult. Depts. | Cleaning Supplies | Sponges |
| Mult. Depts. | Cleaning Supplies | Spray bottle |
| Mult. Depts. | Cleaning Supplies | Squeegees |
| Mult. Depts. | Cleaning Supplies | Stain remover |
| Mult. Depts. | Cleaning Supplies | Stain remover packets |
| Mult. Depts. | Cleaning Supplies | Stain spotter |
| Mult. Depts. | Cleaning Supplies | Stainless steel cleaner |
| Mult. Depts. | Cleaning Supplies | Tile cleaner |
| Mult. Depts. | Cleaning Supplies | Toilet brushes |
| Mult. Depts. | Cleaning Supplies | Towels, cleaning rags |
| Mult. Depts. | Cleaning Supplies | Towels, paper |
| Mult. Depts. | Cleaning Supplies | Trigger sprayer bottles |
| Mult. Depts. | Cleaning Supplies | Upholstery cleaner |
| Mult. Depts. | Cleaning Supplies | Vacuum accessories |
| Mult. Depts. | Cleaning Supplies | Vacuum belts |
| Mult. Depts. | Cleaning Supplies | Vacuum cleaner accessories |
| Mult. Depts. | Cleaning Supplies | Vacuum cleaners |

| Department/ Schedule | Account Name | Item Name |
|---|---|---|
| Mult. Depts. | Cleaning Supplies | Vacuum filters |
| Mult. Depts. | Cleaning Supplies | Vacuums—canister, portable, upright |
| Mult. Depts. | Cleaning Supplies | Waxes |
| Mult. Depts. | Cleaning Supplies | Woolite packets |
| Mult. Depts. | Complimentary Services/Gifts | Amenities, gifts |
| Mult. Depts. | Complimentary Services/Gifts | Baskets, wine (for gratis presentations)—not reusable |
| Mult. Depts. | Complimentary Services/Gifts | Cheese baskets, gratis |
| Mult. Depts. | Complimentary Services/Gifts | Complimentary beverage |
| Mult. Depts. | Complimentary Services/Gifts | Complimentary food |
| Mult. Depts. | Complimentary Services/Gifts | Complimentary parking |
| Mult. Depts. | Complimentary Services/Gifts | Fruit baskets gratis to customers |
| Mult. Depts. | Complimentary Services/Gifts | Gifts to customers |
| Mult. Depts. | Complimentary Services/Gifts | VIP guest gifts |
| Mult. Depts. | Contract Services | Carpet cleaning services |
| Mult. Depts. | Contract Services | Carpet/rug cleaning (outside service) |
| Mult. Depts. | Contract Services | Comment card processing (outside service) |
| Mult. Depts. | Contract Services | Consultant fees |
| Mult. Depts. | Contract Services | Contract cleaning—awning, floors, fumigation, windows |
| Mult. Depts. | Contract Services | Purchasing service fees |
| Mult. Depts. | Contract Services | Rug cleaning services |
| Mult. Depts. | Contract Services | Shopping service |
| Mult. Depts. | Contract Services | Window cleaning services |
| Mult. Depts. | Corporate Office Reimbursables | Management company expenses (travel, entertainment, etc.) |
| Mult. Depts. | Decorations | Cut flowers |
| Mult. Depts. | Decorations | Decorations, holiday and special occasion |
| Mult. Depts. | Decorations | Floral arrangements |
| Mult. Depts. | Decorations | Flowers, fresh and artificial |
| Mult. Depts. | Dues and Subscriptions | Magazine subscriptions |
| Mult. Depts. | Dues and Subscriptions | Membership fees—professional organizations |
| Mult. Depts. | Employee Benefits | Housing and educational |
| Mult. Depts. | Employee Benefits | Payroll, 401(k) costs |
| Mult. Depts. | Employee Benefits | Payroll, automobile |
| Mult. Depts. | Employee Benefits | Payroll, child care, employee |
| Mult. Depts. | Employee Benefits | Payroll, dental insurance |

| Department/<br>Schedule | Account Name | Item Name |
|---|---|---|
| Mult. Depts. | Employee Benefits | Payroll, disability insurance |
| Mult. Depts. | Employee Benefits | Payroll, group life insurance |
| Mult. Depts. | Employee Benefits | Payroll, health insurance |
| Mult. Depts. | Employee Benefits | Payroll, long-term disability |
| Mult. Depts. | Employee Benefits | Payroll, meals (cost allocation from staff dining) |
| Mult. Depts. | Employee Benefits | Payroll, pension costs |
| Mult. Depts. | Employee Benefits | Payroll, profit sharing |
| Mult. Depts. | Employee Benefits | Payroll, union insurance |
| Mult. Depts. | Employee Benefits | Payroll, union other |
| Mult. Depts. | Employee Benefits | Payroll, union pension |
| Mult. Depts. | Employee Benefits | Payroll, workers' compensation insurance |
| Mult. Depts. | Employee Benefits | Stock benefits |
| Mult. Depts. | Employee Benefits | Stock options |
| Mult. Depts. | Entertainment—In-House | Entertainment of non-employees in-house |
| Mult. Depts. | Equipment Rental | Beeper rental |
| Mult. Depts. | Equipment Rental | Copier rental/lease |
| Mult. Depts. | Laundry and Dry Cleaning | Curtains, dry cleaning |
| Mult. Depts. | Laundry and Dry Cleaning | Draperies, dry cleaning |
| Mult. Depts. | Laundry and Dry Cleaning | Dry cleaning costs, non-guest (in-house laundry) |
| Mult. Depts. | Laundry and Dry Cleaning | Dry cleaning services, non-guest (outside laundry) |
| Mult. Depts. | Laundry and Dry Cleaning | Laundry costs, non-guest (in-house laundry) |
| Mult. Depts. | Laundry and Dry Cleaning | Laundry services, non-guest (outside laundry) |
| Mult. Depts. | Licenses and Permits | Inspection fees for licensing |
| Mult. Depts. | Licenses and Permits | Transfer fees, licenses |
| Mult. Depts. | Linen | Linen rental |
| Mult. Depts. | Management Fees | Management fees—specific dept. |
| Mult. Depts. | Miscellaneous | Fines (health, safety, etc.) |
| Mult. Depts. | Operating Supplies | Adapter plug, electrical |
| Mult. Depts. | Operating Supplies | Adding machine tape |
| Mult. Depts. | Operating Supplies | Adding machines |
| Mult. Depts. | Operating Supplies | Adhesive tape |
| Mult. Depts. | Operating Supplies | Air deodorizing accessories/ systems |
| Mult. Depts. | Operating Supplies | Answering machines |
| Mult. Depts. | Operating Supplies | Anti-fatigue mats |

| Department/<br>Schedule | Account Name | Item Name |
|---|---|---|
| Mult. Depts. ............... | Operating Supplies........................................ | Artwork |
| Mult. Depts. ............... | Operating Supplies........................................ | Ash cans |
| Mult. Depts. ............... | Operating Supplies........................................ | Ashtrays |
| Mult. Depts. ............... | Operating Supplies........................................ | Band-Aids |
| Mult. Depts. ............... | Operating Supplies........................................ | Baskets, urinal |
| Mult. Depts. ............... | Operating Supplies........................................ | Baskets, waste liners |
| Mult. Depts. ............... | Operating Supplies........................................ | Baskets, wine (for gratis presentations)— reusable |
| Mult. Depts. ............... | Operating Supplies........................................ | Batteries |
| Mult. Depts. ............... | Operating Supplies........................................ | Binder clips |
| Mult. Depts. ............... | Operating Supplies........................................ | Binders |
| Mult. Depts. ............... | Operating Supplies........................................ | Book matches (guest) |
| Mult. Depts. ............... | Operating Supplies........................................ | Calculators |
| Mult. Depts. ............... | Operating Supplies........................................ | Calendars and diaries |
| Mult. Depts. ............... | Operating Supplies........................................ | Candles |
| Mult. Depts. ............... | Operating Supplies........................................ | Candlesticks |
| Mult. Depts. ............... | Operating Supplies........................................ | Cashier envelopes |
| Mult. Depts. ............... | Operating Supplies........................................ | Cashier forms |
| Mult. Depts. ............... | Operating Supplies........................................ | CD–ROM, writable |
| Mult. Depts. ............... | Operating Supplies........................................ | Cellophane tape |
| Mult. Depts. ............... | Operating Supplies........................................ | Clipboards |
| Mult. Depts. ............... | Operating Supplies........................................ | Coin drawers |
| Mult. Depts. ............... | Operating Supplies........................................ | Computer discs |
| Mult. Depts. ............... | Operating Supplies........................................ | Copier paper |
| Mult. Depts. ............... | Operating Supplies........................................ | Copier toner |
| Mult. Depts. ............... | Operating Supplies........................................ | CPR kits |
| Mult. Depts. ............... | Operating Supplies........................................ | Curtain holdbacks |
| Mult. Depts. ............... | Operating Supplies........................................ | Curtain hooks |
| Mult. Depts. ............... | Operating Supplies........................................ | Curtain rods |
| Mult. Depts. ............... | Operating Supplies........................................ | Curtain stackbacks |
| Mult. Depts. ............... | Operating Supplies........................................ | Curtains |
| Mult. Depts. ............... | Operating Supplies........................................ | Data binders and accessories |
| Mult. Depts. ............... | Operating Supplies........................................ | Defibrillator |
| Mult. Depts. ............... | Operating Supplies........................................ | Desk accessories |
| Mult. Depts. ............... | Operating Supplies........................................ | Desk caddies |
| Mult. Depts. ............... | Operating Supplies........................................ | Desk pad and holder |
| Mult. Depts. ............... | Operating Supplies........................................ | Double-stick tape |
| Mult. Depts. ............... | Operating Supplies........................................ | Drapery baton |
| Mult. Depts. ............... | Operating Supplies........................................ | Drapery cords |
| Mult. Depts. ............... | Operating Supplies........................................ | Drapery liners |

| Department/<br>Schedule | Account Name | Item Name |
|---|---|---|
| Mult. Depts. ............. | Operating Supplies......................................... | Drapes |
| Mult. Depts. ............. | Operating Supplies......................................... | Drapes, blackout |
| Mult. Depts. ............. | Operating Supplies......................................... | Duct tape |
| Mult. Depts. ............. | Operating Supplies......................................... | Electrical adapters |
| Mult. Depts. ............. | Operating Supplies......................................... | Employee pins |
| Mult. Depts. ............. | Operating Supplies......................................... | Erasers |
| Mult. Depts. ............. | Operating Supplies......................................... | Extension cords |
| Mult. Depts. ............. | Operating Supplies......................................... | Fans, portable |
| Mult. Depts. ............. | Operating Supplies......................................... | File folders |
| Mult. Depts. ............. | Operating Supplies......................................... | Film, camera |
| Mult. Depts. ............. | Operating Supplies......................................... | Fireplace lighter |
| Mult. Depts. ............. | Operating Supplies......................................... | Fireplace screen |
| Mult. Depts. ............. | Operating Supplies......................................... | Fireplace tools |
| Mult. Depts. ............. | Operating Supplies......................................... | Firewood |
| Mult. Depts. ............. | Operating Supplies......................................... | First aid kits/supplies |
| Mult. Depts. ............. | Operating Supplies......................................... | Flags |
| Mult. Depts. ............. | Operating Supplies......................................... | Flashlights |
| Mult. Depts. ............. | Operating Supplies......................................... | Frames, art |
| Mult. Depts. ............. | Operating Supplies......................................... | Garbage bags |
| Mult. Depts. ............. | Operating Supplies......................................... | Garbage can liners |
| Mult. Depts. ............. | Operating Supplies......................................... | Garbage cans |
| Mult. Depts. ............. | Operating Supplies......................................... | Gasoline—motor vehicles (company and employee use) |
| Mult. Depts. ............. | Operating Supplies......................................... | Glue |
| Mult. Depts. ............. | Operating Supplies......................................... | Goldfish |
| Mult. Depts. ............. | Operating Supplies......................................... | High chairs |
| Mult. Depts. ............. | Operating Supplies......................................... | Hole punch |
| Mult. Depts. ............. | Operating Supplies......................................... | Hooks, coat |
| Mult. Depts. ............. | Operating Supplies......................................... | Hooks, door |
| Mult. Depts. ............. | Operating Supplies......................................... | Ink |
| Mult. Depts. ............. | Operating Supplies......................................... | Ink cartridges |
| Mult. Depts. ............. | Operating Supplies......................................... | Key chain coils |
| Mult. Depts. ............. | Operating Supplies......................................... | Key chain reels |
| Mult. Depts. ............. | Operating Supplies......................................... | Key lock box |
| Mult. Depts. ............. | Operating Supplies......................................... | Key rings |
| Mult. Depts. ............. | Operating Supplies......................................... | Key tags |
| Mult. Depts. ............. | Operating Supplies......................................... | Keyboard drawers |
| Mult. Depts. ............. | Operating Supplies......................................... | Label maker |
| Mult. Depts. ............. | Operating Supplies......................................... | Label maker supplies |
| Mult. Depts. ............. | Operating Supplies......................................... | Lampshades |

| Department/<br>Schedule | Account Name | Item Name |
|---|---|---|
| Mult. Depts. ............... | Operating Supplies......................................... | Liners, drapery |
| Mult. Depts. ............... | Operating Supplies......................................... | Log books |
| Mult. Depts. ............... | Operating Supplies......................................... | Marking ink |
| Mult. Depts. ............... | Operating Supplies......................................... | Matches, customer use |
| Mult. Depts. ............... | Operating Supplies......................................... | Mats, floor |
| Mult. Depts. ............... | Operating Supplies......................................... | Memo pads |
| Mult. Depts. ............... | Operating Supplies......................................... | Mini-blinds |
| Mult. Depts. ............... | Operating Supplies......................................... | Mouse, computer |
| Mult. Depts. ............... | Operating Supplies......................................... | Mouse pads |
| Mult. Depts. ............... | Operating Supplies......................................... | Name badges |
| Mult. Depts. ............... | Operating Supplies......................................... | Office supplies, general |
| Mult. Depts. ............... | Operating Supplies......................................... | Outlet safety plugs |
| Mult. Depts. ............... | Operating Supplies......................................... | Packing tape |
| Mult. Depts. ............... | Operating Supplies......................................... | Pain relievers |
| Mult. Depts. ............... | Operating Supplies......................................... | Paper clips |
| Mult. Depts. ............... | Operating Supplies......................................... | Paper, copier |
| Mult. Depts. ............... | Operating Supplies......................................... | Paper liners |
| Mult. Depts. ............... | Operating Supplies......................................... | Parchment |
| Mult. Depts. ............... | Operating Supplies......................................... | Paste |
| Mult. Depts. ............... | Operating Supplies......................................... | Pencil holders |
| Mult. Depts. ............... | Operating Supplies......................................... | Pencil sharpeners |
| Mult. Depts. ............... | Operating Supplies......................................... | Pencils |
| Mult. Depts. ............... | Operating Supplies......................................... | Pens |
| Mult. Depts. ............... | Operating Supplies......................................... | Pins—employee, safety, stick, straight |
| Mult. Depts. ............... | Operating Supplies......................................... | Placards |
| Mult. Depts. ............... | Operating Supplies......................................... | Plants |
| Mult. Depts. ............... | Operating Supplies......................................... | Portable fans |
| Mult. Depts. ............... | Operating Supplies......................................... | Portable steam cleaners |
| Mult. Depts. ............... | Operating Supplies......................................... | Poster board |
| Mult. Depts. ............... | Operating Supplies......................................... | Post-it notes |
| Mult. Depts. ............... | Operating Supplies......................................... | Printer supplies and accessories |
| Mult. Depts. ............... | Operating Supplies......................................... | Printing calculator |
| Mult. Depts. ............... | Operating Supplies......................................... | Q-tips |
| Mult. Depts. ............... | Operating Supplies......................................... | Record books |
| Mult. Depts. ............... | Operating Supplies......................................... | Recorders, mini/micro cassette and accessories |
| Mult. Depts. ............... | Operating Supplies......................................... | Recycle bins |
| Mult. Depts. ............... | Operating Supplies......................................... | Reports |
| Mult. Depts. ............... | Operating Supplies......................................... | Ribbons—typewriter, calculator, cash register |

| Department/<br>Schedule | Account Name | Item Name |
|---|---|---|
| Mult. Depts. | Operating Supplies | Roller shades |
| Mult. Depts. | Operating Supplies | Roman shades |
| Mult. Depts. | Operating Supplies | Rubber bands |
| Mult. Depts. | Operating Supplies | Rubber cement |
| Mult. Depts. | Operating Supplies | Rubber stamps |
| Mult. Depts. | Operating Supplies | Rugs, throw |
| Mult. Depts. | Operating Supplies | Rulers |
| Mult. Depts. | Operating Supplies | Safety glasses |
| Mult. Depts. | Operating Supplies | Safety pins |
| Mult. Depts. | Operating Supplies | Scissors |
| Mult. Depts. | Operating Supplies | Shelf paper |
| Mult. Depts. | Operating Supplies | Shipping supplies |
| Mult. Depts. | Operating Supplies | Shipping tags |
| Mult. Depts. | Operating Supplies | Signs and banners |
| Mult. Depts. | Operating Supplies | Smoking urn sand stamp |
| Mult. Depts. | Operating Supplies | Stamp pads |
| Mult. Depts. | Operating Supplies | Stamp pads (ink) |
| Mult. Depts. | Operating Supplies | Stamps, rubber |
| Mult. Depts. | Operating Supplies | Staplers |
| Mult. Depts. | Operating Supplies | Staples |
| Mult. Depts. | Operating Supplies | Stencils |
| Mult. Depts. | Operating Supplies | Surge protectors |
| Mult. Depts. | Operating Supplies | Tape, adhesive |
| Mult. Depts. | Operating Supplies | Tape holder |
| Mult. Depts. | Operating Supplies | Tape, Scotch |
| Mult. Depts. | Operating Supplies | Telephone directory covers and holders |
| Mult. Depts. | Operating Supplies | Trash can liners |
| Mult. Depts. | Operating Supplies | Trash cans/receptacles |
| Mult. Depts. | Operating Supplies | Umbrellas |
| Mult. Depts. | Operating Supplies | Urinal baskets |
| Mult. Depts. | Operating Supplies | Video camera |
| Mult. Depts. | Operating Supplies | Visual planners |
| Mult. Depts. | Operating Supplies | Waste receptacles |
| Mult. Depts. | Operating Supplies | Wastebaskets |
| Mult. Depts. | Operating Supplies | Wastebaskets (employee) |
| Mult. Depts. | Operating Supplies | Wet floor signs |
| Mult. Depts. | Operating Supplies | Wrapping paper |
| Mult. Depts. | Operating Supplies | Writing supplies |
| Mult. Depts. | Payroll Taxes | Federal unemployment tax |

| Department/<br>Schedule | Account Name | Item Name |
|---|---|---|
| Mult. Depts. .............. | Payroll Taxes.................................................... | Payroll, city head tax |
| Mult. Depts. .............. | Payroll Taxes.................................................... | Payroll, national retirement contribution tax (Social Security) |
| Mult. Depts. .............. | Payroll Taxes.................................................... | Payroll, national unemployment tax (FUTA) |
| Mult. Depts. .............. | Payroll Taxes.................................................... | Payroll, state disability insurance |
| Mult. Depts. .............. | Payroll Taxes.................................................... | Payroll, state unemployment tax |
| Mult. Depts. .............. | P&ODC ......................................................... | Postage and overnight delivery charges |
| Mult. Depts. .............. | Printing and Stationery ............................... | Business cards |
| Mult. Depts. .............. | Printing and Stationery ............................... | Charge vouchers |
| Mult. Depts. .............. | Printing and Stationery ............................... | Check/folio/statement presentation folders |
| Mult. Depts. .............. | Printing and Stationery ............................... | Comment cards |
| Mult. Depts. .............. | Printing and Stationery ............................... | Computer forms—commercial, printed |
| Mult. Depts. .............. | Printing and Stationery ............................... | Copying service |
| Mult. Depts. .............. | Printing and Stationery ............................... | Envelopes |
| Mult. Depts. .............. | Printing and Stationery ............................... | Envelopes—cashier |
| Mult. Depts. .............. | Printing and Stationery ............................... | Floor plans |
| Mult. Depts. .............. | Printing and Stationery ............................... | Forms, general |
| Mult. Depts. .............. | Printing and Stationery ............................... | Forms, printed |
| Mult. Depts. .............. | Printing and Stationery ............................... | Guest comment cards |
| Mult. Depts. .............. | Printing and Stationery ............................... | Guest questionnaire forms |
| Mult. Depts. .............. | Printing and Stationery ............................... | Guest suggestion forms |
| Mult. Depts. .............. | Printing and Stationery ............................... | Parking permit cards |
| Mult. Depts. .............. | Printing and Stationery ............................... | Parking violation stickers |
| Mult. Depts. .............. | Printing and Stationery ............................... | Printed forms |
| Mult. Depts. .............. | Printing and Stationery ............................... | Printer paper |
| Mult. Depts. .............. | Printing and Stationery ............................... | Stationery |
| Mult. Depts. .............. | Royalty Fees.................................................... | Royalties for use of third-party brand name |
| Mult. Depts. .............. | Salaries and Wages ........................................ | Payroll, hourly wages |
| Mult. Depts. .............. | Salaries and Wages ........................................ | Payroll, laundry attendant |
| Mult. Depts. .............. | Salaries and Wages ........................................ | Payroll, laundry manager |
| Mult. Depts. .............. | Salaries and Wages ........................................ | Payroll, leased labor |
| Mult. Depts. .............. | Salaries and Wages ........................................ | Payroll, salaried wages |
| Mult. Depts. .............. | Salaries and Wages ........................................ | Payroll, service charges |
| Mult. Depts. .............. | Salaries and Wages ........................................ | Payroll, staff dining attendant |
| Mult. Depts. .............. | Salaries and Wages ........................................ | Payroll, staff dining manager |
| Mult. Depts. .............. | Supplemental Pay.......................................... | Holiday pay |

| Department/ Schedule | Account Name | Item Name |
|---|---|---|
| Mult. Depts. | Supplemental Pay | Paid time off |
| Mult. Depts. | Supplemental Pay | Payroll, bonus pay (discretionary) |
| Mult. Depts. | Supplemental Pay | Payroll, incentive pay (discretionary) |
| Mult. Depts. | Supplemental Pay | Payroll, jury duty pay |
| Mult. Depts. | Supplemental Pay | Payroll, personal days |
| Mult. Depts. | Supplemental Pay | Payroll, relocation pay |
| Mult. Depts. | Supplemental Pay | Payroll, severance pay |
| Mult. Depts. | Supplemental Pay | Payroll, sick pay |
| Mult. Depts. | Supplemental Pay | Payroll, statutory holiday pay |
| Mult. Depts. | Supplemental Pay | Payroll, vacation pay |
| Mult. Depts. | Training | Books, technical |
| Mult. Depts. | Training | Educational activities for employees |
| Mult. Depts. | Training | Educational assistance |
| Mult. Depts. | Training | Educational books/pamphlets for employees |
| Mult. Depts. | Training | Instructor fees, training |
| Mult. Depts. | Training | Manuals, instructional/training |
| Mult. Depts. | Training | Orientation expenses |
| Mult. Depts. | Training | Pamphlets, educational/ instructional (for employees) |
| Mult. Depts. | Training | Publications, house (for employees) |
| Mult. Depts. | Training | Service manuals (employee) |
| Mult. Depts. | Training | Speaker fees, training |
| Mult. Depts. | Training | Training program costs |
| Mult. Depts. | Training | Videotapes, training/safety |
| Mult. Depts. | Travel—Meals & Enter. | Entertainment, outside—employee |
| Mult. Depts. | Travel—Meals & Enter. | Meals and entertainment, outside |
| Mult. Depts. | Travel—Meals & Enter. | Meals, business expense |
| Mult. Depts. | Travel—Meals & Enter. | Travel expenses (food/beverage) |
| Mult. Depts. | Travel—Meals & Enter. | Travel meals |
| Mult. Depts. | Travel—Other | Airfare |
| Mult. Depts. | Travel—Other | Car rental |
| Mult. Depts. | Travel—Other | Mileage reimbursement |
| Mult. Depts. | Travel—Other | Room charges, travel |
| Mult. Depts. | Travel—Other | Taxi fare |
| Mult. Depts. | Travel—Other | Tolls, highway |
| Mult. Depts. | Travel—Other | Travel expenses (non-food/bev.) |
| Mult. Depts. | Uniform Costs | Aprons |
| Mult. Depts. | Uniform Costs | Blouses |
| Mult. Depts. | Uniform Costs | Boots |

| Department/ Schedule | Account Name | Item Name |
| --- | --- | --- |
| Mult. Depts. | Uniform Costs | Caps |
| Mult. Depts. | Uniform Costs | Coats |
| Mult. Depts. | Uniform Costs | Dresses |
| Mult. Depts. | Uniform Costs | Hats |
| Mult. Depts. | Uniform Costs | Jackets |
| Mult. Depts. | Uniform Costs | Jumpers |
| Mult. Depts. | Uniform Costs | Overalls |
| Mult. Depts. | Uniform Costs | Pants |
| Mult. Depts. | Uniform Costs | Repairs, uniforms |
| Mult. Depts. | Uniform Costs | Shirts |
| Mult. Depts. | Uniform Costs | Shoes |
| Mult. Depts. | Uniform Costs | Shorts |
| Mult. Depts. | Uniform Costs | Skirts |
| Mult. Depts. | Uniform Costs | Smocks |
| Mult. Depts. | Uniform Costs | Socks |
| Mult. Depts. | Uniform Costs | Suits |
| Mult. Depts. | Uniform Costs | Ties |
| Mult. Depts. | Uniform Costs | Trousers |
| Mult. Depts. | Uniform Costs | T-shirts |
| Mult. Depts. | Uniform Costs | Uniform repair |
| Mult. Depts. | Uniform Laundry | Uniform cleaning |
| Mult. Depts. | Uniform Laundry | Uniform cleaning allowance |
| A&G | Audit Charges | Audit fees, public accountants |
| A&G | Audit Charges | Internal audit expense |
| A&G | Audit Charges | Internal audit fees (chain properties) |
| A&G | Bank Charges | Bank checks, charges |
| A&G | Bank Charges | Bank related fees and costs |
| A&G | Bank Charges | Exchange on bank checks and currency |
| A&G | Bank Charges | Overdraft fees |
| A&G | Bank Charges | Stop payment charges |
| A&G | Cash Overages/Shortages | Cash overages and shortages |
| A&G | Cent. Acct. Charges | Accounting fees—centralized (management company) |
| A&G | Cent. Acct. Charges | Accounting fees—centralized (owner) |
| A&G | Cluster Services | Cluster accounting office costs |
| A&G | Contract Services | Document destruction fees |
| A&G | Contract Services | Storage of equipment/records (off-site) |
| A&G | Contract Services | Third-party outsourcing |

| Department/ Schedule | Account Name | Item Name |
|---|---|---|
| A&G | Corporate Office Reimbursables | Owners' expenses (travel, entertainment, etc.) |
| A&G | Credit and Collection | Check verification |
| A&G | Credit and Collection | Collection fees |
| A&G | Credit and Collection | Credit reports |
| A&G | Credit and Collection | Credit service expense |
| A&G | Credit and Collection | Fees, attorney, for collections |
| A&G | Credit and Collection | Fees, collection |
| A&G | Credit and Collection | Legal fees/expenses for collections |
| A&G | Credit and Collection | Notary fees, collection of accounts |
| A&G | Credit Card Commissions | Credit card commissions |
| A&G | Decorations | Holiday/special event decorations for A&G areas |
| A&G | Donations | Charitable contributions |
| A&G | Dues and Subscriptions | Dues—hotel associations (non-marketing) |
| A&G | Dues and Subscriptions | Dues—professional associations (non-marketing) |
| A&G | Dues and Subscriptions | Hotel association dues (non-marketing) |
| A&G | Dues and Subscriptions | Magazines—trade (non-marketing) |
| A&G | Dues and Subscriptions | Membership dues—associations (non-marketing) |
| A&G | Dues and Subscriptions | Professional dues (non-marketing) |
| A&G | Dues and Subscriptions | Subscriptions—trade (non-marketing) |
| A&G | Equipment Rental | Copier rental—temporary |
| A&G | Human Resources | Advertising—recruiting |
| A&G | Human Resources | Awards—employees |
| A&G | Human Resources | Christmas gifts—employees |
| A&G | Human Resources | Drug testing of employees |
| A&G | Human Resources | Fees, medical |
| A&G | Human Resources | Help wanted ads |
| A&G | Human Resources | In-house newsletter (for employees) |
| A&G | Human Resources | Interview expenses |
| A&G | Human Resources | Investigation of employees (including background checks) |
| A&G | Human Resources | Lodging of employees |
| A&G | Human Resources | Medical supplies and drugs for employees |
| A&G | Human Resources | Medical supplies for employees |
| A&G | Human Resources | Personnel forms, general |

| Department/ Schedule | Account Name | Item Name |
|---|---|---|
| A&G | Human Resources | Physicians' fees—employees (non-workers' compensation) |
| A&G | Human Resources | Posters, safety |
| A&G | Human Resources | Prizes, employee |
| A&G | Human Resources | Recruiter fees |
| A&G | Human Resources | Reference checking, employee |
| A&G | Human Resources | Relocation costs |
| A&G | Human Resources | Social activities, employees |
| A&G | Human Resources | Sports activities and equipment, employees |
| A&G | Human Resources | Suggestion awards, employees |
| A&G | Human Resources | Temporary housing, employee |
| A&G | Human Resources | Total quality management |
| A&G | Human Resources | Visa costs for an ex-pat employee |
| A&G | Human Resources | Want ads (help wanted) |
| A&G | Legal Services | Court/legal fees—other than collections |
| A&G | Legal Services | Expert witness costs |
| A&G | Legal Services | Legal fees for acquiring visas for ex-pats |
| A&G | Legal Services | Legal retainer |
| A&G | Licenses and Permits | Annual report fee |
| A&G | Licenses and Permits | Business licenses, general |
| A&G | Loss and Damage | Lost and damaged articles— guest non-insured |
| A&G | Operating Supplies | Cash boxes |
| A&G | Operating Supplies | Check writer machines |
| A&G | Operating Supplies | Coin handling equipment |
| A&G | Operating Supplies | Coin wrappers |
| A&G | Operating Supplies | Coin/currency bag seals |
| A&G | Operating Supplies | Coin/currency equipment |
| A&G | Operating Supplies | Correction fluid/tape |
| A&G | Operating Supplies | Currency bill straps |
| A&G | Operating Supplies | Desk pads (employee) |
| A&G | Operating Supplies | Fax machine supplies and accessories |
| A&G | Operating Supplies | Film purchase and developing |
| A&G | Operating Supplies | Letters for bulletin/sign boards |
| A&G | Operating Supplies | Machine stands |
| A&G | Operating Supplies | Mail bags |
| A&G | Operating Supplies | Mail chute rentals |

| Department/ Schedule | Account Name | Item Name |
|---|---|---|
| A&G | Operating Supplies | Presentation binders |
| A&G | Operating Supplies | Report covers |
| A&G | Operating Supplies | Ring binders |
| A&G | Operating Supplies | Storage files |
| A&G | Operating Supplies | Toner for copiers |
| A&G | P&ODC | Express delivery charges |
| A&G | P&ODC | Express mail/UPS (non-marketing) |
| A&G | P&ODC | Freight charges (non-marketing) |
| A&G | P&ODC | Overnight delivery (non-marketing) |
| A&G | P&ODC | Post office box rental |
| A&G | P&ODC | Postage (non-marketing) |
| A&G | P&ODC | Postage meter rentals (non-marketing) |
| A&G | Payroll Processing | Payroll processing fees |
| A&G | Professional Fees | Accountant's fees, consulting |
| A&G | Professional Fees | Commissions, rental agents |
| A&G | Professional Fees | Consultant fees, professional |
| A&G | Professional Fees | Fees, stock transfer agents |
| A&G | Professional Fees | Fees, transfer |
| A&G | Professional Fees | Fees, trustees (handling bond, etc.) |
| A&G | Professional Fees | Notary fees |
| A&G | Professional Fees | Professional fees |
| A&G | Professional Fees | Stock transfer agents, fees |
| A&G | Provision for Doubtful Accounts | Bad debt allowance |
| A&G | Provision for Doubtful Accounts | Provision for doubtful accounts |
| A&G | Provision for Doubtful Accounts | Uncollectible accounts |
| A&G | Salaries and Wages | Payroll, accounting clerk |
| A&G | Salaries and Wages | Payroll, administrative |
| A&G | Salaries and Wages | Payroll, controller |
| A&G | Salaries and Wages | Payroll, director of finance |
| A&G | Salaries and Wages | Payroll, director of human resources |
| A&G | Salaries and Wages | Payroll, director of operations |
| A&G | Salaries and Wages | Payroll, general manager |
| A&G | Salaries and Wages | Payroll, information technology |
| A&G | Salaries and Wages | Payroll, miscellaneous |
| A&G | Salaries and Wages | Payroll, purchasing clerk |
| A&G | Salaries and Wages | Payroll, purchasing manager |
| A&G | Salaries and Wages | Payroll, receiving clerk |
| A&G | Salaries and Wages | Payroll, security director |

| Department/<br>Schedule | Account Name | Item Name |
|---|---|---|
| A&G | Salaries and Wages | Payroll, security officer |
| A&G | Salaries and Wages | Payroll, storeroom clerk |
| A&G | Security | Armored transport fee |
| A&G | Security | Detective service |
| A&G | Security | Protective service |
| A&G | Security | Safe deposit box rentals (off-site) |
| A&G | Security | Security—contracted |
| A&G | Settlement Costs | Claim/litigation settlement costs, contract disputes |
| A&G | Settlement Costs | Claim/litigation settlement costs, EEOC |
| A&G | Settlement Costs | Claim/litigation settlement costs, non-insured |
| A&G | Staff Transportation | Limousine—employee use |
| A&G | Staff Transportation | Transportation of employees |
| A&G | Training | Instructor fees, training |
| A&G | Training | Literature—educational for employees |
| F&B | Audiovisual Cost | Audiovisual equipment rent (charged to customer) |
| F&B | Audiovisual Cost | Cost of Internet—function room |
| F&B | Audiovisual Cost | Easels (charged to customer) |
| F&B | Audiovisual Cost | Flip charts (charged to customers) |
| F&B | Banquet Expense | Table rental (banquet not charged to customer) |
| F&B | Banquet Expense | Tent rental for parties/banquets (not charged to customer) |
| F&B | China | Aluminum trays |
| F&B | China | Ash trays, aluminum, glass |
| F&B | China | Bowls, mixing/preparation (all sizes & materials) |
| F&B | China | Bowls, serving (all sizes & materials) |
| F&B | China | Butter dishes (all materials) |
| F&B | China | Casseroles |
| F&B | China | China |
| F&B | China | China rental |
| F&B | China | Coffee pots (glass, plastic, silver) |
| F&B | China | Creamers |
| F&B | China | Crocks (all materials) |
| F&B | China | Cups/saucers, cappuccino |
| F&B | China | Cups/saucers, coffee |

| Department/ Schedule | Account Name | Item Name |
|---|---|---|
| F&B | China | Cups/saucers, espresso |
| F&B | China | Glass bowls |
| F&B | China | Glass dishes |
| F&B | China | Pitchers, water |
| F&B | China | Plates, all sizes & materials (except paper/plastic) |
| F&B | China | Platters, serving |
| F&B | China | Ramekins (all materials) |
| F&B | China | Salad bowls |
| F&B | China | Salt and pepper shakers |
| F&B | China | Sauce boats (all materials) |
| F&B | China | Soufflé dishes (all materials) |
| F&B | China | Sugar holders |
| F&B | China | Teapots and lids (all materials) |
| F&B | Cleaning Supplies | Cleaning supplies |
| F&B | Commissions | Commissions, travel agent (food & beverage exclusively) |
| F&B | Complimentary Services/Gifts | Gratis food, bar |
| F&B | Complimentary Services/Gifts | Mints, guest (restaurant) |
| F&B | Complimentary Services/Gifts | Parking, gratis F&B guest |
| F&B | Contract Services | Beer coil cleaning (outside service) |
| F&B | Contract Services | Cleaning beer coils (outside service) |
| F&B | Contract Services | Contract cleaning, kitchen hoods |
| F&B | Contract Services | Fumigators, kitchen/restaurant |
| F&B | Contract Services | Kitchen hood cleaning |
| F&B | Contract Services | Knife sharpening |
| F&B | Contract Services | Piano tuning |
| F&B | Contract Services | Public area cleaning service, restaurant/banquet foyers |
| F&B | Contract Services | Public restroom cleaning service |
| F&B | Contract Services | Shopping services (bar spotters) |
| F&B | Corporate Office Reimbursables | Corporate office reimbursables |
| F&B | Cost of Beverage Sales | Bar fruit and garnish |
| F&B | Cost of Beverage Sales | Bar supplies—consumable |
| F&B | Cost of Beverage Sales | Beer—bottle |
| F&B | Cost of Beverage Sales | Beer—draught |
| F&B | Cost of Beverage Sales | Beverage assessment (this is not other tax & assessment) |
| F&B | Cost of Beverage Sales | $CO_2$ for soft drink mix |
| F&B | Cost of Beverage Sales | Cooler/cider |
| F&B | Cost of Beverage Sales | Gas for beer lines |

| Department/<br>Schedule | Account Name | Item Name |
|---|---|---|
| F&B | Cost of Beverage Sales | Juices for cocktail mix |
| F&B | Cost of Beverage Sales | Liquor |
| F&B | Cost of Beverage Sales | Liquor—bottle |
| F&B | Cost of Beverage Sales | Off-premises beer |
| F&B | Cost of Beverage Sales | Off-premises cooler/cider |
| F&B | Cost of Beverage Sales | Off-premises liquor |
| F&B | Cost of Beverage Sales | Off-premises wine |
| F&B | Cost of Beverage Sales | Soft drinks for bar mix |
| F&B | Cost of Beverage Sales | Wine—bottle |
| F&B | Cost of Beverage Sales | Wine—glass |
| F&B | Cost of Food Sales | Baked goods |
| F&B | Cost of Food Sales | Canned food |
| F&B | Cost of Food Sales | $CO_2$ for soft drink mix |
| F&B | Cost of Food Sales | Coffee/tea |
| F&B | Cost of Food Sales | Dairy products |
| F&B | Cost of Food Sales | Dry goods (flour, pasta, etc.) |
| F&B | Cost of Food Sales | Eggs |
| F&B | Cost of Food Sales | Employee meal food cost credit |
| F&B | Cost of Food Sales | Fish |
| F&B | Cost of Food Sales | Fruit |
| F&B | Cost of Food Sales | Juice |
| F&B | Cost of Food Sales | Meat |
| F&B | Cost of Food Sales | Soft drink syrup or premix |
| F&B | Cost of Food Sales | Vegetables |
| F&B | Decorations | Flower vases, glass (tabletop) |
| F&B | Decorations | Flowers, banquet tables |
| F&B | Decorations | Flowers (tabletop) |
| F&B | Decorations | Ice carvings/sculpture |
| F&B | Dishwashing Supplies | Detergents (dish) |
| F&B | Dishwashing Supplies | Dishwashing soaps & rinsing agents |
| F&B | Dishwashing Supplies | Flatware cleaner |
| F&B | Dishwashing Supplies | Scouring pads |
| F&B | Dishwashing Supplies | Scrapers, dish |
| F&B | Dishwashing Supplies | Silver polish |
| F&B | Dishwashing Supplies | Sponges, dishwashing |
| F&B | Dishwashing Supplies | Steel wool |
| F&B | Equipment Rental | Dance floor rental (one time event) |
| F&B | Equipment Rental | Misc. banquet equipment rental (for a function or to meet peak demand) |

| Department/<br>Schedule | Account Name | Item Name |
|---|---|---|
| F&B | Equipment Rental | Table & chair rental<br>(one time event) |
| F&B | Equipment Rental | Table & chair rental (short term<br>or for one time event) |
| F&B | Equipment Rental | Truck rental (food delivery) |
| F&B | Flatware | Flatware (includes silver, stainless) |
| F&B | Flatware | Flatware rental |
| F&B | Flatware | Serving utensils |
| F&B | Flatware | Tongs, serving |
| F&B | Glassware | Carafes |
| F&B | Glassware | Cups, drinking (non-coffee, all<br>sizes & materials) |
| F&B | Glassware | Glasses, drinking (alcoholic<br>beverage/all sizes & materials) |
| F&B | Glassware | Glasses, drinking (non-alcoholic/<br>all sizes & materials) |
| F&B | Glassware | Glassware rental |
| F&B | Glassware | Shot glasses, bar |
| F&B | Ice | Dry ice |
| F&B | Ice | Ice consumption |
| F&B | Kitchen Fuel | Butane fuel |
| F&B | Kitchen Fuel | Charcoal, cooking |
| F&B | Kitchen Fuel | Food warmer fuel |
| F&B | Kitchen Fuel | Fuel, kitchen |
| F&B | Kitchen Fuel | Propane, cooking & preparation |
| F&B | Kitchen Fuel | Sterno for food warming |
| F&B | Kitchen Smallwares | Kitchen smallwares |
| F&B | Laundry and Dry Cleaning | Linen cleaning (all types) |
| F&B | Licenses and Permits | Health permits |
| F&B | Licenses and Permits | Licenses, beverage |
| F&B | Licenses and Permits | Licenses, cabaret |
| F&B | Licenses and Permits | Licenses, checkrooms |
| F&B | Licenses and Permits | Licenses, health permit |
| F&B | Licenses and Permits | Licenses, music copyright |
| F&B | Licenses and Permits | Licenses, public assembly |
| F&B | Licenses and Permits | Licenses, temporary space liquor |
| F&B | Linen | Linen napkins |
| F&B | Linen | Linen rental (all types) |
| F&B | Linen | Linen tablecloth |
| F&B | Linen | Table runners, linen |
| F&B | Linen | Table skirt clips |

| Department/ Schedule | Account Name | Item Name |
|---|---|---|
| F&B | Linen | Table skirts, linen |
| F&B | Linen | Table undercloth, linen |
| F&B | Linen | Tablecloths, linen |
| F&B | Linen | Towels, bar |
| F&B | Management Fees | Management fees |
| F&B | Menus and Beverage Lists | Beverage lists |
| F&B | Menus and Beverage Lists | In-room dining breakfast cards |
| F&B | Menus and Beverage Lists | Menu covers (food or beverage) |
| F&B | Menus and Beverage Lists | Menu design (food or beverage) |
| F&B | Menus and Beverage Lists | Menu printing (food or beverage) |
| F&B | Menus and Beverage Lists | Wine lists |
| F&B | Miscellaneous | Miscellaneous |
| F&B | Misc. Cost (of Other Revenue) | Apparel (for sale in F&B) |
| F&B | Misc. Cost (of Other Revenue) | Banquet/conference/catering recoverable supplies |
| F&B | Misc. Cost (of Other Revenue) | China & glassware (for sale in F&B) |
| F&B | Misc. Cost (of Other Revenue) | Cigar cost |
| F&B | Misc. Cost (of Other Revenue) | Electrical hookup (charged to customer) |
| F&B | Misc. Cost (of Other Revenue) | Freight & shipping charged to banquet customer |
| F&B | Misc. Cost (of Other Revenue) | Logo merchandise (for sale in F&B) |
| F&B | Misc. Cost (of Other Revenue) | Table & chair rental (banquets, charged to customer) |
| F&B | Misc. Cost (of Other Revenue) | Table linen & chair cover rental (banquets, charged to customer) |
| F&B | Misc. Cost (of Other Revenue) | Tent rental (banquets, charged to customer) |
| F&B | Misc. Cost (of Other Revenue) | Tobacco cost |
| F&B | Misc. Cost (of Other Revenue) | Transportation charged to customer, banquets |
| F&B | Music and Entertainment | Meals, musicians and entertainers |
| F&B | Music and Entertainment | Music, live musicians |
| F&B | Music and Entertainment | Music, mechanical |
| F&B | Music and Entertainment | Piano rental (lounge/restaurant entertainment) |
| F&B | Music and Entertainment | Room costs, musicians and entertainers |
| F&B | Music and Entertainment | Sheet music |
| F&B | Operating Supplies | Bar mats |
| F&B | Operating Supplies | Books, outlet reservations log |
| F&B | Operating Supplies | Candle holders, tabletop |

| Department/ Schedule | Account Name | Item Name |
|---|---|---|
| F&B | Operating Supplies | Check presenters |
| F&B | Operating Supplies | Gasoline for food delivery vehicle |
| F&B | Operating Supplies | Glass racks |
| F&B | Operating Supplies | Hair nets for food service employees |
| F&B | Operating Supplies | Ice buckets and liners |
| F&B | Operating Supplies | Markers (flip chart) |
| F&B | Operating Supplies | Mats, rubber (bar) |
| F&B | Operating Supplies | Props, banquets |
| F&B | Operating Supplies | Reservation books |
| F&B | Operating Supplies | Rubber boots, kitchen |
| F&B | Operating Supplies | Sneeze guards |
| F&B | Operating Supplies | Steak markers |
| F&B | Operating Supplies | Table pads |
| F&B | Operating Supplies | Tray jacks |
| F&B | Operating Supplies | Tray liners |
| F&B | Operating Supplies | Trays, serving (all materials) |
| F&B | Operating Supplies | Vases (tabletop) |
| F&B | Operating Supplies | Wine cellar supplies |
| F&B | Paper and Plastics | Aluminum foil |
| F&B | Paper and Plastics | Bags, paper leftover |
| F&B | Paper and Plastics | Boxes, carry out |
| F&B | Paper and Plastics | Boxes, pastry |
| F&B | Paper and Plastics | Cardboard boxes |
| F&B | Paper and Plastics | Carry out containers |
| F&B | Paper and Plastics | Cellophane wrap |
| F&B | Paper and Plastics | Chef hats |
| F&B | Paper and Plastics | Cocktail picks |
| F&B | Paper and Plastics | Coffee filters |
| F&B | Paper and Plastics | Cups, paper/plastic |
| F&B | Paper and Plastics | Doilies, paper |
| F&B | Paper and Plastics | Filter paper |
| F&B | Paper and Plastics | Foam insulated cups |
| F&B | Paper and Plastics | Foil wrapping |
| F&B | Paper and Plastics | Liners, paper |
| F&B | Paper and Plastics | Napkins, cocktail |
| F&B | Paper and Plastics | Napkins, paper |
| F&B | Paper and Plastics | Plastic flatware |
| F&B | Paper and Plastics | Plastic food storage containers |
| F&B | Paper and Plastics | Plastic wrap |
| F&B | Paper and Plastics | Plates, paper/plastic |

| Department/ Schedule | Account Name | Item Name |
|---|---|---|
| F&B | Paper and Plastics | Stir sticks, cocktail |
| F&B | Paper and Plastics | Straws, cocktail |
| F&B | Paper and Plastics | Straws, soft drink |
| F&B | Paper and Plastics | Styrofoam cups |
| F&B | Paper and Plastics | Tablecloths, paper/plastic |
| F&B | Paper and Plastics | Toothpicks |
| F&B | Paper and Plastics | Waxed paper |
| F&B | Printing and Stationery | Guest checks |
| F&B | Printing and Stationery | POS supplies |
| F&B | Printing and Stationery | Table tents |
| F&B | Reservation Fees | Reservation fees |
| F&B | Royalty Fees | Royalty fees |
| F&B | Salaries and Wages | Payroll, baker |
| F&B | Salaries and Wages | Payroll, banquet/conference/ catering attendant |
| F&B | Salaries and Wages | Payroll, banquet/conference/ catering houseperson |
| F&B | Salaries and Wages | Payroll, banquet/conference/ catering porter |
| F&B | Salaries and Wages | Payroll, banquet/conference/ catering runner |
| F&B | Salaries and Wages | Payroll, banquet/conference/ catering server |
| F&B | Salaries and Wages | Payroll, bartender |
| F&B | Salaries and Wages | Payroll, beverage manager |
| F&B | Salaries and Wages | Payroll, butcher |
| F&B | Salaries and Wages | Payroll, chef de partie |
| F&B | Salaries and Wages | Payroll, cleaner |
| F&B | Salaries and Wages | Payroll, conference/event services manager |
| F&B | Salaries and Wages | Payroll, cook |
| F&B | Salaries and Wages | Payroll, director of food and bev. |
| F&B | Salaries and Wages | Payroll, director of outlets |
| F&B | Salaries and Wages | Payroll, dishwasher |
| F&B | Salaries and Wages | Payroll, executive chef |
| F&B | Salaries and Wages | Payroll, executive sous chef |
| F&B | Salaries and Wages | Payroll, food & beverage manager |
| F&B | Salaries and Wages | Payroll, host(ess) |
| F&B | Salaries and Wages | Payroll, in-room dining server |
| F&B | Salaries and Wages | Payroll, kitchen manager |
| F&B | Salaries and Wages | Payroll, kitchen steward |

| Department/ Schedule | Account Name | Item Name |
|---|---|---|
| F&B | Salaries and Wages | Payroll, maître d' |
| F&B | Salaries and Wages | Payroll, outlet attendant |
| F&B | Salaries and Wages | Payroll, outlet busperson |
| F&B | Salaries and Wages | Payroll, outlet cashier |
| F&B | Salaries and Wages | Payroll, outlet houseperson |
| F&B | Salaries and Wages | Payroll, outlet porter |
| F&B | Salaries and Wages | Payroll, outlet runner |
| F&B | Salaries and Wages | Payroll, outlet server |
| F&B | Salaries and Wages | Payroll, restaurant manager |
| F&B | Salaries and Wages | Payroll, service captain |
| F&B | Salaries and Wages | Payroll, sommelier |
| F&B | Salaries and Wages | Payroll, stewarding manager |
| F&B | Training | Training |
| F&B | Travel—Meals & Enter. | Travel—meals & entertainment |
| F&B | Travel—Other | Travel—other |
| F&B | Uniform Costs | Uniform |
| F&B | Uniform Laundry | Uniform laundry |
| F&B | Utensils | Bags, pastry |
| F&B | Utensils | Beaters |
| F&B | Utensils | Blenders, bar |
| F&B | Utensils | Bottle openers |
| F&B | Utensils | Can openers |
| F&B | Utensils | Chafing dishes |
| F&B | Utensils | Coffee urn |
| F&B | Utensils | Colanders |
| F&B | Utensils | Cookie cutters |
| F&B | Utensils | Cooking utensils |
| F&B | Utensils | Corkscrews |
| F&B | Utensils | Cutting boards |
| F&B | Utensils | Food processor |
| F&B | Utensils | Forks, kitchen |
| F&B | Utensils | Ice tongs |
| F&B | Utensils | Knives, kitchen |
| F&B | Utensils | Ladles, kitchen |
| F&B | Utensils | Mixing bowls |
| F&B | Utensils | Mixing cans, bar |
| F&B | Utensils | Molds |
| F&B | Utensils | Pans, baking, broiling, frying |
| F&B | Utensils | Plate cover, dome |
| F&B | Utensils | Pocket thermometers |

| Department/ Schedule | Account Name | Item Name |
|---|---|---|
| F&B | Utensils | Pots |
| F&B | Utensils | Pour spouts, liquor |
| F&B | Utensils | Scissors, kitchen |
| F&B | Utensils | Shakers, bar |
| F&B | Utensils | Spatulas, kitchen |
| F&B | Utensils | Spoons, mixing |
| F&B | Utensils | Stirrers, beverage |
| F&B | Utensils | Stoppers, bottle (bar) |
| F&B | Utensils | Strainers, bar |
| F&B | Utensils | Tongs, cooking |
| F&B | Utensils | Tubes, pastry |
| F&B | Utensils | Utensils, kitchen |
| Golf/Pro Shop | Contract Services | Caddy service |
| Golf/Pro Shop | Contract Services | Pest control, golf course |
| Golf/Pro Shop | Contract Services | Tree removal & trimming service, golf course |
| Golf/Pro Shop | Cost of Clothing Sales | Clothing, golf (for sale) |
| Golf/Pro Shop | Cost of Merch. Sales | Books, golf (for sale) |
| Golf/Pro Shop | Cost of Merch. Sales | Gloves, golf (for sale) |
| Golf/Pro Shop | Cost of Merch. Sales | Golf bags (for sale) |
| Golf/Pro Shop | Cost of Merch. Sales | Golf balls (for sale) |
| Golf/Pro Shop | Cost of Merch. Sales | Golf clubs (for sale) |
| Golf/Pro Shop | Cost of Merch. Sales | Magazines, golf (for sale) |
| Golf/Pro Shop | Cost of Merch. Sales | Pull carts, golf (for sale) |
| Golf/Pro Shop | Cost of Merch. Sales | Shoes, golf (for sale) |
| Golf/Pro Shop | Dues and Subscriptions | Magazines, golf (for staff use) |
| Golf/Pro Shop | Equipment Rental | Golf cart rental |
| Golf/Pro Shop | Gasoline and Lubricants | Gasoline and lubricants, golf cart |
| Golf/Pro Shop | Gasoline and Lubricants | Gasoline and lubricants, mowers (golf course) |
| Golf/Pro Shop | Gasoline and Lubricants | Gasoline and lubricants, tractors/ trucks (golf course) |
| Golf/Pro Shop | Grounds M&L | Fences & bridges maintenance |
| Golf/Pro Shop | Grounds M&L | Fertilizers, golf course |
| Golf/Pro Shop | Grounds M&L | Flowers, golf course |
| Golf/Pro Shop | Grounds M&L | Insecticides, golf course |
| Golf/Pro Shop | Grounds M&L | Mowers, tractors, and trucks maintenance—golf |
| Golf/Pro Shop | Grounds M&L | Plants and shrubs, golf course |
| Golf/Pro Shop | Grounds M&L | Repairs & maintenance, golf cart paths |

| Department/<br>Schedule | Account Name | Item Name |
|---|---|---|
| Golf/Pro Shop | Grounds M&L | Reseeding golf course |
| Golf/Pro Shop | Grounds M&L | Sand, cinders, and top dressing, golf course |
| Golf/Pro Shop | Grounds M&L | Seeds, golf course |
| Golf/Pro Shop | Grounds M&L | Signage, golf maintenance |
| Golf/Pro Shop | Grounds M&L | Topsoil for golf course |
| Golf/Pro Shop | Irrigation | Water and drainage systems maintenance, golf course |
| Golf/Pro Shop | Irrigation | Water controllers, computerized water systems, golf course |
| Golf/Pro Shop | Operating Supplies | Ball washers, golf course |
| Golf/Pro Shop | Operating Supplies | Flag pins, golf |
| Golf/Pro Shop | Operating Supplies | Golf bags (for rental) |
| Golf/Pro Shop | Operating Supplies | Golf balls (practice range) |
| Golf/Pro Shop | Operating Supplies | Golf clubs (for rental) |
| Golf/Pro Shop | Operating Supplies | Pull carts, golf (for rental) |
| Golf/Pro Shop | Operating Supplies | Shoes, golf (for rent) |
| Golf/Pro Shop | Printing and Stationery | Scorecards, golf |
| Golf/Pro Shop | Salaries and Wages | Payroll, golf hourly |
| Golf/Pro Shop | Salaries and Wages | Payroll, golf management |
| Golf/Pro Shop | Tournament Expenses | Banners, golf tournament |
| Golf/Pro Shop | Tournament Expenses | Cart name plates, golf tournament |
| Golf/Pro Shop | Tournament Expenses | Portable sanitary facilities, golf tournament |
| Golf/Pro Shop | Tournament Expenses | Prizes, golf tournament |
| Golf/Pro Shop | Tournament Expenses | Scoreboard rental, golf tournament |
| Golf/Pro Shop | Tournament Expenses | Security, golf tournament |
| Golf/Pro Shop | Tournament Expenses | Software, golf tournament |
| Golf/Pro Shop | Vehicle Rep. & Maint. | Golf cart batteries |
| Golf/Pro Shop | Vehicle Rep. & Maint. | Golf cart repairs & maintenance |
| Golf/Pro Shop | Water | Water usage, golf course |
| Health Club/Spa | Ambience | Aromatherapy oils (health club/spa) |
| Health Club/Spa | Ambience | Diffusers (health club/spa) |
| Health Club/Spa | Ambience | Spa music |
| Health Club/Spa | Athletic Supplies | Fitness class supplies (health club/spa) |
| Health Club/Spa | Athletic Supplies | Non-capitalized gym equipment (health club/spa) |
| Health Club/Spa | Complimentary Services/Gifts | Complimentary beverages for guests (health club/spa) |

| Department/ Schedule | Account Name | Item Name |
|---|---|---|
| Health Club/Spa | Complimentary Services/Gifts | Complimentary cotton swabs and cotton balls for guest use (health club/spa) |
| Health Club/Spa | Complimentary Services/Gifts | Complimentary razors for guest use (health club/spa) |
| Health Club/Spa | Complimentary Services/Gifts | Complimentary snacks for guests (health club/spa) |
| Health Club/Spa | Complimentary Services/Gifts | Complimentary soap and shampoo for guest use (health club/spa) |
| Health Club/Spa | Cost of Sales | Accessories (for sale in health club/spa) |
| Health Club/Spa | Cost of Sales | Apparel (for sale in health club/spa) |
| Health Club/Spa | Cost of Sales | Spa products (for sale in health club/spa) |
| Health Club/Spa | Health and Beauty Products | Elixirs (health club/spa) |
| Health Club/Spa | Health and Beauty Products | Face cream (health club/spa) |
| Health Club/Spa | Health and Beauty Products | Hair shampoo (health club/spa) |
| Health Club/Spa | Health and Beauty Products | Lotions (health club/spa) |
| Health Club/Spa | Health and Beauty Products | Massage oils (health club/spa) |
| Health Club/Spa | Health and Beauty Products | Nail polish (health club/spa) |
| Health Club/Spa | Health and Beauty Products | Tonics (health club/spa) |
| Health Club/Spa | Linen | Bath mats (health club/spa) |
| Health Club/Spa | Linen | Bathrobes (health club/spa) |
| Health Club/Spa | Linen | Blankets (health club/spa) |
| Health Club/Spa | Linen | Slippers (health club/spa) |
| Health Club/Spa | Linen | Towels (health club/spa) |
| Health Club/Spa | Operating Supplies | Clothing hangers (health club/spa) |
| Health Club/Spa | Operating Supplies | Toilet paper (health club/spa) |
| Health Club/Spa | Operating Supplies | Weight scale (health club/spa) |
| Health Club/Spa | Printing and Stationery | Equipment instructions (health club/spa) |
| Health Club/Spa | Printing and Stationery | Guest treatment forms (health club/spa) |
| Health Club/Spa | Salaries and Wages | Payroll, health club hourly |
| Health Club/Spa | Salaries and Wages | Payroll, health club management |
| Health Club/Spa | Salaries and Wages | Payroll, spa hourly |
| Health Club/Spa | Salaries and Wages | Payroll, spa management |
| Health Club/Spa | Salaries and Wages | Payroll, swimming pool attendant (health club/spa operated) |
| Health Club/Spa | Swimming Pool | Life preserver (health club/spa operated) |
| Health Club/Spa | Swimming Pool | Pool chemicals (health club/spa operated) |

| Department/<br>Schedule | Account Name | Item Name |
|---|---|---|
| Health Club/Spa | Swimming Pool | Pool safety equipment (health club/spa operated) |
| Health Club/Spa | Swimming Pool | Pool toys (health club/spa operated) |
| Info & Telecom | A&G | Accounting hardware, small value purchases |
| Info & Telecom | A&G | Accounting software licenses, support and maintenance fees |
| Info & Telecom | A&G | Cameras, security |
| Info & Telecom | A&G | Security hardware, small value purchases |
| Info & Telecom | A&G | Security system licenses, support and maintenance fees |
| Info & Telecom | Cost of Cell Phones | Cell phone equipment |
| Info & Telecom | Cost of Cell Phones | Cost of cell phone plans |
| Info & Telecom | Contract Services | Information and telecommunication hardware maintenance non-system specific |
| Info & Telecom | Cost of Internet Services | Cost of complimentary Internet—function room |
| Info & Telecom | Cost of Internet Services | Cost of complimentary Internet—guest room |
| Info & Telecom | Cost of Internet Services | Internet access charges |
| Info & Telecom | Cost of Internet Services | Internet equipment not subject to capitalization |
| Info & Telecom | Cost of Local Calls | Cost of complimentary local telephone call—guest room |
| Info & Telecom | Cost of Local Calls | Cost of local calls, admin. and guest |
| Info & Telecom | Cost of Local Calls | Telephone access charges |
| Info & Telecom | Cost of Local Calls | Telephone usage fees |
| Info & Telecom | Cost of Local Calls | Telephone utility taxes |
| Info & Telecom | Cost of Local Calls | Trunk line charges |
| Info & Telecom | Cost of Long Distance Calls | Cost of complimentary long distance telephone call—guest room |
| Info & Telecom | Cost of Long Distance Calls | Cost of long distance calls, admin. and guest |
| Info & Telecom | Cost of Long Distance Calls | Telephone access charges |
| Info & Telecom | Cost of Long Distance Calls | Telephone usage fees |
| Info & Telecom | Cost of Long Distance Calls | Telephone utility taxes |
| Info & Telecom | Cost of Long Distance Calls | Trunk line charges |
| Info & Telecom | Energy Management | Energy management hardware, small value purchases |
| Info & Telecom | Energy Management | Energy management software licenses, support & maintenance fees |

| Department/<br>Schedule | Account Name | Item Name |
|---|---|---|
| Info & Telecom........... | Food & Beverage............................................. | Food & beverage software licenses, support and maintenance fees |
| Info & Telecom........... | Food & Beverage............................................. | Food & beverage systems hardware, small value purchases |
| Info & Telecom........... | Golf ................................................................ | Golf course software licenses, support and maintenance fees |
| Info & Telecom........... | Hardware......................................................... | Computer keyboards |
| Info & Telecom........... | Hardware......................................................... | Computer monitors |
| Info & Telecom........... | Hardware......................................................... | Computer mouse |
| Info & Telecom........... | Hardware......................................................... | CPU stands |
| Info & Telecom........... | Hardware......................................................... | Ethernet cables |
| Info & Telecom........... | Hardware......................................................... | Keyboards, computer |
| Info & Telecom........... | Hardware......................................................... | Laptop computers |
| Info & Telecom........... | Hardware......................................................... | Modems |
| Info & Telecom........... | Health Club/Spa............................................. | Health club/spa hardware, small value purchases |
| Info & Telecom........... | Health Club/Spa............................................. | Health club/spa software licenses, support and maintenance fees |
| Info & Telecom........... | Human Resources........................................... | Human resources hardware, small value purchases |
| Info & Telecom........... | Human Resources........................................... | Human resources software licenses, support and maintenance fees |
| Info & Telecom........... | Human Resources........................................... | Timeclocks |
| Info & Telecom........... | Information Security ..................................... | LAN/WAN e-mail hardware, small value purchases |
| Info & Telecom........... | Information Systems ...................................... | LAN/WAN e-mail software licenses, support and maintenance fees |
| Info & Telecom........... | Information Systems ...................................... | PCI compliance costs |
| Info & Telecom........... | Operating Supplies......................................... | Computer manuals, commercial |
| Info & Telecom........... | Operating Supplies......................................... | Computer manuals, printed |
| Info & Telecom........... | Operating Supplies......................................... | Computer printer paper |
| Info & Telecom........... | Operating Supplies......................................... | Computer supplies and accessories |
| Info & Telecom........... | Operating Supplies......................................... | Data cartridges and tapes |
| Info & Telecom........... | Operating Supplies......................................... | Data processing supplies |
| Info & Telecom........... | Other Equipment ........................................... | Computer books |
| Info & Telecom........... | Other Equipment ........................................... | Diskettes |
| Info & Telecom........... | Other Equipment ........................................... | Telecommunications equipment maintenance |
| Info & Telecom........... | Other Equipment ........................................... | Telephone cords |
| Info & Telecom........... | Other Equipment ........................................... | Telephone face plate |
| Info & Telecom........... | Other Equipment ........................................... | Telephone headsets |
| Info & Telecom........... | Other Equipment ........................................... | Wireless cards |

| Department/ Schedule | Account Name | Item Name |
|---|---|---|
| Info & Telecom | POM | Preventive maintenance hardware, small value purchases |
| Info & Telecom | POM | Preventive maintenance software licenses, support & maintenance fees |
| Info & Telecom | Rooms | Property management system hardware, small value purchases |
| Info & Telecom | Rooms | Property management system software license, support and maintenance fees |
| Info & Telecom | Salaries and Wages | Payroll, director of IT |
| Info & Telecom | Sales and Marketing | Sales and marketing hardware, small value purchases |
| Info & Telecom | Sales and Marketing | Sales and marketing software licenses, support & maintenance fees |
| Info & Telecom | System Costs | Software application upgrades |
| Info & Telecom | Telecommunications | Modem lines |
| Info & Telecom | Telecommunications | Music on hold service |
| Info & Telecom | Telecommunications | Switchboard repairs |
| Info & Telecom | Telecommunications | T-1 |
| Info & Telecom | Telecommunications | Telecommunication software license, support and maintenance fees |
| Info & Telecom | Telecommunications | VoIP |
| Minor Oper. Dept. | Guest Communications | Cost of fax—guest room |
| Minor Oper. Dept. | Guest Communications | Cost of internet—guest room |
| Minor Oper. Dept. | Guest Communications | Cost of telephone call—guest room |
| Minor Oper. Dept. | Guest Laundry Revenue | Guest dry cleaning expenses—partially serviced by the hotel |
| Minor Oper. Dept. | Guest Laundry Revenue | Guest laundry expenses—partially serviced by the hotel |
| Minor Oper. Dept. | In-Room Movie Rentals | In-room movie rental expenses—hotel operated |
| Minor Oper. Dept. | Occasional Food and Bev. Rev. | Occasional food and beverage expenses—limited service hotels |
| Minor Oper. Dept. | Retail Kiosk Sales | Kiosk cost of sales operated by the front desk personnel |
| Minor Oper. Dept. | Vending Revenue | Vending machine expenses—hotel operated |
| Minor Oper. Dept. | Video Game Sales | Video game expenses—hotel operated |
| Non Op. I&E | B&O Taxes | Gross receipts taxes not paid by customers—state/county/city |
| Non Op. I&E | B&O Taxes | Other business taxes that cannot be passed on to the customer (non-revenue generating department) |

| Department/<br>Schedule | Account Name | Item Name |
|---|---|---|
| Non Op. I&E | B&O Taxes | Sales and occupancy taxes not paid by customers |
| Non Op. I&E | Building and Contents | Insurance expense, boiler explosion |
| Non Op. I&E | Building and Contents | Insurance expense, building |
| Non Op. I&E | Building and Contents | Insurance expense, business interruption |
| Non Op. I&E | Building and Contents | Insurance expense, earthquake |
| Non Op. I&E | Building and Contents | Insurance expense, fire |
| Non Op. I&E | Building and Contents | Insurance expense, flood |
| Non Op. I&E | Building and Contents | Insurance expense, furnishings and equipment |
| Non Op. I&E | Building and Contents | Insurance expense, property |
| Non Op. I&E | Building and Contents | Insurance expense, terrorism |
| Non Op. I&E | Building and Contents | Insurance expense, tornado |
| Non Op. I&E | Building and Contents | Insurance expense, weather |
| Non Op. I&E | Building and Contents | Insurance—legal or settlement expenses |
| Non Op. I&E | Building and Contents | Underinsured losses, property |
| Non Op. I&E | Deductible | Insurance deductibles—property |
| Non Op. I&E | Deductible | Insurance deductibles—general liability |
| Non Op. I&E | Deductible | Insurance deductibles—liability/ burglary, theft, umbrella, fidelity, auto, innkeeper, liquor, cyber |
| Non Op. I&E | Deductible | Self-insurance retention |
| Non Op. I&E | Land and Buildings | Building lease, base rent |
| Non Op. I&E | Land and Buildings | Building lease, participating rent (based on operating results) |
| Non Op. I&E | Land and Buildings | Employee housing—employee reimbursement (contra) |
| Non Op. I&E | Land and Buildings | Employee housing—property lease |
| Non Op. I&E | Land and Buildings | Land lease |
| Non Op. I&E | Liability | General insurance—legal settlement costs or audit adjustments |
| Non Op. I&E | Liability | Insurance expense, automobile |
| Non Op. I&E | Liability | Insurance expense, burglary |
| Non Op. I&E | Liability | Insurance expense, cyber |
| Non Op. I&E | Liability | Insurance expense, director & officer coverage |
| Non Op. I&E | Liability | Insurance expense, EPLI |
| Non Op. I&E | Liability | Insurance expense, fidelity |
| Non Op. I&E | Liability | Insurance expense, guest liability |

| Department/ Schedule | Account Name | Item Name |
|---|---|---|
| Non Op. I&E | Liability | Insurance expense, innkeepers |
| Non Op. I&E | Liability | Insurance expense, liability |
| Non Op. I&E | Liability | Insurance expense, liquor |
| Non Op. I&E | Liability | Insurance expense, theft |
| Non Op. I&E | Liability | Insurance expense, umbrella |
| Non Op. I&E | Liability | Underinsured losses, liability |
| Non Op. I&E | Other Property and Equipment | Call accounting system lease (non-capital) |
| Non Op. I&E | Other Property and Equipment | Call accounting system software lease (non-capital) |
| Non Op. I&E | Other Property and Equipment | Computer hardware lease (non-capital) |
| Non Op. I&E | Other Property and Equipment | Computer software lease (non-capital) |
| Non Op. I&E | Other Property and Equipment | Copier lease (non-capital) |
| Non Op. I&E | Other Property and Equipment | Off-site storage rent |
| Non Op. I&E | Other Property and Equipment | Personal computer lease (non-capital) |
| Non Op. I&E | Other Property and Equipment | PMS hardware lease (non-capital) |
| Non Op. I&E | Other Property and Equipment | PMS software lease (non-capital) |
| Non Op. I&E | Other Property and Equipment | POS hardware lease (non-capital) |
| Non Op. I&E | Other Property and Equipment | POS software lease (non-capital) |
| Non Op. I&E | Other Property and Equipment | Telephone hardware lease (non-capital) |
| Non Op. I&E | Other Property and Equipment | Telephone software lease (non-capital) |
| Non Op. I&E | Other Property and Equipment | Telephone switch lease (non-capital) |
| Non Op. I&E | Other Property and Equipment | Trash compactor lease (non-capital) |
| Non Op. I&E | Other Property and Equipment | Vehicle lease (non-capital) |
| Non Op. I&E | Other Taxes and Assessments | Association assessment—general. (Not if defined: e.g., snow removal). |
| Non Op. I&E | Owner Expenses | Asset manager fees |
| Non Op. I&E | Owner Expenses | Market studies or audits—owner directed |
| Non Op. I&E | Owner Expenses | Receiver fees |
| Non Op. I&E | Personal Property Taxes | Personal property tax refunds (contra)—state/county/city |
| Non Op. I&E | Personal Property Taxes | Personal property taxes—state/county/city |
| Non Op. I&E | Real Estate Taxes | Attorneys' fees/expenses—real estate taxes |
| Non Op. I&E | Real Estate Taxes | Business improvement district (bid) assessment or tax |

| Department/ Schedule | Account Name | Item Name |
|---|---|---|
| Non Op. I&E | Real Estate Taxes | Consultant fees—real estate property taxes |
| Non Op. I&E | Real Estate Taxes | Legal fees/expenses—real estate taxes |
| Non Op. I&E | Real Estate Taxes | Real property tax refunds (contra)—state/county/city |
| Non Op. I&E | Real Estate Taxes | Real property taxes—state/county/city |
| Non Op. I&E | Unrealized Foreign Exch. Gains or Losses | Foreign exchange gain or loss related to FF&E reserve accounts |
| Non Op. I&E | Unrealized Foreign Exch. Gains or Losses | Foreign exchange gain or loss related to foreign currency account |
| Non Op. I&E | Unrealized Foreign Exch. Gains or Losses | Foreign exchange gain or loss related to foreign denominated debt |
| Parking | Cleaning Supplies | Cleaner, concrete (parking garage) |
| Parking | Contract Services | Customer parking paid to third party |
| Parking | Licenses and Permits | Garage licenses |
| Parking | Printing and Stationery | Parking, gate tickets |
| Parking | Rent | Rent, temporary parking space |
| Parking | Salaries and Wages | Payroll, parking manager |
| Parking | Salaries and Wages | Payroll, valet/parking attendant |
| Parking | Salaries and Wages | Payroll, valet/parking cashier |
| Payroll-Related Exp. | Automobile Allowance | Employee auto leases |
| Payroll-Related Exp. | Child Care | Employee child care |
| Payroll-Related Exp. | Contributory Savings Plan | Administrative fees for contributory savings plans |
| Payroll-Related Exp. | Contributory Savings Plan | Employer 401(k) contributions |
| Payroll-Related Exp. | Contributory Savings Plan | Employer registered retirement savings plan contributions |
| Payroll-Related Exp. | Dental Insurance | Employer cost of dental insurance |
| Payroll-Related Exp. | Disability Insurance | Employer cost of disability insurance |
| Payroll-Related Exp. | Expat Benefits | Cost of living adjustments (COLA) |
| Payroll-Related Exp. | Expat Benefits | Hardship premiums for ex-pats |
| Payroll-Related Exp. | Expat Benefits | Tax equalization payments for ex-pats |
| Payroll-Related Exp. | Expat Benefits | Transportation costs for home leave for ex-pats |
| Payroll-Related Exp. | Expat Benefits | Tuition cost for family members of ex-pats |
| Payroll-Related Exp. | Group Life Insurance | Employer share of group life insurance |
| Payroll-Related Exp. | Health Insurance | Employer share of employee health insurance |

| Department/ Schedule | Account Name | Item Name |
|---|---|---|
| Payroll-Related Exp. | Housing and Educational | Educational cost of non-ex-pat family members |
| Payroll-Related Exp. | Housing and Educational | Off-property housing costs for non-ex-pat employees |
| Payroll-Related Exp. | Meals | Employee meals from cafeteria |
| Payroll-Related Exp. | Meals | Employee meals in hotel restaurants at cost |
| Payroll-Related Exp. | National Disability Insurance | Employer share of national disability insurance program |
| Payroll-Related Exp. | National Medical Insurance | Employer share of governmental medical program |
| Payroll-Related Exp. | National Medical Insurance | Employer share of insurance administered by national insurance system |
| Payroll-Related Exp. | National Medical Insurance | Employer share of Medicare (FICA) |
| Payroll-Related Exp. | National Retirement Contribution | Employer share of a national retirement program |
| Payroll-Related Exp. | National Retirement Contribution | Employer share of retirement administered by national insurance system |
| Payroll-Related Exp. | National Retirement Contribution | Employer share of social security Canadian pension plan |
| Payroll-Related Exp. | National Retirement Contribution | Employer share of Social Security (FICA) |
| Payroll-Related Exp. | National Unemployment Insurance | Employer share of Canadian employment insurance |
| Payroll-Related Exp. | National Unemployment Insurance | Employer share of federal unemployment compensation |
| Payroll-Related Exp. | National Unemployment Insurance | Employer share of unemployment administered by national insurance system |
| Payroll-Related Exp. | National Unemployment Insurance | FUTA |
| Payroll-Related Exp. | Nonunion Insurance | Accident insurance for non-union employees |
| Payroll-Related Exp. | Nonunion Pension | Employer cost for non-union pension plans |
| Payroll-Related Exp. | Profit Sharing | Employer cost of profit sharing plan |
| Payroll-Related Exp. | Public Subsidized Transportation | Subsidized public transportation for employees |
| Payroll-Related Exp. | State Disability Insurance | State disability insurance |
| Payroll-Related Exp. | State Medical Insurance | State medical insurance |
| Payroll-Related Exp. | State Retirement Contribution | Employer share of a state retirement program |
| Payroll-Related Exp. | State Retirement Contribution | Employer share of Quebec pension plan |

| Department/<br>Schedule | Account Name | Item Name |
|---|---|---|
| Payroll-Related Exp. . | State Unemployment Insurance | State unemployment insurance |
| Payroll-Related Exp. . | Stock Benefits | Company issued stock to employees |
| Payroll-Related Exp. . | Union Insurance | Employer share of union employees insurance |
| Payroll-Related Exp. . | Union Other | Union dues |
| Payroll-Related Exp. . | Union Other | Union legal fund |
| Payroll-Related Exp. . | Union Pension | Employer share of union employees' pension plan |
| Payroll-Related Exp. . | Workers' Compensation Insurance | Workers' compensation insurance premium |
| POM | Building | Awning repairs |
| POM | Building | Building repairs |
| POM | Building | Ceiling, wall and floor repairs |
| POM | Building | EIFS repair |
| POM | Building | Key blank, key cards (non-guest-room) and key machine repairs |
| POM | Building | Lock repairs/service |
| POM | Building | Parking lot repair |
| POM | Building | Sign repairs |
| POM | Building | Window repair (glass screen, lock, mechanism, framing etc.) |
| POM | Building | Window shade & treatment repairs |
| POM | Contract Services | Extermination services |
| POM | Contract Services | Fumigation |
| POM | Contract Services | Mechanical, electrical or other recurring contracted service |
| POM | Contract Services | Pest control services |
| POM | Contract Services | Plant services (watering, etc.) |
| POM | Elec. & Mech. | Electric sub-meters maintenance |
| POM | Elec. & Mech. | Electric supplies |
| POM | Elec. & Mech. | Electrical repairs |
| POM | Elec. & Mech. | Generator repairs |
| POM | Elec. & Mech. | Motor repairs (other than vehicles) |
| POM | Elec. & Mech. | Public address system repairs |
| POM | Elec. & Mech. | Sound system repairs |
| POM | Elevators & Escalators | Elevator and escalator repairs |
| POM | Elevators & Escalators | Maintenance contracts, elevators and escalators |
| POM | Engineering Supplies | Pest control supplies (in-house use) |
| POM | Engineering Supplies | Tools |
| POM | Equipment Rental | Generator rentals (property power back-up) |

| Department/<br>Schedule | Account Name | Item Name |
|---|---|---|
| POM | Equipment Rental | Paint sprayer rental |
| POM | Equipment Rental | Platform lift/cherry picker rental |
| POM | Floor Covering | Adhesive, stair tread |
| POM | Floor Covering | Carpet repairs |
| POM | Floor Covering | Floor refinishing |
| POM | Floor Covering | Tape, carpet |
| POM | Floor Covering | Tile repairs (floor) |
| POM | Furniture and Equipment | Furniture refinishing |
| POM | Furniture and Equipment | Furniture repairs |
| POM | Furniture and Equipment | Television repairs |
| POM | Furniture and Equipment | Upholstery repairs |
| POM | Grounds M&L | Fertilizer |
| POM | Grounds M&L | Flower purchases |
| POM | Grounds M&L | Irrigation system repairs |
| POM | Grounds M&L | Landscaping service (indoor and outdoor) |
| POM | Grounds M&L | Plant and tree purchases (indoor and outdoor) |
| POM | Grounds M&L | Plant and tree rentals |
| POM | Grounds M&L | Snow removal service |
| POM | Grounds M&L | Tree purchases |
| POM | HVAC Equipment | Air filters |
| POM | HVAC Equipment | Boiler repairs |
| POM | HVAC Equipment | Ceiling fan repairs |
| POM | HVAC Equipment | Central plant costs |
| POM | HVAC Equipment | Chemicals, cooling tower |
| POM | HVAC Equipment | Cooling system repairs |
| POM | HVAC Equipment | Cooling tower repairs |
| POM | HVAC Equipment | HVAC systems repairs |
| POM | Kitchen Equipment | Kitchen equipment repairs |
| POM | Laundry Equipment | Laundry equipment repairs |
| POM | Licenses and Permits | Inspection fees—boilers, elevators, escalators, life/safety |
| POM | Licenses and Permits | Licenses, building |
| POM | Licenses and Permits | Licenses, canopy |
| POM | Licenses and Permits | Licenses, elevators |
| POM | Licenses and Permits | Licenses, engineering |
| POM | Licenses and Permits | Licenses, locksmith |
| POM | Licenses and Permits | Licenses, sidewalk |
| POM | Life/Safety | ADA compliance items—not capitalized |

| Department/Schedule | Account Name | Item Name |
|---|---|---|
| POM | Life/Safety | Alarm systems repairs |
| POM | Life/Safety | Chemicals, fire extinguishers |
| POM | Life/Safety | Emergency equipment & supplies |
| POM | Life/Safety | Emergency exit signs repairs |
| POM | Life/Safety | Fire alarm service—third party |
| POM | Life/Safety | Fire alarm system repairs (smoke, heat, strobe, attenuators, etc.) |
| POM | Life/Safety | Hazardous materials remediation |
| POM | Light Bulbs | Electric bulbs—all |
| POM | Miscellaneous | Maintenance request forms |
| POM | Operating Supplies | Manuals, service (instructional materials) |
| POM | Operating Supplies | Mats, floor |
| POM | Operating Supplies | Technical books and publications, maintenance |
| POM | Operating Supplies | Vehicle parts and supplies—not capitalized |
| POM | Painting and Decorating | Paint and ancillary chemicals |
| POM | Painting and Decorating | Paint brushes/rollers/sprayers & other supplies |
| POM | Painting and Decorating | Painting, contracted |
| POM | Painting and Decorating | Wall covering repairs, minor replacements |
| POM | Plumbing | Plumbing fixture repair parts |
| POM | Plumbing | Plumbing system repair parts |
| POM | Salaries and Wages | Payroll, chief engineer |
| POM | Salaries and Wages | Payroll, engineer |
| POM | Salaries and Wages | Payroll—plumber, HVAC, electrical, painter, gardener, or other specialized trade |
| POM | Salaries and Wages | Payroll, swimming pool attendant (no health club/spa) |
| POM | Swimming Pool | Swimming pool/spa parts, repairs, and chemicals/maintenance (no health club/spa) |
| POM | Vehicle Repairs | Auto/truck repair—property use |
| POM | Waste Removal | Refuse/compactor container charges |
| POM | Waste Removal | Waste, garbage, debris, and recycling removal |
| Rooms | Cleaning Supplies | Carpet cleaner equipment |
| Rooms | Cleaning Supplies | Deodorizers |
| Rooms | Cleaning Supplies | Soap scum remover, guestroom |
| Rooms | Commissions | Commissions, travel agent (rooms) |

| Department/Schedule | Account Name | Item Name |
|---|---|---|
| Rooms | Commissions & Fees—Group | Commissions, meeting planners |
| Rooms | Comp. In-Room/Media Entertainment | Cable television service |
| Rooms | Comp. In-Room/Media Entertainment | Satellite television service |
| Rooms | Comp. In-Room/Media Entertainment | Subscription TV channels (e.g., HBO) |
| Rooms | Complimentary Services/Gifts | Baskets, welcome |
| Rooms | Complimentary Services/Gifts | Newspapers |
| Rooms | Complimentary Services/Gifts | Welcome baskets, guestroom |
| Rooms | Contract Services | In-room guest account services (check-out) |
| Rooms | Contract Services | Public area cleaning service, lobby/guestroom corridors |
| Rooms | Contract Services | Video check-out service |
| Rooms | Contract Services | Video comment card service |
| Rooms | Guest Relocation | Guest relocation due to lack of room availability |
| Rooms | Guest Relocation | Walks, relocation of guest due to lack of room availability |
| Rooms | Guest Supplies | Aftershave lotion |
| Rooms | Guest Supplies | Amenities, guest |
| Rooms | Guest Supplies | Amenity baskets/containers (not reusable) |
| Rooms | Guest Supplies | Antacid (for use by guests in rooms) |
| Rooms | Guest Supplies | Aspirin (for use by guests in rooms) |
| Rooms | Guest Supplies | Baggage tags (gratis) |
| Rooms | Guest Supplies | Bath gel |
| Rooms | Guest Supplies | Bath salts |
| Rooms | Guest Supplies | Bath sheets |
| Rooms | Guest Supplies | Bath soap |
| Rooms | Guest Supplies | Bath tissue |
| Rooms | Guest Supplies | Bathing cap |
| Rooms | Guest Supplies | Bathing suits, disposable |
| Rooms | Guest Supplies | Body lotion |
| Rooms | Guest Supplies | Bottled water (gratis in rooms) |
| Rooms | Guest Supplies | Buttons (for use by guests in rooms) |
| Rooms | Guest Supplies | Candy (gratis) |
| Rooms | Guest Supplies | Cell phone chargers |
| Rooms | Guest Supplies | Coffee filters |
| Rooms | Guest Supplies | Coffee for use by guests in rooms |
| Rooms | Guest Supplies | Combs |
| Rooms | Guest Supplies | Conditioner, hair |
| Rooms | Guest Supplies | Cookie wrappings, guestroom |

| Department/<br>Schedule | Account Name | Item Name |
|---|---|---|
| Rooms | Guest Supplies | Cookies, guestroom |
| Rooms | Guest Supplies | Cosmetics |
| Rooms | Guest Supplies | Cotton balls |
| Rooms | Guest Supplies | Creamer packets |
| Rooms | Guest Supplies | Creams, body/face (rooms) |
| Rooms | Guest Supplies | Cups, disposable, for use by guests in rooms |
| Rooms | Guest Supplies | Dental floss |
| Rooms | Guest Supplies | Dental kit |
| Rooms | Guest Supplies | Deodorant |
| Rooms | Guest Supplies | Detergent for use by guests in rooms |
| Rooms | Guest Supplies | Dish soap for use by guests in rooms |
| Rooms | Guest Supplies | Dishwasher soap for use by guests in rooms |
| Rooms | Guest Supplies | Dry cleaning bags for use by guests in rooms |
| Rooms | Guest Supplies | Emery boards |
| Rooms | Guest Supplies | Espresso pods for use by guests in rooms |
| Rooms | Guest Supplies | Facial tissue |
| Rooms | Guest Supplies | Fans, paper (for use by guests in rooms) |
| Rooms | Guest Supplies | Filters, coffee |
| Rooms | Guest Supplies | Fingernail file |
| Rooms | Guest Supplies | Fire-starter packets for use by guests in rooms |
| Rooms | Guest Supplies | Fountain pens for use by guests in rooms |
| Rooms | Guest Supplies | Hair nets for use by guests in rooms |
| Rooms | Guest Supplies | Hair pins for use by guests in rooms |
| Rooms | Guest Supplies | Hair spray for use by guests in rooms |
| Rooms | Guest Supplies | Hairbrushes for use by guests in rooms |
| Rooms | Guest Supplies | Hand lotion |
| Rooms | Guest Supplies | Hand sanitizer |
| Rooms | Guest Supplies | Hand soap for use by guests in rooms |
| Rooms | Guest Supplies | Hot chocolate packets for use by guests in rooms |
| Rooms | Guest Supplies | Laundry bags (disposable) for use by guests in rooms |

| Department/<br>Schedule | Account Name | Item Name |
|---|---|---|
| Rooms | Guest Supplies | Liquid soap for use by guests in rooms |
| Rooms | Guest Supplies | Luggage tags for use by guests in rooms |
| Rooms | Guest Supplies | Magazines for use by guests in rooms |
| Rooms | Guest Supplies | Makeup remover for use by guests in rooms |
| Rooms | Guest Supplies | Mouthwash for use by guests in rooms |
| Rooms | Guest Supplies | Nail polish remover for use by guests in rooms |
| Rooms | Guest Supplies | Newspaper bags for use by guests in rooms |
| Rooms | Guest Supplies | Pillow mints |
| Rooms | Guest Supplies | Playing cards for use by guests in rooms |
| Rooms | Guest Supplies | Postcards for use by guests in rooms |
| Rooms | Guest Supplies | Razors for use by guests in rooms |
| Rooms | Guest Supplies | Sanitary pads/tampons |
| Rooms | Guest Supplies | Serving spoons for use by guests in rooms |
| Rooms | Guest Supplies | Sewing kits for use by guests in rooms |
| Rooms | Guest Supplies | Shampoo for use by guests in rooms |
| Rooms | Guest Supplies | Shaving cream/gel for use by guests in rooms |
| Rooms | Guest Supplies | Shoe brushes for use by guests in rooms |
| Rooms | Guest Supplies | Shoe mitts for use by guests in rooms |
| Rooms | Guest Supplies | Shoe polish for use by guests in rooms |
| Rooms | Guest Supplies | Shower caps for use by guests in rooms |
| Rooms | Guest Supplies | Silverware for use by guests in rooms |
| Rooms | Guest Supplies | Soap and soap dishes, guestroom |
| Rooms | Guest Supplies | Soda for use by guests in rooms |
| Rooms | Guest Supplies | Stationery for use by guests in rooms |
| Rooms | Guest Supplies | Stir sticks for use by guests in rooms |
| Rooms | Guest Supplies | Sugar packets for use by guests in rooms |

| Department/ Schedule | Account Name | Item Name |
|---|---|---|
| Rooms | Guest Supplies | Sweetener packets for use by guests in rooms |
| Rooms | Guest Supplies | Swimsuit bags for use by guests in rooms |
| Rooms | Guest Supplies | Swizzle sticks for use by guests in rooms |
| Rooms | Guest Supplies | Tags, baggage (gratis) |
| Rooms | Guest Supplies | Tea bags for use by guests in rooms |
| Rooms | Guest Supplies | Telephone message pads |
| Rooms | Guest Supplies | Thread for use by guests in rooms |
| Rooms | Guest Supplies | Tissue for use by guests in rooms |
| Rooms | Guest Supplies | Toilet tissue |
| Rooms | Guest Supplies | Toothbrushes for use by guests in rooms |
| Rooms | Guest Supplies | Toothpaste for use by guests in rooms |
| Rooms | Guest Supplies | Toothpicks for use by guests in rooms |
| Rooms | Guest Supplies | Towelettes for use by guests in rooms |
| Rooms | Guest Supplies | Tweezers for use by guests in rooms |
| Rooms | Guest Transportation | Airport van maintenance |
| Rooms | Guest Transportation | Auto fuel costs (guest transport) |
| Rooms | Guest Transportation | Car washing (rooms vans, carts, limos) |
| Rooms | Guest Transportation | Carts, fuel costs (guest transport) |
| Rooms | Guest Transportation | Fuel costs, auto (guest transport) |
| Rooms | Guest Transportation | Fuel costs, cart (guest transport) |
| Rooms | Guest Transportation | Guest transportation service contracts |
| Rooms | Guest Transportation | Limousine services, guest (no charge) |
| Rooms | Linen | Bath towels (all sizes) |
| Rooms | Linen | Bathmats |
| Rooms | Linen | Bathroom throw rugs |
| Rooms | Linen | Bed pads |
| Rooms | Linen | Bed ruffles |
| Rooms | Linen | Bed skirts |
| Rooms | Linen | Bedspreads |
| Rooms | Linen | Blanket covers |
| Rooms | Linen | Blankets, guestroom |
| Rooms | Linen | Bumpers, bed |
| Rooms | Linen | Bumpers, crib |

| Department/<br>Schedule | Account Name | Item Name |
|---|---|---|
| Rooms | Linen | Bunting |
| Rooms | Linen | Comforters |
| Rooms | Linen | Duvet covers |
| Rooms | Linen | Duvets |
| Rooms | Linen | Hand towels |
| Rooms | Linen | Mattress cover |
| Rooms | Linen | Mattress pad |
| Rooms | Linen | Pillow cases |
| Rooms | Linen | Pillow shams |
| Rooms | Linen | Pillows, down, foam, polyester, neck, decorative throw |
| Rooms | Linen | Quilt |
| Rooms | Linen | Robes |
| Rooms | Linen | Rubber sheets |
| Rooms | Linen | Rugs, bathroom |
| Rooms | Linen | Shams |
| Rooms | Linen | Sheets, fitted |
| Rooms | Linen | Sheets, flat |
| Rooms | Linen | Towels, bar (guestroom) |
| Rooms | Linen | Towels, bath (all sizes) |
| Rooms | Linen | Towels, hand |
| Rooms | Linen | Washcloths |
| Rooms | Operating Supplies | Afghans, guestroom |
| Rooms | Operating Supplies | Amenity baskets/containers (reusable) |
| Rooms | Operating Supplies | Aquarium, guestroom or lobby |
| Rooms | Operating Supplies | Aquarium supplies, guestroom or lobby |
| Rooms | Operating Supplies | Bags—beverage glass covers, guestroom |
| Rooms | Operating Supplies | Baskets, amenity |
| Rooms | Operating Supplies | Bathroom scale |
| Rooms | Operating Supplies | Bathtub safety mats |
| Rooms | Operating Supplies | Bathtub safety strips |
| Rooms | Operating Supplies | Blackout drapes |
| Rooms | Operating Supplies | Books, in-room guest reading |
| Rooms | Operating Supplies | Bottle openers, guestroom |
| Rooms | Operating Supplies | Bottle warmers |
| Rooms | Operating Supplies | Braille signs |
| Rooms | Operating Supplies | Can openers |

| Department/<br>Schedule | Account Name | Item Name |
|---|---|---|
| Rooms | Operating Supplies | Candy dishes, guestroom<br>(gratis candy for customers) |
| Rooms | Operating Supplies | Canopies, bed |
| Rooms | Operating Supplies | Cappuccino machines |
| Rooms | Operating Supplies | Carafes, guestroom |
| Rooms | Operating Supplies | Carts, housekeeper |
| Rooms | Operating Supplies | Carts, laundry |
| Rooms | Operating Supplies | China, guestroom |
| Rooms | Operating Supplies | Clock radios for guestrooms |
| Rooms | Operating Supplies | Clock/DVD players, Blu-ray,<br>Apple TV for guestrooms |
| Rooms | Operating Supplies | Clocks for guest rooms |
| Rooms | Operating Supplies | Closet rod |
| Rooms | Operating Supplies | Closet sachets |
| Rooms | Operating Supplies | Clothes brushes |
| Rooms | Operating Supplies | Coasters |
| Rooms | Operating Supplies | Coffee mugs |
| Rooms | Operating Supplies | Coffee pots for use by guests<br>in rooms |
| Rooms | Operating Supplies | Computer monitors, guest rooms |
| Rooms | Operating Supplies | Containers, amenity |
| Rooms | Operating Supplies | Cords |
| Rooms | Operating Supplies | Cords, drapery |
| Rooms | Operating Supplies | Corkscrews for use by guests<br>in rooms |
| Rooms | Operating Supplies | Cots |
| Rooms | Operating Supplies | Covers, toilet seats |
| Rooms | Operating Supplies | Crib bumper pads |
| Rooms | Operating Supplies | Crib covers |
| Rooms | Operating Supplies | Crib mattresses |
| Rooms | Operating Supplies | Cribs |
| Rooms | Operating Supplies | Cups, china, for use by guests<br>in rooms |
| Rooms | Operating Supplies | Dish drainer, guestroom |
| Rooms | Operating Supplies | Dishcloths, guestroom |
| Rooms | Operating Supplies | Dishes for use by guests in rooms |
| Rooms | Operating Supplies | Dispensers, bath tissue |
| Rooms | Operating Supplies | Dispensers, lotion |
| Rooms | Operating Supplies | Dispensers, soap |
| Rooms | Operating Supplies | Do not disturb cards |
| Rooms | Operating Supplies | Doilies, guestroom |

| Department/Schedule | Account Name | Item Name |
|---|---|---|
| Rooms | Operating Supplies | Door viewer |
| Rooms | Operating Supplies | Doormats |
| Rooms | Operating Supplies | Doorstop |
| Rooms | Operating Supplies | Dryers, hair |
| Rooms | Operating Supplies | DVD player, guestrooms |
| Rooms | Operating Supplies | Emergency exit instruction card |
| Rooms | Operating Supplies | Espresso maker for use by guests in rooms |
| Rooms | Operating Supplies | Facial tissue box cover |
| Rooms | Operating Supplies | Flatware for use by guests in rooms |
| Rooms | Operating Supplies | Gideon Bibles |
| Rooms | Operating Supplies | Glass bags |
| Rooms | Operating Supplies | Glass covers |
| Rooms | Operating Supplies | Glassware (all types) for use by guests in rooms |
| Rooms | Operating Supplies | Hair dryers |
| Rooms | Operating Supplies | Hangers (all types) |
| Rooms | Operating Supplies | Housekeeper carts |
| Rooms | Operating Supplies | Humidifier |
| Rooms | Operating Supplies | Ice buckets and liners |
| Rooms | Operating Supplies | Ice tongs for use by guests in rooms |
| Rooms | Operating Supplies | Inflatable beds |
| Rooms | Operating Supplies | Innkeepers liability card frames |
| Rooms | Operating Supplies | Iron |
| Rooms | Operating Supplies | Ironing board covers |
| Rooms | Operating Supplies | Ironing board holders |
| Rooms | Operating Supplies | Ironing boards |
| Rooms | Operating Supplies | Key cards |
| Rooms | Operating Supplies | Keys, safe deposit box |
| Rooms | Operating Supplies | Laundry bags (cloth) for use by guests in rooms |
| Rooms | Operating Supplies | Luggage racks |
| Rooms | Operating Supplies | Makeup mirror |
| Rooms | Operating Supplies | Mattress, crib |
| Rooms | Operating Supplies | Mattress protectors |
| Rooms | Operating Supplies | Microwave, guestroom |
| Rooms | Operating Supplies | Mouse traps |
| Rooms | Operating Supplies | Mugs, coffee, for use by guests in rooms |

| Department/ Schedule | Account Name | Item Name |
|---|---|---|
| Rooms | Operating Supplies | Napkins (paper/cloth) for use by guests in rooms |
| Rooms | Operating Supplies | Night lights |
| Rooms | Operating Supplies | Paper towel holders, guestroom |
| Rooms | Operating Supplies | Paper towels, guestroom |
| Rooms | Operating Supplies | Paper tray liners, rooms |
| Rooms | Operating Supplies | Phone books for guestrooms |
| Rooms | Operating Supplies | Pitchers, guestrooms |
| Rooms | Operating Supplies | Placemats, guestrooms |
| Rooms | Operating Supplies | Playpens |
| Rooms | Operating Supplies | Plungers, toilet |
| Rooms | Operating Supplies | Potholder, guestroom |
| Rooms | Operating Supplies | Potholder mitt, guestroom |
| Rooms | Operating Supplies | Presto logs, guestroom |
| Rooms | Operating Supplies | Quilt rack |
| Rooms | Operating Supplies | Radios, guestroom |
| Rooms | Operating Supplies | Rollaway beds |
| Rooms | Operating Supplies | Rubber tub mat |
| Rooms | Operating Supplies | Safe deposit box keys |
| Rooms | Operating Supplies | Shaving mirror, guestroom |
| Rooms | Operating Supplies | Sheers |
| Rooms | Operating Supplies | Shower curtain liners |
| Rooms | Operating Supplies | Shower curtain rings |
| Rooms | Operating Supplies | Shower curtains |
| Rooms | Operating Supplies | Shower slippers |
| Rooms | Operating Supplies | Slippers for use by guests in rooms |
| Rooms | Operating Supplies | Speakers, stereo, guestroom |
| Rooms | Operating Supplies | Spoons for use by guests in rooms |
| Rooms | Operating Supplies | Stationery portfolio |
| Rooms | Operating Supplies | Strainers, guestroom |
| Rooms | Operating Supplies | Sugar caddy, guestroom |
| Rooms | Operating Supplies | Table pads, guestroom |
| Rooms | Operating Supplies | Table protectors, guestroom |
| Rooms | Operating Supplies | Table tent cards, guestroom |
| Rooms | Operating Supplies | Tablecloths, guestroom |
| Rooms | Operating Supplies | Teapots, guestroom |
| Rooms | Operating Supplies | Telephone directories for guestrooms |
| Rooms | Operating Supplies | Television remote |

| Department/ Schedule | Account Name | Item Name |
|---|---|---|
| Rooms | Operating Supplies | Throw, guestroom |
| Rooms | Operating Supplies | Tissue box covers, guestroom |
| Rooms | Operating Supplies | Toothbrush holders, guestroom |
| Rooms | Operating Supplies | Toys for use by guests in rooms |
| Rooms | Operating Supplies | Trays, guestroom |
| Rooms | Operating Supplies | Tumblers, guestroom |
| Rooms | Operating Supplies | *TV Guides*, guestroom |
| Rooms | Operating Supplies | Water pitchers, guestroom |
| Rooms | Printing and Stationery | Cable guide cover |
| Rooms | Printing and Stationery | Check-out folders |
| Rooms | Printing and Stationery | Check-out notices |
| Rooms | Printing and Stationery | Folios |
| Rooms | Printing and Stationery | Guest guide |
| Rooms | Printing and Stationery | Hotel maps |
| Rooms | Printing and Stationery | Housekeeping reports |
| Rooms | Printing and Stationery | Innkeepers liability cards |
| Rooms | Printing and Stationery | Maps |
| Rooms | Printing and Stationery | Room attendant reports |
| Rooms | Printing and Stationery | Room directories |
| Rooms | Printing and Stationery | Room directory binders |
| Rooms | Printing and Stationery | Room rack forms |
| Rooms | Printing and Stationery | Safe deposit record cards |
| Rooms | Printing and Stationery | Telephone message cards |
| Rooms | Printing and Stationery | Water conservation cards |
| Rooms | Reservations | Internet web page, reservations |
| Rooms | Reservations | Reservation fees (chain assessment) |
| Rooms | Reservations | Reservation fees (GDS) |
| Rooms | Reservations | Reservation fees (OTA) |
| Rooms | Reservations | Reservation telephone expense |
| Rooms | Reservations | Reservation website building and maintenance |
| Rooms | Salaries and Wages | Payroll, bell service |
| Rooms | Salaries and Wages | Payroll, breakfast attendant |
| Rooms | Salaries and Wages | Payroll, club floor attendant |
| Rooms | Salaries and Wages | Payroll, concierge |
| Rooms | Salaries and Wages | Payroll, desk clerk |
| Rooms | Salaries and Wages | Payroll, director of reservations |
| Rooms | Salaries and Wages | Payroll, door attendant |
| Rooms | Salaries and Wages | Payroll, front office manager |

| Department/ Schedule | Account Name | Item Name |
|---|---|---|
| Rooms | Salaries and Wages | Payroll, guest services |
| Rooms | Salaries and Wages | Payroll, housekeeping attendant |
| Rooms | Salaries and Wages | Payroll, housekeeping director/ manager |
| Rooms | Salaries and Wages | Payroll, night manager |
| Rooms | Salaries and Wages | Payroll, reservations agent |
| Rooms | Salaries and Wages | Payroll, room director |
| Rooms | Salaries and Wages | Payroll, transportation driver |
| Sales/Marketing | Agency Fees | Advertising agency fees |
| Sales/Marketing | Agency Fees | Public relations |
| Sales/Marketing | Cluster Services | Cluster allocation from brand or management (no breakdown) |
| Sales/Marketing | Collateral Material | Banquet space map & floor plans |
| Sales/Marketing | Collateral Material | Brochures |
| Sales/Marketing | Collateral Material | Coupons |
| Sales/Marketing | Collateral Material | Flyers |
| Sales/Marketing | Collateral Material | Meeting space map & floor plans |
| Sales/Marketing | Collateral Material | Postcards |
| Sales/Marketing | Collateral Material | Rack cards |
| Sales/Marketing | Collateral Material | Sales kits |
| Sales/Marketing | Complimentary Services/Gifts | Logoed items for marketing |
| Sales/Marketing | Complimentary Services/Gifts | Promotional gifts |
| Sales/Marketing | Complimentary Services/Gifts | Sales initiated client amenities |
| Sales/Marketing | Contract Services | Guest surveys (outside service) |
| Sales/Marketing | Contract Services | Revenue management fee (3rd party) |
| Sales/Marketing | Contract Services | Revenue optimization fee (3rd party) |
| Sales/Marketing | Contract Services | Survey—meeting planner |
| Sales/Marketing | Corporate Office Reimbursables | Airfare—corporate—sales and marketing |
| Sales/Marketing | Corporate Office Reimbursables | Car rental—corporate—sales and marketing |
| Sales/Marketing | Corporate Office Reimbursables | Meals—corporate—sales and marketing |
| Sales/Marketing | Corporate Office Reimbursables | Travel—corporate—sales and marketing |
| Sales/Marketing | Decorations | Christmas decorations (inside & outside, visible to guests) |
| Sales/Marketing | Decorations | Decorations—inside—special events |
| Sales/Marketing | Decorations | Holiday decorations (inside & outside, visible to guests) |

| Department/ Schedule | Account Name | Item Name |
|---|---|---|
| Sales/Marketing | Direct Mail | Address list maintenance/ purchase/rental |
| Sales/Marketing | Direct Mail | Advertising—direct mail |
| Sales/Marketing | Direct Mail | Copy writing for direct mail |
| Sales/Marketing | Direct Mail | Database purchase |
| Sales/Marketing | Direct Mail | Direct mail expenses— outside service |
| Sales/Marketing | Direct Mail | Email blasts |
| Sales/Marketing | Direct Mail | Mailing lists |
| Sales/Marketing | Direct Mail | Newsletter production |
| Sales/Marketing | Direct Mail | Postage for direct mail |
| Sales/Marketing | Dues and Subscriptions | Association dues—sales and marketing staff |
| Sales/Marketing | Dues and Subscriptions | Chamber of commerce dues |
| Sales/Marketing | Dues and Subscriptions | Convention bureau dues |
| Sales/Marketing | Dues and Subscriptions | Dues, associations (marketing) |
| Sales/Marketing | Dues and Subscriptions | Hotel sales and marketing association dues |
| Sales/Marketing | Dues and Subscriptions | Magazine subscriptions, trade (marketing) |
| Sales/Marketing | Dues and Subscriptions | Membership dues—associations (marketing) |
| Sales/Marketing | Dues and Subscriptions | Newspaper subscriptions |
| Sales/Marketing | Dues and Subscriptions | Professional dues (marketing) |
| Sales/Marketing | Dues and Subscriptions | Subscriptions (marketing) |
| Sales/Marketing | Dues and Subscriptions | Tourist board/bureau fees |
| Sales/Marketing | Dues and Subscriptions | Trade publication subscriptions (marketing) |
| Sales/Marketing | Dues and Subscriptions | Visitors bureau dues |
| Sales/Marketing | Familiarization Trips | Beverages for fam trip attendees |
| Sales/Marketing | Familiarization Trips | Familiarization (fam) tour expenses |
| Sales/Marketing | Familiarization Trips | Meals for fam trip attendees |
| Sales/Marketing | Franchise & Affiliation Fees—Royalties | Franchise fee (chain royalty) |
| Sales/Marketing | Franchise & Affiliation Fees—Royalties | Franchise royalty |
| Sales/Marketing | Franchise & Affiliation Fees—Royalties | Royalty fee—franchise or affiliation |
| Sales/Marketing | Franchise and Affiliation Marketing | Advertising assessments |
| Sales/Marketing | Franchise and Affiliation Marketing | Affiliation advertising fee |
| Sales/Marketing | Franchise and Affiliation Marketing | Affiliation marketing fee |
| Sales/Marketing | Franchise and Affiliation Marketing | Cooperative marketing charges |
| Sales/Marketing | Franchise and Affiliation Marketing | Franchise advertising fee |

| Department/<br>Schedule | Account Name | Item Name |
|---|---|---|
| Sales/Marketing | Franchise and Affiliation Marketing | Franchise marketing fee |
| Sales/Marketing | Franchise and Affiliation Marketing | Marketing assessments |
| Sales/Marketing | In-House Graphics | Advertising signs, interior |
| Sales/Marketing | In-House Graphics | Posters |
| Sales/Marketing | In-House Graphics | Promotional signs, interior |
| Sales/Marketing | In-House Graphics | Signs (inside) |
| Sales/Marketing | In-House Graphics | Table top promotion printing |
| Sales/Marketing | Loyalty Programs | Airline loyalty program fees |
| Sales/Marketing | Loyalty Programs | Car rental loyalty program fees |
| Sales/Marketing | Loyalty Programs | Frequent car rental fees |
| Sales/Marketing | Loyalty Programs | Frequent flyer fees |
| Sales/Marketing | Loyalty Programs | Frequent guest fees |
| Sales/Marketing | Loyalty Programs | Guest loyalty fees |
| Sales/Marketing | Loyalty Programs | Referral programs |
| Sales/Marketing | Media | Ad design & creative |
| Sales/Marketing | Media | Advertising—directories |
| Sales/Marketing | Media | Advertising—Internet incl. OTA |
| Sales/Marketing | Media | Advertising—magazines |
| Sales/Marketing | Media | Advertising—newspapers |
| Sales/Marketing | Media | Advertising production—magazines |
| Sales/Marketing | Media | Advertising production—misc. |
| Sales/Marketing | Media | Advertising production—newspaper |
| Sales/Marketing | Media | Advertising production—TV & radio |
| Sales/Marketing | Media | Advertising—radio |
| Sales/Marketing | Media | Barter/contra agreement |
| Sales/Marketing | Media | Consortia ads |
| Sales/Marketing | Media | Copy writing for advertising |
| Sales/Marketing | Media | Directory advertising |
| Sales/Marketing | Media | Directory listing |
| Sales/Marketing | Media | Internet advertising |
| Sales/Marketing | Media | Magazine advertising |
| Sales/Marketing | Media | Meeting guides advertising |
| Sales/Marketing | Media | Meeting guides listing |
| Sales/Marketing | Media | Newspaper advertising |
| Sales/Marketing | Media | Online travel agency (OTA) ads |
| Sales/Marketing | Media | Production—magazines |
| Sales/Marketing | Media | Production—newspapers |
| Sales/Marketing | Media | Production—other |

| Department/ Schedule | Account Name | Item Name |
|---|---|---|
| Sales/Marketing | Media | Production—TV |
| Sales/Marketing | Media | Radio advertising |
| Sales/Marketing | Media | Telephone directory advertising |
| Sales/Marketing | Media | Television ad |
| Sales/Marketing | Media | Tourist guide ad |
| Sales/Marketing | Media | Tourist guide listing |
| Sales/Marketing | Media | TV advertising |
| Sales/Marketing | Media | Video—welcome channel |
| Sales/Marketing | Media | Visitors guide ad |
| Sales/Marketing | Media | Visitors guide listing |
| Sales/Marketing | Media | Yellow Pages ad |
| Sales/Marketing | Operating Supplies | Telephone directories for departmental use |
| Sales/Marketing | Outside Sales Representation | Representation firms |
| Sales/Marketing | Outside Services Market Research | Consultant fees, market research |
| Sales/Marketing | Outside Services Market Research | Customer research/survey—outside service |
| Sales/Marketing | Outside Services Market Research | Hotelligence fee |
| Sales/Marketing | Outside Services Market Research | Internet review monitoring fees |
| Sales/Marketing | Outside Services Market Research | Reader board service fee |
| Sales/Marketing | Outside Services Market Research | Reputation management fee |
| Sales/Marketing | Outside Services Market Research | Review monitoring fees |
| Sales/Marketing | Outside Services Market Research | Social media monitoring service |
| Sales/Marketing | Outside Services Market Research | STAR report fee |
| Sales/Marketing | Outside Services Market Research | STR fee |
| Sales/Marketing | Outside Services Market Research | Travel click fee |
| Sales/Marketing | Outside Signage | Advertising—outdoor |
| Sales/Marketing | Outside Signage | Billboards |
| Sales/Marketing | Outside Signage | Directional signs (outside) |
| Sales/Marketing | Outside Signage | Highway signs |
| Sales/Marketing | Outside Signage | Outdoor advertising |
| Sales/Marketing | Outside Signage | Road signs |
| Sales/Marketing | Outside Signage | Signs (outside) |
| Sales/Marketing | P&ODC | Overnight delivery (marketing) |
| Sales/Marketing | P&ODC | Postage (marketing) |
| Sales/Marketing | P&ODC | Postage meter rentals (marketing) |
| Sales/Marketing | P&ODC | Stamps (marketing) |
| Sales/Marketing | Photography | Model fees |
| Sales/Marketing | Photography | Photos |
| Sales/Marketing | Promotion | Charity events (fees, donations, registrations) |

| Department/ Schedule | Account Name | Item Name |
|---|---|---|
| Sales/Marketing | Promotion | Client gifts |
| Sales/Marketing | Promotion | Donations |
| Sales/Marketing | Promotion | Gift certificates donated |
| Sales/Marketing | Promotion | Sponsorships |
| Sales/Marketing | Salaries and Wages | Cluster allocation from brand or management (payroll) |
| Sales/Marketing | Trade Shows | Booths at trade shows |
| Sales/Marketing | Trade Shows | Trade show booth construction |
| Sales/Marketing | Trade Shows | Trade show promotional items |
| Sales/Marketing | Trade Shows | Trade show registration |
| Sales/Marketing | Travel—Other | Brand meetings fee |
| Sales/Marketing | Travel—Other | Chamber of commerce events/ registration |
| Sales/Marketing | Travel—Other | Conference registration |
| Sales/Marketing | Travel—Other | Visitors bureau events/registration |
| Sales/Marketing | Travel—Meals & Enter. | Entertainment while traveling |
| Sales/Marketing | Travel—Meals & Enter. | Meals |
| Sales/Marketing | Website | Domain name registration |
| Sales/Marketing | Website | Key word buys |
| Sales/Marketing | Website | PPC fees |
| Sales/Marketing | Website | Search engine optimization costs |
| Sales/Marketing | Website | SEO costs |
| Sales/Marketing | Website | Virtual tour production |
| Sales/Marketing | Website | Website design & maintenance |
| Sales/Marketing | Website | Website development |
| Utilities | Electricity | Electricity |
| Utilities | Gas | Consultant fees (shared savings plans) |
| Utilities | Gas | Gas (for utility use) |
| Utilities | Oil | Oil (for utility use) |
| Utilities | Other Fuels | Geothermal power |
| Utilities | Other Fuels | Propane (for utility use) |
| Utilities | Other Fuels | Solar power |
| Utilities | Other Fuels | Wind power |
| Utilities | Steam | Steam (for utility use) |
| Utilities | Water/Sewer | Cogeneration of water |
| Utilities | Water/Sewer | Desalinization of water |
| Utilities | Water/Sewer | Sewer |
| Utilities | Water/Sewer | Wastewater surcharge |
| Utilities | Water/Sewer | Water |

# Part V
# Gross vs. Net Reporting

The determination to report revenue on a net or gross basis influences the classification of a revenue source as Miscellaneous Income or an Other Operated Department. An entity must determine whether it is acting as an agent or as a principal in the transaction.

The decision to recognize revenue based on the net amount retained (i.e., the amount billed to the customer less the amount paid to a supplier) as an agent or the gross amount billed to a customer as a principal is based on a comparison of the revenue source to a series of indicators. The determination to report a revenue source on a net or gross basis is made based on the predominance of indicators describing the production, execution, collection risk, and delivery of the revenue. Note that the evaluation of whether an indicator exists may not result in a clear yes or no answer; rather, an indicator may partially exist (or the risk may be partially mitigated) based on the specific facts and circumstances of the arrangement. None of the indicators should be considered presumptive or determinative. The relative strength of each indicator should be considered in the overall evaluation.

The following paragraphs summarize the indicators that provide guidance for the determination of reporting hotel revenues on a net or gross basis.

## Indicators of Net Revenue Reporting

1. *The supplier (not the property) is the primary obligor.* The primary obligor is the party responsible for fulfillment, including the acceptability of the product or service ordered or purchased by the customer. Representations (written or otherwise) made by a property during marketing and the terms of the sales contract generally will provide evidence as to a customer's understanding of whether the property or the supplier is responsible for fulfilling the ordered product or service.

2. *The amount the property earns is fixed.* This may be a fixed dollar amount per customer transaction regardless of the amount billed to a customer or a stated percentage of the amount billed to a customer. The percentage may vary based on discounts or negotiated terms with the customer.

3. *Credit/collection risk is with the supplier.* This fact may indicate that the property is an agent of the supplier and should record revenue on a net basis. If the property collects revenue as a convenience for the customer or supplier, this doesn't imply credit risk is with the property.

## Indicators of Gross Revenue Reporting

1. *The property is the primary obligor in the transaction.* The customer's perspective that the property is responsible for providing the product or service desired, including remedies if the customer is dissatisfied, is a strong indicator the property has risks and rewards as a principal in the transaction. Representations made by the property during marketing and the terms of the sales contract generally will provide evidence as to whether the property or the supplier is the primary obligor. In the case where the property is responsible for the customer remedies, but the supplier is responsible for the fulfillment of the goods/services, the hotel's risk as primary obligor would be partially mitigated.

2. *The property has credit/collection risk.* The property is responsible for collecting the sales price from a customer, but must pay the amount owed to a supplier after the supplier performs, regardless of whether the sales price is fully collected. The risk of loss is an indicator that the company has risks and rewards as a principal in the transaction. Credit risk is not present if:

   - a property returns or refunds only the net amount it earned in the transaction if the transaction is cancelled or reversed;

   - a property fully collects the sales price prior to the delivery of the product or service to the customer (in other words, before the property incurs an obligation to the supplier); and

   - a customer pays by debit or credit card and a property obtains authorization for the charge in advance of product shipment or service performance.

3. *The property determines the nature, type, characteristics, or specifications of the product(s) or service(s) ordered by the customer.* This is an indicator that the property is primarily responsible for fulfillment.

4. *The property has multiple suppliers for a customer-ordered product or service and discretion to select the supplier at the time of the transaction.* This is an indicator that the property is primarily responsible for fulfillment.

5. *Unmitigated general inventory risk is a strong indicator that the property has risks and rewards as a principal in the transaction and, therefore, that it should record gross revenue based on the amount billed to the customer.* Inventory risk exists if a property takes title to a product before that product is ordered by a customer (the property maintains the product in inventory) or will take title to the product if the customer returns it (back-end inventory risk) and the customer has a right of return. An equally strong indicator of gross reporting exists if a customer arrangement involves services and the entity is obligated to compensate the individual service provider for work performed, regardless of whether the customer accepts that work.

6. *Physical loss inventory risk is present.* Although not as applicable in the hospitality industry, physical loss inventory risk exists if title to the product is transferred to an entity at the shipping point and is transferred from that entity to the customer upon delivery. This indicator, although less persuasive than general inventory risk, may be applicable in the case of property retail sales. If the service contract provides to the property a fixed level of adjustment (i.e., dollar or percentage) to the amount due to account for service credits issued to the customer, the property's general inventory risk would be partially mitigated.

7. *The property has reasonable latitude, within economic constraints, to establish the exchange price with a customer for the product or service.* This fact may indicate that the property has risks and rewards of a principal in the transaction and that it should record gross revenue based on the amount billed to the customer. A requirement imposed by the supplier to sell products or services

at specified prices is not an indicator that a company should record revenue only at the net amount earned in the transaction. Conversely, the property may require the supplier to provide prices that are commercially reasonable in order to be competitive in the market. This requirement does not constitute evidence that the property has latitude in establishing pricing for purposes of gross versus net calculations, but rather establishes a parameter for conducting business with the customer.

8. *The property adds meaningful value to the product or provides a significant portion of the services ordered by the customer.* This is an indicator that the property is primarily responsible for fulfillment. Meaningful value is evaluated from the perspective of the product or service ordered by the customer such that the selling price of that product is greater as a result of the property's addition.

## Case Study Examples of Gross vs. Net Revenue Reporting

The following case studies provide examples of applications of the preceding indicators to common property revenue sources. Many more revenue instances will fall into these types of determinations. In each case, it is the reporting entity that determines if the revenues are reported as gross or net. Each case will depend on the facts and circumstances of the arrangement, written or otherwise, between the property and the supplier.

# Laundry and Dry Cleaning

### Scenario One: In-House Operation

*Structure.* Property A operates a laundry facility that performs laundry and dry cleaning services for the guests of the hotel. All employees are employed by the property. In addition, the equipment and supplies are also owned (or leased) by the property.

*Evaluation.* Since Property A is responsible for providing the service to the guest, sets the prices charged, and assumes the risk of collection, the revenues and expenses under Scenario One are reported on a gross basis within a Guest Laundry on Other Operated Departments.

### Scenario Two: Outside Contract

*Structure.* Property B issues an RFP to several local laundries that specifies quality standards, delivery and pickup times, and other elements of providing laundry and dry cleaning services to its guests. After evaluating all proposals submitted, Property B contracts with XYZ Cleaners to launder and dry clean clothing for its guests. Property B collects the clothing from the guest, passes the clothing on to XYZ Cleaners for laundering or dry cleaning, and then returns the clothing to the guest's room. XYZ Cleaner charges Property B the contracted amount to clean each item of clothing. Property B then marks up the cost charged by XYZ (by a fixed dollar amount or percentage) and charges the guest the higher amount. Property B is the primary obligor in providing the service and takes all responsibility for resolving guest service issues. Property B also has discretion in selecting which outside laundry service to use.

*Evaluation.* Since Property B is the primary obligor, does provide a moderate degree of service to the guest (pick up and return of the clothing), sets the standards of service and prices charged to the guest, and assumes the risk of collection, the revenues and expenses under Scenario Two are reported on a gross basis as either an Other Operated Department or as a Minor Operated Department.

### Scenario Three: Outside Concessionaire

*Structure.* XYZ Cleaners approaches Property C to provide laundry and dry cleaning services for the property's guests. Guests of Property C bring their clothing to the front desk with a completed laundry service request form. The property then passes the clothing on to XYZ Cleaners for laundering or dry cleaning. Upon return to the property, the clothing is stored at the front desk for guest pick-up. Property C passes on the cost of the charge received from XYZ Cleaners directly to the guest without a markup. Property C then pays XYZ Cleaners the amount of laundry/dry cleaning revenue collected by the property, minus a commission (percentage of revenue or fixed dollar amount per item).

*Evaluation.* Since Property C provides only a limited degree of service to the guest, does not mark up the price from that charged by XYZ Cleaners, and receives a fixed commission, the revenue to the property under Scenario Three (the commission) is reported in Miscellaneous Income on a net basis.

## In-Room TV Entertainment

### Scenario One: In-House Operation

*Structure.* Property A owns its own TVs and MATV system and provides free local, basic, and some premium cable channels to guests. Each room has its own DVD player and the property maintains a library of DVDs for rent by guests. In-room promotions list the titles available and the charges to rent a DVD.

*Evaluation.* Since Property A is responsible for providing the service to the guest, sets the prices charged, carries the inventory of DVDs, and assumes the risk of collection, the revenues and expenses under Scenario One are reported on a gross basis as either an Other Operated Department or as a Minor Operated Department.

### Scenario Two: Outside TV Entertainment Service Agreement

*Structure.* Property B enters into a service agreement with XYZ Video Corporation (XYZ Video) to provide pay-per-view movies and other electronic guest services which may include on-demand music, video games, TV on demand, music on demand, and Internet access, all charged to the guest on a per-usage basis. The guest is made aware through in-room literature and/or video content that XYZ Video is providing these electronic video and guest services. XYZ Video sets the pricing of all services charged to the guest.

Property B owns or leases its TVs and MATV system. XYZ Video owns and maintains its "system" of in-room electronic services.

Property B bills the guests the gross amount of the pay-per-view service as recorded by XYZ Video's monitoring system, plus any applicable sales and use taxes. On a monthly basis, XYZ Video invoices Property B for the pay-per-view/usage fees recorded by its monitoring device. Property B is allowed to deduct a commission from its remittance to XYZ Video that is typically a percentage of the pay-per-view/usage fees.

XYZ Video provides training to Property B's personnel in operating the system, using in-room electronic services, managing guest issues and complaints, and programming content, among other things. XYZ Video may permit a set number of monthly adjustments to guest pay-per-view charges, permit a flat percentage of total pay-per-view revenue to be adjusted on the monthly invoice, or permit Property B's management to determine all rebates to accommodate guest complaints, depending on the contract.

*Evaluation.* Since Property B receives a percentage commission of the pay-per-view/usage fees charged to the guest, it would record the net commission in Miscellaneous Income. Although it does provide some level of service, Property B has no inventory risk, little collection risk, and also has the adjustments allowed by XYZ Video to mitigate guests' disputes. To the guest, XYZ Video is prominently featured in all in-room advertising and equipment as the provider (primary obligor) of the movies and other electronic guest services.

# Parking

### Scenario One: Property Operation

*Structure.* Property A operates the parking lot and performs all services for guests using the facility. Property A sets the prices, collects the revenue, employs the parking employees, and is responsible for the costs of operating the facility.

*Evaluation.* As Property A directly provides the services to the guests, controls the pricing, and has retained the risks and rewards of ownership, the revenue and expenses under this scenario are properly recorded on a gross basis and Parking is considered an Other Operated Department.

### Scenario Two: Outside Contractor

*Structure.* Property B contracts with Contractor Z to provide parking administration and valet parking services for Property B's guests. Property B owns the parking structure, employs the personnel, is responsible for costs of maintenance of the facility (including liability insurance), and has approval rights over the price to be charged to guests. Contractor Z charges the property a contracted amount (percentage of revenue or fixed amount) to provide the parking services. Property B is responsible for collecting the amounts charged to guests' folios.

*Evaluation.* As Property B provides the facility for the service, assumes the risk of collection, retains control over pricing, and bears the risk of departmental loss, the revenues and expenses are reported on a gross basis under this scenario and Parking is considered an Other Operated Department.

## Scenario Three: Outside Concessionaire

*Structure.* Property C contracts with Company Z to provide parking facilities in a preferred provider relationship with the property. Company Z owns and operates the parking lot. Property C passes the charge set by Company Z on to its guests without a mark-up and is responsible for the collection from the guest. The amounts collected on behalf of Company Z are remitted to Company Z on a periodic basis net of a contracted commission.

*Evaluation.* As Property C has not assumed the risk and rewards of operating the parking, the revenues are recorded on a net basis, with Property C only recording the amount of the commission in Miscellaneous Income.

## Scenario Four: Lease to Outside Concessionaire

*Structure.* Property D leases a parking facility to a third party (Company Z) that operates the parking lot. Under the terms of the lease, the parking facility is to provide parking services for the property. Company Z establishes the price to be charged for the service with input from Property D. The parking employees are employed by Company Z, but wear uniforms similar to those worn by the employees of Property D; it is not explicitly communicated to the guests of Property D that the parking employees are working for Company Z. Guests are able to charge the parking fees to their folios, in which case Property D remits the amount of collections back to Company Z on a periodic basis. Property D is not responsible for uncollectable parking fees from guests. Property D is not responsible for vehicle losses and/or damage.

*Evaluation.* Some indicators point toward gross recording, while other indicators point toward net recording. The facts that Company Z is the primary provider of the service and has the predominant credit risk are strong indicators that support recording on a net basis.

Factors that support recording on a gross basis are that the guests of Property D may believe that Property D is providing the services, since the employees wear a uniform similar to other employees at Property D. Property D also had several other third-party concessionaires to select from before choosing Company Z to lease out Property D's parking facility and, therefore, had discretion in supplier selection.

Although indicators of gross recording exist for this example, those indicators are not sufficient to overcome the stronger indicators that revenues should be recorded on a net basis as part of Property D's revenues in Miscellaneous Income.

# Audiovisual

## Scenario One: Property Operation

*Structure.* Property A operates its audiovisual services, owns or rents the necessary equipment, sets the sales price, invoices the guests, and performs all services for guests requiring the services.

*Evaluation.* As Property A directly provides the services to the guest, controls the pricing, and has retained the risks and rewards of ownership, the revenue and expenses under this scenario are properly recorded on a gross basis. If Property A has a Food and Beverage department, it reports these revenues and expenses as Audiovisual and Audiovisual Cost on *Food and Beverage—Schedule 2*. If Property A does not have a Food and Beverage department, it reports these revenues and expenses as a Minor Operated Department in Other Operated Departments.

## Scenario Two: Outside Contractor

*Structure.* Property B contracts with Contractor Z as the exclusive recommended vendor to provide audiovisual services for Property B's guests. Contractor Z employs the personnel to provide the service and is responsible for the costs to purchase and maintain the equipment (including liability insurance). Property B employs the sales managers who coordinate the services of Contractor Z with its guests and is responsible for collecting the revenue from guests. The sales contract between Property B and guests does not explicitly mention Contractor Z. Property B coordinates and satisfies customer disputes. Property B and Contractor Z agree jointly upon the prices to charge and the standard of service. Contractor Z pays Property B a contracted amount (percentage of revenue or fixed amount) to provide the audiovisual services. Property B is responsible to pay Contractor Z for the services once they are performed, regardless of whether the sales price is fully collected.

*Evaluation.* Some indicators point toward gross recording while others point toward net recording. Strong indicators that support recording on a gross basis include the fact that Property B acts as the primary obligor from the customer's perspective; it has assumed credit risk and it has the ability to set pricing within certain economic constraints.

A factor that supports recording on a net basis is that the amount earned by Property B is fixed (whether this is a percentage of revenue or a fixed dollar amount).

Although an indicator of net recording exists for this example, it is not sufficient to overcome the stronger indicators that revenues should be recorded on a gross basis. If Property B has a Food and Beverage department, it reports these revenues and expenses as Audiovisual and Audiovisual Cost in *Food and Beverage—Schedule 2*. If Property B does not have a Food and Beverage department, it reports these revenues and expenses as a Minor Operated Department on Other Operated Departments.

## Scenario Three: Outside Contractor

*Structure.* Property C contracts with Contractor Z as the exclusive recommended vendor to provide audiovisual services for Property C's guests. Contractor Z employs the personnel to provide the service and is responsible for costs of purchase and maintenance of the equipment (including liability insurance). Contractor Z determines the prices to charge for services to guests, but Property C has the ability to require Contractor Z to change its prices if it determines that Contractor Z's prices are unreasonable. The sales contract between Property C and its guests states that the audiovisual services will be provided by Contractor Z and that Contractor Z is solely responsible or that Contractor Z has a contract with guests directly. Contractor Z pays Property C a contracted amount (percentage of revenue or fixed amount) to provide the audiovisual services. Property C is responsible for collecting the revenue and remitting it to Contractor Z for the services once they are performed. However, if a guest fails to pay, Property C is not liable to Contractor Z.

*Evaluation.* Property C has not assumed the risk and rewards of operating the audiovisual services as Contractor Z is the primary obligor from the customers' perspective and has assumed credit and inventory risk. Although Property C has the ultimate ability to adjust prices if it determines Contractor Z's prices are unreasonable, this is not a strong enough indicator to support recording revenue on a gross basis. Revenue should be recorded on a net basis. If Property C has a Food and Beverage department, it reports this net revenue as Audiovisual on *Food and Beverage—Schedule 2.* If Property C does not have a Food and Beverage department, it reports this net revenue as Miscellaneous Income.

# Retail Outlets

### Scenario One: Property Operation

*Structure.* Property A operates an on-premises retail outlet, employs the staff, owns or rents the necessary fixtures for the shop, and purchases the inventory.

*Evaluation.* As Property A directly owns the inventory, controls the pricing, and has retained the risks and rewards of ownership, the revenue and expenses under this scenario are properly recorded on a gross basis and the retail outlet is considered an Other Operated Department.

### Scenario Two: Leased Space

*Structure.* Property B rents space on the premises to Retailer Z. Retailer Z operates the retail outlet, employs the staff, owns or rents the necessary fixtures for the shop, and purchases the inventory. The rental agreement between Property B and Retailer Z details what goods and services Retailer Z is allowed to sell, as well as the minimum or maximum price that certain products or services can be sold at. Retailer Z pays a fixed rent and/or a percentage rent to Property B. Property B can collect the outlet's retail sales charged to guestrooms through its guestroom billing and remit the amount to Retailer Z.

*Evaluation.* Some indicators point toward gross recording, while other indicators point toward net recording. Strong indicators that support recording on a net basis include the fact that Retailer Z is the primary obligor of the services and products provided in the retail store. In addition, Property B earns a fixed dollar and/or percentage of sales amount.

A factor that supports recording on a gross basis is that Property B may have some credit risk on the amount it collects from guests.

Although an indicator of gross recording exists for this example, this indicator is not sufficient to overcome the stronger indicators that revenues should be recorded on a net basis in Miscellaneous Income.

# Recreational Activities

## Scenario One: Property Operation

*Structure.* Property A operates the tennis center at the resort. Staff and instructors are either full-time or commissioned employees of Property A, which also purchases the equipment and insurance coverage. Property A charges guests for the use of the services and is responsible for collection of the revenues and payment of the expenses.

*Evaluation.* As Property A directly provides the services to guests, controls the pricing, and has retained the risks and rewards of ownership, the revenue and expenses under this scenario are properly recorded on a gross basis and the tennis center is considered an Other Operated Department.

## Scenario Two: Outside Contractor

*Structure.* Property B contracts with Contractor Z to provide tennis instruction, rental equipment, and court maintenance for Property B's guests. Contractor Z employs the personnel to provide the service and is responsible for the costs of purchasing and maintaining the equipment (including liability insurance). Contractor Z requires guests to sign a liability waiver in its legal operating name prior to delivery of the services. Contractor Z pays Property B a contracted amount (percentage of revenue or fixed amount) to provide the tennis services and retail. Property B collects the amounts charged to guests' rooms and remits it to Contractor Z.

*Evaluation.* Contractor Z is responsible for fulfillment of the service and assumes the risks and rewards of ownership. While certain credit risk may be borne by Property B, the predominance of factors indicates that revenues should be reported on a net basis in Miscellaneous Income.

## Scenario Three: Third-Party Management

*Structure.* Property C has certain facilities for use as a tennis center, but not the in-house expertise to operate it. Property C therefore enters into an agreement with Contractor Z to provide advice on tennis instruction, rentals, and services for Property C's guests. Contractor Z provides recommendations on employees for Property C to hire and the levels and quality of insurance, equipment, and retail items for Property C to purchase (including liability insurance). In return for providing this service, Contractor Z receives a management fee based on the revenue and an incentive fee based on the profit of the tennis center. All of the revenues and expenses of the tennis center are the responsibility of Property C, including the fees.

*Evaluation.* Property C is responsible for fulfillment and has retained all of the risk for the operation inclusive of inventory risk and credit risk. Under this scenario, revenue is properly recorded on a gross basis and the tennis center is considered an Other Operated Department.

# Surcharges, Service Charges, and Gratuities

Surcharges, service charges, and gratuities should be evaluated to determine whether they should be reported revenue. While this is different from determining whether to record revenue at gross or net, the same indicators and process used in examining gross versus net recording apply when classifying surcharges, service charges, and gratuities. The property must determine whether it is acting as an agent or as a principal in the transaction in order to properly report that transaction.

Surcharges and service charges generally include any mandatory, non-discretionary, or other charge automatically added to a customer account in respect of the service or use of an amenity. They may include, but are not restricted to, such items as the following:

| Item | Revenue Recorded in Department |
|---|---|
| Resort fees | Miscellaneous Income |
| Bag handling charges | Rooms Other Revenue |
| Banquet service charge | F&B Other Revenue |
| Restaurant service charge | F&B Other Revenue |
| Room service delivery charge | F&B Other Revenue |
| Corkage charge | F&B Other Revenue |
| Pool towel charge | Health Club/Spa Other Revenue |
| Spa service charge | Health Club/Spa Other Revenue |

GAAP related to revenue recognition is fully applicable to both surcharges and service charges.

When such charges are mandatory and the client does not have the ability to alter the amount or direct where the payment of the service charge should be made, the property is considered to:

- be the primary obligor;

- establish the price;

- determine the product or service specification;

- retain the general credit risk.

In such cases, surcharges and service charges should be recorded as revenue and may not be credited to any expense account.

All mandatory non-discretionary fees that are disclosed to the client as a service charge should be classified as a service charge. Those would include the service charges added to rooms (usually outside the United States), banquet service charges, in-room dining service charges, etc.

Those mandatory non-discretionary fees that do not contain the words "service charge" in their name would be surcharges. Included in this group would be resort fees, bag handling fees, corkage charges, and pool towel charges.

In contrast, a gratuity is generally a discretionary amount added to an account or left directly with an employee by the customer.

When the customer establishes the price through the unrestricted right to determine the amount of the charge, makes the pricing decision free from compulsion, and the charge is not the subject of negotiation or dictated by the property's employment policies, an evaluation of GAAP would likely determine the amount to be a gratuity, notwithstanding that the property remains the primary obligor.

Gratuities are generally retained by the employee at the time of the transaction in the case of cash or disbursed by the employer as trustee for the employees in the case of charged gratuities.

A gratuity is not income to the property. It is treated as income directly in the hands of the employee.

Following are some examples relating to food and beverage venues and spas.

### Food and Beverage Venue

*Structure 1.* The policy of the food and beverage venue is to charge an 18 percent fee on parties larger than eight people. The guest does not decide the amount of the charge or even whether he or she actually wanted to leave any amount in respect of the service provided.

*Evaluation.* In such cases, the amount would be considered a service charge and should be recorded as Other Revenue—Surcharges and Service Charges in *Food and Beverage—Schedule 2.* In many jurisdictions, the amount is also subject to sales tax.

*Structure 2.* The food and beverage venue has no minimum gratuity policy and relies on guest to freely decide how much, if anything, to leave the service staff.

*Evaluation.* In this case, any amount the guest provides would be considered a gratuity. The determination is independent of whether the guest voucher provides a blank line for the client to add a gratuity.

*Structure 3.* The food and beverage venue adds a suggested charge of 15 percent on all guest checks, as a matter of convenience for customers, with full disclosure (on menus and guest checks) that guests have the right to change the amount at their discretion.

*Evaluation.* In this case, the amount the guest provides would be considered a gratuity.

### Spa

*Structure 1.* The policy of the spa is to charge a 20 percent fee on all treatments. Following a spa treatment, the guest is presented with a charge voucher to sign that includes the additional 20 percent; the guest has no discretion to eliminate or change the amount.

*Evaluation.* In this case, the amount would be considered a service charge and should be recorded as Other Revenue in *Health Club/Spa—Sub-schedule 3-2.* In many jurisdictions, the amount is also subject to sales tax.

*Structure 2.* The spa has no minimum gratuity policy and relies on the guest to freely decide how much, if anything, to leave the spa staff.

*Evaluation.* In this case, the amount is considered a gratuity. The determination is independent of whether the guest voucher provides a blank line for the client to add a gratuity.

*Structure 3.* It is the policy of the spa to add an 18 percent charge on all spa bills, which is paid to the therapist providing the service. The policy evolved due to the profile of the customer who is unfamiliar with the local tipping policy. There is no communication or disclosure made to the guest in respect of any discretion allowed in the amount charged unless the guest initiates such enquiry or complains about the charge.

*Evaluation.* In this case, guests are unaware that they have the ability to decide either the amount of the charge or whether they actually want to leave any amount in respect of the service provided. The amount would be considered a service charge and should be recorded as Other Revenue in *Health Club/Spa—Sub-schedule 3-2*. In many jurisdictions, the amount is also subject to sales tax.